DEMOSTHENES, SPEECHES 1–17

THE ORATORY OF CLASSICAL GREECE

Translated with Notes • Michael Gagarin, Series Editor

VOLUME 14

DEMOSTHENES, SPEECHES 1–17

Translated with introduction and notes by
Jeremy Trevett

 UNIVERSITY OF TEXAS PRESS, AUSTIN

This book has been supported by an endowment dedicated to classics and the ancient world and funded by the Areté Foundation; the Gladys Krieble Delmas Foundation; the Dougherty Foundation; the James R. Dougherty, Jr. Foundation; the Rachael and Ben Vaughan Foundation; and the National Endowment for the Humanities.

Requests for permission to reproduce material from this work should be sent to:
>   Permissions
>   University of Texas Press
>   P.O. Box 7819
>   Austin, TX 78713-7819
>   www.utexas.edu/utpress/about/bpermission.html

♾ The paper used in this book meets the minimum requirements of ANSI/NISO z39.48-1992 (R1997) (Permanence of Paper).

Library of Congress Cataloging-in-Publication Data

Demosthenes.
    [Selections. English. 2011]
    Demosthenes, speeches 1–17 / translated with introduction and notes by Jeremy Trevett. — 1st ed.
        p.   cm. — (The oratory of classical Greece ; v. 14) Includes bibliographical references and index.

ISBN 978-0-292-72909-4

    1. Demosthenes—Translations into English.   2. Speeches, addresses, etc., Greek—Translations into English.   3. Athens (Greece)—Politics and government—Early works to 1800.
I. Trevett, Jeremy.   II. Title.   III. Title: Speeches 1–17.
    PA3951.E5   2011b
    885'.01—dc23

                                                        2011022824

For Karin, Oliver, and Alice

CONTENTS

DEMOSTHENES (Jeremy Trevett)

SERIES EDITOR'S PREFACE

This is the fourteenth volume in a series of translations of *The Oratory of Classical Greece.* The aim of the series is to make available primarily for those who do not read Greek up-to-date, accurate, and readable translations with introductions and explanatory notes of all the surviving works and major fragments of the Attic orators of the classical period (ca. 420–320 BC): Aeschines, Andocides, Antiphon, Demosthenes, Dinarchus, Hyperides, Isaeus, Isocrates, Lycurgus, and Lysias. This volume contains sixteen speeches, two of them almost certainly not by Demosthenes, that were purportedly written for delivery in the assembly, together with a letter from Philip of Macedon that is traditionally included among the speeches of Demosthenes. They include the highly polemical Olynthiacs and Philippics and other speeches that provide considerable information about Athenian politics and public finance in the middle of the fourth century.

This volume, like the others in the series, has benefited greatly from the careful attention of many at the University of Texas Press, including Director Joanna Hitchcock, Humanities Editor Jim Burr, manuscript editor Lynne Chapman, and copy editor Nancy Moore. As always, they have been a pleasure to work with.

—M.G.

TRANSLATOR'S PREFACE

I should like to thank Alan Boegehold, who read the manuscript for the Press and made a number of helpful suggestions; Jim Burr and Lynne Chapman of the University of Texas Press, and Nancy Moore, my copy editor, for their extremely professional editorial guidance; and Brian Turner of the Ancient World Mapping Center at UNC Chapel Hill for creating the maps. Above all, I owe a deep debt of gratitude to Michael Gagarin, first for his invitation to contribute to this series, then for his patient encouragement in the face of my slow progress, and above all for the numerous improvements that he has made to the book. Needless to say, all remaining errors are my own.

—J.T.

Greece. Map © 2011, Ancient World Mapping Center (www.unc.edu/awmc). Used by permission.

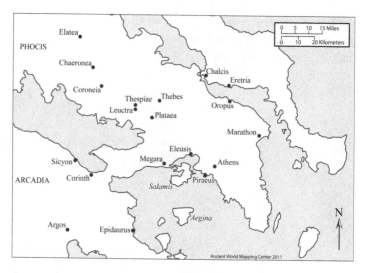

Attica and surrounding region. Map © 2011, Ancient World Mapping Center (www.unc.edu/awmc). Used by permission.

SERIES INTRODUCTION

Greek Oratory

〰〰〰〰〰〰〰〰〰〰〰〰〰〰〰〰〰〰〰〰〰〰〰〰〰〰〰〰〰〰〰

By Michael Gagarin

ORATORY IN CLASSICAL ATHENS

From as early as Homer (and undoubtedly much earlier) the Greeks placed a high value on effective speaking. Even Achilles, whose greatness was primarily established on the battlefield, was brought up to be "a speaker of words and a doer of deeds" (*Iliad* 9.443); and Athenian leaders of the sixth and fifth centuries,[1] such as Solon, Themistocles, and Pericles, were all accomplished orators. Most Greek literary genres—notably epic, tragedy, and history—underscore the importance of oratory by their inclusion of set speeches. The formal pleadings of the envoys to Achilles in the *Iliad*, the messenger speeches in tragedy reporting events like the battle of Salamis in Aeschylus' *Persians* or the gruesome death of Pentheus in Euripides' *Bacchae*, and the powerful political oratory of Pericles' funeral oration in Thucydides are but a few of the most notable examples of the Greeks' never-ending fascination with formal public speaking, which was to reach its height in the public oratory of the fourth century.

In early times, oratory was not a specialized subject of study but was learned by practice and example. The formal study of rhetoric as an "art" (*technē*) began, we are told, in the middle of the fifth century in Sicily with the work of Corax and his pupil Tisias.[2] These two are scarcely more than names to us, but

---

[1] All dates in this volume are BC unless the contrary is either indicated or obvious.

[2] See Kennedy 1963: 26–51. Cole 1991 has challenged this traditional picture, arguing that the term "rhetoric" was coined by Plato to designate and denigrate an activity he strongly opposed. Cole's own reconstruction is not

another famous Sicilian, Gorgias of Leontini (ca. 490–390), developed a new style of argument and is reported to have dazzled the Athenians with a speech delivered when he visited Athens in 427. Gorgias initiated the practice, which continued into the early fourth century, of composing speeches for mythical or imaginary occasions. The surviving examples reveal a lively intellectual climate in the late fifth and early fourth centuries, in which oratory served to display new ideas, new forms of expression, and new methods of argument.[3] This tradition of "intellectual" oratory was continued by the fourth-century educator Isocrates and played a large role in later Greek and Roman education.

In addition to this intellectual oratory, at about the same time the practice also began of writing speeches for real occasions in public life, which we may designate "practical" oratory. For centuries Athenians had been delivering speeches in public settings (primarily the courts and the Assembly), but these had always been composed and delivered impromptu, without being written down and thus without being preserved. The practice of writing speeches began in the courts and then expanded to include the Assembly and other settings. Athens was one of the leading cities of Greece in the fifth and fourth centuries, and its political and legal systems depended on direct participation by a large number of citizens; all important decisions were made by these large bodies, and the primary means of influencing these decisions was oratory.[4] Thus, it is not surprising that oratory flourished in Athens,[5] but it may not be immediately obvious why it should be written down.

---

without problems, but he does well to remind us how thoroughly the traditional view of rhetoric depends on one of its most ardent opponents.

[3]Of these only Antiphon's Tetralogies are included in this series. Gorgias' *Helen* and *Palamedes*, Alcidamas' *Odysseus*, and Antisthenes' *Ajax* and *Odysseus* are translated in Gagarin and Woodruff 1995.

[4]Yunis 1996 has a good treatment of political oratory from Pericles to Demosthenes.

[5]All our evidence for practical oratory comes from Athens, with the exception of Isocrates 19, written for a trial in Aegina. Many speeches were undoubtedly delivered in courts and political forums in other Greek cities, but it may be that such speeches were written down only in Athens.

The pivotal figure in this development was Antiphon, one of the fifth-century intellectuals who are often grouped together under the name "Sophists."[6] Like some of the other sophists he contributed to the intellectual oratory of the period, but he also had a strong practical interest in law. At the same time, Antiphon had an aversion to public speaking and did not directly involve himself in legal or political affairs (Thucydides 8.68). However, he began giving general advice to other citizens who were engaged in litigation and were thus expected to address the court themselves. As this practice grew, Antiphon went further, and around 430 he began writing out whole speeches for others to memorize and deliver. Thus began the practice of "logography," which continued through the next century and beyond.[7] Logography particularly appealed to men like Lysias, who were metics, or noncitizen residents of Athens. Since they were not Athenian citizens, they were barred from direct participation in public life, but they could contribute by writing speeches for others.

Antiphon was also the first (to our knowledge) to write down a speech he would himself deliver, writing the speech for his own defense at his trial for treason in 411. His motive was probably to publicize and preserve his views, and others continued this practice of writing down speeches they would themselves deliver in the courts and (more rarely) the Assembly.[8] Finally, one other type of practical oratory was the special tribute delivered on certain important public occasions, the best known of which is the funeral oration. It is convenient to designate these three types of

---

[6]The term "sophist" was loosely used through the fifth and fourth centuries to designate various intellectuals and orators, but under the influence of Plato, who attacked certain figures under this name, the term is now used of a specific group of thinkers; see Kerferd 1981.

[7]For Antiphon as the first to write speeches, see Photius, *Bibliotheca* 486a7–11 and [Plut.], *Moralia* 832c–d. The latest extant speech can be dated to 320, but we know that at least one orator, Dinarchus, continued the practice after that date.

[8]Unlike forensic speeches, speeches for delivery in the Assembly were usually not composed beforehand in writing, since the speaker could not know exactly when or in what context he would be speaking; see further Trevett 1996.

oratory by the terms Aristotle later uses: forensic (for the courts), deliberative (for the Assembly), and epideictic (for display).[9]

THE ORATORS

In the century from about 420 to 320, dozens—perhaps even hundreds—of now unknown orators and logographers must have composed speeches that are now lost, but only ten of these men were selected for preservation and study by ancient scholars, and only works collected under the names of these ten have been preserved. Some of these works are undoubtedly spurious, though in most cases they are fourth-century works by a different author rather than later "forgeries." Indeed, modern scholars suspect that as many as seven of the speeches attributed to Demosthenes may have been written by Apollodorus, son of Pasion, who is sometimes called "the eleventh orator."[10] Including these speeches among the works of Demosthenes may have been an honest mistake, or perhaps a bookseller felt he could sell more copies of these speeches if they were attributed to a more famous orator.

In alphabetical order the Ten Orators are as follows:[11]

+ AESCHINES (ca. 390–ca. 322) rose from obscure origins to become an important Athenian political figure, first an ally, then a bitter enemy of Demosthenes. His three speeches all concern major public issues. The best known of these (Aes. 3) was delivered at the trial in 330, when Demosthenes responded with *On the Crown* (Dem. 18). Aeschines lost the case and was forced to leave Athens and live the rest of his life in exile.

---

[9] *Rhetoric* 1.3. Intellectual orations, like Gorgias' *Helen*, do not easily fit into Aristotle's classification. For a fuller (but still brief) introduction to Attic oratory and the orators, see Edwards 1994.

[10] See Trevett 1992.

[11] The Loeb volumes of *Minor Attic Orators* also include the prominent Athenian political figure Demades (ca. 385–319), who was not one of the Ten; but the only speech that has come down to us under his name is a later forgery. It is possible that Demades and other fourth-century politicians who had a high reputation for public speaking did not put any speeches in writing, especially if they rarely spoke in the courts (see above n. 8).

- ANDOCIDES (ca. 440–ca. 390) is best known for his role in the scandal of 415, when just before the departure of the fateful Athenian expedition to Sicily during the Peloponnesian War (431–404), a band of young men mutilated statues of Hermes, and at the same time information was revealed about the secret rites of Demeter. Andocides was exiled but later returned. Two of the four speeches in his name give us a contemporary view of the scandal: one pleads for his return, the other argues against a second period of exile.

- ANTIPHON (ca. 480–411), as already noted, wrote forensic speeches for others and only once spoke himself. In 411 he participated in an oligarchic coup by a group of 400, and when the democrats regained power he was tried for treason and executed. His six surviving speeches include three for delivery in court and the three Tetralogies—imaginary intellectual exercises for display or teaching that consist of four speeches each, two on each side. All six of Antiphon's speeches concern homicide, probably because these stood at the beginning of the collection of his works. Fragments of some thirty other speeches cover many different topics.

- DEMOSTHENES (384–322) is generally considered the best of the Attic orators. Although his nationalistic message is less highly regarded today, his powerful mastery of and ability to combine many different rhetorical styles continue to impress readers. Demosthenes was still a child when his wealthy father died. The trustees of the estate apparently misappropriated much of it, and when he came of age, he sued them in a series of cases (27–31), regaining some of his fortune and making a name as a powerful speaker. He then wrote speeches for others in a variety of cases, public and private, and for his own use in court (where many cases involved major public issues), and in the Assembly, where he opposed the growing power of Philip of Macedon. The triumph of Philip and his son Alexander the Great eventually put an end to Demosthenes' career. Some sixty speeches have come down under his name, about a third of them of questionable authenticity.

- DINARCHUS (ca. 360–ca. 290) was born in Corinth but spent much of his life in Athens as a metic (a noncitizen resident).

His public fame came primarily from writing speeches for the prosecutions surrounding the Harpalus affair in 324, when several prominent figures (including Demosthenes) were accused of bribery. After 322 he had a profitable career as a logographer.

- HYPERIDES (389/8–322) was a political leader and logographer of so many different talents that he was called the pentathlete of orators. He was a leader of the Athenian resistance to Philip and Alexander and (like Demosthenes) was condemned to death after Athens' final surrender. One speech and substantial fragments of five others have been recovered from papyrus remains; otherwise, only fragments survive.

- ISAEUS (ca. 415–ca. 340) wrote speeches on a wide range of topics, but the eleven complete speeches that survive, dating from ca. 390 to ca. 344, all concern inheritance. As with Antiphon, the survival of these particular speeches may have been the result of the later ordering of his speeches by subject; we have part of a twelfth speech and fragments and titles of some forty other works. Isaeus is said to have been a pupil of Isocrates and the teacher of Demosthenes.

- ISOCRATES (436–338) considered himself a philosopher and educator, not an orator or rhetorician. He came from a wealthy Athenian family but lost most of his property in the Peloponnesian War, and in 403 he took up logography. About 390 he abandoned this practice and turned to writing and teaching, setting forth his educational, philosophical, and political views in essays that took the form of speeches but were not meant for oral delivery. He favored accommodation with the growing power of Philip of Macedon and panhellenic unity. His school was based on a broad concept of rhetoric and applied philosophy; it attracted pupils from the entire Greek world (including Isaeus, Lycurgus, and Hyperides) and became the main rival of Plato's Academy. Isocrates greatly influenced education and rhetoric in the Hellenistic, Roman, and modern periods until the eighteenth century.

- LYCURGUS (ca. 390–ca. 324) was a leading public official who restored the financial condition of Athens after 338 and played a large role in the city for the next dozen years. He brought charges of corruption or treason against many other officials, usually with success. Only one speech survives.

• LYSIAS (ca. 445–ca. 380) was a metic—an official resident of Athens but not a citizen. Much of his property was seized by the Thirty during their short-lived oligarchic coup in 404–403. Perhaps as a result he turned to logography. More than thirty speeches survive in whole or in part, though the authenticity of some is doubted. We also have fragments or know the titles of more than a hundred others. The speeches cover a wide range of cases, and he may have delivered one himself (Lys. 12), on the death of his brother at the hands of the Thirty. Lysias is particularly known for his vivid narratives, his *ēthopoiïa*, or "creation of character," and his prose style, which became a model of clarity and vividness.

THE WORKS OF THE ORATORS

As soon as speeches began to be written down, they could be preserved. We know little about the conditions of book "publication" (i.e., making copies for distribution) in the fourth century, but there was an active market for books in Athens, and some of the speeches may have achieved wide circulation.[12] An orator (or his family) may have preserved his own speeches, perhaps to advertise his ability or demonstrate his success, or booksellers may have collected and copied them in order to make money.

We do not know how closely the preserved text of these speeches corresponded to the version actually delivered in court or in the Assembly. Speakers undoubtedly extemporized or varied from their text on occasion, but there is no good evidence that deliberative speeches were substantially revised for publication.[13] In forensic oratory a logographer's reputation would derive first and

---

[12]Dover's discussion (1968) of the preservation and transmission of the works of Lysias (and perhaps others under his name) is useful not just for Lysias but for the other orators too. His theory of shared authorship between logographer and litigant, however, is unconvincing (see Usher 1976).

[13]See further Trevett 1996: 437–439.

foremost from his success with jurors. If a forensic speech was victorious, there would be no reason to alter it for publication, and if it lost, alteration would probably not deceive potential clients. Thus, the published texts of forensic speeches were probably quite faithful to the texts that were provided to clients, and we have little reason to suspect substantial alteration in the century or so before they were collected by scholars in Alexandria (see below).

In addition to the speaker's text, most forensic speeches have breaks for the inclusion of documents. The logographer inserted a notation in his text—such as *nomos* ("law") or *martyria* ("testimony")—and the speaker would pause while the clerk read out the text of a law or the testimony of witnesses. Many speeches survive with only a notation that a *nomos* or *martyria* was read at that point, but in some cases the text of the document is included. It used to be thought that these documents were all creations of later scholars, but many (though not all) are now accepted as genuine.[14]

With the foundation of the famous library in Alexandria early in the third century, scholars began to collect and catalogue texts of the orators, along with many other classical authors. Only the best orators were preserved in the library, many of them represented by over 100 speeches each (some undoubtedly spurious). Only some of these works survived in manuscript form to the modern era; more recently a few others have been discovered on ancient sheets of papyrus, so that today the corpus of Attic Oratory consists of about 150 speeches, together with a few letters and other works. The subject matter ranges from important public issues and serious crimes to business affairs, lovers' quarrels, inheritance disputes, and other personal or family matters.

In the centuries after these works were collected, ancient scholars gathered biographical facts about their authors, produced grammatical and lexicographic notes, and used some of the speeches as evidence for Athenian political history. But the ancient scholars who were most interested in the orators were those who studied prose style, the most notable of these being Diony-

---

[14]See MacDowell 1990: 43–47; Todd 1993: 44–45.

sius of Halicarnassus (first century BC), who wrote treatises on
several of the orators,[15] and Hermogenes of Tarsus (second century AD), who wrote several literary studies, including *On Types of
Style*.[16] But relative to epic or tragedy, oratory was little studied;
and even scholars of rhetoric whose interests were broader than
style, like Cicero and Quintilian, paid little attention to the orators, except for the acknowledged master, Demosthenes.

Most modern scholars until the second half of the twentieth
century continued to treat the orators primarily as prose stylists.[17]
The reevaluation of Athenian democracy by George Grote and
others in the nineteenth century stimulated renewed interest in
Greek oratory among historians; and increasing interest in Athenian law during that century led a few legal scholars to read the
orators. But in comparison with the interest shown in the other
literary genres—epic, lyric, tragedy, comedy, and even history—
Attic oratory has been relatively neglected until the last third of
the twentieth century. More recently, however, scholars have discovered the value of the orators for the broader study of Athenian culture and society. Since Dover's ground-breaking works
on popular morality and homosexuality,[18] interest in the orators
has been increasing rapidly, and they are now seen as primary
representatives of Athenian moral and social values, and as evidence for social and economic conditions, political and social ide-

---

[15] Dionysius' literary studies are collected and translated in Usher
1974–1985.

[16] Wooten 1987. Stylistic considerations probably also influenced the selection of the "canon" of ten orators; see Worthington 1994.

[17] For example, the most popular and influential book ever written on
the orators, Jebb's *The Attic Orators* (1875), was presented as an "attempt
to aid in giving Attic Oratory its due place in the history of Attic Prose"
(I.xiii). This modern focus on prose style can plausibly be connected to the
large role played by prose composition (the translation of English prose into
Greek, usually in imitation of specific authors or styles) in the Classics cur-
riculum, especially in Britain.

[18] Dover (1974, 1978). Dover recently commented (1994: 157), "When I
began to mine the riches of Attic forensic oratory I was astonished to dis-
cover that the mine had never been exploited."

ology, and in general those aspects of Athenian culture that in the past were commonly ignored by historians of ancient Greece but are of increasing interest and importance today, including women and the family, slavery, and the economy.

GOVERNMENT AND LAW IN CLASSICAL ATHENS

The hallmark of the Athenian political and legal systems was its amateurism. Most public officials, including those who supervised the courts, were selected by lot and held office for a limited period, typically a year. Thus a great many citizens held public office at some point in their lives, but almost none served for an extended period of time or developed the experience or expertise that would make them professionals. All significant policy decisions were debated and voted on in the Assembly, where the quorum was 6,000 citizens, and all significant legal cases were judged by bodies of 200 to 500 jurors or more. Public prominence was not achieved by election (or selection) to public office but depended rather on a man's ability to sway the majority of citizens in the Assembly or jurors in court to vote in favor of a proposed course of action or for one of the litigants in a trial. Success was never permanent, and a victory on one policy issue or a verdict in one case could be quickly reversed in another.[19] In such a system the value of public oratory is obvious, and in the fourth century, oratory became the most important cultural institution in Athens, replacing drama as the forum where major ideological concerns were displayed and debated.

Several recent books give good detailed accounts of Athenian government and law,[20] and so a brief sketch can suffice here. The

---

[19]In the Assembly this could be accomplished by a reconsideration of the question, as in the famous Mytilenean debate (Thuc. 3.36–50); in court a verdict was final, but its practical effects could be thwarted or reversed by later litigation on a related issue.

[20]For government, see Sinclair 1988, Hansen 1991; for law, MacDowell 1978, Todd 1993, and Boegehold 1995 (Bonner 1927 is still helpful). Much of our information about the legal and political systems comes from a work attributed to Aristotle but perhaps written by a pupil of his, *The Athenian*

main policy-making body was the Assembly, open to all adult male citizens; a small payment for attendance enabled at least some of the poor to attend along with the leisured rich. In addition, a Council of 500 citizens, selected each year by lot with no one allowed to serve more than two years, prepared material for and made recommendations to the Assembly; a rotating subgroup of this Council served as an executive committee, the Prytaneis. Finally, numerous officials, most of them selected by lot for one-year terms, supervised different areas of administration and finance. The most important of these were the nine Archons (lit. "rulers"): the eponymous Archon after whom the year was named, the Basileus ("king"),[21] the Polemarch, and the six Thesmothetae. Councilors and almost all these officials underwent a preliminary examination (*dokimasia*) before taking office, and officials submitted to a final accounting (*euthynai*) upon leaving; at these times any citizen who wished could challenge a person's fitness for his new position or his performance in his recent position.

There was no general taxation of Athenian citizens. Sources of public funding included the annual tax levied on metics, various fees and import duties, and (in the fifth century) tribute from allied cities; but the source that figures most prominently in the orators is the Athenian system of liturgies (*leitourgiai*), by which in a regular rotation the rich provided funding for certain special public needs. The main liturgies were the *chorēgia*, in which a sponsor (*chorēgos*) supervised and paid for the training and performance of a chorus which sang and danced at a public festival,[22] and the trierarchy, in which a sponsor (trierarch) paid to equip and usually commanded a trireme, or warship, for a year. Some of these liturgies required substantial expenditures, but even so, some men

---

Constitution (*Ath. Pol.*—conveniently translated with notes by Rhodes 1984). The discovery of this work on a papyrus in Egypt in 1890 caused a major resurgence of interest in Athenian government.

[21] Modern scholars often use the term *archōn basileus* or "king archon," but Athenian sources (e.g., *Ath. Pol.* 57) simply call him the *basileus*.

[22] These included the productions of tragedy and comedy, for which the main expense was for the chorus.

spent far more than required in order to promote themselves and their public careers, and litigants often tried to impress the jurors by referring to liturgies they had undertaken (see, e.g., Lys. 21.1–5). A further twist on this system was that if a man thought he had been assigned a liturgy that should have gone to someone else who was richer than he, he could propose an exchange of property (*antidosis*), giving the other man a choice of either taking over the liturgy or exchanging property with him. Finally, the rich were also subject to special taxes (*eisphorai*) levied as a percentage of their property in times of need.

The Athenian legal system remained similarly resistant to professionalization. Trials and the procedures leading up to them were supervised by officials, primarily the nine Archons, but their role was purely administrative, and they were in no way equivalent to modern judges. All significant questions about what we would call points of law were presented to the jurors, who considered them together with all other issues when they delivered their verdict at the end of the trial.[23] Trials were "contests" (*agōnes*) between two litigants, each of whom presented his own case to the jurors in a speech, plaintiff first, then defendant; in some cases each party then spoke again, probably in rebuttal. Since a litigant had only one or two speeches in which to present his entire case, and no issue was decided separately by a judge, all the necessary factual information and every important argument on substance or procedure, fact or law, had to be presented together. A single speech might thus combine narrative, argument, emotional appeal, and various digressions, all with the goal of obtaining a favorable verdict. Even more than today, a litigant's primary task was to control the issue—to determine which issues the jurors would consider most important and which questions they would have in their minds as they cast their votes. We only

---

[23]Certain religious "interpreters" (*exēgētai*) were occasionally asked to give their opinion on a legal matter that had a religious dimension (such as the prosecution of a homicide), but although these opinions could be reported in court (e.g., Dem. 47.68–73), they had no official legal standing. The most significant administrative decision we hear of is the refusal of the Basileus to accept the case in Antiphon 6 (see 6.37–46).

rarely have both speeches from a trial,[24] and we usually have little or no external evidence for the facts of a case or the verdict. We must thus infer both the facts and the opponent's strategy from the speech we have, and any assessment of the overall effectiveness of a speech and of the logographer's strategy is to some extent speculative.

Before a trial there were usually several preliminary hearings for presenting evidence; arbitration, public and private, was available and sometimes required. These hearings and arbitration sessions allowed each side to become familiar with the other side's case, so that discussions of "what my opponent will say" could be included in one's speech. Normally a litigant presented his own case, but he was often assisted by family or friends. If he wished (and could afford it), he could enlist the services of a logographer, who presumably gave strategic advice in addition to writing a speech. The speeches were timed to ensure an equal hearing for both sides,[25] and all trials were completed within a day. Two hundred or more jurors decided each case in the popular courts, which met in the Agora.[26] Homicide cases and certain other religious trials (e.g., Lys. 7) were heard by the Council of the Areopagus or an associated group of fifty-one Ephetae. The Areopagus was composed of all former Archons—perhaps 150–200 members at most times. It met on a hill called the Areopagus ("rock of Ares") near the Acropolis.

Jurors for the regular courts were selected by lot from those citizens who registered each year and who appeared for duty that day; as with the Assembly, a small payment allowed the poor to serve. After the speakers had finished, the jurors voted immediately without any formal discussion. The side with the majority won; a tie vote decided the case for the defendant. In some cases where the penalty was not fixed, after a conviction the ju-

---

[24]The exceptions are Demosthenes 19 and Aeschines 2, Aeschines 3 and Demosthenes 18, and Lysias 6 (one of several prosecution speeches) and Andocides 1; all were written for major public cases.

[25]Timing was done by means of a water clock, which in most cases was stopped during the reading of documents.

[26]See Boegehold 1995.

rors voted again on the penalty, choosing between penalties proposed by each side. Even when we know the verdict, we cannot know which of the speaker's arguments contributed most to his success or failure. However, a logographer could probably learn from jurors which points had or had not been successful, so that arguments that are found repeatedly in speeches probably were known to be effective in most cases.

The first written laws in Athens were enacted by Draco (ca. 620) and Solon (ca. 590), and new laws were regularly added. At the end of the fifth century the existing laws were reorganized, and a new procedure for enacting laws was instituted; thereafter a group of Law-Givers (*nomothetai*) had to certify that a proposed law did not conflict with any existing laws. There was no attempt, however, to organize legislation systematically, and although Plato, Aristotle, and other philosophers wrote various works on law and law-giving, these were either theoretical or descriptive and had no apparent influence on legislation. Written statutes generally used ordinary language rather than precise legal definitions in designating offenses, and questions concerning precisely what constituted a specific offense or what was the correct interpretation of a written statute were decided (together with other issues) by the jurors in each case. A litigant might, of course, assert a certain definition or interpretation as "something you all know" or "what the lawgiver intended," but such remarks are evidently tendentious and cannot be taken as authoritative.

The result of these procedural and substantive features was that the verdict depended largely on each litigant's speech (or speeches). As one speaker puts it (Ant. 6.18), "When there are no witnesses, you (jurors) are forced to reach a verdict about the case on the basis of the prosecutor's and defendant's words alone; you must be suspicious and examine their accounts in detail, and your vote will necessarily be cast on the basis of likelihood rather than clear knowledge." Even the testimony of witnesses (usually on both sides) is rarely decisive. On the other hand, most speakers make a considerable effort to establish facts and provide legitimate arguments in conformity with established law. Plato's view of rhetoric as a clever technique for persuading an ignorant crowd that the false is true is not borne out by the speeches, and the legal system does not appear to have produced many arbitrary or clearly unjust results.

The main form of legal procedure was a *dikē* ("suit") in which the injured party (or his relatives in a case of homicide) brought suit against the offender. Suits for injuries to slaves would be brought by the slave's master, and injuries to women would be prosecuted by a male relative. Strictly speaking, a *dikē* was a private matter between individuals, though like all cases, *dikai* often had public dimensions. The other major form of procedure was a *graphē* ("writing" or "indictment") in which "anyone who wished" (i.e., any citizen) could bring a prosecution for wrongdoing. *Graphai* were instituted by Solon, probably in order to allow prosecution of offenses where the victim was unable or unlikely to bring suit himself, such as selling a dependent into slavery; but the number of areas covered by *graphai* increased to cover many types of public offenses as well as some apparently private crimes, such as *hybris*.

The system of prosecution by "anyone who wished" also extended to several other more specialized forms of prosecution, like *eisangelia* ("impeachment"), used in cases of treason. Another specialized prosecution was *apagōgē* ("summary arrest"), in which someone could arrest a common criminal (*kakourgos*, lit. "evildoer"), or have him arrested, on the spot. The reliance on private initiative meant that Athenians never developed a system of public prosecution; rather, they presumed that everyone would keep an eye on the behavior of his political enemies and bring suit as soon as he suspected a crime, both to harm his opponents and to advance his own career. In this way all public officials would be watched by someone. There was no disgrace in admitting that a prosecution was motivated by private enmity.

By the end of the fifth century the system of prosecution by "anyone who wished" was apparently being abused by so-called sykophants (*sykophantai*), who allegedly brought or threatened to bring false suits against rich men, either to gain part of the fine that would be levied or to induce an out-of-court settlement in which the accused would pay to have the matter dropped. We cannot gauge the true extent of this problem, since speakers usually provide little evidence to support their claims that their opponents are sykophants, but the Athenians did make sykophancy a crime. They also specified that in many public procedures a plaintiff who either dropped the case or failed to obtain one-fifth of the votes would have to pay a heavy fine of 1,000 drachmas. Despite this, it appears that litigation was common in Athens and was seen by some as excessive.

Over the course of time, the Athenian legal and political systems have more often been judged negatively than positively. Philosophers and political theorists have generally followed the lead of Plato (427–347), who lived and worked in Athens his entire life while severely criticizing its system of government as well as many other aspects of its culture. For Plato, democracy amounted to the tyranny of the masses over the educated elite and was destined to collapse from its own instability. The legal system was capricious and depended entirely on the rhetorical ability of litigants with no regard for truth or justice. These criticisms have often been echoed by modern scholars, who particularly complain that law was much too closely interwoven with politics and did not have the autonomous status it achieved in Roman law and continues to have, at least in theory, in modern legal systems.

Plato's judgments are valid if one accepts the underlying presuppositions, that the aim of law is absolute truth and abstract justice and that achieving the highest good of the state requires thorough and systematic organization. Most Athenians do not seem to have subscribed to either the criticisms or the presuppositions, and most scholars now accept the long-ignored fact that despite major external disruptions in the form of wars and two short-lived coups brought about by one of these wars, the Athenian legal and political systems remained remarkably stable for almost two hundred years (508–320). Moreover, like all other Greek cities at the time, whatever their form of government, Athenian democracy was brought to an end not by internal forces but by the external power of Philip of Macedon and his son Alexander. The legal system never became autonomous, and the rich sometimes complained that they were victims of unscrupulous litigants, but there is no indication that the people wanted to yield control of the legal process to a professional class, as Plato recommended. For most Athenians—Plato being an exception in this and many other matters—one purpose of the legal system was to give every-one the opportunity to have his case heard by other citizens and have it heard quickly and cheaply; and in this it clearly succeeded.

Indeed, the Athenian legal system also served the interests of the rich, even the very rich, as well as the common people, in that it provided a forum for the competition that since Homer had been an important part of aristocratic life. In this competition, the rich used the courts as battlegrounds, though their main weapon was the rhetoric of popular ideology, which hailed the rule of law and promoted the ideal of moderation and restraint.[27] But those who aspired to political leadership and the honor and status that accompanied it repeatedly entered the legal arena, bringing suit against their political enemies whenever possible and defending themselves against suits brought by others whenever necessary. The ultimate judges of these public competitions were the common people, who seem to have relished the dramatic clash of individuals and ideologies. In this respect fourth-century oratory was the cultural heir of fifth-century drama and was similarly appreciated by the citizens. Despite the disapproval of intellectuals like Plato, most Athenians legitimately considered their legal system a hallmark of their democracy and a vital presence in their culture.

THE TRANSLATION OF GREEK ORATORY

The purpose of this series is to provide students and scholars in all fields with accurate, readable translations of all surviving classical Attic oratory, including speeches whose authenticity is disputed, as well as the substantial surviving fragments. In keeping with the originals, the language is for the most part nontechnical. Names of persons and places are given in the (generally more familiar) Latinized forms, and names of officials or legal procedures have been translated into English equivalents, where possible. Notes are intended to provide the necessary historical and cultural background; scholarly controversies are generally not dis-

---

[27] Ober 1989 is fundamental; see also Cohen 1995.

cussed. The notes and introductions refer to scholarly treatments in addition to those listed below, which the reader may consult for further information.

Cross-references to other speeches follow the standard numbering system, which is now well established except in the case of Hyperides (for whom the numbering of the Oxford Classical Text is used).[28] References are by work and section (e.g., Dem. 24.73); spurious works are not specially marked; when no author is named (e.g., 24.73), the reference is to the same author as the annotated passage.

ABBREVIATIONS

Aes.	= Aeschines
And.	= Andocides
Ant.	= Antiphon
Arist.	= Aristotle
Aristoph.	= Aristophanes
Ath. Pol.	= *The Athenian Constitution*
Dem.	= Demosthenes
Din.	= Dinarchus
Herod.	= Herodotus
Hyp.	= Hyperides
Is.	= Isaeus
Isoc.	= Isocrates
Lyc.	= Lycurgus
Lys.	= Lysias
Plut.	= Plutarch
Thuc.	= Thucydides
Xen.	= Xenophon

NOTE ON CURRENCY: The main unit of Athenian currency was the drachma; this was divided into obols and larger amounts were designated minas and talents.

---

[28]For a listing of all the orators and their works, with classifications (forensic, deliberative, epideictic) and rough dates, see Edwards 1994: 74–79.

1 drachma = 6 obols
1 mina   = 100 drachmas
1 talent   = 60 minas (6,000 drachmas)

It is impossible to give an accurate equivalence in terms of modern currency, but it may be helpful to remember that the daily wage of some skilled workers was a drachma in the mid-fifth century and 2–2½ drachmas in the later fourth century. Thus it may not be too misleading to think of a drachma as worth about $50 or £33 and a talent as about $300,000 or £200,000 in 1997 currency.

BIBLIOGRAPHY OF WORKS CITED

Boegehold, Alan L., 1995: *The Lawcourts at Athens: Sites, Buildings, Equipment, Procedure, and Testimonia*. Princeton.

Bonner, Robert J., 1927: *Lawyers and Litigants in Ancient Athens*. Chicago.

Carey, Christopher, 1997: *Trials from Classical Athens*. London.

Cohen, David, 1995: *Law, Violence and Community in Classical Athens*. Cambridge.

Cole, Thomas, 1991: *The Origins of Rhetoric in Ancient Greece*. Baltimore.

Dover, Kenneth J., 1968: *Lysias and the Corpus Lysiacum*. Berkeley.

———, 1974: *Greek Popular Morality in the Time of Plato and Aristotle*. Oxford.

———, 1978: *Greek Homosexuality*. London.

———, 1994: *Marginal Comment*. London.

Edwards, Michael, 1994: *The Attic Orators*. London.

Gagarin, Michael, and Paul Woodruff, 1995: *Early Greek Political Thought from Homer to the Sophists*. Cambridge.

Hansen, Mogens Herman, 1991: *The Athenian Democracy in the Age of Demosthenes*. Oxford.

Jebb, Richard, 1875: *The Attic Orators*, 2 vols. London.

Kennedy, George A., 1963: *The Art of Persuasion in Greece*. Princeton.

Kerferd, G. B., 1981: *The Sophistic Movement*. Cambridge.

MacDowell, Douglas M., 1978: *The Law in Classical Athens*. London.

———, ed. 1990: *Demosthenes, Against Meidias*. Oxford.

Ober, Josiah, 1989: *Mass and Elite in Democratic Athens*. Princeton.

Rhodes, P. J., trans., 1984: *Aristotle, The Athenian Constitution*. Penguin Books.

Sinclair, R. K., 1988: *Democracy and Participation in Athens*. Cambridge.

Todd, Stephen, 1993: *The Shape of Athenian Law*. Oxford.

Trevett, Jeremy, 1992: *Apollodoros the Son of Pasion*. Oxford.

———, 1996: "Did Demosthenes Publish His Deliberative Speeches?" *Hermes* 124: 425–441.

Usher, Stephen, 1976: "Lysias and His Clients," *Greek, Roman and Byzantine Studies* 17: 31–40.

———, trans., 1974–1985: *Dionysius of Halicarnassus, Critical Essays*. 2 vols. Loeb Classical Library. Cambridge, MA.

———, 1999: *Greek Oratory: Tradition and Originality*. Oxford.

Wooten, Cecil W., trans., 1987: *Hermogenes' On Types of Style*. Chapel Hill, NC.

Worthington, Ian, 1994: "The Canon of the Ten Attic Orators," in *Persuasion: Greek Rhetoric in Action*, ed. Ian Worthington. London: 244–263.

Yunis, Harvey, 1996: *Taming Democracy: Models of Political Rhetoric in Classical Athens*. Ithaca, NY.

DEMOSTHENES, SPEECHES 1–17

INTRODUCTION TO DEMOSTHENES

By Michael Gagarin

Since antiquity Demosthenes (384–322 BC) has usually been judged the greatest of the Attic orators. Although the patriotic and nationalistic tenor of his message has been more highly regarded in some periods of history than in others, he is unique in his mastery of so many different rhetorical styles and his ability to blend them into a powerful ensemble.

LIFE

Demosthenes was born into an old wealthy Athenian family. His father Demosthenes owned workshops that made swords and furniture. His maternal grandfather, Gylon, had been exiled from Athens and lived in the Crimea, where his mother Cleobule was born (perhaps to a Scythian mother). When Demosthenes was seven, his father died leaving his estate in the trust of several guardians. According to Demosthenes' own account, the guardians mismanaged and defrauded the estate to the point that when he turned eighteen, the age of majority, he received almost nothing. He devoted the next several years to recovering his property, first studying forensic pleading and then bringing a series of suits against the guardians to recover his patrimony (speeches 27–31). He won the first case (27, *Against Aphobus I*), but then had to bring several more suits in order to collect the amount awarded him by the court. In the course of these trials he gained a reputation as a successful speaker, became sought after by others, and began to write speeches for a wide range of private suits, including inheritance, shipping loans, assault, and trespass. His clients included one of the richest men in Athens, the banker Phormio;

the speech *For Phormio* (36) involves a dispute over twenty talents (equivalent to several million dollars today). Demosthenes' vivid characterization of the honest, hard-working Phormio and his malicious and extravagant opponent proved so convincing that the jurors reportedly refused to listen to the other side and took the highly unusual step of voting immediately for Phormio.

In 355 Demosthenes became involved in his first major public case (22, *Against Androtion*). By this time it was common for ambitious or influential citizens to bring legal charges against their political opponents on matters of public interest. Charges of proposing an illegal decree (the *graphē paranomōn*) were particularly common; these involved the indictment of the proposer of a decree on the ground that it conflicted with existing law.[1] Although these speeches addressed the specific issue of a conflict between laws, it was generally accepted that the merits of the decree, and of its proposer, were also relevant factors, and these cases formed a major arena for the ongoing political struggles between leading figures in the city.

About the same time Demosthenes also began to publish speeches on public issues which he delivered in the Assembly, and after 350, although he continued from time to time to write speeches for private disputes, he turned his attention primarily to public policy, especially relations between Athens and the growing power of Macedon under King Philip. Demosthenes' strategy throughout was to increase Athens' military readiness, to oppose Philip's expansion and to support other Greek cities in their resistance to it. Most notable in support of these objectives were the three *Olynthiacs* (1–3) in 349 unsuccessfully urging support for the city of Olynthus (which soon afterwards fell to Philip) and the four *Philippics* (4, 6, 9, 10) in 351–341 urging greater opposition to Philip. But Philip continued to extend his power into Greece, and in 338 he defeated a combined Greek force (including Athens)

---

[1]One might compare the U.S. procedure of challenging the constitutionality of a law in court. Differences include the fact that today no charge is brought against the proposer of the law and that the case is heard by a small panel of professional judges, not the hundreds of untrained jurors who would have heard the case in Athens.

at the battle of Chaeronea in Boeotia, north of Attica. This battle
is usually taken to mark the end of the Greek cities' struggle to remain independent.

After Chaeronea Demosthenes continued to urge resistance to
Philip, but his efforts were largely ineffectual and his successes
and failures are more a matter of internal Athenian politics. His
most prominent opponent during this period was Aeschines, who
had been acquitted earlier (343) when Demosthenes brought a suit
against him in connection with a delegation to Philip on which
both men had served (19, cf. Aeschines 2). After Chaeronea, when
a minor ally of Demosthenes named Ctesiphon proposed a decree awarding a crown to Demosthenes in recognition of his service to the city, Aeschines brought a *graphē paranomōn* against
Ctesiphon (Aeschines 3). The suit, which was not tried until 330,
raised legal objections to the proposed decree but also attacked
the person and career of Demosthenes at considerable length. Demosthenes responded with his most famous speech *On the Crown*
(18), often known by its Latin name *De Corona*. The verdict was
so one-sided that Aeschines was fined for not receiving one-fifth
of the votes and went into exile. This was Demosthenes' greatest
triumph. The last years of his life, however, resulted in notable de-
feats, first in the rather shadowy Harpalus affair (324–323), from
which no speech of his survives (but see Dinarchus 1). Shortly afterwards he was condemned to death at the instigation of pro-
Macedonian forces and committed suicide.

WORKS

Sixty-one speeches and some miscellaneous works, including a
collection of letters, have come down to us under Demosthenes'
name. The authenticity of many of these has been challenged, often because of the allegedly poor quality of the work; but this reason is less often accepted today, and most of the public speeches
and many of the private speeches are now thought to be authentic. Among the main exceptions are a group of private speeches
(45, 46, 49, 50, 52, 53, 59 and possibly 47 and 51) that were delivered by Apollodorus and are now commonly thought to have
been composed by him (Trevett 1992).

Apart from a funeral oration (60) and collections of proems and letters, Demosthenes' works fall into two groups, the Assembly speeches (1–17) and the court speeches (18–59); the latter can be further divided into public and private speeches, though these are not formal legal categories. Notable among the public forensic speeches are *Against Meidias* (21), which has recently drawn attention for its pronouncements on Athenian public values, and his last surviving speech, *On the Crown* (18), generally recognized as his masterpiece. In this speech he uses his entire repertory of rhetorical strategies to defend his life and political career. He treats the legal issues of the case briefly, as being of minor concern, and then defends his conduct during the past three decades of Athenian history, arguing that even when his policy did not succeed, on each occasion it was the best policy for the city, in contrast to Aeschines' policies, which, when he ventured to propose any, were disastrous. Demosthenes' extensive personal attack on Aeschines' life and family may be too harsh for modern taste, but the blending of facts, innuendoes, sarcasm, rhetorical questions, and other devices is undeniably effective.

Demosthenes' private speeches have recently begun to attract more interest from scholars, who draw from them insight into Athenian social, political, and economic life. Only the speeches concerned with recovering his inheritance (27–31) were delivered by Demosthenes himself; the rest were written for delivery by other litigants. We have already noted *For Phormio*, which is one of several having to do with banking. *Against Conon* (54) alleges an assault by several young rowdies spurred on by their father, and *Against Neaera* (59), delivered and probably written by Apollodorus, recounts the life of a former slave woman and her affairs with different Athenian men.

STYLE

Demosthenes is a master of Greek prose style; he paid careful attention to style, and to the oral delivery of his speeches. His Roman counterpart, Cicero, modeled his oratorical style (and some other features of his work) in part on Demosthenes' Greek. Although Demosthenes' style varied considerably over the course of time and among the different types of speeches, later assessments of his style are based primarily on the public forensic speeches, and especially the last of these, *On the Crown*. Long and sometimes elaborate sentences are one feature of his style, but Demosthenes' true greatness is his ability to write in many styles and to vary his style, mixing different features together both to suit the topic and to give variety and vigor to his speeches. The final product required great skill and practice to deliver effectively, and the stories about Demosthenes' rigorous training in delivery (see in general Plutarch, *Life of Demosthenes* 6–7), even if not literally true, accurately reflect his priorities. Indeed, only by reading aloud sections of *On the Crown* in Greek can one truly appreciate the power and authority of his prose.

SIGNIFICANCE

Demosthenes played a vital role in Athenian public affairs for some thirty years. His advocacy of the vigilant defense of Greece against foreign invaders, though ultimately unsuccessful in preserving Greek freedom, inspired his fellow Athenians with patriotic loyalty, and has similarly inspired many others in later times. In recent times political rhetoric has not been so widely admired as in the past, and Demosthenes is less read today than he used to be. But he still represents the greatest achievement of Greek oratory and stands as one of the greatest orators of any age.

INTRODUCTION TO THIS VOLUME

‹›

By Jeremy Trevett

This volume contains translations of all the surviving deliberative speeches of Demosthenes, including several whose authenticity has been questioned (Dem. 7, 10, 11, 13, 17), as well as the text
of a letter of Philip of Macedon to the Athenians (Dem. 12). Collectively these form the first seventeen "speeches" of the corpus of
Demosthenes' works. All the speeches were, or at least purported
to be, written to be delivered to the Athenian Assembly and are in
fact almost the only examples in Attic oratory of the genre of deliberative oratory.

POLITICAL LIFE IN FOURTH-CENTURY ATHENS

The sovereign decision-making body of democratic Athens
was the Assembly (*ekklēsia*), a public meeting, held approximately
forty times a year, that was open to all adult Athenian citizens.[1]
Attendance varied, but on occasions over six thousand citizens,
perhaps a quarter of the citizen body, will have been present. The
agenda was prepared in advance by the Council (*boulē*), which for
each item on the agenda might either make a definite proposal
or simply put the matter forward for discussion. When the herald asked "who wishes to speak?" it was open to any Athenian to
come forward, ascend the speaker's platform (*bēma*), and address

---

[1]Hansen 1991 is an accessible account of the institutions of Athens'
fourth-century democracy. Rhodes 1986 provides a useful, brief introduction to the practice of politics at Athens. On political participation of various kinds, see Sinclair 1988.

his fellow-citizens, either speaking for or against the proposal already before the Assembly or making a new proposal himself.

This prospect must have been daunting for many Athenians, and in practice the speakers tended to come from a relatively small number of citizens, who are referred to variously as "the speakers" (*hoi rhētores*) or "those who engage in politics" (*hoi politeuomenoi*). These "politicians," as it is convenient to describe them, were generally wealthy enough to be able to devote much of their time to political activity without the need to work for a living. In addition to speaking in the Assembly and proposing decrees, they are also found serving on embassies and engaging in politically motivated litigation. Some, but by no means all, also put themselves forward for election to hold the military post of general (*stratēgos*), although this was less common in the fourth century than in the fifth.[2]

Classical Athens wholly lacked the political parties of modern parliamentary democracies. In theory its political leaders needed no organization behind them, and Demosthenes often gives the impression that he is quite alone in addressing the Athenian Assembly. In practice, however, politicians did cooperate with each other, either on the basis of personal ties or because they agreed on matters of policy, although such alliances were often impermanent and ad hoc. Demosthenes indeed complains that the Athenians conduct their politics "by symmories," that is, by means of "parties," each dominated by a politician and a general (2.29). In one passage, he refers to the proposal that "we" have devised (4.30), offering a fleeting glimpse of those others who shared his views and collaborated with him. Political associates might cooperate in other areas, for example, on embassies (see 9.72) or in court. Moreover, it is in the 340s that we find a clear polarization on the issue of relations with Macedon, with Demosthenes the leading figure in what may fairly be called an anti-Macedonian party, together with men such as Hyperides and Hegesippus. Demosthenes often alleges that rival politicians are conspiring together to advance Philip's interests. These men are almost never

---

[2]Demosthenes himself never held military command.

named in his speeches to the Assembly (cf. 10.70–74), but the identity of several of them, such as Eubulus and Aeschines, is known.

ATHENS IN THE MIDDLE OF THE FOURTH CENTURY

Although Athens was the richest and most powerful city of mainland Greece, its prospects at the time when Demosthenes delivered his first deliberative speech (Dem. 14 of 354/3) were uncertain.[3] The central issues with which Demosthenes was concerned were foreign policy and public finance. Athens' external interests and commitments were many and complex. First, it had hegemonic ambitions in the Aegean and was the leader of an (originally anti-Spartan) league known by modern historians as the Second Athenian Confederacy, which consisted of many Greek cities of the Aegean and beyond.[4] But the Athenians had recently suffered a humiliating reverse in the Social War (357–355) at the hands of several leading members of the league, who had become disenchanted with Athenian leadership and had forcibly seceded from it.[5]

Second, Athens had long-standing strategic interests in the north Aegean, with a particular wish to regain Amphipolis and control the Chersonese. Amphipolis, a city on the river Strymon in Thrace, was founded by Athens in the fifth century but had been lost during the Peloponnesian War; its recovery became an *idée fixe*.[6] The Chersonese (modern Gallipoli peninsula) controls the Hellespont, the straits connecting the Sea of Marmara and the Aegean Sea, and it was vital for Athens' ability to import from the Black Sea region the wheat on which it depended to feed its population.

---

[3]Developments in the earlier part of the fourth century are surveyed by Sealey 1993; see also the relevant chapters of Hornblower 2002 and Rhodes 2006.

[4]On the Second Athenian Confederacy, see Cargill 1981.

[5]See the Introduction to Dem. 15. On defections from the league, see Cargill 1981: 161–188.

[6]On Athenian imperialism in this period, see Badian 1995 and Harding 1995.

Third, Athens had strained relations with the Persian Empire, in part because of the involvement of the satrap (i.e., Persian provincial governor) Mausolus in the Social War against Athens (see Dem. 15) and in part because of the recent assistance provided by the Athenian general Chares to the rebel satrap Artabazus.[7] Fourth, Athens had interests in mainland Greece. There the long-standing rivalry between the three leading states—Athens, Sparta and Thebes—had been upset first by Sparta's rapid decline after its defeat by Thebes at the battle of Leuctra in 371, and then by Thebes' involvement in a draining war with its northern neighbor Phocis in the Third Sacred War of 356–346.[8] As a result, there developed a power vacuum in Greece.[9]

A major constraint on Athens' foreign policy in this period was the weakness of its public finances. Athens in the fourth century was no longer buoyed by tribute from its empire, as it had been in the fifth, and it was chronically short of money. Demosthenes' claim (made in 341) that in the recent past Athens' total annual revenues had amounted to no more than 130 talents (10.37) probably refers to the 350s. Money was in short supply for naval campaigning, and Athenian generals were often forced to scrounge resources where they could: hence their harassment of Athens' allies for money, which was a precipitating cause of the Social War, and Chares' taking service with Artabazus (see above). As a result, the cost of waging war fell more directly on the rich: in addition to their role in financing Athens' navy through the system of trierarchies and symmories (see Dem. 14), they were also liable to pay the wealth tax (*eisphora*), which was levied on the assets of richer Athenians. Demosthenes complains that this led many rich men to conceal the extent of their wealth. A particular source of contention was the theoric ("festival") fund. This fund had been established earlier in the century to allow poorer citizens to attend performances of plays staged as part of religious festivals. By the 350s the theoric fund was being used for other nonmilitary

---

[7] See the Introduction to Dem. 14.
[8] On the Third Sacred War, see the detailed study of Buckler 1989.
[9] See the Introduction to Dem. 16.

expenditure as well, and was fenced around by laws that made it difficult, and dangerous, to propose that the money be used for other purposes. Although the total amount of money handled by the theoric fund may not have been large in absolute terms, the use of that money for civilian expenditure came to be a matter of dispute, with Demosthenes and his supporters seeking to have it used to pay for military activity against Philip of Macedon.[10]

PHILIP OF MACEDON

The majority of Demosthenes' deliberative speeches are concerned with Athens' relations with Philip of Macedon, the ruler of a large kingdom to the north of Greece, which had previously played only a peripheral role in Greek history.[11]

Although populous and agriculturally rich, Macedonia[12] suffered from chronic dynastic and internal instability and was also regularly under threat from its non-Greek tribal neighbors to the west, north and east (Illyrians, Paeonians, and Thracians respectively). Moreover, it had long been subject to intervention on the part of the Greeks, and in particular the Athenians, who were drawn above all by access to the ship-building timber of which the region had an abundant supply. In addition to the numerous Greek cities of the Chalcidic peninsula to its east, there were also Greek settlements on the coast of Macedonia itself. Greek writers of the time generally describe the Macedonians as non-Greek, though often such statements are marked by anti-Macedonian prejudice, and the "Greekness" of the Macedonians remains an open question.[13] What is clear is that both politically and culturally Macedonia was unlike Greek cities such as Athens. At the same time the Macedonian court was strongly Hellenized: Greek

---

[10]On the theoric fund, see Sealey 1993: 256–258; Harris 1996.

[11]The fullest study of Philip's reign is Hammond and Griffith 1979. See also Ellis 1976; Cawkwell 1978; Worthington 2008. On earlier Macedonian history, see Borza 1990.

[12]The kingdom is properly called Macedonia, but Philip is traditionally identified (in English) as Philip of Macedon.

[13]See 9.31n; Badian 1982.

artists and writers were patronized, and Philip himself was well versed in Greek (see Dem. 12).

Philip succeeded to the throne of Macedonia in 359, after the death of the previous king in a disastrous military defeat at the hands of the Illyrians. The early years of his reign were largely devoted to securing his kingdom, both internally and against its non-Greek neighbors. He also started to annex nearby Greek cities: Amphipolis and Pydna in 357; Potideia in 356; and Methone probably in 354. The seizure of Amphipolis, which was originally an Athenian possession (see above), impelled the Athenians to declare war, but, distracted by the Social War and apparently deceived by Philip, they were unable to prevent his seizure of cities that they had recently controlled or that they claimed for themselves.

In the same period, Philip extended his influence eastwards into Thrace and southwards into northern Greece, where he intervened on behalf of his Thessalian allies against the Phocians. Defeated by the Phocian army in 353, he secured a crushing revenge at the battle of the Crocus Field in 352 and marched towards the strategically vital pass of Thermopylae, which controlled the passage to southern Greece. Here, however, he was thwarted by the dispatch of an Athenian expeditionary force, which blocked the pass against him. Philip followed this with continued campaigning in Thrace (see the Introduction to Dem. 4). In the late 350s his relations with the neighboring Greek cities of the Chalcidic League, headed by Olynthus, started to deteriorate, even though they were allied to him (see the Introduction to Dem. 1–3), and in 349 he invaded its territory. The Olynthians appealed to Athens for help, and the Athenians eventually sent three separate relief forces. But the effort was in vain: Philip captured Olynthus in 348, razed the city to the ground, and acquired a substantial number of Athenian prisoners in the process.

After the fall of Olynthus, the Athenians, unable to persuade any of the other Greeks to join them in further resistance to Philip, had little choice but to accept his offer to negotiate peace terms. The resulting peace, known as the Peace of Philocrates after its chief Athenian negotiator, was concluded in summer 346, on the basis of each side keeping what it possessed. The members

of Athens' league were included, but the Phocians and the independent Thracian king Cersobleptes were (despite Athenian pro-
tests) excluded. Over the same summer, Philip marched south,
took control of Thermopylae, and brought an end to the Sacred
War in favor of his ally Thebes, by destroying the cities of the
Phocians. Demosthenes, who participated in the Athenian embassies to Philip to negotiate the peace, claimed that Philip tricked
the Athenians into believing that Phocis would be saved and (less
plausibly) that he thereby prevented them occupying Thermopylae as they had done in 352.

The following years saw Philip extend his influence over
Greece. Demosthenes alleges that there was (usually indirect)
Macedonian intervention in the Peloponnese in support of anti-
Spartan states such as Elis, Argos, and Messenia and in central
Greece at Megara and on the island of Euboea. Moreover, from
342 Philip resumed campaigning against Cersobleptes in eastern Thrace. None of this activity directly involved Athens, but all
of it could be—and was—construed by anti-Macedonian politicians as threatening its interests: Sparta was Athens' ally; Megara
and Euboea were its neighbors; and Philip's Thracian campaign
brought his army close to both Byzantium and the Chersonese—
the two places that controlled Athens' economic lifeline to the
Black Sea. Public opinion at Athens became polarized between
those who thought that the city had no realistic choice but to
keep the peace and try to maintain good relations with Philip,[14]
and those who argued that Philip was plotting Athens' ruin under cover of the peace and that the Athenians needed to take action against him. Philip offered to renegotiate the peace in 344/3,
but his offer was rebuffed (see Dem. 6 and 7), and in 341 fighting broke out between Athenian forces in the Chersonese and the
neighboring Greek city of Cardia, which was allied to Philip (see
Dem. 8). As the threat of war loomed, Athens tried to build support in Greece (see Dem. 9). The events that precipitated war were
Philip's siege first of the Greek city of Perinthus, on the Sea of

---

[14]Demosthenes' main political opponents in this period were Eubulus
(see Cawkwell 1963a and *OCD*³ s.v. Eubulus) and Aeschines, on whom see
Carey 2000 in this series.

Marmara, and then of Byzantium itself (see Dem. 10). Assistance was sent to Byzantium both by Athens and by the Persians, who feared that Philip's territorial ambitions now extended to the Persian Empire itself. Philip retaliated by seizing a fleet of grain ships bound for Athens. The Athenians interpreted these actions as acts of war and renounced the peace.

Although Athens succeeded in detaching Thebes from its alliance with Philip, the resulting coalition was no match for the Macedonians, and in 338 Philip won a decisive victory over the Greeks at the battle of Chaeronea in Boeotia. As a result, all of Greece fell under Macedonian rule, and Greek independence was at an end.[15]

DEMOSTHENES' POLICIES

Demosthenes' deliberative speeches fall into two groups: those delivered before he identified Philip as an overriding threat to Athens (Dem. 13–16) and those that are concerned with Philip (what ancient critics called the "Philippics": Dem. 1–11).[16] The earlier speeches lack focus, at least by comparison, as Demosthenes addresses a number of topical issues. The first, *On the Symmories* (Dem. 14), uses perhaps exaggerated rumors of a planned Persian campaign against Athens to propose a number of reforms to the Athenian system for funding the operation of the navy. An interest in institutional reform appears also in the speech *On Organization* (Dem. 13), in which Demosthenes advocates a system whereby Athenian citizens will be paid for undertaking public services of various kinds and will no longer receive money for doing nothing (an early swipe at theoric payments: see below). In the speech *On the Freedom of the Rhodians* (Dem. 15), he ar-

---

[15]For subsequent events, see the Introduction to Dem. 17 (a speech dating to the reign of Philip's son Alexander).

[16]On Demosthenes' political career, see Pickard-Cambridge 1914; Montgomery 1983; Carlier 1990 (in French; the most balanced biography); Sealey 1993. Also influential are a series of articles by G. L. Cawkwell, some of which are cited in the bibliography. MacDowell 2009 is an excellent survey of all the speeches of Demosthenes.

gues that the Athenians should accept a request from exiled democrats from the island of Rhodes to support the restoration of democracy there. Demosthenes asserts that it is in Athens' interest to support democracy everywhere in Greece, but in seeking to persuade the Athenians to help the Rhodians, he faced an uphill task, since Rhodes had recently participated in the Social War against Athens. Moreover, his attempt to explain how such an intervention would not antagonize the satrap of Caria, who supported the oligarchs on Rhodes, or the Persian King, who was campaigning nearby against Egypt, seem unconvincing. The remaining early speech, *For the Megalopolitans* (Dem. 16), argues in favor of accepting a request from the central Peloponnesian city of Megalopolis for an alliance, in the face of the threat of Spartan attack. In this speech Demosthenes shows a keen awareness of the principle of the balance of power, and he uses complex arguments to argue that Athens' paramount strategic goal was to prevent the resurgence of Spartan power in the Peloponnese. The speech is contrarian, since Athens and Sparta were firm allies at this time, and it is not surprising that it, like the other early speeches, failed to persuade its audience.

These speeches, which have tended to be criticized as opportunistic and immature, certainly make blithe assumptions about the likely behavior of others (e.g., the Spartans in Dem. 16, Artemisia in Dem. 15), but they also show Demosthenes to be a serious student of foreign policy, capable of independent thought, and seeking in a sense to redeem Athens as an active and principled participant in the affairs of Greece after the fiasco of the Social War. Even at this early stage we see his concern for institutional reform and still more for a change of attitude on the part of the Athenians towards public service.

The *First Philippic* (Dem. 4) marks a turning point in Demosthenes' political career. In this speech, delivered only a year or so later than those discussed above, he focuses exclusively on the threat that Philip poses to Athens. Philip's decisive victory at the battle of the Crocus Field in 352, his march south on Thermopylae, and his subsequent campaigning in eastern Thrace all convinced Demosthenes that Athens' strategic situation had changed, radically and for the worse. To deal with the threat posed by

Philip, Demosthenes makes specific military proposals: for the creation of a rapid-response force based in Athens and a permanent raiding force to be stationed in the north Aegean. He also encourages the Athenians not to despair, while criticizing them for their laxness and demanding that they show greater willingness to serve in person. The three *Olynthiacs*, Dem. 1–3, were delivered during Philip's campaign against the cities of the Chalcidic League. In them Demosthenes advocates that Athens send help to the beleaguered city of Olynthus. He argues that Philip's unprovoked attack on the league is a heaven-sent opportunity for Athens (Dem. 1), and he belittles Philip as being much weaker than he appears (Dem. 2). By the time of the last speech of the series (Dem. 3), Olynthus' military situation seems to have deteriorated, and Demosthenes' tone is less optimistic. In this speech too he states bluntly what he had only alluded to earlier: that the Athenians should divert money from the theoric fund to pay for the war.

The remaining deliberative speeches all belong to the period between the making of the Peace of Philocrates in 346 and the outbreak of war between Athens and Philip in 340.[17] *On the Peace* (Dem. 5) was delivered shortly after the peace was ratified, and it reverts to the cautious attitude of Dem. 14. Demosthenes argues that, although the peace is a bad deal for Athens, it would be foolish to oppose Philip in his desire to participate in the Delphic Amphictyony, a religious organization based at Delphi, and thereby risk his organizing a broadly based coalition against Athens. By the time of the *Second Philippic* (Dem. 6) of 344/3, Demosthenes' approach is more aggressive. This speech was apparently delivered in response to an overture from Philip to the Athenians to renegotiate those terms of the Peace of Philocrates with which they were dissatisfied. Demosthenes largely passes over this offer and uses the speech to denounce both Philip and his Greek allies. Philip, he claims, has violated the terms of the peace and is plotting against Athens. At the same time, he sharply attacks un-

---

[17] Dem. 17 dates to the reign of Philip's son Alexander, but it is probably not a genuine speech of Demosthenes.

named Athenian politicians who, he alleges, have been bribed by Philip to advance his interests.

The remaining three major speeches[18] belong closely together in time, when the likelihood of war had sharply increased. In the first of them, *On the Chersonese* (Dem. 8), Demosthenes argues that the Athenians need to support Diopeithes, their general in the Chersonese, who is conducting an aggressive policy against Philip's interests in the region. The *Third Philippic* (Dem. 9) addresses the state of Greece as a whole. In it Demosthenes criticizes Philip for a series of interventions in various cities of southern and central Greece, and the rest of the Greeks for their abandonment of the love of liberty that had characterized Greece in the fifth century. Demosthenes argues that the Greeks should unite against Philip, whom he vilifies as a wretched foreigner. In the *Fourth Philippic* (Dem. 10) he addresses many of the same themes—there is considerable recycling of material from Dem. 8 in particular— but also discusses the possibility of Persia joining Athens against Philip. Prompted in part by the prospect of Persian financial aid, Demosthenes withdraws his opposition to the use of the theoric fund for nonmilitary expenditure and asks rich and poor Athenians to stop squabbling over public finances.

The "Philippic" speeches of Demosthenes were delivered over the course of an eleven-year period, and each responds to the circumstances of the time. Thus, in *On the Peace* (Dem. 5) he seeks to defuse pressure to go to war with Philip, and in the *Fourth Philippic* (Dem. 10) he changes his earlier views about the theoric fund. Nevertheless there is considerable thematic unity over the speeches as a whole—a unity that is reinforced by the frequent repetition of material from one speech to another. Demosthenes argues strongly that Philip is an inveterate enemy to Athens: his actions are all ultimately directed against the city, and his protes-

---

[18]Dem. 8–10. Of the others, Dem. 11 is short and derivative of Demosthenes' earlier speeches. It is also generally regarded as not by Demosthenes, though see the Speech Introduction for a recent defense of its authenticity. Dem. 7 is generally taken to be a work of another Athenian politician, Hegesippus. It is a belligerent response to Philip's diplomatic overtures and represents a cruder version of Demosthenes' policy at the time.

tations of goodwill are deceitful. The Athenians should not fear him too much, but they must recognize the danger, be prepared to raise taxes, and undertake military service in person. Demosthenes also alleges that many politicians (i.e., those who disagree with him) have been bribed by Philip. He consistently represents himself as the one speaker who discerns the danger posed by Philip and advocates the correct policies to deal with him. In polarizing the issues in such a way, and in attacking the moral failures of the Athenians and their leaders, he avoids seriously addressing the views of his opponents, who presumably disagreed (with equal sincerity) with his analysis of Philip's intentions and over the policies that Athens should adopt towards him.[19]

Whether Demosthenes was right to pursue such strongly anti-Macedonian policies is much debated. Against older views that accepted his allegations, both about Philip and about some of his fellow political leaders, at face value and that saw him as fighting a lone patriotic hand against Athens' deadly enemy, it has more recently been argued that his repeated allegations of bribery are unfounded; that some of his complaints of Macedonian interference in the affairs of Greek cities are tendentious at best, mendacious at worst; and that his entire strategy was based on a false view of Philip as ill disposed towards Athens. The result, it is argued, was to provoke a war that Athens had no chance of winning.[20] There

---

[19]Demosthenes maintains that the appropriate policies are clear but that what is lacking is the will to carry them out. He very rarely seeks to counter the actual *arguments* of rival speakers. The techniques by which he seeks to manipulate Athenian opinion to support his policies are examined in a series of recent articles by G. Mader (e.g., 2005, 2006).

[20]The former view is represented by older works such as Pickard-Cambridge 1914 and Jaeger 1938. The chief architect of the revisionist view is G. L. Cawkwell, in a series of influential articles. In particular, Cawkwell 1962a argues that Demosthenes' policy of sending troops to defend Olynthus and fight Philip in the north (see Dem. 1–4) was misguided; Cawkwell 1963b argues that Demosthenes exaggerates (esp. in Dem. 6) the extent of Philip's interference in the affairs of Greek cities in the second half of the 340s. Harding 1987 provides a useful survey of Demosthenes' fluctuating reputation.

is some plausibility in this view, but the reaction against previous adulation of Demosthenes has gone too far. Philip's motives were inherently unclear, but the fact of his growing domination of Greece was undeniable. Even if Demosthenes' political opponents at Athens were not bribed by Philip, they might well be regarded as his dupes.

Demosthenes clearly does exaggerate at times, but it would be naïve to brand him a liar (and there were surely limits to how far any politician could safely misrepresent current events to the Assembly); rather, such exaggeration was a rhetorical strategy in the service of his overriding goal, which was to persuade the Athenians of the reality of the danger that Philip posed. If different policies had been followed, Athens might indeed have avoided war. But in a Greece dominated by Macedonia, it would inevitably have been reduced to the level of a vassal state, its security wholly in Philip's hands. For the majority of Athenians, as eventually for the Thebans too, such a prospect was intolerable.

COMPOSITION, DELIVERY, AND PUBLICATION

The set of deliberative speeches attributed to Demosthenes in the manuscripts (Dem. 1–17) is a somewhat miscellaneous collection, since it contains one work that is obviously neither a speech nor by Demosthenes (Dem. 12, the *Letter of Philip*) and two speeches (Dem. 7 and 17) that were rightly judged in antiquity to be dissimilar in style to the genuine speeches of Demosthenes. Of the other speeches, doubts have been raised about the authenticity of Dem. 10, 11, and 13. It has also been proposed that Dem. 17 is not a genuine speech of Alexander's reign but a later composition. Many of the doubts that have been raised about these speeches are the product of a hypercritical attitude prevalent in nineteenth-century scholarship, and it is now generally, though not universally, agreed that Dem. 10 and 13 are genuine; even Dem. 11 may be by Demosthenes, it has recently been suggested. In addition, there is no reason to deny that Dem. 12 is a genuine letter of Philip (whether or not he wrote it himself), and the view is taken in this volume that Dem. 17, although not written by Demosthenes, is the work of a contemporary anti-Macedonian politician.

How, when, and by whom these works were collected is unclear. It presumably happened after Demosthenes' lifetime, and a likely candidate is his nephew Demochares, in the early third century. It seems plausible that he, or whoever the compiler was, bundled in with the genuine speeches some works—perhaps found among Demosthenes' papers—that related to the speeches (i.e., Dem. 12) or that were written by his supporters and were taken to reflect his views (Dem. 7 and 17). Also included were a set of *Prologues* (*prooimia* in Greek) to deliberative speeches: several of these correspond to the prologues of surviving speeches, and they are best regarded as written by Demosthenes to form the basis for largely improvised speeches.[21]

Deliberative oratory seems not to have lent itself to written composition,[22] and it is striking that these speeches are almost the only examples of the genre from classical Athens.[23] Moreover, literary scholars of antiquity mention almost no other (now lost) written deliberative speeches, and so their small number is not an accident of survival.[24] Most speeches to the Assembly will have been made extemporaneously; almost by definition politicians had to be capable public speakers, who could participate in a debate without being tied to a prepared text.[25] Demosthenes may have been unusual if not unique in writing his speeches out

---

[21] *Prologues* 3, 7, 8, and 27 correspond to Dem. 1, 14, 16, and 15 respectively. For translations of the *Prologues*, see Worthington 2006 in this series. The *Prologues* are helpfully discussed by Yunis 1996: 247–257.

[22] See Hudson-Williams 1951; Tuplin 1998: 292–295.

[23] The only other surviving deliberative speech is Andocides 3, though its authenticity has been doubted (see Harris 2000). In addition, two of the works in this volume, Dem. 7 and 17, are (or purport to be) genuine deliberative speeches to the Athenian Assembly and are almost certainly not the work of Demosthenes.

[24] Thus Hansen 1984: 60–66; cf. Yunis 1996: 243 n. 14.

[25] Cf. p. 7 above on politicians as "the speakers." By contrast, lawcourt speeches could be written out in advance and delivered from memory without significant interruption (though see Bers 1985 for heckling in court) and within a set period of time. It is therefore not surprising that many more lawcourt speeches have survived from classical Athens.

in advance.[26] In this regard it is significant that the biographical tradition about him, especially as transmitted by Plutarch in his *Life of Demosthenes*, emphasizes his use of writing: Demosthenes' speeches, his opponents sneered, "smelled of the lamp" (Plut. *Demosthenes* 8). It seems likely therefore that the texts we have were written, at least in the first instance, as drafts of the speeches that Demosthenes intended to make to the Assembly.[27]

Given our ignorance of what Demosthenes said on any occasion, the precise relationship between the texts we have and the speeches that he delivered is largely unknowable. In Dem. 15 he refers (6) to his having previously delivered a speech that is presumably identical, or very similar, to Dem. 14. If he wrote out his speeches in advance (see above), we cannot know whether he delivered any individual speech as written (or indeed whether he delivered it at all). Presumably at a minimum there was a certain amount of extemporizing, for example, to respond to points made by other speakers. On the whole, however, it is probably safe to suppose that the surviving speeches represent more or less what Demosthenes intended to say on a particular occasion, although dating them is a difficult matter.[28]

Whether Demosthenes published the texts of his deliberative speeches, and whether he revised them before doing so, are two separate though related questions, since he is likely to have revised a speech after its delivery only if he intended to publish it, that is, to make copies to be circulated among his friends and support-

---

[26]Yunis 1996: 242 suggests that he may have been the first politician to do so, in part because of his background as a writer of lawcourt speeches (see previous note). This background may indeed be relevant, but there is no evidence, as Yunis implies, that other politicians followed his example.

[27]On Demosthenes' nervousness as a public speaker, see Aes. 2.34; Plut. *Demosthenes* 11; and MacDowell 2009: 6. It is possible that the lack of Assembly speeches from the period after 340 is due to his increased confidence as a speaker, which meant that he did not feel the need to write out his speeches in advance.

[28]See pp. 23–24 below on the dates provided by the ancient critic Dionysius of Halicarnassus.

ers, either in Athens or elsewhere.[29] Earlier scholars were overly inclined to find evidence of revision in Demosthenes' speeches, on the assumption that (like the Roman orator Cicero) he carefully revised his speeches before publishing them. An example is the reference to Philip's raid on the territory of Olynthus in Dem. 4, delivered in 351, which was once wrongly believed to be an interpolated reference to the war of 349/8, rather than a contemporary reference to an earlier incursion.[30] In fact, the evidence for revision is very limited.[31] It has been argued that Dem. 8 is a revised speech that includes material originally written for the later Dem. 10, although this is uncertain.[32] Revision has also been proposed to explain why some medieval manuscripts of Demosthenes' speeches contain a slightly longer version of Dem. 9 and others, a shorter one. If the material found only in the longer text is genuine, as it seems to be, then it is possible that the speech was edited by Demosthenes himself, to distribute it outside Athens. In my view, however, a different explanation is more likely.[33]

Whether or not the surviving deliberative speeches show signs of revision, it is commonly believed that Demosthenes himself published them.[34] His purpose in doing so is unlikely to have been to influence public policy at Athens, since as an active politician he could achieve that end much more effectively by addressing the Assembly. It is conceivable that he published some of his speeches to influence opinion elsewhere in Greece, though it can be objected that this aim would have been better served

---

[29]Since all copies of a text had to be made by hand, there was no equivalent in the ancient world to modern publication, and the total number of copies of even "published" speeches must have been small.

[30]See 4.17n.

[31]See in general Trevett 1996.

[32]See the Introduction to Dem. 10 for discussion.

[33]The issue has recently been discussed by Wooten 2008: 167–173, who argues this case. For doubts, see MacDowell 2009: 353. See more fully the Introduction to Dem. 9.

[34]See Hansen 1984: 60–66; Sealey 1993: 221–229; Yunis 1996: 241–247; Tuplin 1998.

by speeches, whether circulated in writing or delivered in person, that were composed for the purpose and that addressed their intended audience directly.[35] It seems most likely, therefore, that if he published his speeches, he did so to vindicate himself, in the eyes both of his contemporaries and of posterity, and in the face of heated criticism from his political rivals,[36] as a farsighted and honest adviser of the people, and a significant political thinker.[37] It is not certain, however, that Demosthenes did publish his speeches at all. An alternative, and in my view more likely, explanation is that the texts of his speeches are simply drafts of what he intended to say to the Assembly, were for the most part filed away once they had served their purpose, and remained substantially unpublished until after his death.[38]

ANCIENT COMMENTATORS ON DEMOSTHENES

The speeches of Demosthenes were much read, studied, and written about in antiquity, and since the ancient commentators are important sources of information about their date, content, and authorship, and are frequently referred to in this volume, it

---

[35]In any case, some of the speeches, especially the pre-Philippic speeches Dem. 14–16, are unlikely to have been of much *political* interest outside Athens.

[36]The trial "on the crown" of 330, in which Aeschines prosecuted Demosthenes' supporter Ctesiphon, was concerned largely with the assessment of Demosthenes' political record: see Aes. 3; Dem. 18.

[37]The strongest argument that some of the speeches were distributed in Demosthenes' lifetime is an anecdote that suggests that a contemporary of his named Aesion had *read* them (Plut. *Demosthenes* 11.4: "the speeches of Demosthenes, when read out, were far superior . . ."). Tuplin 1998 argues that the corpus of deliberative speeches that in his view were published (Dem. 1–6, 8, 9, 14–16) demonstrates various patterns that are "consciously informed by considerations of a literary and paradigmatic nature" (p. 319), i.e., that Demosthenes carefully selected and arranged the speeches. I find this implausible.

[38]Thus, Trevett 1996. See too MacDowell 2009: 8, "In the majority of cases I think it likely that Demosthenes did not revise or distribute the texts of his speeches but simply kept them at home."

may be useful to make some general remarks about them.[39] The manuscripts of Dem. 1–17 contain introductions (*hypotheseis* in Greek) to each of the speeches written by the fourth-century AD scholar Libanius of Antioch, as well as anonymous commentaries on them (*scholia* in Greek, referred to as ancient commentary or commentator in this volume). These commentaries deal mostly with rhetorical matters, but they also contain discussion of historical questions.[40]

One very important commentary, partially preserved on papyrus, was discovered in Egypt at the end of the nineteenth century. It is the work of Didymus, a scholar of the first century nicknamed "brass guts" because of his prodigious industriousness.[41] It covers Dem. 9 (the end only), 10, 12 and the beginning of 13: presumably the complete work dealt with all the deliberative speeches. Didymus is particularly important because he argues for his views and cites excerpts from the (otherwise lost) works of fourth- and third-century historians that covered the period. Of these, the two most important are Theopompus of Chios, whose substantial contemporary *Philippic History* covered Greek history during the years of Philip's reign (359–336), and Philochorus of Athens, who wrote an annalistic *Atthis* (i.e., a year-by-year history of Athens) that covered the same period in great detail.[42] Last, the first-century rhetorician Dionysius of Halicarnassus, in the course of a work (the *First Letter to Ammaeus*) in which he seeks to prove that Aristotle's *Rhetoric* was a later work than any of Demosthenes' deliberative speeches, provides dates for all the speeches (ex-

---

[39] See in general Dickey 2007: 51–53; Gibson 2002.

[40] These are cited by page and line numbers from the Greek text of Dilts 1983.

[41] Harding 2006 provides a very useful translation of and commentary on Didymus' text. Didymus is cited by column and line number from the papyrus roll.

[42] Translations of the surviving fragments of Theopompus can be found in Shrimpton 1991; of Philochorus, in Harding 2008. The only surviving narrative history that covers this period is the *Library of History* of Diodorus Siculus, a Greek historian of the first century BC, which lacks detail and is unreliable on matters of chronology.

cept Dem. 13). It seems likely that Dionysius took over these dates from another source, and it is a matter of debate how much confidence should be put in them.[43]

LIST OF WORKS IN THIS VOLUME

For discussion of questions of date and authorship, see the introductions to the individual speeches.

1. *First Olynthiac*, 349/8.

2. *Second Olynthiac*, 349/8.

3. *Third Olynthiac*, 349/8.

4. *First Philippic*, 351.

5. *On the Peace*, 346.

6. *Second Philippic*, 344/3.

7. *On Halonnesus*, 343/2 (by Hegesippus, not Demosthenes).

8. *On the Chersonese*, 341.

9. *Third Philippic*, 341.

10. *Fourth Philippic*, 341.

11. *Response to the Letter of Philip*, 340 (perhaps spurious).

12. *Letter of Philip*, 340 (probably a genuine letter from Philip).

13. *On Organization*, Late 350s.

14. *On the Symmories*, 354/3.

15. *On the Freedom of the Rhodians*, Late 350s.

16. *For the Megalopolitans*, 353/2.

17. *On the Agreement with Alexander*, 331? (not by Demosthenes).

---

[43]See Sealey 1955; Lane Fox 1997; Lewis 1997: 230–251. The dates of individual speeches are discussed in the speech introductions.

CHRONOLOGY

359	Accession of Philip as king of Macedonia.
357	Philip captures Amphipolis and Pydna. Athens declares war on Philip.
357–355	Social War between Athens and several of its disaffected allies.
356–346	Third Sacred War between Thebes and Phocis.
356	Philip captures Potidaea.
354	Philip captures Methone.
354/3	*On the Symmories* (Dem. 14).
353/2	*For the Megalopolitans* (Dem. 16).
352	Philip defeats Phocian army at the battle of Crocus Field in Thessaly. Athenian army occupies the pass of Thermopylae.
352–350	Philip campaigns in Thrace; *On the Freedom of the Rhodians* (Dem. 15); *On Organization* (Dem. 13).
351	*First Philippic* (Dem. 4).
349/8	Philip attacks Chalcidic League and besieges Olynthus. Athens sends relief forces to Olynthus. *First, Second, Third Olynthiacs* (Dem. 1–3).
348	Fall of Olynthus.
346	Peace of Philocrates between Philip and Athens. End of the Third Sacred War and defeat of Phocis. Philip gains control of Thermopylae. *On the Peace* (Dem. 5).
344/3	Persian embassy to Athens. Philip offers to revise the Peace of Philocrates. *Second Philippic* (Dem. 6).
343	*On the Dishonest Embassy* (Dem. 19).
343/2	*On Halonnesus* (Dem. 7).
342–340	Philip campaigns in Thrace and defeats Cersobleptes.
341	Hostilities between the Athenian force in the Chersonese and Philip's ally Cardia. *On the Chersonese* (Dem. 8); *Third Philippic* (Dem. 9); *Fourth Philippic* (Dem. 10).

340	Philip besieges Perinthus and Byzantium. Outbreak of war between Philip and Athens. *Letter of Philip* (Dem. 12); *Response to the Letter of Philip* (Dem. 11).
339	Alliance between Thebes and Athens.
338	Philip defeats the Greek army at the battle of Chaeronea.
337	Establishment of the League of Corinth.
336	Murder of Philip; accession of Alexander as king of Macedonia. Initial Macedonian invasion of Asia Minor.
335	Revolt and sack of Thebes.
334	Launch of the major Macedonian invasion of the Persian Empire.
331	Spartan revolt against Macedonian rule led by King Agis. Possible date of *On the Agreement with Alexander* (Dem. 17).
330	*On the Crown* (Dem. 18).

1. FIRST OLYNTHIAC

∻∻

INTRODUCTION TO DEMOSTHENES 1–3

Olynthus was a city in the Chalcidic peninsula and the head of the Chalcidic League, the only significant Greek power in the north Aegean.[1] The league had made an alliance with Philip of Macedon in 357, when he offered to recover for them the nearby city of Potidaea, which was controlled by Athens and had a garrison of Athenian "cleruchs," that is, settlers.[2] Philip and his new allies proceeded to lay siege to Potidaea, probably in early 356 (Diodorus 16.8.5). Demosthenes states that the Athenians voted to send a relief expedition, but that nothing came of it (4.35), no doubt in part because Athens at the time was embroiled in the Social War against some of its allies who were in revolt. When Potidaea fell, the Athenian settlers were sent home, but the Potidaeans themselves were sold into slavery, and their city and land were handed over to the Chalcidic League. Philip also gave it Anthemous, a city that had previously been a bone of contention between Macedonia and Olynthus (Libanius *Introduction to Dem. 1* 2).

Nevertheless, relations between Philip and Olynthus started to deteriorate in the late 350s. Philip's growing power alarmed the Olynthians, who started to turn towards Athens instead. Demosthenes claimed in a speech of 352 (Dem. 23.107–109) that after the

---

[1] This general introduction deals with the background to the three *Olynthiacs*, which have a common subject matter and were all delivered within a short period. Each speech also has a shorter individual introduction. On these speeches, see MacDowell 2009: 229–239.

[2] See Dem. 23.107–109; Diodorus 16.8.3–4; Tod 1948: no. 158.

Olynthians started to be alarmed by Philip's strength, "they have made friendship with you [the Athenians] and say that they will make alliance." In the *First Philippic* (probably of 351) he refers to Philip's "sudden campaigns from his own land against Thermopylae and the Chersonese and Olynthus and anywhere else he wishes" (4.17). Since he mentions Olynthus only in passing, some less serious incident than outright war was evidently involved.[3] In addition, the historian Theopompus, in a passage describing events of 351/0 (*FGH* 115 fragment 127), reports that Philip told the Chalcidians a fable, that War follows close on the heels of Arrogance (*hybris*).

Taken together, these passages suggest that Philip was angered by the Olynthians' recent rapprochement with Athens and staged a show of force to try to coerce them back into line. The latter were evidently divided on this issue. Before Philip declared war on them, the pro-Athenian Apollonides was exiled (Dem. 59.91), and two supporters of Macedonia, Lasthenes and Euthycrates, were appointed as cavalry commanders (9.56–66; Dem. 19.265). Nevertheless, according to a later speech of Demosthenes (9.11), Philip told the Olynthians bluntly that either they must stop living in Olynthus or he, in Macedonia. Finally, in autumn 349, he invaded their territory, intimidating and forcing some of their cities into submission. Torone and Mecyberna, the port of Olynthus, were captured by treachery, the league's army was defeated, and the city of Olynthus was put under siege (Diodorus 16.52.9, 53.2).

In the face of this crisis the Olynthians turned to Athens for help. The main narrative source for the Athenian response is the historian Philochorus, who in his history of Athens recorded, under the year 349/8, first an alliance between Athens and Olynthus (the first entry for the year, and so probably in late summer 349) and then three separate expeditionary forces sent out from Athens (the last of which was too late to help).[4] These comprised respectively:

---

[3]See the Introduction to Dem. 4 for the chronology.

[4]*FGH* 328 fragments 49–51 = Harding 1985: no. 80. Demosthenes' policy of fighting Philip in the north and reinforcing Olynthus is the subject of a sharp, and influential, critique by Cawkwell (1962a).

+ 2,000 [mercenary] peltasts (i.e., light infantry) and 38 ships;

+ 4,000 peltasts, 150 cavalry, and 18 triremes under the command of Charidemus, which engaged in joint operations with the Olynthians at Pellene and Bottiaea (places in the Chalcidic peninsula);

+ 2,000 citizen hoplites, 300 cavalry, and 17 triremes.

But Athens' intervention did not save Olynthus, which was betrayed to Philip by his partisans Euthycrates and Lasthenes (on whom see above; Diodorus 16.53.2). Demosthenes later claimed that in the course of a single year the Olynthians lost every city in the Chalcidic peninsula by treachery and that five hundred cavalry were betrayed by their officers, presumably the men just named (Dem. 19.265–267). Most of the inhabitants were killed or sold into slavery, and the cities of the league were destroyed (9.26). Refugees are attested at Athens and on the Athenian-controlled island of Lemnos.[5] The site of the destroyed city of Olynthus, which was never resettled, is ironically now the most complete excavated classical Greek city.[6]

All three *Olynthiacs* belong to the year of Philip's campaign against Olynthus (349/8), but it is not clear in what order they were delivered or what intervals there were between them.[7] The issue was debated already in antiquity: the traditional arrangement (1–2–3) reflects the order of the speeches in one of the medieval manuscripts of Demosthenes, which the Roman critic Caecilius had also argued for; another scholar, Dionysius of Halicarnassus, ordered them 2–3–1, on what (if any) authority we do not know.[8] This latter sequence is unlikely to be correct, and it is generally

---

[5]Athens: Tod 1948: no. 166; Lemnos: *IG* XII.8.4 = Harding 1985: no. 81.

[6]On the excavations at Olynthus, see Cahill 2002.

[7]For the date, see Dionysius of Halicarnassus, *First Letter to Ammaeus* 4. The Athenian year ran from roughly mid summer to mid summer, and so does not correspond to our calendar year. Here 349/8 was the year in which Callimachus was *archōn* (magistrate) at Athens and ran from summer 349 to summer 348.

[8]See the ancient commentary on Dem. 2.1 (Dilts 1983: 49.4) for Caecilius; Dionysius of Halicarnassus, *First Letter to Ammaeus* 4.

agreed that Dem. 3 is the latest, both because its tone is markedly more pessimistic than that of the other two speeches and because in it Demosthenes speaks directly about the need to divert money from the theoric fund, whereas in Dem. 1 his remarks on this topic are guarded (1.19), and in Dem. 2 he does not mention it at all. The order of the other two speeches is unclear, although it has plausibly been argued, from a comparison of the accounts of affairs in Thessaly in the two speeches, that Dem. 2 is the earlier.[9] At any rate, Dem. 1 and 2 appear to have been delivered close in time to each other, and they, if not all three speeches, seem to predate the first of the three Athenian expeditions to relieve Olynthus.[10]

INTRODUCTION

In the *First Olynthiac* Demosthenes proposes that the Athenians send a relief force to Olynthus (2). He goes on to argue that they should in fact send two forces to the north: one to relieve Olynthus and another to raid Philip's territory (17–18). The idea of creating two separate forces is found in a different form in a slightly earlier speech, Dem. 4, where he proposes both a rapid-response force and a force permanently stationed in the north Aegean. Demosthenes suggests that the Athenians already have the money to pay for these, but that they choose to distribute it in other ways. His allusion is to the theoric fund (*ta theōrika*), a fund of public money whose primary purpose was to subsidize Athenian citizens' attendance at the theater but which had grown to cover other civilian expenditure as well. It was politically risky, and may indeed have been illegal, to propose that this money be used for military purposes, and Demosthenes pointedly refuses to do so (18–19).[11]

Instead, as in the speech *On Organization* (Dem. 13), Demos-

---

[9] Ellis 1967: see 1.22n.

[10] The issue is discussed in detail by Tuplin 1998: 276–291. He is skeptical of previous attempts to determine their "historical order," i.e., the order in which they were actually given, but on the basis of a literary analysis detects a "rising tone of alarm" in the sequence 1–2–3.

[11] See, more fully, the Introduction to Dem. 3.

thenes argues for the introduction of a single system of state pay that would be limited to citizens who served in person, in whatever capacity was required. He also urges the Athenians to be willing to pay the wealth-tax (*eisphora*). This was an occasional tax, levied as a fixed proportion of the assessed wealth of the richest Athenians.[12] Since Athens had no other means of raising money in a hurry, and since its public finances were overstretched, the wealth-tax became a regular means to fund military activity. It tended to be unpopular with the rich, who often sought to conceal the true extent of their wealth and who also had a financial interest in avoiding war.

The tone of the speech is optimistic, emphasizing the heaven-sent opportunity of joining the Olynthians in fighting Philip (7) at a safe distance from Athens. Demosthenes argues that Philip is not invincible: his reputation as a rogue and a liar makes him untrustworthy to any free state (3–5), and he is not succeeding as he would wish (21–23). He claims that Philip's successes are due in large part to Athenian laxness (11); on the other hand, if the Athenians fail to take vigorous action, Philip's record shows that he will not stop at Olynthus (12–14). If the Athenians do not defeat him in the north, they may find themselves having to repel him from Attica itself (15, 26–27). Therefore, he argues, they must take advantage of Philip's ill-judged attack on Olynthus, and be willing to pay taxes and campaign in person to deal with him (6).

There are texts of this speech with commentary by Sandys 1910 and McQueen 1986 and a translation with commentary by Ellis and Milns 1970.

I. FIRST OLYNTHIAC

[1] I imagine that you would give much, men of Athens, to know what will benefit the city in the matter we are considering.

---

[12]This tax was collected through a system of contribution groups called symmories (*symmoriai*), among which wealthy Athenians were distributed. Each symmory was required to raise a fixed proportion of the total needed. See further 2.29n and (for the extension of the symmory system to the funding of the navy) the Introduction to Dem. 14.

Since this is the case, you should listen attentively to those who wish to offer you advice. If a speaker comes forward with a useful proposal already prepared,[13] you should listen to his advice and accept it; but in addition I regard it as a sign of your good fortune that it may occur to some speakers to say much that is needed on the spur of the moment, so that from all that is said you will easily be able to choose what is to your advantage.

[2] The present situation,[14] men of Athens, all but takes voice and says that you must take control of the Olynthians' affairs, if indeed you are concerned about their preservation—though I find it difficult to describe our attitude towards them. In my opinion, you should vote for an immediate relief force, and make preparations as quickly as possible to send help from here, to avoid suffering a recurrence of what happened previously, and should send an embassy to announce these decisions and observe what is happening. [3] My particular fear is that, since he[15] is a rogue and a clever manipulator of events, sometimes making concessions, whenever it is in his interest, sometimes making threats, which might reasonably be regarded as credible, sometimes slandering us and our failure to intervene, he may turn around and snatch some advantage from this whole situation. [4] However, men of Athens, one might say that the hardest thing about Philip to fight against is the best for you: the fact that he, as an individual, controls everything, both what is public and what is secret, and is simultaneously general and ruler and paymaster, and is present everywhere with his army. As a result, he has a considerable advantage for the rapid and timely conduct of war,[16] but the opposite is the case as regards the agreements that he would like to make with the Olynthians.[17] [5] For the Olynthians now

---

[13]Demosthenes distinguishes between speakers such as himself (see the Introduction to this volume, pp. 19–20) who prepare their speeches in advance and those who speak off the cuff.

[14]I.e., Philip's attack on Olynthus: see the Introduction to Dem. 1–3.

[15]Philip.

[16]On Philip's military superiority on land, see also 9.47–50.

[17]Demosthenes here presumably refers to the possibility of the negotiated surrender of Olynthus.

see clearly that they are fighting not for glory or over the division of land but to prevent the destruction and enslavement of their country, and they know how he treated those Amphipolitans[18] who handed over their city to him, and those Pydnans who let him into their city.[19] Free states, I believe, have no trust in tyranny, especially if they share a common border with it.[20] [6] And so, men of Athens, if you acknowledge these facts and keep in mind everything else that you should, I urge you to be resolute and aroused to action and to apply yourselves to the war as never before, willingly contributing money[21] and going on campaign in person and neglecting nothing. For there is no reason or excuse left for you to refuse to do what is needed. [7] Now what everyone was chattering about recently—that we must induce the Olynthians to go to war with Philip—has come about of its own accord and in a way that may prove most advantageous to you. For if they had been persuaded by you to go to war, they would be unreliable allies and might only partially acknowledge that they were at war; but since they hate him on account of their own grievances,[22] their hatred of him will probably be assured because of what they fear and of what they have suffered. [8] You must not

[18]Philip captured the Greek city of Amphipolis in Thrace in 357: see 4.12n. According to the ancient commentary on this passage (Dilts 1983: 26.3–10), Philip had the Amphipolitans who had betrayed the city to him put to death first, saying that he feared they would show the same disloyalty to him as they had to their own citizens.

[19]The Greek city of Pydna on the west coast of the Thermaic Gulf in Macedonia had been seized by the Athenian general Timotheus in 364 (see 3.28n) and was captured by Philip in 357 (Diodorus 16.8.2–3). On its betrayal, see also Dem. 20.63. The ancient commentary (Dilts 1983: 26.13–19) says that the traitors fled to the shrine of Philip's father Amyntas when they learned they would not be spared, but that Philip falsely promised they would come to no harm if they left it and then had them killed.

[20]Philip controlled the territory to the north of the Chalcidic peninsula and so shared a land border with the Chalcidic League.

[21]Demosthenes refers to the wealth-tax (*eisphora*): see the Speech Introduction.

[22]There was growing tension between Philip and Olynthus in the period before the outbreak of war in 349: see the Introduction to Dem. 1–3.

pass up such an opportunity, men of Athens, when it has fallen into your lap, nor suffer the same fate as you have suffered many times already. For if, when we had returned from helping the Euboeans,[23] and the Amphipolitans Hierax and Stratocles[24] were here on this very platform urging us to sail and take possession of their city, we had shown the same concern for our own interests as we had for the security of the Euboeans, we would have held on to Amphipolis then and would have avoided all our subsequent troubles. [9] Again, when it was announced that Pydna, Potidaea, Methone, Pagasae,[25] and the other places—I do not wish to waste time talking about them individually—were being besieged, if we had energetically dispatched an appropriate relief force to the first of these, we would now be dealing with a more tractable and much weaker Philip. But as things are, men of Athens, we always abandon any opportunity that presents itself and hope that the future will turn out well of its own accord, and as a result we have made Philip stronger and more powerful than any previous king of Macedonia. But now indeed in the case of Olynthus, as great an opportunity has come to us of its own accord as any of those previous ones. [10] And it seems to me at any rate,

---

[23] On the Athenian expedition to Euboea in 357, see 8.74n.

[24] On the fall of Amphipolis, see 5n above. It is unclear whether these men came to Athens as official ambassadors or as unofficial representatives of a pro-Athenian faction.

[25] Demosthenes lists the four sieges in chronological order. On Pydna, see 5n above. The Greek city of Potidaea, on the narrow isthmus separating the peninsula of Pallene from the Chalcidice, had been captured by the Athenian general Timotheus in 364 and settled with Athenians: see 3.28n. Philip successfully besieged it in 356 (Diodorus 16.8.5). The Greek city of Methone on the Thermaic Gulf just to the north of Pydna had also been won by Timotheus in 364 (see 3.28n) and was captured by Philip probably in 354 (Diodorus 16.31.6 records it under the year 354/3). Pagasae was the port of Pherae in southern Thessaly. It was captured by Philip, most probably in 352, in the course of his intervention in the Third Sacred War against Pherae (see Diodorus 16.37.3, 38.1). Diodorus elsewhere records Philip's capture of an unknown place called "Pagae" under the year 354/3 (16.31.6), and some scholars emend this to "Pagasae," but there is no other evidence that Philip campaigned in Thessaly in this year.

men of Athens, that if someone were appointed to give a fair appraisal of your treatment at the hands of the gods, although many things are not as they should be, he would nevertheless be very grateful to them, and with good reason. For the fact that we have suffered many reverses in the war might justly be attributed to our carelessness, whereas the fact that we did not suffer these reverses long ago, and that to counterbalance them an alliance has been presented to us, if we are willing to take advantage of it, I would regard as a beneficial result of their goodwill. [11] And yet we conduct ourselves, I believe, like those who have acquired a sum of money: if someone keeps all the money that he acquires, he is very grateful to Fortune; but if it slips through his fingers, he forgets his gratitude too. Similarly in public affairs, those who misuse their opportunities forget whatever benefit they have received from the gods, since every previous benefit is judged according to its eventual outcome. For this reason, men of Athens, you must give full thought for the future, so that by making these corrections, you may wipe away the dishonor you have incurred for your past conduct. [12] But if we also abandon these men, men of Athens, and he then captures Olynthus, will someone tell me what is to prevent him marching wherever he wishes? Does any of you observe or reflect on the means by which Philip, who was weak, has become strong? First, he took Amphipolis, then Pydna, and then Potidaea, next Methone, and then he attacked Thessaly, [13] and after that, Pherae, Pagasae, and Magnesia.[26] After winning over the whole country[27] in the way he wanted, he invaded Thrace.[28] Then, after expelling some of the kings there

---

[26]On these places, see 8–9nn above. Magnesia is a region in the east of Thessaly.

[27]The "whole country" refers to Thessaly, of which Philip was elected chief magistrate (*archōn*) for life after his decisive victory over the Phocians at the battle of the Crocus Field in 352: see Justin *Epitome* 7.3.2.

[28]Thrace was the large region extending east of Macedonia as far as the Black Sea. In this period it was ruled by several independent kings. Philip began campaigning in Thrace in late 352, perhaps in response to Athens' occupation of the Chersonese and negotiations with the Thracian king Cersobleptes (see Diodorus 16.34.3–4). See further 3.4–5.

and installing others, he fell sick.[29] When he recovered his health, he did not sink into idleness but immediately made an attempt on the Olynthians.[30] And I pass over his campaigns against the Illyrians and Paeonians and Arybbas and wherever else one might mention.[31]

[14] But why, it might be asked, are you telling us this now? My purpose is to make you understand, men of Athens, both the harm done by our continual neglect of our affairs, one after another, and Philip's habitual meddlesomeness, which prevents him from being content with what he has achieved and remaining at peace. If he is always determined to surpass his existing achievements, while we refuse to apply ourselves robustly to any situation, how can matters be expected to end? [15] By the gods, who of you is so foolish as to be unaware that the war will move from there to here, if we neglect it? And if that happens, men of Athens, I fear that, like those who thoughtlessly borrow at high rates of interest and prosper for a short while but later lose even their principal, so we may be seen to have paid a high price for our neglect and, in our constant search to do what brings pleasure, may later be forced to do many hard things against our will, and our very homeland may be at risk.

[16] Perhaps it will be said that criticism is easy and open to all but that the duty of the adviser is to reveal what should be done in the present situation. I am well aware, men of Athens, that you are often angry not at those who are at fault but at the most recent speakers about the political situation, if anything turns out

---

[29]On rumors of Philip's illness or death, see 4.11, delivered in 351.

[30]This "attempt" refers to an earlier incursion (see 7n above) rather than the current war: see Hammond and Griffith 1979: 298 n. 3.

[31]These campaigns against various non-Greek peoples to the north and west of Macedonia probably took place in 351/0, after Philip's operations in Thrace. The Illyrians to the west had been defeated by Philip at the start of his reign: this later campaign is also mentioned (as a rumor) at 4.48. The Paeonians were a tribe to the north of Macedonia. Arybbas was king of the Molossians of Epirus, to the southwest of Macedonia, and uncle of Philip's wife Olympias: see also 7.32n. These campaigns are discussed by Hammond and Griffith 1979: 304–308.

contrary to your expectation. But I certainly do not think that out of concern for one's personal safety one should refrain from saying what is to your advantage. [17] I say that you should relieve the situation in two ways: both by rescuing the cities of the Olynthians and sending the soldiers to do so and by ravaging his territory with triremes and other soldiers. If you neglect either of these, I fear that the campaign may be in vain. [18] For if, while you are ravaging his territory, he submits to this attack and reduces Olynthus, he will easily return to his own land and defend it.[32] But if you send help only to Olynthus, he will see that there is no danger at home, will keep a careful watch, and will eventually take the city by siege. It is therefore necessary that the relief force be large and be divided into two parts.

[19] That is my opinion about the relief force. As for the provision of money, you have money, men of Athens, you have more than anyone else: this money you receive in the form you wish.[33] If we hand it over to those who are on campaign, you will need no further source of money. But if you do not, you will need a further source, or rather, you will be in need of the whole amount. "What is this?" someone may say, "Do you propose that this money be transferred to the military fund?" No, by God, I do not propose that.[34] [20] But I do believe that soldiers must be provided, and that there should be a military fund,[35] and a single system for receiving pay and for performing one's duty, whereas you think that somehow you should receive this money for attending festivals in

---

[32]I.e., Demosthenes predicts that if Athens attacks the coast of Macedonia Philip will remain in the territory of Olynthus until he has reduced the city, and will then return to Macedonia to deal with the Athenian attacks there.

[33]Demosthenes refers in guarded terms to payments from the theoric fund, on which see 3.11–13 and the Introduction to Dem. 3.

[34]Demosthenes is afraid of being prosecuted if he should make such an unpopular, and perhaps also illegal, proposal: see the Introduction to Dem. 3 on the precise nature of the danger.

[35]The military fund (*to stratiōtikon*) was almost certainly already in existence by this date, although almost nothing is known of its operation: see Cawkwell 1962b.

much the same way as you do now, without any trouble.[36] The only course left, I believe, is for everyone to pay taxes,[37] much if much is needed, a little if little is needed. But we do need money, and without it we can do none of the things that we need. Other men speak about certain other sources of revenue: choose whichever you think is advantageous and take control of the situation while the opportunity is here.

[21] It is worthwhile to consider and evaluate how Philip's affairs now stand. His present situation is not one of readiness, even though it appears to be and a careless observer might so describe it, nor is it as satisfactory as it could be, nor would he ever have started this war if he thought that he would actually have to fight, but he expected that as soon as he attacked, he would carry off everything. But he was mistaken. This indeed is the first thing that has turned out contrary to his plan, and it rattles him and causes him great distress. And then there is the situation in Thessaly. [22] The Thessalians are always naturally untrustworthy to everybody, as you know, and are behaving towards him exactly as they have in the past.[38] For indeed they have voted to demand that he return Pagasae to them, and they have prevented him from fortifying Magnesia.[39] And I have heard some people say that they will no longer even allow him to derive profit from their harbors and marketplaces, on the ground that these revenues should be used to manage the common affairs of the Thessalians, not be taken by Philip.[40] If he is deprived of these funds,

---

[36] The original purpose of the theoric fund was to subsidize Athenian citizens' attendance at theater performances, for which there was an admission charge.

[37] Demosthenes seeks to scare the Athenians with the threat that liability to pay the *eisphora* may need to be extended from the rich to all citizens.

[38] On the Thessalians' reputation for unreliability, see also Dem. 24.112. It probably arose in the main from the factionalism and instability of Thessalian politics, on which see (for the fourth century) Westlake 1935.

[39] On Pagasae and Magnesia, see 13n above.

[40] Philip enjoyed effective control of Thessaly, but the Thessalians are reported to object to his treating Pagasae and Magnesia as his personal possessions, as well as to his handling of the public finances of the country.

he will be hard pressed to provide supplies for his mercenaries. [23] Moreover, it must be supposed that the Paeonians and the Illyrians and, in general, all these people would rather be free and autonomous than slaves.[41] For they are not accustomed to take orders from anybody, and the fellow is said to be overbearing. And, by Zeus, that is perhaps quite credible, since undeserved success leads the foolish to make poor judgments. As a result, it often seems more difficult to preserve one's wealth than it was to acquire it. [24] Therefore, men of Athens, you ought to consider his difficulty as your opportunity, and readily share the burdens, and send ambassadors for what is needed, and campaign in person, and spur on everyone else. Consider: if Philip were to seize such an opportunity against us, and war were to come against our land, how readily do you think that he would attack us? Are you not then ashamed if you will not dare, when you have the chance, to do to him the very things that he would do to you, if he could?

[25] Moreover, men of Athens, you should not forget that now is the moment that will decide whether you are to wage war there or he is to do so here. If Olynthus holds out, you will be waging war there and ravaging his territory, while enjoying your own land without fear. But if Philip takes Olynthus, who will prevent him from marching here? [26] The Thebans? I fear it may be rather harsh to say so, but they will readily join in attacking us.[42] The Phocians then? But they are unable to defend their own territory without your help.[43] Or some other city? But, my dear sir, no one will be willing. It would be the height of absurdity if, when he can, he should fail to do the very thing that he now rants about doing, at the risk of seeming foolish. [27] Nothing more, I think, needs be said about the great difference between fighting here and

---

[41] On these non-Greek allies of Philip, see 13n above.

[42] On the generally poor relations between Athens and Thebes in this period, see Dem. 16 and the Introduction to this volume.

[43] Demosthenes is referring to an Athenian expedition to Thermopylae in 352, in the aftermath of Philip's defeat of the Phocian army at the battle of the Crocus Field, which prevented Philip from securing this strategically vital pass: see Diodorus 16.37.3, 38.2.

fighting there. For if you had to take the field in person for only thirty days, and to draw the supplies that you needed from our territory—when there was no war in it, I mean—I think that the damage the farmers among you would suffer would exceed all you have spent on the previous war in its entirety. But if war comes, how much damage must you suppose they will suffer? There is also the insult and the shame that you would feel at the situation—for decent men, there is no greater punishment than this.

[28] Since you know all this, you all must help push war away from here to there: the well-off so that, by spending a little of their wealth for the sake of the many things that they possess in their prosperity, they may enjoy the rest without fear; those in their prime, so that, by acquiring experience of war in Philip's territory, they may become fearsome guardians of their own land and keep it inviolate; and the public speakers, so that their political conduct may stand up to scrutiny,[44] since you will judge their actions according to how events turn out. May the results then be excellent, for all our sakes!

---

[44] All Athenian public officials underwent an official scrutiny (*euthynai*) at the end of their term in office. Public speakers were not liable to this scrutiny unless they had held some official position such as ambassador.

2. SECOND OLYNTHIAC

INTRODUCTION

This speech was delivered in 349/8 (see the Introduction to Dem. 1–3), apparently before the Athenians had sent any assistance to Olynthus, since at 12 Demosthenes calls for them to take action. As in the *First Olynthiac*, he represents the Olynthian appeal to Athens as a marvelous opportunity that must be taken (1–2). He proposes that the Athenians send help to Olynthus and also send an embassy to Thessaly, which has grown restive under Macedonian rule (11).

The bulk of the speech is devoted to belittling Philip and seeking to persuade the Athenians that he is far from invincible. Many of Philip's successes are attributed to deception (6–8), and his apparent power is said to be insecurely based (10–11). Macedonia is militarily useful only as a supplement to others, not in its own right (14). It is also disunited, since ordinary Macedonians do not share their king's ambition and are exhausted by continuous war (15–16). The infantry are mediocre (17); those Macedonians who are competent are pushed aside by the king out of jealousy, while any who are morally upright are repulsed by the moral laxity of the court (18–19). Philip's success obscures the underlying weakness of his position (20–21); he has been lucky, but the gods are more likely to support Athens (22). Yet the Athenians are idle, while Philip is at least energetic (23). This is surprising both in light of Athens' history and because the Athenians are now fighting for their own property (24). They procrastinate but must be willing to serve in person (25–27). The generals are neither committed to the war (28) nor held to account, while the Athenian people are disunited (29). They must be willing to cooperate and serve in person (30–31).

Demosthenes' complaints about the Athenians' inactivity and the need for them to serve in person are regular features of his deliberative oratory. More striking are his critical remarks about Philip and the Macedonians. Demosthenes attributes his information about the poor quality of the Macedonian infantry, the jealousy of the king, and the degeneracy of the Macedonian court to "someone who has been in that country, and who is incapable of lying" (17). Many Greeks visited the Macedonian court, and it is not unlikely that Demosthenes had informants with first-hand knowledge of it. The nature and tone of these remarks resemble those of his contemporary, the historian Theopompus of Chios, whose *Philippic History* (of which only fragments survive) was a detailed history of Greece during the years of Philip's reign. Theopompus was familiar with life in Macedonia, and in surviving fragments he makes very sharp criticism of the moral laxity of Philip's court: the king's favoritism, drunkenness, and homosexual liaisons. Although there is no evidence, or even likelihood, that Theopompus was Demosthenes' informant, the similarity of their views indicates the currency among at least some educated Greeks of a scornful attitude toward Philip and his entourage.

There is some measure of truth to the picture of Macedonia that Demosthenes paints, and the heavy drinking and factionalism of the court are familiar from the better-documented reign of Philip's son Alexander. But Demosthenes presents a fundamentally misleading picture of the strengths and weaknesses of Philip's position. First, he downplays Macedonian military capabilities. The strength of the army lay in its cavalry, but the infantry of the phalanx, armed with the distinctive long pike (*sarissa*), was more than a match for Greek hoplites. Demosthenes' claim that the Macedonian army made a contribution only in an auxiliary capacity (14) was wholly untrue, at least as regards Philip's reign. Second, his assertion that Philip's control of his kingdom was insecure amounts to wishful thinking, since although Macedonia had a history of dynastic instability, there were no plausible rivals to Philip for the throne. Moreover, Philip's unparalleled successes made his position virtually unchallengeable. Demosthenes' claim that ordinary Macedonians were war weary was almost certainly unfounded. Finally, although life at the Macedonian court was, by southern Greek standards, raucous and at times uncouth, there is no evidence that its hard-drinking culture was a source of weakness. Demosthenes understandably wished to convince the Athenians that they had a chance to defeat Philip, but the claims that he makes in this section are half-truths at best.

There are texts with commentary of this speech by Sandys 1910 and McQueen 1986 and a translation with commentary by Ellis and Milns 1970.

2. SECOND OLYNTHIAC

[1] On many occasions, it seems to me, men of Athens, the gods have clearly revealed their goodwill to the city, and not least in the present situation. For the appearance of people who will wage war on Philip,[1] whose territory borders on his and who have a considerable force and, most important of all, whose attitude towards the war is such that they regard their agreement[2] with him as untrustworthy and leading to the destruction of their country—this situation seems to have come about by some miraculous and altogether divine benefaction. [2] We, men of Athens, must now avoid giving the impression that we treat ourselves worse than the present situation treats us, since it would be shameful—indeed most shameful—to be seen to have given up not only the cities and places that we once controlled but also the allies and the opportunities that Fortune has provided.

[3] It is in my opinion a mistake, men of Athens, to seek to persuade you to do your duty by recounting Philip's strength to you. Why? Because all the facts that one might mention seem to me to bring credit to him but to be blunders on our part. The

---

[1] I.e., the Olynthians.

[2] Philip made an alliance with the Chalcidic League headed by Olynthus in 357/6: see Dem. 23.107–109; Diodorus 16.8.3–4; Rhodes and Osborne 2003: no. 50. In the years preceding the outbreak of war relations between Philip and Olynthus had deteriorated: see the Introduction to Dem. 1–3.

more he has achieved beyond what he deserves, the more amazing
he seems to everybody; but as for you, the worse your handling of
the situation, the greater the shame you have incurred. [4] These
matters, then, I shall leave to one side. For indeed, men of Athens, if one were to examine the matter carefully, one would see
that Philip's rise to greatness is due to us, not him. Nor do I think
that now is the time to talk about the activities of those who engage in politics on his behalf, for which he owes them a debt of
gratitude and for which you should punish them. I shall, however, undertake to talk about other matters, which it will be more
advantageous for you to hear and which, men of Athens, anyone
who is willing to examine the matter correctly will see are greatly
to his discredit.

[5] To call him a liar and a perjurer without showing what he
has done might be called empty abuse, and rightly so. But to recount all his actions so far, and to convict him on all of these
counts, fortunately requires only a short speech. It also serves,
I think, two useful purposes: both to make him appear worthless—which he is—and to show those who are overly impressed
by Philip and think him invincible that all the sources of his previous duplicitous rise to greatness are now gone and that his affairs have come to a dead end. [6] I, too, men of Athens, would be
convinced that Philip is fearsome and remarkable if I saw that he
had risen to power as a result of acting with justice. As it is, by ob-
servation and examination I see that at the outset, when certain
men sought to drive away the Olynthians who wished to reach an
agreement with you,³ he got the better of us in our innocence by
saying that he would hand over Amphipolis to us and by devis-
ing that once much talked about secret.⁴ [7] And subsequently he

---

³Olynthus sent an embassy to Athens in 357/6 in the context of competition between Athens and Philip to secure the support of the Chalcidic
League (Diodorus 16.8.4, and see above, 1n, on the alliance between Olynthus and Philip).

⁴In 357 Philip allegedly offered to hand over the Greek city of Amphipolis in Thrace to Athens. According to the fourth-century historian Theopompus (*FGH* 115 fragment 30), two Athenian ambassadors to Philip had
proposed ceding to him the nearby city of Pydna in return for it. Despite

won the friendship of the Olynthians by seizing Potidaea, which belonged to you, and did his former allies[5] an injustice by handing it over to them,[6] and now finally he has won over the Thessalians by promising that he will give them Magnesia and by undertaking to conduct the war against Phocis on their behalf.[7] In short, there is no associate of his whom he has not cheated, since it is by deceiving and winning over all of those who are ignorant of him, one after another, that he has grown in power. [8] And so, just as it was through these people[8] that he has reached this highpoint, when each of them thought that he would do something to their advantage, so it is through these same people that he is bound to be destroyed, when it has been demonstrated that all his actions were for his own benefit. This is the critical pass, men of Athens, to which Philip's affairs have come. Or else let someone come forward and show me, or rather show you, that I am not telling the truth, that those whom he deceived at the start will

---

the doubts of de Ste. Croix (1963), who argued that the political institutions of democratic Athens prevented the city from engaging in secret diplomacy, it is likely that Theopompus is broadly correct. Certainly it was in Athens' interest to keep any such negotiations secret from the Pydnans. See also 7.27.

[5]The ancient commentary on this passage (Dilts 1983: 61.21) states that by "former allies" Demosthenes means the Potidaeans, and the Athenian politician Hegesippus claims (Dem. 7.10) that Potidaea was an ally of Philip when he attacked it in 356. The word "you" (i.e., "you, his former allies") appears in the manuscripts but is generally deleted by editors as a later (and incorrect) insertion. Philip made peace with the Athenians soon after his accession in 359 (Diodorus 16.4.1) and offered them an alliance (Dem. 23.121), but almost certainly no alliance was made.

[6]Philip captured the Athenian-controlled city of Potidaea in the Chalcidic peninsula in 356 (see 1.9n). When he was making his alliance with the Chalcidic League (1n), he promised to secure Potidaea for it: see Diodorus 16.8.5.

[7]On Thessalian opposition to Philip's control of the region of Magnesia, see 11 below; 1.13, 22. The "war against Phocis" is the Third Sacred War, in which much of Thessaly was fighting on the side of the Thebans against the Phocians.

[8]I.e., the Olynthians and the Thessalians.

trust him in the future, or that those whom he has wrongly en-slaved would not now be glad to be freed.

[9] If any of you accepts that this is true, but thinks that Philip will retain control by force, since he has already seized the towns and harbors and the like, he is wrong. For whenever affairs are organized in a spirit of goodwill, and all the participants in a war share a common interest, then men are willing to work to-gether and endure setbacks and stand fast; but whenever someone like Philip grows strong as a result of greed and villainy, the first excuse and a small stumble overturns and destroys everything. [10] It is impossible, quite impossible, men of Athens, that a crim-inal and perjurer and liar should acquire power that is securely based; rather, such things last for a moment or a short time, and flourish on the basis of hopes if they are lucky, but in time are found out and fall apart. Just as the lower parts of a house, I be-lieve, or of a ship or similar structure must be the strongest, so the beginning and basic conception of any action must be true and just. But this is now impossible in the case of Philip's actions.

[11] I say that we should help the Olynthians, and I support the best and quickest way of doing so that anyone might pro-pose; and we should send an embassy to the Thessalians to in-form some of them about these matters and to spur on the rest, since they have now voted to demand the return of Pagasae and to open negotiations about Magnesia.⁹ [12] You should see to it, men of Athens, that our ambassadors not only make speeches but are also able to demonstrate some achievement on our part—that we have marched out in a manner worthy of our city and are en-gaged in action, since all speech, if it is not accompanied by ac-tion, seems vain and empty, especially in the case of our city. For the more we are ready to make speeches, the more everyone dis-trusts them. [13] You must demonstrate that your conduct has un-dergone a substantial change for the better—by raising taxes, and campaigning, and doing everything energetically—if you want people to pay attention to you. And if you are willing to do these things as you should, men of Athens, not only will Philip's alli-

---

⁹On Pagasae and Magnesia, see 1.22n.

ances be shown to be weak and unreliable but his very kingdom and power will be proved to be in a parlous state.

[14] For, on the whole, the power and empire of Macedonia are of some value as a supplementary force, as was the case at the time of Timotheus' campaign against Olynthus;[10] and again it proved to be of some use in combination with the Olynthians against Potidaea;[11] and just recently it helped[12] the Thessalians, who were weak and disordered, against the family of tyrants.[13] And in general, I think, even a small force is very helpful wherever it is brought to bear, but on its own it is weak and riddled with deficiencies. [15] All the things that one might suppose would make him great—his wars and expeditions—have in fact made his kingdom less secure than it naturally is. For you should not suppose, men of Athens, that Philip and his subjects take pleasure in the same things. Rather, he desires and strives for glory, and chooses to be active and take risks, and to suffer whatever may befall, preferring the glory of achieving more than any previous Macedonian king to a life of security.

[16] But his subjects do not share in the glory of his achievements; instead, they are always being pounded by this to-and-fro campaigning, and are distressed and endure constant hardship, and are not allowed to spend time at their work or their private affairs; nor are they able to dispose of the little that they produce, since the markets have been closed on account of the

---

[10]The Athenian general Timotheus campaigned successfully in 364/3 against the Chalcidic League, with the assistance of the Macedonian king Perdiccas III. See Nepos *Timotheus* 1.2; Polyaenus *Stratagems* 3.10.7 and 14.

[11]On Philip's capture of Potidaea, see 7n. Demosthenes' claim that this was an achievement of the Olynthians, with help from Philip, is wholly misleading: it was Philip's Macedonian forces that captured the city.

[12]The word "helped" (*eboēthēsen*) is deleted by Dilts as an interpolation, though the meaning is not significantly affected.

[13]In 353 and 352 Philip intervened in Thessaly in support of the Thessalian League against the rulers of Pherae in southern Thessaly, who were allies of the Phocians. After defeating the Phocian army at the battle of the Crocus Field in 352, he captured Pherae and its port Pagasae and installed a pro-Macedonian regime there: see 1.9, 12–13; Diodorus 16.38.1.

war.[14] [17] The attitude of most Macedonians to Philip can easily be gathered from these facts: the mercenaries and Foot Companions[15] in his entourage have the reputation of being wonderful and disciplined fighters, but I have heard from someone who has been in that country, and who is incapable of lying, that they are no better than anyone else. [18] For, he says, any of them who are experienced in war and battle are removed by Philip out of jealousy, since he wishes to give the impression that every achievement is his alone—in addition to everything else, he reports that Philip's jealousy is unsurpassable. And if anyone is sober or generally upright, and is unable to tolerate the constant loose living and drunkenness[16] and lewd dancing,[17] such a man is pushed aside and treated as a nobody. [19] The rest of his company, he says, are brigands and flatterers and men whose drunken dancing is so vile that I shrink from describing it to you. And this is clearly true: for those men whom everyone drove away[18] from here for being far more disgusting than conjurers,[19] that public slave Cal-

---

[14]The majority of Macedonian overseas trade was probably in the hands either of Athenians or of cities of the Chalcidic League, both of whom were now enemies of Macedon. In any case, Athens' naval superiority will have made any Macedonian seaborne trade very precarious.

[15]The identity of the "Foot Companions" (*pezhetairoi*) under Philip is uncertain. According to Theopompus (*FGH* 115 fragment 348), they were an elite Royal Guard, but in the reign of Philip's son Alexander III, this title was applied to all the infantrymen of the Macedonian phalanx. The historian Anaximenes attributes the creation of the Foot Companions to Alexander, but it is unclear to which of the three Macedonian kings of that name he is referring (*FGH* 72 fragment 4). See further Hammond and Griffith 1979: 705–709.

[16]The Macedonians were regarded by the Greeks as heavy drinkers, and Greek authors record several drunken parties in the courts of both Philip and his son Alexander: see, e.g., Diodorus 16.55, 87; Theopompus *FGH* 115 fragments 27 and 282 (on Theopompus, see 19n below).

[17]The reference is to a sexually suggestive dance called the *kordax*.

[18]The Greek word used here (*apēlaunon*) indicates that these men were shunned, not formally exiled.

[19]Lit. "wonder workers," i.e., public entertainers of low status, such as conjurers and magicians.

lias and men of his stamp,[20] pantomime actors[21] of the ridiculous and poets of shameful songs, which they compose for their associates in order to raise a laugh—these are the men he loves and keeps about himself.[22] [20] Such things, men of Athens, even if they seem relatively unimportant, provide thoughtful observers with clear proof of his disgusting nature. But at the moment, I think, his success obscures them. Success is good at concealing such disgraces; but if someone stumbles, then these aspects of his life are exposed to intense scrutiny. And in my opinion, men of Athens, Philip will be exposed quite soon, if the gods are willing, and if you desire it. [21] For just as in our bodies, so long as a person is strong things go unnoticed, but when some weakness befalls him, be it a fracture or a sprain or some other underlying problem, everything is disturbed; so in the case of cities and tyrants: as long as they wage war abroad their troubles are invisible to most people, but when they are entangled in a war on their own borders, everything is exposed.

[22] If any of you, men of Athens, sees Philip's success and concludes that he is a formidable enemy, he is thinking like a sensible man. For fortune is a vital element—rather it is everything—in all human affairs. Nevertheless, if I were given the choice, I would personally choose the fortune of our city, so long as you are willing to do your duty in person, even to a limited degree, rather than his, since I observe that you have many more avenues than he has for gaining the favor of the gods. [23] And yet we seem to sit around doing nothing. But an idler cannot call on his

---

[20]Nothing further is known of this Callias. Publicly owned slaves were employed at Athens to assist various office holders in their duties, e.g., as clerks. See also 8.47n.

[21]*Mimos* was a genre of dramatic performance, often depicting scenes from everyday life in a humorous fashion. It somewhat resembled modern pantomime and was thus quite different from modern mime.

[22]The historian Theopompus of Chios (*FGH* 115), who spent time at Philip's court, wrote in similarly disapproving terms about the dissolute conduct at it, including the prevalence of drunkenness and Philip's taste for low company. See the Speech Introduction; Shrimpton 1977 and 1991: 157–180; Flower 1997: 98–115.

friends to act on his behalf, still less on the gods! Indeed, it is no wonder that Philip, who goes on campaign and engages in hard work and attends to everything, and who leaves aside no opportunity or season, gets the better of us who delay and take votes and hold enquiries. Nor do I find this surprising. Indeed, the opposite would have been amazing: if we, who do none of the things that those who are at war must do, were to get the better of one who does everything. [24] But I am amazed at this: that in the past you rose up against the Spartans in the cause of justice for the Greeks, and refused many opportunities to make large private gains, but instead spent your own money by raising taxes and were the first to risk your lives on campaign,[23] so that the majority of the Greeks should get justice, whereas now you shrink from marching out and put off paying taxes, even to protect your own possessions! Indeed, I am amazed that you, who have often rescued the other Greeks, both collectively and individually, now sit about, even when you have been deprived of your own property. [25] These things amaze me, but it amazes me even more, men of Athens, that none of you is able to reckon how long you have been at war with Philip[24] and what you have been doing during that period. Surely you realize that you have spent the whole time procrastinating, hoping others will act, blaming each other, holding trials, hoping again, doing pretty much the same as you are doing now! [26] Are you so senseless, men of Athens, that you hope to improve our city's situation by following the very same policies that led to its decline? This would be unreasonable and contrary to nature, since it is much easier to keep what you have than to acquire anything. In our case, as a result of the war, we no longer have any of our previous possessions to defend, but must reacquire them.[25] This is now the task that we face. [27] I tell you,

---

[23]In 395 Athens joined Thebes, Corinth and Argos in launching the Corinthian War against Sparta.

[24]Athens had been at war with Philip since his capture of Amphipolis in 357 (see 1.5n), which was treated by the Athenians as an act of war (see Aes. 2.70; Isoc. 5.2).

[25]Demosthenes refers both to Amphipolis and to the coastal cities in Thrace and Macedonia—Pydna, Potidaea, and Methone—that the Athenian general Timotheus had captured in 364: see 1.9n, 3.28n.

we must raise funds, eagerly march out in person, blame no one until you have gained control of the situation, and then, on the basis of the facts alone, honor those who deserve praise and punish those who do wrong, and get rid of the excuses and omissions on your part. For it is not possible to make a strict examination of what others have done, if you have not first done your own duty. [28] Why, men of Athens, do you suppose that all the generals that you dispatch avoid this war, and find private ones,[26] if I must speak truthfully even about the generals? The reason is that in the war against Philip, the prizes for which the war is being fought belong to you—if Amphipolis is captured, it will immediately revert to you[27]—but the risks belong exclusively to your commanders, and there is no pay available to them. Elsewhere, however, the dangers are fewer, and there are profits to be made by the commanders and their troops—Lampsacus, Sigeum, the ships that they can plunder.[28] Each of the generals seeks his own profit. [29] When you notice the disastrous state of your affairs, you put the commanders on trial; but then, when you allow them to speak, you hear about these constraints and let them go. The result is that you dispute and quarrel with each other—some have one opinion, others another, and our collective interest suffers. Previously, men of Athens, you paid taxes by symmory, but now you engage in public life by symmory: a politician is the leader of each group, with a general beneath him and three hundred assistants. The rest of you are assigned, some to one group and others to

---

[26]Most notably, the Athenian general Chares had recently taken service with the rebel satrap Artabazus: see 4.24n.

[27]On Amphipolis in Thrace, see 1.5n. Originally founded by Athens, the Athenians still regarded it as theirs even though they had not controlled it at any point in the fourth century.

[28]Lampsacus and Sigeum were Greek cities of northwestern Asia Minor, at the northern and southern ends of the Hellespont respectively. Both were in the Persian Empire. Demosthenes in a later speech refers to Athenian generals demanding "goodwill payments" from Aegean islanders and (Persian ruled) Asian cities (8.24). For Athenian privateering, see also Dem. 21.173, 24.12, 51.13; Aes. 2.71. Such activity was almost inevitable because the Athenians failed to provide adequate financial support to their generals.

another.[29] [30] You must put such conduct aside and even now recover your self-control, and join together in deliberating, speaking, and taking action for the common good. But if you grant some citizens the right to give orders as if in a tyranny, compel others to serve as trierarchs, to pay the wealth-tax, and to campaign, and allow others still to do nothing but vote against them and make no other contribution to the collective effort, you will fail to accomplish any of the things you need to do in a timely fashion. For whichever part of the citizenry feels it has been wronged will always be remiss, and you will have the opportunity to punish these men, but not the enemy! [31] I say, in summary, that you should all contribute equitably according to your means; you should all go on campaign in turn until everyone has served; you should give a hearing to all who come forward to speak; and you should choose the best proposals that you hear, rather than whatever this man or that should say. If you do these things, you will be able to congratulate not only the speaker at the time but also yourselves later, when your whole situation has improved.

---

[29] Demosthenes should not be taken to mean that the symmory system (on which, see 14.26n) was no longer in operation; his point is that in the past symmories had been used only for tax collection, whereas now they also form the (metaphorical) basis for Athens' political organization. In each symmory the man who contributed the most was called the "leader" (see Dem. 28.4). A feature of Athenian public life in the fourth century (by contrast with earlier periods) was the tendency for different men to serve as political and military leaders and for individual (civilian) politicians and generals to collaborate with each other: see Isoc. 8.54–55; Hansen 1991: 268–277.

3. THIRD OLYNTHIAC

〜〜〜〜〜〜〜〜〜〜〜〜〜〜〜〜〜〜〜〜〜〜〜〜〜〜〜〜〜〜〜〜〜〜〜〜〜

INTRODUCTION

This is probably the third in order of writing of the three speeches that Demosthenes delivered in 349/8, arguing that Athens should send help to the northern Greek city of Olynthus, which was under attack from Philip of Macedon (see the Introduction to Dem. 1–3).

The military situation had apparently deteriorated since Demosthenes delivered the first two *Olynthiacs*. Now the Athenians cannot effectively retaliate against Philip and are reduced to defending themselves and their allies (1–2), and their affairs are in an "utterly wretched state" (3). Although it is impossible to determine exactly when the speech was delivered, its solemn and anxious tone suggests that Philip's campaign against Olynthus was well advanced. Whether the first Athenian relief force had yet sailed is unclear, but on balance it is unlikely; certainly Demosthenes makes no mention of it. The Athenians have let slip one opportunity (in the late 350s) (5) and cannot afford to do so again (6). Moreover, the situation in central Greece is now so disadvantageous to Athens that if Olynthus should be allowed to fall, there will be nothing to prevent Philip penetrating further into Greece (8; cf. similar fears at 1.12, 25).

In addition to his familiar appeals for action, Demosthenes' response to Athens' situation in this speech is twofold. For the first theme, he argues forthrightly for the repeal of some of the laws regulating the theoric fund (11), with a view to transferring money from civilian to military use. In the *First Olynthiac* he had already touched on this subject (1.19), but in that speech he denies that he is proposing the transfer of money to the military fund. Now, he claims that there is no alternative source of money (19).

The theoric fund (*ta theōrika*) took its name from *theōria*, the Greek word for observing, and by extension for attendance as a spectator at a religious festival. The original purpose of the fund was to subsidize the attendance of poorer Athenian citizens at theatrical performances at the Dionysia and Lenaea festivals. It was instituted probably in the first half of the fourth century, although the evidence is contradictory.[1] By the middle of the century, however, the theoric fund was being used for other civilian purposes as well. The amount of money spent each year is unknown, but the fund had considerable ideological significance. For some, it was the "glue" that held Athenian democracy together.[2] For Demosthenes and his supporters, who advocated a vigorous and inevitably expensive military response to Philip, the theoric fund was a symbol of what was wrong with Athens: money that could have been used to help pay for the war was being squandered.[3] It appears that the theoric fund was itself funded partly from an annual allocation and partly, during wartime, from the surplus of the city's annual budget (see Dem. 59.4, which is, however, not entirely coherent). The administration of the theoric fund was regulated by one or more laws, which could be altered or overturned only by the establishment of a panel of Lawgivers (*Nomothetai*): see 10. Anyone who attempted to do so by other means would be immediately liable to prosecution by a *graphē paranomōn* (a public suit for making an illegal proposal).

Libanius in his introduction to Dem. 1 claims that there was a clause imposing the death penalty on anyone who sought to divert money from the theoric to the military fund, and that this is why Demosthenes is so circumspect in that speech (1.19), and why here he tells the Athenians not to expect any politician to risk destruction (12).[4] Such harsh penalty clauses are attested in

---

[1] See Harding 1985: no. 75 for the evidence.

[2] The metaphor is attributed to the Athenian politician Demades by Plutarch (*Moralia* 1011b).

[3] In 29 Demosthenes scornfully dismisses the spending of money on public works.

[4] See Libanius *Introduction to Dem. 1* 5.

fourth-century Athens,[5] but it may be that Libanius drew an erroneous inference from this passage and that the destruction Demosthenes fears at the hands of the Athenians is political ruin rather than death—what we might call political suicide. By proposing that those politicians who were responsible for the passing of the law should also propose its repeal, he is offering a gentleman's agreement that he and his supporters will not prosecute them for doing so.[6]

Demosthenes (as usual in his deliberative speeches; 10.70 is the one exception) does not name his opponents, but it is generally agreed that he is referring primarily to Eubulus and his supporters. Eubulus was a leading politician of the period and was instrumental in reforming Athens' public finances. He served as commissioner of the theoric fund in the 350s and apparently resisted what he regarded as the waste of public money on overambitious military campaigns.[7] Demosthenes advocates in place of the theoric distributions a new system of payment, according to which Athenian citizens would receive public money for doing different tasks, depending on their age and on whether Athens was at war or peace (34–35). This system had already been sketched out in Dem. 13.

The second main theme of the speech is the contrast between Athens in its fifth-century heyday and in its present state (21–31), a section that is substantially taken over from the earlier speech Dem. 13.[8] Demosthenes' mood is downbeat: Athens' leaders in the past put the public interest ahead of their own, whereas present-day politicians flatter the people (21–22); its fifth-century leaders caused Athens to flourish abroad and at home but themselves lived modestly (23–26), whereas its present-day leaders have failed to take advantage of the decline of Sparta and Thebes and have presided over a series of foreign policy disasters and the squandering of large sums of public money (27–28). Their domestic expen-

---

[5] Lewis 1974.

[6] On Demosthenes and the theoric fund, see Sealey 1993: 256–258; Harris 1996.

[7] On Eubulus' career, see Cawkwell 1963a and (in brief) *OCD*[3] s.v. Eubulus; on his financial office holding, see Lewis 1997: 212–229.

[8] Cf. 13.25–31 and see the Introduction to Dem. 13.

diture is wasteful and unnecessary, and they have lined their own pockets (29). In the past, politicians were servants of the people (30); now, they are their masters (31).

There are texts of this speech with commentaries by Sandys 1910 and McQueen 1986 and a translation with commentary by Ellis and Milns 1970.

3. THIRD OLYNTHIAC

[1] I find myself facing quite different opinions, men of Athens, when I look at our situation and when I reflect on the speeches that I hear. For the speeches deal with how to punish Philip, but our situation has deteriorated so badly that we are reduced to examining how to prevent him from harming us first. As a result, I believe that those who deliver speeches of this nature are simply mistaken and have set before you an untrue basis for deliberation. [2] I know very well that there was a time when the city could be secure and could punish Philip, for in my own lifetime not so long ago both were possible. Now, however, I am convinced that it is enough for us to secure as our primary goal the protection of our allies. Only if we achieve this will we be able to consider whom to punish and how. But before we have made a sound beginning, I think it pointless to say anything about the end.

[3] The present situation, more than any previous one, requires much thought and deliberation, but I do not consider it particularly difficult to advise you what to do in our current circumstances. I am, however, at a loss, men of Athens, as to the manner in which I should speak to you about them. For I am convinced, both from personal experience and from what I have heard, that we have lost control of the situation more because of our unwillingness to do our duty than from any lack of intelligence on our part. I ask you, if I speak freely, to bear with me and to see whether I am telling the truth and am aiming to bring about some improvement in the future, since you see that it is as a result of the speeches that certain men address to you in the Assembly in order to gain your approval that our affairs have reached an utterly wretched state.

[4] I suppose that I should first summarize for you in a few

words what has happened. You remember, men of Athens, that it was announced to you two or three years ago that Philip was in Thrace besieging Fort Heraeum.[9] That was in the month of Maimacterion.[10] Many speeches were made on that occasion and there was a great uproar, and you voted to launch forty triremes and man them with those up to forty-five years old[11] and to levy a wealth-tax of sixty talents.[12] [5] After that, the rest of the year passed and then the months Hecatombaion, Metageitnion, and Boedromion.[13] In that month, shortly after the Mysteries,[14] you dispatched Charidemus[15] with ten empty ships and five talents of silver.[16] For when it was announced that Philip was sick

---

[9]Fort Heraeum (Heraion Teichos) was a site in eastern Thrace near both the Sea of Marmara and the Chersonese. On the date of its siege, see the following note.

[10]Maimacterion was the fifth month of the Athenian year, which started in midsummer: the approximate date is November 352. This is the Thracian campaign referred to at 1.13.

[11]Athenians were liable for military service from the ages of 18 to 59 and were called up by age classes.

[12]The wealth-tax (*eisphora*) was levied as a variable percentage of the total available wealth of the richest Athenians (which at this period was 6,000 talents: see 14.27n); hence, 60 talents represented an *eisphora* of one percent.

[13]Boedromion was the third month (of the following year, 351/0), i.e., roughly September 351.

[14]The Mysteries were a very important initiation ceremony, forming part of the cult of the two goddesses Demeter and Persephone at Eleusis in western Attica. The "Greater" Mysteries took place in the month Boedromion and lasted for ten days. See in general Parker 2005: 327–368.

[15]Charidemus was one of the ten generals for 351/0. Originally from Oreus in Euboea, he served Athens as a mercenary commander and was granted Athenian citizenship at some point before the delivery of Dem. 23 in 353/2 (Dem. 23.149–151; Osborne 1983: T51). In that year the Athenian politician Aristocrates proposed a grant of special legal protection for him; this was challenged by a *graphē paranomōn* for which Demosthenes wrote the speech (= Dem. 23).

[16]An "empty" ship was one for which the commander rather than the city was responsible for finding rowers (see Gabrielsen 1994: 108). Demosthenes treats the Athenians' failure to provide rowers, together with the

or dead—both were reported—you thought that you no longer needed to send a relief force and disbanded the expedition.[17] But this was the moment of opportunity: if on that occasion we had enthusiastically sent a relief force there, as we had voted, Philip, even if he survived, would not now be bothering us.

[6] What was done at that time cannot be undone. But now a further opportunity for war has come, and this is why I have reminded you of that occasion, so that you do not suffer the same fate as before. How then shall we make use of this opportunity, men of Athens? For if you fail to send help "at full strength to the best of your ability,"[18] observe how you will have been acting in every respect to Philip's advantage. [7] The Olynthians possessed considerable force, and the situation was that Philip had no confidence in them, nor they in him. We made peace with them.[19] This was an obstacle and annoyance to Philip, that a great city should be reconciled with us and be lying in wait for any opportunities he might provide. We thought we should involve these people[20] in war by whatever means we could, and what everyone was chattering about then has now somehow or other come to pass. [8] What remains then for us to do, men of Athens, but to send help resolutely and enthusiastically? I see no other option. For apart from the shame that would envelop us, if we were to surrender any of our interests, the danger in doing so would in my opinion be considerable, in view of the Thebans' attitude towards us,

---

small size of the squadron and the inadequate funds voted for it, as an indication that they did not take the expedition seriously. See also 4.43, where the reference to empty ships has the same rhetorical purpose.

[17]These rumors are reported as recent at 4.10–11 (delivered probably in 351); Philip's illness is also mentioned at 1.13.

[18]These words are identified by Sandys (1910) in his commentary as a formula of diplomacy, commonly found in alliances where one party promises to aid the other.

[19]On this peace, see Dem. 23.107–109; Libanius *Introduction to Dem. 1* 2. Its date is uncertain, but the claim by Libanius that it was made when Philip was away might suggest the period while he was in Thessaly, in 352. See Hammond and Griffith 1979: 298–299.

[20]The Olynthians.

and the fact that the Phocians have exhausted their money,[21] and that there is nothing to stop Philip, after he has subdued what is before him, from turning against us here. [9] If any of you wishes to put off doing his duty until that time, then he is choosing to see suffering close at hand when he could be hearing of it happening elsewhere, and wishes to be forced to look for people who will help him when he could now be helping others. For I imagine that we are all well aware that this is how things will turn out, if we discard the present opportunity.

[10] Perhaps someone may say: "We all recognize that we must help, and help we shall, but tell us how." Do not be amazed, men of Athens, if I say something that most of you will find unexpected. You should appoint lawmakers. Use these lawmakers not to pass a law—you have enough of them—but to repeal those laws that are presently harming your interests.[22] [11] I am referring directly to the laws relating to the theoric fund and to certain of the laws relating to those who go on campaign. Some of these laws distribute military funds as theoric payments to those who stay at home; others let those who shirk military service get off scot-free and make even those who wish to do their duty more despondent. When you have repealed these laws and made it safe to offer the best advice, only then should you look for someone to propose the measures that you all know to be beneficial.[23] [12] Until that is done, do not expect anyone to be willing to give you the best advice and then be destroyed by you.[24] You will not find anyone, especially when the only likely result is that whoever speaks and makes these proposals will be unjustly punished and, far from improving the situation, will make people even more

---

[21]Thebes was hostile to Athens: see 1.26n. The Phocians depended for money on the resources of the sanctuary of Apollo at Delphi, which they had appropriated early in their war with the Thebans.

[22]In fourth-century Athens, laws could be passed or repealed only by specially chosen panels of citizens called *Nomothetai* (Law-Givers): see Rhodes 1985.

[23]I.e., to use the theoric fund for military purposes.

[24]On the sense in which the giver of such advice would be "destroyed," see the Speech Introduction.

afraid to give good advice than they already are. Moreover, men of Athens, we should ask the same men to propose the repeal of these laws as passed them.[25] [13] For it is not right that those who at that time passed laws that damaged the whole city should be popular for having done so, whereas anyone who now gives the best advice, which will result in all of us faring better, should be punished with your hatred for doing so. Before you set this matter right, men of Athens, you should certainly not suppose that anyone is so prominent as to be able to break these laws with impunity, or so foolish as to throw himself into obvious trouble.

[14] You must also know, men of Athens, that a decree is worthless if it is not accompanied by the will to carry out the decision with enthusiasm. For if decrees alone had the power either to compel you to do your duty or to accomplish the goals for which they were proposed, you would not find yourselves voting for many things but accomplishing few if any of them; nor would Philip have been insulting you for such a long time, since, to judge by your decrees at any rate, he would long ago have been punished. [15] But that is not the case. For although action comes after speaking and voting in time, it precedes them in effectiveness and is more powerful than them. Action, then, is what you must add, since you have the other things already. You have men who can tell you your duty, men of Athens, and you are yourselves the smartest of people at understanding what has been said; and you will be able to act now, if you do what is right. [16] What occasion or opportunity, men of Athens, do you seek that will be better than the present one? When will you do your duty, if not now? Has this man not taken all our territories? If he becomes master of this land,[26] shall we not suffer the utmost ignominy? Are those people, whom we promised to support if they were to go to war, not now at war with him? Is he not our enemy? Does he not possess what is ours? Is he not a foreigner (*barbaros*)?[27] Can

---

[25]According to the ancient commentary on this passage (Dilts 1983: 92.12–13), the reference is to the leading politician Eubulus, on whom see the Speech Introduction.

[26]I.e., the territory of the Olynthians.

[27]The primary meaning of the Greek word *barbaros* is one who does not speak Greek, but by this period it had acquired pejorative connota-

anyone find words to describe him? [17] But, by the gods, after
we have neglected everything and all but helped him in his preparations, are we now to inquire who was responsible for this state
of affairs? For we shall not admit that we are responsible—that I
know for certain! Even in the dangers of war no deserter accuses
himself but instead blames the general and his neighbors and
everyone else, even though (as you know) it is because of all the
deserters that they are defeated. For the man who blames other
people could have held his position; and if each man had done
this, they would have been victorious. [18] So too now. Suppose
someone does not give the best advice: let someone else stand up
and speak, but without accusing the former. If someone makes a
better speech, do what he proposes, and good luck to you. If his
proposals are unpleasant, it is not the fault of the speaker, unless
he omits to pray when he should.[28] Prayer is easy, men of Athens, for a speaker who has collected together into a short compass
everything that one might wish to hear. To make a choice, however, when serious matters are under discussion, is not so easy, but
one must choose what is best over what is pleasant, if one cannot
have both.

[19] But if someone is able to leave the theoric fund to one side
and identify other sources of money for military spending, is this
not preferable, it might be asked. I agree, men of Athens, if this
is really possible. But I would be amazed if it has ever happened
to anybody, or ever will happen, that after spending what he has
on things that he does not need, he should be able to afford the
things that he does need from the money that he no longer has.
Each man's wishes, I believe, contribute greatly to such proposals, and that is why it is the easiest thing in the world to deceive
oneself. What each man wishes, this he also believes to be true,
although the facts are often not so. [20] So, men of Athens, you
should examine what is possible in our situation and how you will

---

tions and had some of the implications of the English word "barbarian"
which derives from it. The Macedonian royal house regarded itself as Greek,
but this was denied by anti-Macedonian politicians such as Demosthenes.
See 9.31n.

[28]Demosthenes' deliberative speeches often end with prayers for Athens' success.

be able to go on campaign *and* receive pay.[29] Prudent and honorable men do not neglect their military responsibilities for want of money or take the resulting criticism lightly; nor, after taking up arms against the Corinthians or Megarians,[30] do they permit Philip to enslave Greek cities for want of subsistence money for those who are on campaign.

[21] I have chosen to say these things not with the senseless aim of making myself an object of hatred to some of you. For I am not so foolish or perverse as to wish to be hated, when I do not think that I am doing any good. But I judge it to be the mark of a good citizen to put the safety of the community before his own popularity as a speaker. For, I have heard, as perhaps you have too, that the public speakers in the time of our ancestors—men whom all the speakers praise, even though they do not imitate them at all—adopted this manner of political conduct: the famous Aristides, Nicias, my namesake, and Pericles.[31] [22] But ever since the

---

[29]The provision of pay for military service was a recurring problem for Athens in the fourth century. See further Dem. 8, on the general Diopeithes' financial troubles; Pritchett 1971–1991: 1.3–29.

[30]Demosthenes distinguishes between land campaigns against nearby cities, such as Corinth and Megara, whose territory could easily be reached by the Athenian army, and naval expeditions to the northern Aegean. He fails to address the obvious objection that land operations of the former kind were much cheaper for Athens. For very recent friction between Megara and Athens over an area of borderland called the Hiera Orgas ("Sacred Land"), see 13.32n and more generally the Introduction to Dem. 13.

[31]Aristides was an important political leader of the period after the Persian Wars; Nicias and Demosthenes were Athenian leaders during the Peloponnesian War; Pericles was a prominent figure from the 460s onwards and dominated Athenian politics from the mid 440s until his death in 429. It is possible to see why Demosthenes chose three of the four to illustrate his argument: Aristides was famously upright and was nicknamed "the just"; Nicias unsuccessfully sought to persuade the Athenians to reject the popular proposal to send a naval expedition to Sicily in 415; Pericles is described by Thucydides as leading the Athenian people rather than being led by them (2.65.8). Demosthenes was linked to Nicias by their being the two final commanders of the disastrous Sicilian Expedition; he may also have been chosen to link the speaker to a famous figure of the past, though the two men were not related (see MacDowell 2009: 237 n. 93).

appearance of these politicians who ask you "What do you want? What shall I propose? What favor can I do you?" the affairs of the city have been pledged in exchange for immediate gratification, and this is the result: all their affairs prosper, while yours are in a shameful state. [23] Consider, men of Athens, how one might summarize the achievements of your ancestors' time and those of your own time. My account will be brief and well-known to you, since it is by using examples from home rather than from elsewhere, men of Athens, that you will be able to prosper. [24] Our ancestors, whom the speakers of the day neither indulged nor loved, as these men now do you, ruled the Greeks as willing subjects for forty-five years,[32] carried up more than ten thousand talents to the Acropolis,[33] and had the king who possesses this land as their subject,[34] which is the proper relationship between a foreigner[35] and Greeks, and erected many fine trophies, fighting in person both on land and at sea, and alone among men left behind glorious achievements that are beyond the reach of envy.[36]

---

[32]This is a round number: the period to which Demosthenes refers ran from the establishment of the Delian League in 478/7 to the outbreak of the Peloponnesian War in 431. His claim that the Greek cities of Athens' fifth-century empire were willing subjects is wishful thinking, as is clear from the number of cities that tried to revolt from it, from Thucydides' blunt characterization of it as a tyranny, and from the list of fifth-century abuses that the Athenians promised not to repeat when they established the Second Athenian Confederacy in 377.

[33]According to Thucydides (2.13.3), Athens' financial reserve during the period in question had been as high as 9,700 talents.

[34]At no time in the fifth century was a Macedonian king subject to Athens, but almost all the cities of the north Aegean coast, including some in Macedonian territory, were tribute-paying members of the Athenian empire. There is a possibility that Philip's father Amyntas was a (contribution-paying) member of the Second Athenian Confederacy: thus Cargill 1981: 85–87. Arrian (*Anabasis* 7.9.4) writing in the second century AD makes the same claim. See further Harding 2006: 232.

[35]On the Macedonian royal family as non-Greek (*barbaros*), see 16n; 9.31n.

[36]Trophies (*tropaia*) were monuments created out of captured armor and weapons that were erected on the battlefield by the victors, as symbols of their victory. See Pritchett 1971–1991: 2.246–275.

[25] This is how they acted in the affairs of Greece. Now examine how they conducted themselves as regards the city, both in public and in private matters. In public they created buildings and objects of beauty of such kind and size—temples and the offerings in them—that none of their descendants could surpass them. In private they were so restrained and so true to the nature of their constitution[37] [26] that if any of you knows which is the house of Aristides or of Miltiades or of the distinguished men of that time, he sees that it is no grander than that of its neighbor.[38] For they did not conduct the affairs of the city with a view to their own profit, but each of them thought it right to make the commonwealth more prosperous. Because they managed the affairs of Greece honestly, and matters relating to the gods piously, and their own affairs in a spirit of equality, they rightly enjoyed great good fortune.

[27] Such was our fortune then, under the leadership of the men whom I have named. How do we fare nowadays, under the leadership of these men who are now deemed admirable? Do we fare the same, or nearly so? I pass over other matters—although I have much that I could say—but you all see how much freedom we have to act, since the Spartans have been ruined, the Thebans are preoccupied, and none of the others is sufficiently prominent to rival us for supremacy;[39] but when we could both keep a firm grip on our own possessions and arbitrate over the rights of others, [28] we have been deprived of our own territory[40] and

---

[37]I.e., they conducted themselves in an appropriately democratic manner.

[38]On Aristides, see 21n. Miltiades was an important Athenian political and military leader of the early fifth century: see also 13.21n. In the parallel passage at 13.29, Demosthenes gives a slightly different selection of fifth-century leaders. Private houses in Greece were not at all large in either the fifth or fourth centuries.

[39]Following its defeat by Thebes at the battle of Leuctra in 371 and its subsequent loss of Messenia, Sparta was much reduced in power and influence. Thebes had meanwhile become bogged down in the lengthy Third Sacred War against Phocis. See the Introduction to this volume.

[40]The Athenians regarded Amphipolis in Thrace as their own possession, because it was originally an Athenian settlement (albeit on land that

have spent more than fifteen hundred talents in vain,[41] these men have destroyed the allies whom we secured in the war,[42] and we have trained a great enemy against ourselves. Or does someone wish to come forward and tell me how Philip has grown strong other than through our own actions? [29] "But, my dear sir, even if these things are unsatisfactory, the city itself is now in a better state." Why, what improvement can you name? The battlements we plaster, the roads we repair, the fountains, and similar rubbish? Look at the politicians who are responsible for these things. Some of them were beggars and are now rich; others were obscure and are now prominent. Some have built private houses that are grander than our public buildings. The more our city has declined, the more these men have flourished.

[30] What is the reason for this? Why is it that everything was fine in the past, but is in a wretched state now? Because then the people had the courage to act and campaign in person, and were the masters of the politicians, and controlled all good things, and each of the others[43] was content to receive a share of honor or office or any other benefit from the hands of the people. [31] But now the opposite is the case: the politicians control the good things, and everything is done through them, and you the people are hamstrung.[44] Deprived of money and allies, you now play the part of a servant and an extra, content if these men give you

---

had been taken from the Thracians): see 2.28n. For later wrangling between anti-Macedonian politicians at Athens and Philip, see 7.23–29 (Hegesippus' complaints) and 12.20–23 (Philip's retort).

[41] The ancient commentary on this passage (Dilts 1983: 98.25) claims that the money was spent on (campaigns to recover) Amphipolis, and Aeschines complains about the money the general Chares had wasted on campaign in the north (2.71). In the parallel passage in Dem. 13, it is claimed that this sum was squandered on the poor (13.27); this probably refers to mercenaries, who were often believed to have enlisted to escape extreme poverty. How this figure was calculated is not known.

[42] Demosthenes refers to the cities of the north Aegean coast (Potidaea, Methone, and Pydna) that were won over by the Athenian general Timotheus in 364 but taken by Philip during the 350s. See 1.9n.

[43] I.e., the politicians.

[44] Lit. "have had your sinews cut."

a share of the theoric fund[45] or dispatch the procession at the Boedromia,[46] and, bravest of all, you even thank them for your own possessions! They have confined you to the city and entice you to these things and tame you, turning you into docile pets. [32] It is never possible, I think, for those whose actions are small and trivial to adopt a strong and vigorous spirit: whatever men's habits are, so must their spirit be too. By Demeter, I would not be surprised if I were to suffer greater harm at your hands for saying these things than do those men who are responsible for them, since you do not always grant freedom of speech on every subject, and I am amazed that you have granted it now.

[33] If then, even now, you abandon these habits and are willing to go on campaign and to act in a way that is worthy of yourselves, and to use these domestic surpluses[47] as a starting point for external success, perhaps, men of Athens, perhaps you may acquire some great and lasting benefit and rid yourself of such payments, which are like the foods that doctors prescribe: they neither build strength nor allow the patient to die. In the same way, these sums that you now distribute among yourselves are not large enough to have any lasting benefit, nor would renouncing them allow you to do anything else, but they serve to make each of you more idle. [34] "Do you mean military pay?" someone will ask. Yes I do, and I mean the same system for everyone, men of Athens, in order that each man, in taking his share of public funds,

---

[45]On payments from the theoric fund, see 11n and the Speech Introduction.

[46]The Boedromia was a festival in honor of Apollo, held in the month Boedromion. It is not clear why Demosthenes singles out this particular festival. An alternative manuscript reading, *boidia* ("little cattle"), is perhaps to be preferred. In this case, the reference would be to a procession of cattle to be sacrificed, after which the meat would be distributed to the people. See MacDowell 2009: 237 n. 94.

[47]I.e., theoric payments. Demosthenes apparently refers to them as "surpluses" in the sense that in his opinion the payments are unnecessary, and the money could be used for other purposes; he is not referring to the vexed question of how the annual budget surplus (if any) should be allocated, on which see 1.19n.

should play whatever role the city requires. Suppose we are able to keep the peace: in that case, he is better off staying at home, freed from the pressure to do something shameful out of poverty. Suppose the situation is much as it is now: in that case, he serves as a soldier and draws pay from these same funds, doing his patriotic duty as he should. If any of you is no longer in his prime, he is better off receiving the money, which he now receives under no system and with no benefit to the city, in return for supervising and managing whatever needs to be done.[48] [35] In short, without subtracting or adding anything, except for small sums, I have eliminated the existing confusion and brought order to the city, with a uniform system for receiving pay, going on campaign, serving as jurors, and doing what is appropriate to each man's age and to our situation. I emphatically deny that money should be taken from those who are active and distributed to those who do nothing, or that you should be idle and have leisure and not know what to do, or that you should learn that so-and-so's mercenaries have won a victory—which is what happens now. [36] I am not blaming anyone who is doing his duty on your behalf, but I do urge you to do for yourselves the things for which you honor others, and not withdraw from the position of virtue that was left to you, men of Athens, by your ancestors, who acquired it by undergoing many glorious dangers.

I have told you almost everything I think you should hear. May you choose what will benefit both the city and all of you!

---

[48] The same system is proposed at 13.4.

4. FIRST PHILIPPIC

~~~~~~

INTRODUCTION

The *First Philippic* marks a turning point in Demosthenes' political career: although he had made a glancing reference to Philip in an (arguably) earlier speech (15.24), this is the first speech in which he directly addresses the danger to Athens arising from the growth of Macedonian power. From now on, all his surviving deliberative speeches are characterized by ancient critics as "Philippics," that is, as speeches concerned with policy towards Philip.[1]

Dionysius of Halicarnassus dates the speech to 352/1, but his testimony is not entirely straightforward,[2] and the question of its

---

[1]See Harding 2006: 244: Demosthenes "became a one-issue politician in 351 with the *First Philippic*" (at any rate, so far as the surviving speeches are concerned). We know four of the deliberative speeches (Dem. 4, 6, 9, and 10) as *Philippics*, but ancient critics also regarded Dem. 1–3, 5, [7], 8, and 11 as "Philippic."

[2]Dionysius (*First Letter to Ammaeus* 4) identifies the speech not by its title or opening words, as is his usual practice, but by its content ("a speech before the people on the dispatch of the mercenary force and the squadron of ten triremes of exiles [generally emended to "ten swift triremes] to Macedonia"). Later in the same work, however, he mentions a speech, which he calls the "fifth Philippic," on "the protection of the islanders and the cities of the Hellespont," and gives as its opening words the first words of 30. This latter speech he dates to 347/6 (10). It appears therefore that he regarded 4.1–29 as a separate speech, delivered in 352/1. His division of the single speech that we know as the *First Philippic* into two shorter speeches is not found elsewhere and is regarded by scholars as mistaken.

date continues to be debated.[3] One important passage for dating the speech is 17, where Demosthenes refers to Philip's "sudden campaigns to Thermopylae and the Chersonese and Olynthus" (cf. 41). The events to which he refers are as follows. First is Philip's march southwards in summer 352, after his victory over the Phocians at the battle of the Crocus Field, towards the strategically vital pass of Thermopylae, where he was thwarted by an Athenian expeditionary force that had occupied the site.[4] Second is his expedition to eastern Thrace in autumn 352 (though some scholars have argued that this occurred in 351: see 3.4n).[5] Third is an early incursion into the territory of the Chalcidic League in northern Greece, perhaps on his return from Thrace.[6] Other references in the speech—to Philip's raids on Athenian territory and shipping (34), to his letter to the Euboeans (37), and to his operations in Illyria (48)—are not closely dateable, although the Illyrian campaign probably occurred in early 351 (see 1.13n). The speech also refers to rumors that Philip is ill or dead (11); it is clear from the sequence of events reported at Dem. 3.4–5 that these rumors were circulating at some point before the dispatch from Athens of a force commanded by Charidemus in September 351. In short, a date in late 352/1, that is, summer 351, is possible, but we cannot exclude the possibility that Dionysius is mistaken and that the speech belongs in the following Athenian year, 351/0.[7]

---

[3]See most recently MacDowell 2009: 211–213.

[4]Demosthenes describes this as taking place "recently" or "the other day" (*prōēn*; 17), but this adverb is too imprecise in its range of meaning to allow any conclusions to be drawn about the date of this speech.

[5]In the *Third Olynthiac* of 349/8 Demosthenes refers to Philip's seizure of a place in Thrace in November "two or three years ago" (3.4), which would be consistent with either date.

[6]The suggestion that the reference is to the campaign of 349/8, and has been interpolated into a speech of 352/1, is now rightly rejected. At the same time, the casualness of the reference to Olynthus at 17 rules out the possibility that the speech as a whole belongs as late as 349/8, when that city was at war with Philip. See the Introduction to Dem. 1–3 for relations between Philip and Olynthus in the late 350s.

[7]See Lane Fox 1997: 195–199.

If the exact circumstances that gave rise to the speech are debatable, its general context is abundantly clear. Although Philip had been at war with Athens since his seizure of Amphipolis in 357, and had wrested control of a number of cities on the north Aegean coast to which Athens laid claim, two events opened Demosthenes' eyes to the threat that he posed to Athens. The first was his victory at the Battle of the Crocus Field in 352 and his subsequent thrust southwards towards the pass of Thermopylae. The second was his campaign in Thrace in 352/1 and specifically his advance as far east as Fort Heraeum. This brought him dangerously close to the Chersonese and the Hellespont and to the sea route between the Aegean and the Black Sea on which Athens depended for much of its food imports.

The core of this speech is a detailed proposal for military preparations that will allow Athens to deal effectively with Philip. Demosthenes argues for the creation of two separate forces. The first is to be a standing force of fifty triremes, crewed by citizens, which will be able to respond rapidly to any new campaign by Philip (16–18). The second is a permanent force, mainly of mercenaries but with a citizen component, and with only ten triremes, to engage continuously with Philip in the north Aegean (19–22). Demosthenes also discusses the funding of this second force (28–29). It is a clear indication of Athens' financial weakness that he proposes to provide only subsistence money, with no pay, and expects the troops to make good the shortfall from plunder (but without harming any of Athens' allies!).

The early part of the speech encourages the Athenians not to despair at Philip's apparent strength but to match the resolution that he has shown. After setting out his proposal, Demosthenes turns to criticize the Athenians for their laxness in the waging of war: they take more care for the smooth running of religious festivals than for taking prompt military action (35–37), and they react to Philip's actions rather than take the initiative, and do so too slowly (38–41). A recurrent demand, repeated in several of his later speeches, is that the Athenians must serve in person, to keep an eye on their generals and ensure that the war is prosecuted energetically, rather than rely on mercenaries (24–25, 44–47). Demosthenes, here as elsewhere, attributes Athens' lack of success against Philip to a failure of will on the part of its citizens, rather than a pragmatic reluctance to expend their limited resources on military operations that were unlikely to substantially weaken Philip's power.

There are texts of this speech with commentaries by Sandys 1910 and (very fully) Wooten 2008 and a translation with commentary by Ellis and Milns 1970.

4. FIRST PHILIPPIC

[1] If some new matter were the topic of discussion, men of Athens, I would have waited until most of the regular speakers had given their opinion, and if anything they said pleased me, I would have kept quiet; only if it did not would I have ventured to state my own opinion.[8] But since we are dealing with matters that these men have often addressed on previous occasions, I think that I can reasonably be forgiven for standing up to speak first. For if they had given the necessary advice in the past, there would be no need for you to be deliberating now.

[2] First, men of Athens, you must not despair at the present situation, even if it seems dreadful. For its worst aspect in the past holds out our best hope for the future. What am I referring to? To the fact, men of Athens, that our situation has deteriorated so badly while you have been doing none of the things you needed to do. For if our situation were so poor when you had been doing all that you should, there would be no hope of improving matters. [3] Next, you must consider, whether you hear it from others or remember it from personal knowledge, how powerful the Spartans once were, not long ago, and how well and appropriately you acted, in keeping with the reputation of the city, and endured war against them for the sake of justice.[9] Why do I mention this? To make you see, men of Athens, and understand that

---

[8] It was conventional for more senior politicians to speak first in the Assembly.

[9] Athens fought Sparta both in the Corinthian War of 395–386 and in collaboration with Thebes in the 370s.

nothing frightens you when you are on your guard, but that if you are contemptuous, nothing is as you might wish, using as my examples the Spartans' strength then, which you defeated by applying your intelligence to the situation, and this man's arrogance now, which alarms us because we fail to attend to any of the things that we should. [4] And if any of you, men of Athens, thinks that Philip is hard to wage war against, considering the size of the forces at his disposal and our city's loss of all its possessions, he is quite correct. But let him consider this. Once, men of Athens, Pydna and Potidaea and Methone and the whole surrounding region were on good terms with us,[10] and many of the peoples that are now on his side were autonomous and free and preferred to be on good terms with us more than with him.[11] [5] But if Philip at that time had decided that it would be difficult for him to wage war on the Athenians, since they had such strong outposts in his own territory, whereas he was without allies, he would not have achieved any of the things that he has, nor would he have acquired so much power. But he knew very well, men of Athens, that all these places lie in the open as the prizes of war, and that it is natural for those who are present to take the possessions of those who are absent, and for those who are willing to toil and face danger to get the possessions of those who are negligent. [6] In consequence, and with this resolve, he has conquered and now possesses places everywhere, some as one would possess them after taking them in war, others after making them his allies and well disposed towards him: for they are all willing to ally themselves to and obey anyone whom they see to be well prepared and willing to do what is needed. [7] If, men of Athens, you too are prepared to adopt such a resolve now, since indeed you were not previously, and each of you is willing to drop all pretence and take

---

[10] These places had belonged to Athens' fifth-century empire, but Demosthenes is presumably thinking about their capture in 364 by the Athenian general Timotheus: see 1.9n, 3.28n.

[11] By "peoples" (*ethnē*) Demosthenes means those whose political organization is not based on the city-state (*polis*). These were chiefly such non-Greek people as the Thracians, Paeonians, and Illyrians, but he may also have in mind the Thessalians (see 9.26n on their enslavement "by *ethnos*").

action wherever it is needed and wherever he may be able to benefit the city, those with money by paying taxes, those in the prime
of life by going on campaign, in short if you are simply willing to
get a grip on yourselves, and stop each hoping that you can get
away with doing nothing, while your neighbor does everything
on your behalf, you will recover what is yours, god willing, and
will regain what has been negligently lost, and will punish that
man. [8] Do not imagine that he has fixed the present situation
immutably, as if he were a god. Rather, someone hates and fears
him, men of Athens, and envies him, even from among those who
now seem to be on very good terms with him; and one must suppose that his supporters have the same feelings as any other people would. All these feelings are now repressed, since they have
no outlet because of your slowness and apathy—of which, I say,
you must immediately rid yourselves. [9] You see the situation,
men of Athens: how insolent that man is, who does not even allow you to choose between taking action and living quietly, but
threatens and makes arrogant speeches (so it is reported) and is
unable to be content with possession of the places that he has already conquered, but is always bringing something more under
his power, and surrounds us on all sides as if with nets,[12] while
we sit and wait. [10] When, men of Athens, when will you do
what is needed? What are you waiting for? For some necessity to
arise, by Zeus? What, then, should we call the present developments? For, I believe, the strongest necessity for free men is shame
at their situation. Or, tell me, do you wish to go around asking
each other, "Is there any news?" What could be graver news than
that a Macedonian is waging war on Athens and is in control of
the affairs of Greece? [11] "Is Philip dead?" "No, by Zeus, but he is
sick."[13] What difference does it make to you? Even if something
were to happen to him,[14] you would soon create another Philip, if
this is how you apply yourselves to the situation, since even he has

---

[12]The simile is taken from the hunting of animals with nets.

[13]Rumors about Philip's health circulated in 352/1 while he was on campaign in Thrace (3.5) and would therefore have been recent if this speech
was delivered in 351 (see the Speech Introduction for discussion of its date).

[14]This is a euphemism for "if he dies."

not prospered by reason of his own strength as much as because of our neglect. [12] Moreover, if Fortune, which always takes better care of us than we do of ourselves, should arrange for something to happen to him, you know that if you were on the scene, you might step in and in the general state of confusion arrange matters as you wish. But as you are now, even if the opportunity were to present itself, you would be unable to take Amphipolis,[15] since you are disunited in your preparations and in your resolve.

[13] I shall now stop urging you all to be ready and willing to do your duty, since you acknowledge it and are persuaded to do so. But the kind of force that, in my view, would rid us of the serious troubles we have, and its size, and the sources of money for it, and the other steps that I think would lead to the creation of the most effective force as quickly as possible—these I shall attempt to tell you, men of Athens. In doing so, I make the following request of you. [14] Make your decision only after you have heard all that I have to say; do not prejudge the matter. If anyone thinks that I am describing an entirely new kind of force, he should not suppose that I am prevaricating. It is not those who say "quickly" and "tomorrow" who best address our needs—sending a relief force now will not allow us to prevent what has already happened. [15] Rather, it is whoever can show what kind of force, of what size and funded from what sources, will be able to resist until either we agree to bring the war to an end or we defeat the enemy. Only in this way will we put an end to the harm we are suffering. I believe that I can tell you what needs to be done, but I will not stand in the way of anyone else who has advice to offer. This is the extent of the promise I make; events will give the proof, and you shall be the judges.

[16] First of all, men of Athens, I say that you should prepare fifty triremes. Then you must be resolved, if the need should arise, to embark and sail on them in person. In addition, you should make ready horse-transporting triremes and enough supply ships

---

[15]The strategically important city of Amphipolis on the river Strymon in Thrace was founded by Athens in the fifth century, lost during the Peloponnesian War, and captured by Philip in 357. Its recovery was a central element of Athenian foreign policy.

for half the cavalrymen.[16] [17] These, in my view, are needed to counter his sudden campaigns from his own land to Thermopylae and the Chersonese and Olynthus and anywhere else he wishes.[17] For we must plant the expectation in his mind that you will shake off your excessive lethargy and hurry out, as you did to Euboea and on a previous occasion, it is said, to Haliartus and recently to Thermopylae.[18] [18] Such a force would not be easy for him to despise utterly, even if you do not do as I say you should. Its purpose is either to keep him quiet out of fear, in the knowledge that you are prepared—for he will know it, since there are those of us—yes, there are, more than there should be—who report everything to him; or, if he should despise it, to take him off guard, since there will be nothing to prevent your sailing against his territory if he should give you the opportunity. [19] These are the resolutions that are in my view called for and the preparations that need to be made. But before these, men of Athens, I urge you to mobilize a force to wage war continuously and to damage his interests. None of your ten or twenty thousand mercenaries[19] for me, nor

---

[16]Demosthenes proposes the creation of a substantial rapid-response force. A trireme (*triērēs*, the standard Greek warship of the period) regularly had 170 rowers (out of a total crew of 200), and so the number of those involved could be in excess of 9,000. The regular number of Athenian cavalry was 1,000 (see 14.13n).

[17]On the importance of this passage for dating the speech, see the Speech Introduction. Philip marched on Thermopylae after his victory over the Phocian army in 352 (see the next note) and threatened the Chersonese by his campaign in Thrace in autumn of that year (see 3.4n). His military threat to Olynthus, which is distinct from and predates the outbreak of war, occurred probably in early 351.

[18]Demosthenes refers to Athens' intervention on the island of Euboea in 357 (see 8.74–75), its contribution to the coalition that fought the Spartans at Haliartus in Boeotia during the Corinthian War in 395, and its occupation of Thermopylae in 352 to prevent Philip marching against Phocis (see also below, 41).

[19]Ten thousand (a "myriad") was regularly used by the Greeks to denote a very large number. In fact, Athens is never known to have employed anything like this many mercenaries. See below, 24n, for the ancient commentary on this passage.

these paper forces, but one that will belong to the city and that, whether you elect one man or many or this man or that as its general, will follow and obey him. I also urge you to provide supplies for it. [20] What kind of force do I mean, and of what size, and where will it get its supplies from, and how will it be motivated to take these actions? I shall tell you, dealing with each of these points separately. I am talking about mercenaries—and please beware of the attitude that has often harmed you before: you think that everything is on too small a scale and so in your decrees you choose the most grandiose options, but when it comes to action, you fail to take even small measures. Instead, you should take small measures, and provide for them, and then add to them if they seem inadequate. [21] What I propose is that there be two thousand soldiers in all, of whom five hundred should be Athenian, of whatever age you decide, and that they should campaign for a set period, not for a long time as they do now but for as long as you think appropriate, taking turns; the rest should be mercenaries. There should also be two hundred cavalrymen, of whom at least fifty should be Athenian, serving on the same basis as the infantry, and horse-transport ships for them.[20] [22] Very well, what else? Ten fast triremes.[21] Since he has a fleet,[22] we too need fast triremes to allow our force to sail in safety. How are these to be supplied? I shall tell you, after I have explained why I think so small a force is sufficient, and why I insist that those who go on campaign be citizens.

[23] The reason for a force of this size, men of Athens, is that we cannot now provide one that is capable of meeting him in battle but must act as raiders and wage this kind of war at first. The

---

[20]Athenians were liable to serve in the army from the ages of 18 to 59, and their army was mobilized by age groups (see, e.g., 3.4, where all those up to the age of 45 are to be called up).

[21]Athenian triremes were divided into classes according to their sailing qualities: see 14.18n. Demosthenes is probably calling for ships of either the "select" or "first" class.

[22]The Macedonian fleet was doubtless small, if Demosthenes thought that ten triremes were sufficient to deal with it, but it was capable of causing trouble to Athens: see 34 below. See in general Hammond and Griffith 1979: 310–312.

force should not be excessively large, since there is no money and no supplies, but neither should it be utterly weak. [24] The reason why I say that citizens should participate and sail with the force is that in the past, I am told, the city supported a mercenary force at Corinth, led by Polystratus and Iphicrates and Chabrias and certain others, and you yourselves joined in the campaign.[23] And I know from what I have heard that these mercenaries, drawn up alongside you against the Spartans, and you alongside them, were victorious.[24] But ever since your mercenaries have campaigned on their own, they have defeated our friends and allies, while our enemies have grown stronger than they should. They give a passing glance to the war that the city is waging and then sail off to Artabazus and anywhere else instead, and the general follows them. And this is reasonable enough, since it is impossible for someone who does not provide pay to exercise command.[25] [25] What then do I propose? That you prevent the general and his troops from making excuses by providing them with pay and by stationing your own soldiers alongside them, like supervisors of his actions, because the way we handle things at present is laughable. If anyone were to ask you, "Are you at peace, Athenians?" you would say, "By Zeus, we are not; we are at war with

---

[23]During the Corinthian War against Sparta, the Athenian general Iphicrates commanded a force of light-armed mercenary soldiers of a type known as "peltasts" (see *OCD*[3] s.v. peltasts). This force was based at Corinth and famously defeated a regiment of the Spartan army at Lechaeum in 390: see 13.22. Iphicrates was succeeded as commander by Chabrias. Both men were prominent military leaders until the mid 350s: see 13.20n on the statues erected in the Agora in their honor. Polystratus is not otherwise known, but he may be the man mentioned at Dem. 20.84.

[24]The victory is that of Lechaeum (see the previous note).

[25]According to the ancient commentary on this speech (commenting on 19: Dilts 1983: 116.20–117.2), in 355 the Athenian general Chares augmented his mercenary force with approximately 1,000 mercenaries who had previously served in the satrapal armies of the western Persian Empire. Since he was unable to support these troops, he took service with the rebel satrap Artabazus and defeated a larger Persian army in a battle that he boastfully described to the Athenians as a "second Marathon," i.e., as a great triumph (on the original battle of Marathon, see 13.21n).

Philip."²⁶ [26] Have you not elected from among yourselves ten taxiarchs and generals and phylarchs and two hipparchs?²⁷ What do these men do? Except for whichever individual commander you dispatch to the war, the rest marshal your ceremonial processions alongside the priests.²⁸ Just like the makers of clay figurines, you elect the taxiarchs and phylarchs for the marketplace, not for war.²⁹ [27] But shouldn't the taxiarchs be chosen from among you, men of Athens, and the hipparch, and shouldn't the office holders be from among you, if the force is to be truly Athenian? But your hipparch has to sail to Lemnos,³⁰ while it is Menelaus who commands the cavalry that is fighting for the city's possessions.³¹ I do not mean any criticism of the individual, but the man, whoever he is, should have been elected by you.³²

[28] Perhaps you think that this is well said, but what you most

---

²⁶A state of war existed between Athens and Philip after the latter's capture of Amphipolis in 357: see 2.25n.

²⁷The ten generals had overall command of Athens' armed forces on land and at sea. The taxiarchs each commanded one of the ten tribal contingents (*taxeis*) of the Athenian army. The cavalry was commanded by two hipparchs, with a phylarch leading each of the ten tribal cavalry contingents. On the election of these military officials, see *Ath. Pol.* 61.

²⁸The cavalry often took part in religious processions (Xen. *Hipparchicus* 3.1), and the hoplites participated in the Panathenaic procession. In addition, the generals poured libations at the City Dionysia (see Plut. *Cimon* 8; *IG* II² 1496). Demosthenes' complaint is that Athens' military leaders are underemployed.

²⁹Demosthenes appears to be thinking of clay figurines of soldiers which would be sold in the marketplace (*agora*). The Agora was also an important venue for religious processions.

³⁰Lemnos was an island in the northern Aegean that belonged to Athens and was occupied by Athenian settlers. The Athenians elected a hipparch (distinct from the two cavalry commanders mentioned in 26) to command the cavalry stationed there: see *Ath. Pol.* 61.6.

³¹Menelaus, clearly originally a foreigner, is possibly to be identified with the man of that name from Pelagonia in Upper Macedonia who is praised in an Athenian decree of 362 (*IG* II² 110 = Rhodes and Osborne 2003: no. 38); he may be the Menelaus son of Arrhabaeus of Athens mentioned in a decree of the city of Ilion (Tod 1948: no. 148). See Osborne 1983: T56.

³²The circumstances of Menelaus' appointment are unknown.

wish to hear is how much money is needed and where it will come from. This I shall also do. As for the money, the maintenance—subsistence only—of this force will cost a little more than ninety talents: for ten fast ships, forty talents, at twenty minas per ship per month; for two thousand soldiers, the same amount again, with each soldier receiving ten drachmas a month for maintenance; and for the two hundred cavalrymen, if each receives thirty drachmas a month, twelve talents.[33] [29] If anyone thinks that this is scant provision—for those on campaign to receive maintenance money only—he is wrong. I am sure that if this proposal is accepted the army itself will make good the rest from the war, without wronging any of the Greeks or our allies, and as a result will receive full pay.[34] I am willing to join the expedition myself as a volunteer[35] and suffer any punishment, if this is not the case. Where will the money that I am urging you to provide come from? I shall now tell you.[36]

[STATEMENT OF FINANCIAL RESOURCES]

[30] This, men of Athens, is what we have been able to come up with.[37] When you vote to make your decision, if this plan pleases

---

[33]See 22 on the ships. In the Athenian monetary system, one talent = 60 minas = 6,000 drachmas. Demosthenes' calculations are as follows. Cost of squadron: 10 ships × 12 months × 20 minas = 2,400 minas = 40 talents. Maintenance: 2,000 soldiers × 10 drachmas × 12 months = 240,000 drachmas = 40 talents. Cavalry: 200 cavalry × 30 drachmas × 12 months = 72,000 drachmas = 12 talents. The exact total is 92 talents. The crew of each trireme is assumed to number 200, and the monthly cost for the maintenance of the crew of an individual ship (20 minas = 2,000 drachmas) implies that maintenance for each crew member will be 10 drachmas per month (which is the same as the amount for the soldiers).

[34]On rates of military pay and subsistence money, see Pritchett 1971–1991: 1.14–23.

[35]On volunteering for military service, see Pritchett 1971–1991: 2.110–112.

[36]The document that Demosthenes read out at this point, like the letter in 37, was not preserved in the manuscripts of the speech.

[37]The ancient critic Dionysius of Halicarnassus mistakenly believed that this is the start of a new speech: see the Speech Introduction. Demosthenes'

you, you will be voting to wage war on Philip not only by your decrees and letters but also by your actions.

[31] It seems to me, men of Athens, that your deliberation about the war and your general armaments would be improved if you were to bear in mind the nature of the place against which you are waging war, and observe that Philip often achieves his aims by getting a head start on us, by means of the winds and the seasons of the year; and that he launches his attacks after waiting for the Etesian winds or for winter,[38] whenever we are unable to get there. [32] We need to bear these things in mind and to wage war not by means of relief forces—since if we do so we will be too late for everything—but by means of a permanent standing force. As winter quarters for this force we can use Lemnos and Thasos and Sciathos and the islands in the region,[39] where there are harbors and food and everything that an army needs. During the campaigning season, when it is easy to put in to land and when the winds are safe, it will be easy to put in to the mainland and the entrances of the trading ports.

[33] How and when to employ the force is a decision to be taken at the appropriate time by the commander you appoint; it is what you must provide that I have written down.[40] If you make these provisions, men of Athens, organizing first the sum of money that I specify and then the rest, you will legally compel the soldiers, triremes, cavalrymen, in short the entire force, to stick with the war. As regards money, you will be your own treasurers and providers; and as regards action, you will hold the gen-

---

use of the first-person plural offers a rare glimpse (in these speeches) of the collaboration that undoubtedly took place between politicians.

[38]The Etesian (i.e., "summer") winds (modern Greek "meltemi") are strong north winds of the Aegean Sea that blow up suddenly during the summer months. Their appearance could delay Athenian naval expeditions to the northern Aegean. See also 8.14.

[39]On Lemnos, see 27 above. The large island of Thasos off the northern coast of the Aegean and the island of Sciathos to the north of Euboea were both allies of Athens by virtue of their membership in the Second Athenian Confederacy.

[40]Demosthenes here refers to the decree that he has drafted.

eral accountable and will stop constantly deliberating about the same things but doing nothing further. [34] Furthermore, men of Athens, you will deprive Philip of his greatest financial resource. What is this? The fact that he wages war against you from your own allies, by plundering those who sail the sea. What else? You will no longer suffer harm, unlike in the past when he attacked Lemnos and Imbros and carried off your citizens as prisoners,[41] and captured the cargo ships off Geraestus and levied an incalculable sum from them,[42] and lastly disembarked at Marathon[43] and seized the sacred trireme[44] from there, and you are able neither to prevent such things nor to send assistance at the times that you have set. [35] Why is it, men of Athens, that the festivals of the Panathenaea and the Dionysia always take place at the appointed time, whether experts or amateurs are selected[45] to administer them, when as much money is spent on them as

---

[41]The neighboring islands of Lemnos (cf. 27 and 32 above) and Imbros in the northern Aegean were Athenian possessions, settled by citizens sent from Athens. This and the following examples show that Philip certainly had some naval capability: see 22n above.

[42]Geraestus was at the southern tip of the island of Euboea. The cargo ships mentioned were probably carrying wheat bound for Athens' port of Piraeus.

[43]Marathon was a coastal town of northeastern Attica and the site of a famous battle in 490 in which a Persian expeditionary force was defeated by the Athenian army. See 13.21, 14.30.

[44]There were two so-called sacred triremes in the Athenian fleet, the *Paralus* and the *Salaminia*, which were used on diplomatic and religious missions (on the former, see 8.29n). Each year Athens sent a delegation to participate in a religious festival (the "lesser" Delia) on the island of Delos, which stopped en route to sacrifice at the shrine of Delian Apollo at Marathon. This provides a possible context for Philip's action.

[45]The Greek word *lachōsin* implies selection by lot, though it is known that until at least 349/8 the managers of the Dionysia were elected. MacDowell 2009: 213 n. 23 correctly rejects an older theory that this is evidence that the speech was revised after delivery, and he argues that the reference is to other magistrates, the *archōn* and the board of *athlothētai*, who had responsibility for the processions at the Dionysia and Panathenaea respectively and who were selected by lot.

on any single naval expedition, and they involve as much bustle and preparation as any other occasion I know of,[46] whereas
your naval expeditions all miss their opportunities—the ones to
Methone, to Pagasae, and to Potidaea?[47] [36] The reason is that
the festivals are all regulated by law,[48] and each of you knows far
in advance who will be the chorus master or gymnasiarch[49] of
the tribe, and what he must do and when, and what he should receive from whom, and nothing is overlooked or left unclear out of
neglect. But none of our military preparations are organized, or
kept up to date, or properly defined. As a result, as soon as we receive some news, we appoint trierarchs,[50] and make exchanges of
property for them,[51] and look into the provision of money, and
after this we decide to embark the metics[52] and the slaves who

---

[46] The Panathenaea in honor of Athena and the City Dionysia in honor
of Dionysus were the two most important religious festivals in the Athenian calendar.

[47] See 1.9n.

[48] For the text of such a law, see Dem. 21.10.

[49] These two positions were both liturgies, i.e., public duties that wealthy
individuals were required to finance out of their pocket. A chorus master
(*chorēgos*) was responsible for the training of a dramatic chorus (see *OCD*[3]
s.v. *chorēgia*); a gymnasiarch was responsible for his tribe's runners in the
torchraces that were part of several religious festivals: see Dem. 20.21.

[50] Trierarchs were wealthy Athenians who were appointed to perform the
liturgy (see the previous note) of commanding a ship of the Athenian navy.
They were expected to use their own money to defray the costs of equipping and maintaining the ship. On the trierarchic system, see the Introduction to Dem. 14.

[51] Liability for the performance of liturgies was based on wealth. To ensure that wealthy citizens did not evade their responsibilities, the Athenians
devised a legal procedure called *antidosis* ("exchange"). Any Athenian who
was chosen to perform a liturgy could challenge another to do it in his stead
if he believed the other to be wealthier. The person challenged could either
agree to take over the liturgy (thereby acknowledging that he was richer) or
exchange properties with the challenger (if he thought that he was in fact
poorer). See Christ 1990.

[52] Metics (*metoikoi*) were non-Athenians resident in Attica. They lacked
political rights but were obliged to serve in Athens' armed forces.

live apart from their masters,[53] then ourselves, then we change the crew again, [37] and during all this delay we lose the object of our expedition before we have begun. We spend the time for action on preparation, but the opportunities offered by circumstance do not wait on our slowness and dissimulation.[54] In the meantime, the forces we think we have are shown to be unable to do anything even when opportunities do arise. And that man has reached such a pitch of arrogance that he has already sent letters like this to the Euboeans.[55]

[READING OF LETTER]

[38] Most of what has been read out, men of Athens, is true—would that it were not—though it is perhaps unpleasant to hear.[56] If everything a speaker passes over, in order not to cause distress, is also passed over by events, it would be right to speak with a view to pleasing the audience. But since pleasant speeches—if they are inappropriate—lead to disastrous consequences, it is shameful to deceive ourselves and, by putting off everything that is disagreeable, be too late in all that we do, [39] and be unable to learn even this lesson—that those who wage war properly must anticipate events rather than follow them; and, just as one would expect a general to lead his army, so those who deliberate should lead events, so that all their decisions lead to action and they are not forced to chase after events. [40] But you, men of Athens,

---

[53] Some particularly trusted slaves were permitted by their owners to live and work independently, on condition that they pay them a part of their earnings.

[54] Demosthenes' point is that behind all their bustle, the Athenians have no real intention of getting ready for war.

[55] The ancient commentary on the passage (Dilts 1983: 118.5–7) claims that the letter advised the Euboeans not to put their hopes on alliance with the Athenians, since the latter were unable even to save themselves. There were four separate cities on Euboea (Chalcis, Eretria, Carystus, and Oreus): perhaps Philip sent the same letter to all of them (see MacDowell 2009: 217 n. 38). For Athenian military intervention in Euboea in early 348, see 5.5n.

[56] The text of the letter is not included in the manuscripts of this speech.

who possess greater forces than anyone else—triremes, hoplites, cavalry, revenues—have never yet, to the present day, used any of them as you should, but instead you wage war on Philip in the same way that a foreigner boxes.[57] For when one of them is struck, he always moves his hands to that spot, and if he is struck on the other side, his hands go to that place: he has neither the knowledge nor the will to put up his guard or watch for the next blow. [41] It is the same with you. If you hear that Philip is in the Chersonese, you vote to send a relief force there, and likewise if you hear that he is at Thermopylae.[58] And if you hear that he is somewhere else, you run up and down at his heels and are at his command; you have no plan to turn the war to your advantage, and fail to anticipate any eventuality until you learn that it has happened or is happening. This was perhaps inherent in previous situations, but now things have reached the point that it is no longer supportable. [42] It seems to me, men of Athens, that some god is ashamed at what is being done in the name of our city and is putting this restlessness in Philip. If Philip were willing to be quiet, keeping the places he has defeated and seized before we could act but doing nothing further, I think some of you would be satisfied with this—although we would get a collective reputation for dishonor and cowardice and all the most shameful things. But now, by his constant attacks on people and his grasping for more, perhaps he may summon you forth—if indeed you have not entirely given up. [43] I am amazed if none of you, men of Athens, is concerned or angry when he considers that when the war began, our object was to punish Philip, but now that it is coming to an end, it is to avoid suffering harm at his hands. Yet it is clear that he will not stand still, unless he is stopped. Should we just wait for this to happen? Or, if you were to dispatch empty ships[59] and hopes inspired by so-and-so, do you suppose that everything would be all right? [44] Shall we not embark? Shall we not go out now, even if

---

[57] Demosthenes both assumes that foreigners (*barbaroi*: cf. 3.16n) would be unfamiliar with the Greek sport of boxing and reflects the Greek prejudice that foreigners were by nature inferior to Greeks.

[58] For these two episodes, see 17n above.

[59] On the meaning of "empty ships," see 3.4n.

we did not do so previously, with at least a part of our own forces? Shall we not sail against his territory? "Where shall we find anchorage?" someone may ask. The war itself, men of Athens, will find out the rotten parts of his affairs, if we set to work. But if we sit at home, listening to speakers abuse and blame each other, I fear that we will never achieve any of the things that we need to. [45] For, I believe, wherever a part or even all of the city's forces are dispatched, the gods are kindly and fortune fights on our side; but wherever you send out a general and an empty decree and hopes from the speaker's platform, you achieve nothing that you should, while your enemies laugh at such expeditions, and your allies die of fear.[60] [46] One man on his own can never, never, I say, do everything that you wish: but he can make promises and speeches and blame this man or that and, as a result, your affairs lie in ruins. For when our general is leading wretched unpaid mercenaries, and these men here are smoothly lying to you about what Philip is doing, and you are voting at random on the basis of whatever you hear, what can you expect?

[47] How then will this state of affairs be brought to an end? As soon as you, men of Athens, appoint the same men to be both soldiers and witnesses of the general's conduct and, once they have returned home, judges at the examinations into the conduct of the magistrates,[61] so that you not only hear about your affairs but also observe them in person. As it is, things are so shameful that each general is tried by you two or three times on a capital charge,[62] but none of them dares to engage even once in a life-

---

[60]I.e., fear of Athenian abuses, on which see 24 above.

[61]On the scrutiny (*euthynai*) that all magistrates had to undergo at the end of their year in office, see 1.28. Demosthenes means if the soldiers are Athenian citizens, they can later be witnesses and judges at the general's scrutiny.

[62]Generals and politicians were particularly liable to impeachment (*eisangelia*) on a charge of treason; often such prosecutions were prompted by frustration at their lack of success rather than any real evidence of corruption. See Pritchett 1971–1991: 2.4–33; Hansen 1975; Hamel 1998: 122–157. See also 8.28 on the possibility of recalling the general Diopeithes from the Chersonese under this procedure.

and-death struggle with the enemy. Instead, they prefer the death of kidnappers and clothes-stealers[63] to a fitting end, since a criminal dies after he is tried and convicted, but a general dies fighting the enemy.[64] [48] We go around, some of us saying that Philip is working with the Spartans to ruin Thebes[65] and is overturning constitutions, others claiming that he has sent ambassadors to the King,[66] or that he is fortifying cities in Illyria,[67] or just fabricating speeches on their own. [49] By the gods, men of Athens, I think that Philip is drunk[68] at the scale of his achievements and dreams of doing many similar things, when he sees that there is no one to prevent him, and is elated by what he has accomplished. But, by Zeus, I do not suppose that he chooses to act in such a way that even the stupidest of us will know what he intends to do— for the makers of speeches are the most stupid. [50] But if we put aside such behavior and recognize that he is our enemy and is depriving us of our possessions and has for a long time been insulting us, and that everything we ever hoped someone would do for us is found to have been done against us, and that the future is in our own hands, and if we are not now willing to wage war on him there we shall perhaps be compelled to do so here—if we recognize these things, we will have recognized what is needed and will have rid ourselves of empty rhetoric. What we need to do is not to

---

[63]Under Athenian law kidnappers (*andrapodistai*) and clothes-stealers (*lōpodytai*) could be either seized and dragged off to one of the board of magistrates called the Eleven or reported to one of them. In either case, if they were caught red-handed and admitted their guilt, they were put to death without trial. See MacDowell 1978: 148–149.

[64]Hamel 1998: 204–209 catalogues and discusses the deaths of Athenian generals on campaign.

[65]Philip and Sparta were on opposite sides of the Third Sacred War: he was allied to Thebes, and Sparta supported Phocis. If Philip was intending to collaborate with Sparta against Thebes, this would represent a complete reversal of policy on his part.

[66]There is no other evidence for a Macedonian embassy to Persia at this date, although it is quite possible that one was sent.

[67]On Philip's campaign against the Illyrians, see 1.13n.

[68]Demosthenes refers to metaphorical drunkenness, but the Greeks regarded the Macedonians as conspicuously heavy drinkers: see 2.18n.

contemplate what may possibly happen but to realize that the future will be miserable unless you attend to your obligations and are willing to do your duty.

[51] I have never yet tried to win your favor by saying anything that I did not believe to be to your advantage, and now I have shared everything I know with you candidly, holding nothing back. Just as I know that it is in your interest to hear the best advice, so I wish I knew that the giving of such advice would benefit the man who composed the best speech—I would be much happier if that were the case. As it is, although the consequences for me are unclear, nevertheless I choose to speak in the firm conviction that you will benefit from agreeing to this policy—so long as you put it into practice. May what will benefit all win out.

5. ON THE PEACE

〰〰〰〰〰〰〰〰〰〰〰〰〰〰〰〰〰〰〰〰〰〰〰〰〰〰〰〰〰〰〰

INTRODUCTION

Demosthenes' speech *On the Peace* was delivered in the aftermath of the making of the Peace of Philocrates between Athens and Philip in summer 346.[1] It is correctly dated 346/5 by Dionysius of Halicarnassus[2] and was probably delivered in autumn 346.

Philip's capture of Olynthus in 348 (see the Introduction to Dem. 1–3) meant the failure of Athens' attempt to resist him in the north, and he also now held many Athenians as prisoners of war. Athens tried to organize other states in Greece to unite against him, but without success. The city was isolated, war weary, and keen to secure the return of the prisoners. Meanwhile Philip indicated that he wished to put an end to the state of war with Athens that had existed since 357, and the Athenians agreed to enter negotiations.

In the background to these negotiations were the long-running war (the Third Sacred War) between Thebes and Phocis, allies of Philip and Athens respectively, and control of the strategically vital pass of Thermopylae in northern Greece. Already in 352 Philip had marched south towards Thermopylae but had been prevented from gaining control of it by the dispatch of an expeditionary force from Athens. Among the Phocian generals some wished to hand the pass over to Athens and Sparta, but others inclined towards Philip. As a result, the Athenians could not be sure that

---

[1] The peace takes its name from the most prominent negotiator on the Athenian side.

[2] *First Letter to Ammaeus* 10.

Thermopylae would remain in friendly hands, and they feared that Philip would gain control of it and then march his army south against them. They therefore had little choice but to make peace with him.

The negotiation of the Peace of Philocrates involved a series of embassies between Athens and Philip in the first half of 346. The main sources for what happened are two long lawcourt speeches, Dem. 19 and Aes. 2, delivered in 343 in the course of a prosecution brought by Demosthenes against his political rival Aeschines. Both men were part of the delegations in 346 that negotiated the peace and then witnessed Philip's swearing to accept it; but by 343 the peace had become unpopular at Athens, and each sought to shift responsibility for it onto the other. Demosthenes prosecuted Aeschines on a charge of misconduct as an ambassador, alleging that he had been bribed by Philip, but failed to secure his conviction. They returned to the issue in 330 in the trial "on the Crown," from which again both very long speeches have survived (Dem. 18 and Aes. 3). In these four speeches the two men go into great detail about what happened in 346, but they often contradict each other on matters of fact.[3]

Already in the autumn of 346 many Athenians felt that the peace had not turned out as they had hoped and that Philip had tricked them. Two aspects of the peace were regarded as particularly hard to accept. The first was Philip's insistence that only those allies of Athens who were members of the Second Athenian Confederacy should be included in the peace, whereas the Athenians had wanted to extend its protection to both the Thracian king Cersobleptes and the Thessalian city of Halus. Philip would not agree to this, and in the summer of 346 he continued operations in Thrace and also captured Halus. The second Athenian grievance arose from the way in which Philip had brought the Sacred War between Thebes and Phocis to an end. Aeschines and Philocrates were apparently led to believe by Philip, and an-

---

[3]There is disagreement about many aspects of the negotiation of the Peace of Philocrates. See Hammond and Griffith 1979: 329–347; Sealey 1993: 143–159; MacDowell 2009: 314–342. See also on these four speeches Carey 2000 and Yunis 2005 in this series.

nounced to the Athenians, that Philip would (contrary to his previous policy) turn against his ally Thebes and save Phocis, whereas in fact he continued to support Thebes and destroyed the cities of the Phocians (9–10). Aeschines was accused by Demosthenes of taking bribes from Philip to persuade the Athenians of this (see above; cf. 12), but it is not necessary to believe that he was guilty of anything worse than self-deception. These tricks of Philip are staple complaints in Demosthenes' speeches of the second half of the 340s.[4]

The specific issue that this speech addresses is the transfer of two of the twenty-four seats on the council of the Delphic Amphictyony from Phocis to Philip. The Delphic Amphictyony was a long-established organization comprising the various peoples who "lived around" the sanctuary of the god Apollo at Delphi in central Greece, each of whom sent representatives to the Amphictyonic council. The council administered the sanctuary and could impose penalties for offenses against it, including the declaration of a sacred war, that is, a war in the name of Apollo. The Third Sacred War (356–346) had been declared against the Phocians because they had occupied the sanctuary at Delphi and used its wealth to pay for mercenaries. In bringing this war to an end and punishing the Phocians, Philip represented himself as the champion of Delphi. As ruler of Thessaly, he already had considerable influence over the Amphictyonic council, since many of the members were Thessalian (see 23), but the transfer of the two Phocian seats to him would cement his control of it, as well as being a potent symbol of his power in Greece.

Demosthenes later claimed that a joint Thessalian and Macedonian embassy came to Athens requesting that the Athenians support Philip's membership of the Amphictyonic council (i.e., the transfer of the Phocian seats to him) and that Aeschines was the only man to support this request (19.111–113, delivered in 343). Be that as it may,[5] Demosthenes argues in this speech that the

---

[4]On the mistreatment of the Phocians, see already 10 of this speech.

[5]Libanius argues in his *Introduction* to this speech (3) that it was not delivered, because in it Demosthenes advises the Athenians to agree to Philip's request, whereas in Dem. 19 he criticizes the defendant, Aeschines, for the

Athenians have no choice but to agree to the request, whether or not they like it (19). His main concern is that the Athenians, if they are intransigent on this point, may precipitate united Amphictyonic action (i.e., a sacred war) against themselves, involving not only Philip but also Thessaly, Thebes, and much of the Peloponnese (14, 17). Each of these states, he argues, has its individual quarrel with Athens (18–19) and might be persuaded to go along with Philip for its own advantage, just as happened in 346 when an unholy alliance of Thebes and Thessaly supported his destruction of Phocis (19–23). Demosthenes frankly criticizes the peace (13: its terms are bad and unworthy of the city) but insists that the Athenians cannot afford to break it: since they have already had to endure numerous wrongs at the hands of others, it would be absurd to risk a potentially disastrous war over "the shadow at Delphi," that is, over a purely symbolic addition to Philip's standing at the sanctuary (24–25). This line of argument, reminiscent in some respects of his attempt in Dem. 14 to rein in the aggressive impulses of some Athenians towards the Persian empire, was under the circumstances eminently sensible.

There is a text of this speech with commentary by Sandys 1900 and a translation with commentary by Ellis and Milns 1970.

5. ON THE PEACE

[1] I see, men of Athens, that our present predicament is giving rise to great difficulty and confusion not only because it is pointless to make fine speeches about everything that has been squandered but also because there is absolutely no agreement about where our future interest lies, but some take one view and others another. [2] Deliberation is inherently difficult and irksome, but you, men of Athens, have made it considerably harder. For all other people are in the habit of deliberating before they act, but you do so afterwards! As a result, for as long as I can remember, anyone who criticizes those things that might lead you into trou-

---

very same thing. This weak argument is rightly rejected by MacDowell 2000: 251.

ble wins a good reputation and is thought to speak well, but the actual situation about which you are deliberating gets away from you. [3] Nevertheless I stand before you convinced that if you are willing to listen, without making a disturbance or showing ill will, as is appropriate for those who are deliberating on behalf of the city about matters of such importance, I will be able to speak and to advise you how the present situation may be improved and how what has been squandered may be regained.

[4] Although I am well aware, men of Athens, that it is always very profitable for a speaker to talk to you about himself and his previous speeches, if he has the nerve to do so, I consider it to be such a tiresome and tedious practice that I shrink from doing so myself, even when I see the need for it. But I do think it will help you to judge what I am about to say now if I remind you briefly of what I said on previous occasions. [5] First, men of Athens, at a time when affairs in Euboea were in disarray, and certain people were trying to persuade you to help Plutarchus and undertake an inglorious and costly war,[6] I was the first, indeed the only one to come forward and oppose it,[7] and I was virtually torn apart by those who were trying to persuade you, for the sake of small profits, to commit many great errors. And a short time later, when we had incurred a further burden of shame, and had suffered such things as no men have ever suffered at the hands of those whom they had helped, you all realized that the men who had then persuaded you of that course of action were worthless and that what I had said was best. [6] Again, men of Athens, when I saw that Neoptolemus the actor was free to go about as he pleased, shielded by his profession,[8] and was doing the greatest harm to our city,

---

[6]In early 348 Athens intervened on the island of Euboea in response to an appeal from Plutarchus, the ruler of Eretria. During this campaign Plutarchus was expelled from the island by Phocion, the Athenian commander, but later seized and held to ransom a number of Athenian soldiers (ancient commentary on this passage = Dilts 1983: 122.27–33; Plut. *Phocion* 12–14.1).

[7]Presumably Demosthenes argued that intervention in the affairs of Euboea would be a distraction from the war for Olynthus.

[8]The tragic actor Neoptolemus of Scyros had a successful career at Athens and also enjoyed the favor of Philip, with whom he advocated that Ath-

and was managing and controlling your affairs for the benefit of Philip, I came forward and addressed you, not out of any private enmity or maliciousness, as has become clear from subsequent events. [7] In that case, the people I criticize are not those who spoke on Neoptolemus' behalf, since not a single person did so, but you! For even if you had been watching tragedies in the Theater of Dionysus,[9] rather than a debate about the safety of the city, you would not have listened to him with so much favor or to me with so much hostility. [8] And yet I think that you all now recognize this at least, that after he had arrived at that time in the enemy's country, wishing (so he said) to bring a sum of money that was owed to him there back here to pay for the performance of a liturgy,[10] and after he had made extensive use of the argument that it was terrible for anyone to criticize those who were bringing wealth from Macedonia to Athens, when the peace provided him with immunity from prosecution, he turned the visible assets[11] that he had acquired here into cash and went off to Philip. [9] These two predictions that I made prove that my speeches were right and just and truthful. The third, men of Athens—and as soon as I have said just this one thing I will return to the things I have passed over—relates to the occasion when we ambassadors had returned after accepting the oaths relating to the peace.[12]

---

ens make peace. As an actor he was evidently free to travel without arousing suspicion.

[9]The Theater of Dionysus at the foot of the Acropolis formed part of the sanctuary of Dionysus and was the venue for the production of plays at the City Dionysia. In a theatrical performance it was only to be expected that an actor would outshine a politician.

[10]Liturgies were obligations imposed on wealthy men to perform certain tasks for the state using their own money. See 4.36n.

[11]Visible assets (*phanera ousia*) were assets such as land, property, or slaves that could not be easily concealed, as opposed to cash, bank deposits, and loans. See 14.25n on "invisible wealth."

[12]Demosthenes refers to the making of the Peace of Philocrates in summer 346 and specifically to the second Athenian embassy to Philip that was sent to witness his swearing to accept the peace. See the Speech Introduction.

[10] At that time some men[13] were promising that Thespiae and Plataea would be restored,[14] and that Philip would preserve the Phocians, if he got control of them, and would disperse the city of Thebes into villages,[15] and that Oropus would be given to us,[16] and that Euboea would be surrendered in return for Amphipolis,[17] and were offering such hopes and deceiving you with promises, by which you were induced, neither to your advantage nor perhaps to your credit, to abandon the Phocians.[18] But I shall show that I did not deceive you and was not silent about any of these matters but declared to you, as I am sure you remember, that I neither knew nor expected that any of these things would happen, and that I thought the speaker was talking nonsense.

[11] If I have been more successful than others in predicting the future in all these matters, I do not attribute this to my cleverness or to any talent I might boast of, nor do I claim any other reasons for my special understanding and perception than these two. The first, men of Athens, is good luck, which, I observe, is more powerful than any human cleverness or wisdom. [12] The second is that I judge and calculate matters without being paid to do so, and no one can point to any profit that attaches to my political actions and speeches. As a result, our advantage is revealed to me directly from the facts themselves. But whenever you add

---

[13]Aeschines and Philocrates, whom Demosthenes accuses of misleading the Athenians by asserting that Philip would settle the Third Sacred War to the benefit of Athens' ally Phocis.

[14]The Boeotian cities of Thespiae and Plataea had been destroyed in the 370s by Thebes, the largest city of the region, which consistently sought to dominate the other cities of Boeotia. See also 16.4n, and 18 below on the reception of Plataean exiles at Athens.

[15]On *dioikismos*, the practice of destroying a defeated city and forcibly resettling its population into villages, see 16.30n.

[16]Athens and Thebes had a long-running dispute over the border town of Oropus, which was at the time in Theban hands.

[17]On Amphipolis, see 4.12n. Philip's offer was apparently to give Athens free rein in Euboea in return for an acknowledgement of his claim to Amphipolis (cf. 6.30).

[18]On Athens' failure to protect Phocis, see the Speech Introduction.

money to either side, as if to a pair of scales, it drops down and drags judgment with it, and whoever does so will no longer offer a straight or sound opinion about any matter.

[13] Now then, I say that one condition should hold, that if anyone wishes to provide allies or financial contributions[19] or anything else for our city, he should do so without breaking the existing peace—not because the peace is wonderful or worthy of you but because, whatever its character, it would be better for us that it had never been made than that we should break it now that it has been made. For we have squandered many things, the possession of which would have made war easier and safer for us then than it is now. [14] Second, men of Athens, we must see that we do not provide these people who have come together and now claim to be Amphictyons with the need or excuse for a common war against us.[20] For if war should break out between Philip and us over Amphipolis[21] or some similar private grievance in which the Thessalians and Argives and Thebans are not involved, I do not imagine that any of these would go to war with us, [15] and least of all—and let no one interrupt me before he hears what I have to say—the Thebans,[22] not because they are well disposed to us or because they would not wish to do Philip a favor but because they know perfectly well—however much they are described as stupid[23]—that if war should break out between them and you, they will incur all the losses, but someone else will be

---

[19]"Contributions" (*syntaxeis*) was the term used to describe the sums of money that the members of the Second Athenian Confederacy paid to help defray the costs of its operations; it was intended to be less opprobrious than the word *phoros* ("tribute") used in Athens' fifth-century empire. See Cargill 1981: 124–127.

[20]The council of the Delphic Amphictyony could declare a sacred war against any state that it found guilty of sacrilege against the god Apollo. See the Speech Introduction.

[21]See 10n above.

[22]Demosthenes anticipates heckling from those members of the Assembly who are convinced that Thebes is Athens' inveterate enemy.

[23]The Athenians routinely characterized the Thebans as dull and stupid and referred to them as "Boeotian swine."

ready to reap the benefits.[24] They will not therefore give themselves up to this, unless the war is jointly declared and has a common cause. [16] Nor, on the other hand, do I think that we would suffer any harm if we were to go to war with the Thebans over Oropus or some other private dispute,[25] since I believe that people would come to help either us or them, if anyone were to invade our territory,[26] but would not join either city in making war. Every worthwhile alliance is of this kind, and the result is naturally as follows. [17] No individual is so well disposed towards either us or the Thebans as to wish either of us both to be safe and to dominate others; rather, they would all wish us to be safe for their own sake, but none of them wishes either of us to defeat the other and thereby become their masters. What then do I find a frightening prospect, and what is it that you must guard against? It is that the coming war may offer everybody a common pretext and a shared ground of complaint against us. [18] For if the Argives and Messenians and Megalopolitans, and those other Peloponnesians who agree with them, are going to be hostile to us because of our embassy to Sparta,[27] and because they think that we are in some way supporting Spartan actions,[28] and if the Thebans are ill disposed to us, as people say they are, and will be even more hostile because we are harboring those who are in flight from them and because in every way we display our enmity to-

---

[24]Demosthenes envisages a war on land in which the Theban army would bear the brunt of the fighting, and Thebes' territory would be in danger of Athenian invasion. The beneficiary of such a war would be Philip.

[25]On Oropus, see 10n above.

[26]Greek alliances were generally defensive: i.e., they required one ally to come to the aid of the other if it was attacked but not to join it in a war of aggression.

[27]These three Peloponnesian states were all hostile to Sparta. This embassy is not recorded elsewhere, but Philip's support for the enemies of Sparta, and negotiations between Athens and Sparta, are a central concern of Demosthenes' *Second Philippic* (Dem. 6) of the following year.

[28]The Spartans were seeking to reestablish their traditional hegemony over the Peloponnese by regaining control of Messenia and Arcadia.

wards them,[29] [19] and if the Thessalians are hostile because we are harboring the exiles from Phocis,[30] and if Philip is hostile to us because we are trying to prevent him joining the Amphictyony,[31] then my fear is that all of these, each angry about their own individual grievances, may launch a joint war against us, using the decrees of the Amphictyons as a pretext, and as a result may be drawn in beyond what is to their own advantage, just as happened in the case of Phocis.[32] [20] For surely you know that the Thebans and Philip and the Thessalians all acted in concert, although each had different aims. For example, the Thebans were unable to prevent Philip from passing through and seizing the pass or from coming at the last minute and taking for himself the glory of their own labors.[33] [21] Now in terms of the recovery of their land, the Thebans have achieved some success, but in terms of honor and reputation, the result has brought great shame on them. For if Philip had not passed through,[34] they knew that they would have gained nothing. These results were not what they desired, but since they wished to capture Orchomenus and Coroneia but were unable to do so, they put up with them all.[35] [22] And yet some men dare to assert that Philip did not in fact wish to hand over Orchomenus and Coroneia to the Thebans but was forced to do so. Let them think so. I know that these things were of less concern to him than his wish to take the pass of Ther-

---

[29]Athens accepted refugees from the cities of Boeotia that had been destroyed by the Thebans in the 370s, and it granted Athenian citizenship to those from Plataea (see 16.4n).

[30]After the destruction of their cities, many Phocians sought refuge in Athens.

[31]I.e., to prevent Philip receiving the two seats on the Amphictyonic council that had belonged to Phocis. See the Speech Introduction.

[32]Earlier in 346, when Philip and his allies dealt with the Phocians.

[33]Thebes had fought Phocis for ten years (355–346); the war was rapidly ended as a result of Philip's intervention in 346.

[34]I.e., through the pass of Thermopylae.

[35]The Boeotian cities of Coroneia and Orchomenus had been seized by the Phocians in the course of the Third Sacred War.

mopylae and the glory of claiming responsibility for bringing the war to an end and the presidency of the Pythian festival—these were what he aimed for.[36] [23] But the Thessalians did not want either Thebes or Philip to become great, since they thought that all this was directed against themselves; what they wanted was to secure two assets: the Pylaea[37] and Delphi. It was their desire for these that induced them to collaborate in what was done. You will find that each party was induced by private concerns to do much that it did not wish to do. This, this, is what we must guard against.

[24] "Must we then do as we are told, for fear of these consequences? Is this what you are telling us to do?" Far from it. Rather, I think that we should not act in any way that is unworthy of ourselves, or so as to bring about war, but should let everyone see that we are sensible and that what we say is just. That is what I think we should do. Those who rashly think that we should expose ourselves to any danger whatsoever, and who do not foresee the nature of such a war, I would invite to consider the following. We allow the Thebans to keep Oropus: if anyone should ask us why we do so, insisting that we tell the truth, we should reply "in order to avoid war." [25] And now we have ceded Amphipolis to Philip in accordance with the treaty,[38] and we allow the Cardians to be treated as separate from the other inhabitants of the Chersonese,[39]

---

[36]Philip's possession of Thermopylae meant that the Greeks could no longer block the passage of his army into central Greece, as the Athenians had done in 352 (see 1.26n). The Panhellenic Pythian festival was held every fourth year at Delphi in honor of Pythian Apollo. By a vote of the Amphictyonic council Philip was chosen to preside over the festival of late summer 346 (Diodorus 16.60.2).

[37]The Pylaea was the council meeting of the Delphic Amphictyony. The Amphictyony was now dominated by the Thessalians, since they controlled a majority of the seats on the council.

[38]The Peace of Philocrates was made on the basis of each party retaining what it possessed, and therefore Philip kept control of Amphipolis.

[39]Cardia, a city at the northern end of the Chersonese, retained its independence when the rest of the peninsula was occupied by Athens in 352 and was now an ally of Philip: see Dem. 19.174. For subsequent Athenian dealings with Cardia, see Dem. 8, delivered in 341.

and the Carian⁴⁰ to seize the islands—Chios, Cos, and Rhodes—
and the Byzantines to detain ships,⁴¹ clearly believing that the
tranquility resulting from the peace benefits us more than aggression and contentiousness about these issues. It would therefore be
foolish and quite shocking for us, who are acting in this way towards each party individually about our own vital interests, to go
to war now against all of them over that shadow at Delphi.⁴²

---

⁴⁰Idrieus, brother of Mausolus and Artemisia, who succeeded his sister
as satrap (Persian-appointed governor) of Caria in southwestern Asia Minor in 351. He is identified as "the Carian" because his family were native
Carians, not Persians. Earlier Carian encroachment on nearby Greek islands, especially Rhodes, is addressed in Dem. 15, a speech of the late 350s.

⁴¹The city of Byzantium (modern Istanbul) on the Bosporus controlled
passage between the Black Sea and the Sea of Marmara. The Byzantines
were presumably motivated by a shortage of food to force passing grain
ships en route to Athens to sell their cargo to them instead. In response
to similar action by Byzantium and other cities in 362, the Athenians dispatched a naval squadron to escort the grain ships: see Dem. 50.6, 17–19.

⁴²Demosthenes adapts the proverb "to fight over the shadow of an ass,"
i.e., to fight over nothing.

6. SECOND PHILIPPIC

〰️

INTRODUCTION

The *Second Philippic* is dated to 344/3, according to Dionysius of Halicarnassus, who adds the information that it was delivered in reply to an embassy "from the Peloponnese."[1] This was
a year of important diplomatic activity for Athens. First, the Persian King sent ambassadors to the city, as well as to others, asking
for friendship and alliance, in the hope of securing Greek help for
his attempt to reconquer Egypt.[2] Second, there was at least one
embassy from Philip that offered to renegotiate those terms of the
Peace of Philocrates with which the Athenians were unhappy.[3]
This diplomatic overture is referred to by a number of sources:

1. Didymus writes of an embassy from Philip about peace in 344/3
   coinciding with the Persian appeal noted above (col. 8.8).

2. Libanius, in his *Introduction* to this speech, relates it to an embassy to Athens of Macedonians, Messenians, and Argives
   (i.e., from Philip and some of his Peloponnesian allies) that he
   found recorded in "the Philippic histories," by which he probably means the *Philippic History* of Theopompus.

3. Philip, in his letter to the Athenians of 340, refers to an embassy that he had previously sent them, containing representa-

---

[1] *First Letter to Ammaeus* 10. This date is generally accepted as correct.
[2] Philochorus *FGH* 328 fragment 157; Diodorus 16.44.
[3] The Peace of Philocrates was negotiated between Athens and Philip
in 346.

tives "from the whole alliance," to which they had refused to listen (Dem. 12.18).

4. The author of the speech *On Halonnesus*, attributed to Demosthenes (probably by the Athenian politician Hegesippus: see the Introduction to Dem. 7), refers in 343/2 to an embassy from Philip to Athens that offered to negotiate changes to the Peace of Philocrates, one of whose members was the orator Python of Byzantium (7.18–23).

5. Demosthenes boasted in 330 of having taken this opportunity to accuse Philip of acting unjustly "when Philip dispatched Python of Byzantium together with delegates from all his other allies to humiliate the city and prove that we were at fault" (18.136).

It is likely that all these sources refer to the same Macedonian embassy, led by Python of Byzantium, accompanied by representatives from Philip's allies, and offering to renegotiate the peace, probably in spring 343.[4] It is also likely that this is the embassy that prompted Demosthenes to write the present speech (28 implies the presence in Athens of ambassadors from somewhere). An alternative suggestion, that the ambassadors referred to in the speech were in fact from the Peloponnesian city of Sparta, which was hostile to Philip, has not generally found favor.[5]

In this speech Demosthenes accuses Philip of violating the Peace of Philocrates (1–2) and of plotting (18) against the whole of Greece, and in particular against Athens, which is now his only rival (17). The Athenians need to realize that his massive, and growing, power is directed against them (6). Demosthenes refers to Philip's dealings with Messenia and Argos, which were both enemies of Athens' ally Sparta: he not only is sending them mercenaries and money but is expected in person with a large force (15, cf. 9), and is ordering the Spartans to leave Messenia alone (13). Demosthenes also summarizes a speech that he had previously given as an Athenian ambassador to the Messenian Assembly, in

---

[4]See Cawkwell 1963b: 123–126.
[5]The proposal is that of Calhoun 1933.

which he reminded his audience of Philip's deceitfulness and encouraged them to distrust him, although he failed to persuade them to change their allegiance (20–26).

The speech is notably chauvinistic in tone. Demosthenes repeatedly contrasts Athens with two of the other leading (pro-Macedonian) states in Greece: Thebes and Argos. Athens, he claims, is the only Greek state that is concerned for Greece as a whole (10): it resisted the Persian king Xerxes in the fifth century, whereas Thebes, Argos, and Macedonia either collaborated or stayed neutral (11). Philip naturally sides with Thebes and Argos, since these states are selfish and have no concern for the Greeks as a whole (12). In 346 Philip chose to side with the self-centered Thebans against the Phocians (9); the Messenians and other Peloponnesians are stupidly acting against their own interest, whereas the Athenians are intelligent (27).

Demosthenes is sharply critical of those Athenian politicians who, he claims, made untrue promises in 346 about Philip's intentions, on the basis of which the Athenians were persuaded to accept the peace, and who disparaged him when he warned them of Philip's true intentions (28–35). He refers to unnamed Athenian ambassadors who took bribes (34) and to men who deserve to suffer the death penalty (37). As usual in his deliberative speeches, Demosthenes does not name his political enemies, but it is obvious that one of the men he is referring to is Aeschines, and it should be recalled that this speech was in the same year that Demosthenes prosecuted Aeschines for misconduct as an ambassador to Philip in 346 (Dem. 19).[6] Clearly, feelings were running high.

If the speech is correctly associated with Python's embassy to Athens in 344/3, it might seem surprising that it makes no mention of the subject of that embassy: Philip's offer to negotiate changes to the Peace of Philocrates. One possibility is that in the debate this issue was addressed by Demosthenes' political collaborators, men such as Hyperides and Hegesippus,[7] whereas he used

---

[6] See Dem. 19.12, 19–24 for the names of some of the others.

[7] In a speech delivered in the summer of 343, Demosthenes refers to an Athenian embassy to Philip, which included the virulently anti-Macedonian

his own speech to stir up feeling against Philip and his Greek allies.[8] Another is that at the time he wrote the speech, Demosthenes did not know what proposals Python would make, and so he would have had to extemporize his response to them.[9] A third possibility is that his failure even to address the issue of revision of the peace, combined with his pointed criticism of several of the Greek states that had sent ambassadors to Athens, and who were in the audience (28), was its own reply: Philip's offer was not even worth discussing.

There is a text of this speech with commentary by Sandys 1900.

6. SECOND PHILIPPIC

[1] Whenever, men of Athens, we discuss Philip's actions and his violent breaches of the peace, I always observe that the speeches on our side are manifestly just and considerate, and those who accuse Philip always seem to say what needs to be said, but virtually no necessary action is taken, which would make the speeches worth hearing. [2] But our entire situation has already reached the point that the more fully and clearly Philip is convicted of breaking the peace with you and of plotting against all of Greece, the more difficult it is to advise you what to do. [3] The blame belongs to all of us, men of Athens. At a time when those who are greedy and ambitious should be punished by deeds and actions, not by words, first we speakers shrink from making proposals and offering advice, fearing that we will incur your enmity, but we go on about how terrible his behavior is and the like; then you who sit there are better prepared than Philip to make and listen to speeches that are just, but you are utterly idle when it comes to preventing him from carrying out his current plans. [4] The re-

---

Hegesippus, who spoke his mind and irritated Philip (Dem. 19.331). On Hegesippus, see further Introduction to Dem. 7; on Hyperides, see *OCD*[3] s.v. Hyperides; Worthington, Cooper, and Harris 2001 in this series.

[8]Hegesippus (the probable author of Dem. 7) refers back to this debate at 7.18–25.

[9]This suggestion is made by MacDowell 2009: 331–332.

sult is inevitable, I suppose, and perhaps even reasonable—each of you surpasses the other in the things that you spend time on and that you take seriously—he in action, and you in words. If, even now, you are content to speak with more justice than he, it is easy for you to do so, and no additional effort is required from you. [5] But if we must examine how to correct the present situation, and to prevent matters going even further without our noticing them, and the establishment against us of a massive and irresistible power, we must change our previous manner of deliberation, and all of us, speakers and audience, must choose those policies that are the best and will save us, instead of those that are easiest and most agreeable.

[6] First, men of Athens, if anyone is confident when he sees how great Philip is and how much he controls, and thinks that this carries no danger to our city, and that these preparations of his are not all directed against us, I am amazed and wish to ask all of you to listen briefly to the reasons why I expect the opposite result and judge Philip to be our enemy, so that you may be persuaded by me, if you think that I show better foresight; but if you think that those who confidently put their trust in him show more foresight, you may side with them. [7] For my part, men of Athens, I reckon as follows. Which places did Philip first get control of after the making of the peace? Thermopylae and Phocis.[10] Well then, how did he treat them? He chose to act in the Thebans' interest, not in ours.[11] Why did he do this? I think that he examined his options with a view to his greed and to bringing everything under his control, not to peace or quiet or justice. [8] And he saw correctly that our city and our national character are such that nothing he could offer or do would induce us to abandon any of the other Greeks to him for our own benefit, but that you would take account of justice, shun the infamy associated with betrayal, make all necessary plans, and resist him,

---

[10] In 346 Philip got control of the pass of Thermopylae in central Greece and brought the Third Sacred War between Thebes and Phocis to an end.

[11] Contrary to the hopes of many Athenians, Philip treated the Phocians harshly and rewarded his allies the Thebans by giving them a free hand in Boeotia.

if he tried to do anything of this kind, just as if you were at war. [9] But he thought, correctly as it turned out, that the Thebans, in return for his treatment of them, would allow him to do as he wished in other respects, and not only would not hinder or oppose him but would campaign with him, if he told them to. So too now he is conferring benefits on the Messenians and Argives, in the same belief.[12] And in doing so, he is paying you the highest compliment, men of Athens. [10] For these developments show that he judges you to be the only people who will not abandon the common rights of the Greeks in return for any profit and will not trade your goodwill towards the Greeks for any benefit or advantage. And he naturally took this view of you, and the opposite view of the Argives and Thebans, in the light not only of present circumstances but also of past history. [11] For he finds it recorded, I think, and hears it said that your ancestors, when they had the chance to rule the rest of Greece on condition that they obey the King, not only rejected this proposal, when Alexander, the ancestor of these people, came as a herald on this matter, but chose to abandon their land and endured suffering anything at all, and subsequently did things that everyone longs to tell but no one has been able to recount worthily, which is why I too will omit them, and rightly so—for their deeds are greater than anyone could do justice to in words[13]—whereas the Thebans' ancestors campaigned with the foreigner (*barbaros*),[14] and the Argives

---

[12]Messenia in the southwestern Peloponnese had been subject to Sparta, and its people had been treated as public slaves (*heilōtai*, "helots") of the Spartans, until it was liberated by the Theban general Epaminondas in 370. Thereafter it was an independent state. Argos in the northeastern Peloponnese had been consistently hostile to Sparta ever since the archaic period (cf. 15.23 for the Argives standing up to the Spartans).

[13]When the Persian king Xerxes ("the King") invaded Greece in 480, the Athenians evacuated Attica, and Athens itself was sacked and occupied by the Persians. For the mission of the Macedonian king Alexander to the Athenians, and their response, see Herod. 8.136, 140–143.

[14]On the term *barbaros*, see 3.16n. The Thebans notoriously gave the Persian king symbolic gifts of earth and water as tokens of their surrender (Herod. 7.132).

did not resist.[15] [12] He knows, therefore, that each of these cities will be content with their private advantage and will not look to the common good of Greece. He reckons that if he were to choose you, he would be choosing friends on the principle of justice, but if he were to side with them, he would have accomplices in his own greed. For these reasons he chose them instead of you, both then and now. It is surely not that he sees that they have more ships than you,[16] nor has he found some empire in the interior and thus renounced rule over coastal sites and harbors;[17] nor does he forget the speeches and promises on the basis of which he secured the peace.

[13] "But, by Zeus," someone might say, pretending to know all about the matter, "he acted at that time not out of greed or for the reasons that you allege but because the Thebans' claim was more just than yours."[18] But this is the one claim that he cannot now make. How could he, who is ordering the Spartans to leave Messenia alone,[19] claim that he previously handed over Orchomenus and Coroneia[20] to the Thebans on the ground that their claim to them was just?[21]

[14] "But, by Zeus, he was forced to do so" (for that is the only

---

[15]Argos refused to join the Greek alliance against Persia because of its hatred of Sparta (see 9n; Herod. 7.148–152).

[16]Neither Thebes nor Argos had a significant navy, whereas Athens had over 300 triremes.

[17]Demosthenes discounts the possibility that Philip is rejecting Athens because his imperial ambitions are now directed towards expansion into the non-Greek territories bordering Macedonia to the west and north, for which Athens' naval power would be of no use to him.

[18]Demosthenes addresses the argument that Thebes had a right to rule all Boeotia. Although the cities of Boeotia shared common religious cults and had a history of federalism, they were also independent cities and in many cases suspicious of the Thebans' desire for regional hegemony, as is clear from Thebes' forcible unification of the region in the 370s and 360s.

[19]In this period the Spartans tried, without success, to regain control of Messenia. See the Introduction to Dem. 16.

[20]See 5.21n.

[21]If Philip was seriously concerned for the autonomy of smaller cities, he would not be backing Thebes against the other cities of Boeotia.

remaining alternative), "and made these concessions against his wishes, since he was trapped between the Thessalian cavalry and the Theban hoplites."[22] Fine! Consequently they say that he intends to regard Thebes with suspicion,[23] and certain men are going around pronouncing that he will fortify Elateia.[24] [15] He intends these things, and in my view will go on intending them;[25] but he is not intending to help the Messenians and Argives against the Spartans—he is actually sending them mercenaries and money and is expected in person with a large army.[26] Is he destroying the Spartans, the existing enemies of the Thebans, while at the same time rescuing the Phocians, whom he previously ruined? Who could believe that? [16] For my part, I do not believe that Philip, even if he acted at first under compulsion and against his will, or if he were now renouncing the Thebans, would be so unremittingly opposed to their enemies.[27] But from his present conduct it is clear that he did those things deliberately; and from his every action, if one looks at them correctly, it is evident that he is directing all his efforts against our city. [17] And this is, now at least, in a sense inevitable. Think about it: he wishes to rule and regards you as his only rivals in this. He has been acting unjustly for a long time now and is himself fully conscious of do-

---

[22]The Thessalian cavalry was numerous and strong (see Herod. 7.196), and Thebes had the strongest hoplite army in Greece. In view of the military strength of Macedonia, it is unlikely that either the Thessalians (who were in any case ruled by Philip) or the Thebans (who were his allies) were in a position to threaten Philip.

[23]According to Demosthenes, some Athenian politicians claimed in 346 that Philip would turn against his Theban allies and settle the Third Sacred War in favor of the Phocians. See the Introduction to Dem. 5.

[24]Elateia was a town in Phocis that controlled the road south into Boeotia. Its fortifications were destroyed by Philip in 346; rebuilding them would have been viewed by the Thebans as a threat to them (as indeed happened in 339: see Dem. 18.152, 168; Aes. 3.140; Diodorus 16.84).

[25]That is to say, he will never actually do them.

[26]Philip did not in fact campaign in person in support of either city.

[27]I.e., to the Thebans' enemies. Demosthenes' point is that Philip's consistent hostility to cities such as Sparta gives the lie to the claim that he wishes to turn against Thebes.

ing so, since his secure control of everything else depends on his keeping hold of your possessions. He thinks that if he were to abandon Amphipolis and Potidaea,[28] he would not even be safe at home. [18] He is therefore deliberately plotting against you and knows that you are aware of this. He believes that you are intelligent, and that you justifiably hate him, and is spurred on by the expectation that he will suffer some reverse at your hands, if you seize the opportunity to do so, unless he anticipates you by acting first. [19] For these reasons, he is alert; he stands against you; he courts certain people—the Thebans and those of the Peloponnesians[29] who agree with them—who he thinks will be satisfied with the present situation because of their greed, and will foresee none of the consequences because of their stupidity.[30] And yet to even moderately thoughtful men there are clear signs to be seen; I had occasion to talk about them to the Messenians and Argives, but they are perhaps better related to you.[31]

[20] "How much irritation, Messenians," I said, "do you suppose the Olynthians felt when they heard anyone say anything against Philip at the time when he had ceded to them Anthemous, a place to which all previous Macedonian kings had laid claim, and was giving them Potidaea and driving out the Athenian settlers from there, and had incurred our hatred, while giving them the land to enjoy?[32] Do you suppose that they expected

---

[28] Philip seized Amphipolis in Thrace in 357, and Potidaea in the Chalcidic peninsula in 356 (see also 20n below). The Athenians claimed both these strategically important cities and had held Potidaea from 364 to 356. See 1.9n (Potidaea) and 4.12n (Amphipolis).

[29] During the 360s Thebes had sought to prevent a revival of Sparta's power by supporting its enemies in the Peloponnese—primarily Messene, Megalopolis, and Argos. Although during the period of the Third Sacred War (356–346) Thebes was distracted by its war with Phocis, it nevertheless retained influence in the Peloponnese. See Dem. 16 for Athens' dealings with Megalopolis in this period.

[30] Cf. 5.15, also referring to Theban stupidity.

[31] Demosthenes was sent as an ambassador to the Peloponnese in 344 to try to counter Philip's influence over the enemies of Sparta: see Dem. 18.79.

[32] In 356. On Philip's offer to give Potidaea to the Olynthians, see 1.9n, 2.7n.

to suffer such things or would have believed anyone who told them that they would? [21] Despite all this," I said, "after enjoying other people's land for a short time, they have now been deprived by him for a long time[33] of their own land, and have been shamefully exiled, and have been not only defeated but also betrayed by each other and sold. Becoming too closely associated with tyrants is dangerous for constitutionally governed states. [22] What about the Thessalians?" I asked. "Do you suppose that they expected to have the Ten-man Council that has now been established,[34] at the time when Philip was expelling their tyrants and was giving them Nicaea and Magnesia?[35] Or that the same man who gave them the presidency of the Delphic Amphictyony would deprive them of their private revenues? Of course not! And yet this is what has happened, and it is a matter of public knowledge.[36] [23] You," I said, "watch Philip dispensing gifts and promises. Yet if you are prudent, you should pray that you do not find yourselves being tricked and deceived by him. By Zeus," I said, "cities have all kind of resources for their security and safety, such as palisades and walls and ditches and the like, [24] all of which require labor and expense. But there is one safeguard with which

---

[33]Although Olynthus had been razed to the ground by Philip, Demosthenes holds out the possibility that it may be rebuilt. In fact the site was never resettled.

[34]Demosthenes refers to the establishment of an oligarchy, but he uses the term (*dekadarchia*, lit. "rule of ten men") that had been applied to the oligarchies (of whatever size) set up throughout the cities of Athens' empire, including Athens itself, by the Spartan general Lysander in 405–404. This would have had particular resonance with the strongly anti-Spartan Messenians. The suggestion that the Greek word *dekadarchia* should be emended to *tetrarchia* (tetrarchy, "rule of four"), with reference to the well-attested division of Thessaly into four regional administrative units (see 9.26n), is generally rejected.

[35]Philip replaced the rulers of the Thessalian city of Pherae in 352 (1.13n, 2.14n; Diodorus 16.37.3, 38.1). On his promise to return Magnesia to the Thessalians, see 2.7n. Nicaea in eastern Locris was one of the sites that controlled access to the pass of Thermopylae: see 11.4n.

[36]On Thessalian domination of the Delphic Amphictyony after 346, see 5.23n. Demosthenes had reported in 351 that the Thessalians were unhappy about Philip's appropriation of their revenues (1.22).

all right-thinking people are naturally endowed, and which is a benefit and a source of salvation for everybody, but particularly for democracies in their dealings with tyrants. What is this? Mistrust. Guard it; hold onto it. If you keep it, you will avoid disaster. [25] What do you seek?" I said. "Freedom? Then do you not see that Philip's very titles are inimical to this? Every king and tyrant is an enemy of freedom and an opponent of law. You should be on your guard," I said, "lest, in seeking to escape war, you find yourselves saddled with a master."

[26] But after hearing both this speech—and they shouted out that I was right—and many others from the ambassadors, both when I was there and subsequently, they are apparently no more willing to reject Philip's friendship and promises. [27] Now, it is not strange that the Messenians and some of the other Peloponnesians are acting against what they know to be their own interest. But you, who are intelligent and listen to us speakers telling you how you are being plotted against and ensnared, if you do not act promptly, will find, I think, that without realizing it, you have submitted to everything—so much stronger are immediate gratification and idleness than any consideration of future benefit. [28] You may deliberate later by yourselves about what we need to do, if you are sensible: but now I shall tell you what response you should vote for.[37]

It would have been just, men of Athens, to summon those men who conveyed the promises, on the strength of which you were persuaded to make the peace.[38] [29] For I would not have remained as an ambassador, nor (I know) would you have stopped waging war, if you had thought that Philip would act as he did after he had secured peace.[39] But what was said then was quite contrary to these actions of his. And again, there are others who should be summoned. Who? Those who spoke on the occasion after the making of the peace when I, on my return from the

---

[37] At this point Demosthenes may have extemporized a response to Python's proposal: see the Speech Introduction.

[38] The men are named as Aristodemus, Neoptolemus, and Ctesiphon (among others) at Dem. 19.12.

[39] Demosthenes was a member both of the embassy to Philip to negotiate terms and of the later embassy to administer the oaths to him.

later embassy relating to the oaths, saw that the city was being deceived by false hopes, and warned and protested and tried to prevent the loss of Thermopylae and of the Phocians.[40] [30] They said that I drink water and so am naturally an intractable and disagreeable fellow,[41] whereas Philip would answer your prayers, if he should pass through Thermopylae, and would rebuild Thespiae and Plataea, and put an end to Thebes' arrogance, and dig through the Chersonese at his own expense, and would give you Euboea and Oropus in return for Amphipolis.[42] I know you recall all these claims being made from the speaker's platform, although you are not good at remembering those who injure you. [31] And, most shameful of all, you voted on the basis of these hopes that this same peace should apply to his and our descendants too,[43] so completely were you led on. Why am I speaking about these matters now, and urging you to summon these men? I shall tell you the truth frankly, by the gods, concealing nothing. [32] My purpose is neither to permit myself, by descending to abuse, to speak before you on the same level as my opponents, and thereby provide those who have clashed with me from the beginning a further excuse to take something more from Philip, nor to babble in vain. On the contrary, I think that Philip's actions will harm you more in the future than they do now. [33] For I see trouble coming, and although I hope I am wrong, I fear that it is already all too close at hand. When you can no longer ignore what is happening, and when you no longer hear that these activ-

---

[40]Demosthenes means Aeschines and Philocrates: see 5.10n. He makes the same claim at 19.18. If Demosthenes seriously argued for a last-minute attempt to seize Thermopylae, he was undoubtedly too late, since the Phocian commanders had already surrendered the pass to Philip.

[41]This remark was made by Philocrates (see Dem. 19.46). Drinking water meant avoiding the company of his fellow ambassadors, who would be drinking wine, and was thus interpreted as a sign of his antisocial character.

[42]To the similar list at 5.10 (see the note), Demosthenes here adds the proposal to cut a canal across the neck of the Chersonese peninsula to protect the Athenian settlers there from Thracian attacks (see also 7.39). The neck was already protected by a wall.

[43]See Dem. 19.48, 55–56.

ities are directed against you from me or from someone else, but all see it for yourselves and know it for a fact, then I think you will be angry and resentful. [34] And I am afraid that, since the ambassadors[44] are silent about those matters for which they know they were bribed, your anger may be directed against those of us who are trying to repair some of the damage caused by their actions. For I see that in most cases, people vent their anger not on those who are guilty but on those who are most under their control. [35] While the trouble is still in the future and is only gathering, and we are still listening to each other, I want each of you—even though you know the answer perfectly well—nevertheless to remind yourselves who it was that persuaded you to abandon the Phocians and Thermopylae,[45] the possession of which gives Philip control of the roads to Attica and the Peloponnese, and has caused you to be deliberating not about your rights or your overseas interests but about the inhabitants of your land and about a war against Attica, which will hurt each of you, when it arrives, but which started on that day. [36] If you had not been deceived then, there would be no danger to our city, since surely Philip would never be able to attack Attica either with a fleet, by defeating you at sea, or with an army, by marching through Thermopylae and Phocis,[46] but either he would be acting justly and keeping quiet, upholding the peace, or he would immediately find himself in a war similar to the one which led him at that time to desire peace.[47] [37] Enough has now been said by way of reminding you. As to a strict test of my fears, may that not come about, all you gods! For I would not wish anyone to be punished, even if he deserves to die, if it involves danger and punishment for all.

---

[44] I.e., the (other) Athenian ambassadors to Philip.

[45] See 29n for the identity of these men.

[46] Philip did not possess a fleet remotely large enough to challenge Athens at sea (see 4.22n), and if Thermopylae had remained in friendly hands, the Athenians would have been able to block the pass with their army, as they did in 352 (see 1.26n, 4.17n).

[47] Demosthenes' claim that Philip had been embroiled in war when he opened negotiations with Athens after the fall of Olynthus is misleading. On the contrary, his capture of the city left him in a dominant position in Greece.

7. ON HALONNESUS

〰〰〰〰〰〰〰〰〰〰〰〰〰〰〰〰〰〰〰〰〰〰〰〰〰〰〰〰〰〰〰〰〰〰〰〰〰〰〰

INTRODUCTION

The authorship of the speech *On Halonnesus* was debated in antiquity. Dionysius of Halicarnassus accepts it as the work of Demosthenes without discussion,[1] but Libanius denies this attribution on the ground that some of its vocabulary is too vulgar to have been used by Demosthenes (see 45n) and reports the view of previous scholars that it was the work of a contemporary of Demosthenes named Hegesippus. This attribution was based partly on the speech's style and partly on the speaker's claim to have prosecuted a man named Callippus (43), since it was known that Hegesippus, and not Demosthenes, had prosecuted him. Analysis of the prose rhythm of the speech also suggests that it is not the work of Demosthenes.[2] Although we have no speech of Hegesippus with which to compare it, the modern consensus is that he is its author, and this view is accepted here.

Hegesippus son of Hegesias was a prominent anti-Macedonian politician of the 340s and a political ally of Demosthenes. He was nicknamed "Top-knot" because of his distinctively old-fashioned hairstyle. Hegesippus' earliest political activity dates to the 360s (Diogenes Laertius 3.24), but he was most prominent in the years after the making of the Peace of Philocrates. He took the lead in resisting Philip's diplomatic overtures in 346[3] and joined Demosthenes in defending their political ally Timarchus when

---

[1] *First Letter to Ammaeus* 10.

[2] McCabe 1981.

[3] See the ancient commentary on Dem. 19.72.

he was prosecuted in 345 (Aes. 1.71). He was also active in anti-Macedonian diplomacy: in a speech of 343 Demosthenes says that on an embassy to Macedonia, Hegesippus irritated Philip by his blunt speaking (19.331), and he refers in 341 to embassies that he and Hegesippus had undertaken to the Peloponnese, where they tried to stir up anti-Macedonian sentiment (9.72). Hegesippus also played a leading role in the establishment of an alliance of Greek states opposed to Philip in 340 (Plut. *Demosthenes* 17). He was still alive in 325/4 (*IG* II² 1623 line 185, 1629 line 543). What we know of Hegesippus' strongly anti-Macedonian views and forthright manner is certainly consistent with his authorship of this speech.

The speech is dated by Dionysius of Halicarnassus to 343/2 (see p. 113 n. 1) and probably belongs in the first half of 342 since Philip's campaign in Ambracia, referred to in 32, took place early in that year. It was delivered to the Assembly in response both to a letter from Philip to Athens and to the speeches of the ambassadors who brought the letter (1, 46).[4]

In his letter Philip evidently addressed a number of Athenian complaints and made proposals to try to resolve them. The first issue (in the order that Hegesippus addresses them, if not in importance) was the ownership of Halonnesus, a small island off the coast of Thessaly between the two larger, Athenian-owned, islands of Lemnos and Scyros.[5] Halonnesus too had once belonged to Athens but had been occupied at an unknown date by pirates. Philip drove the pirates out, perhaps in the course of his campaign in central Greece in 346, but retained control of the island. When the Athenians demanded that it be given back to them (implying by their choice of words that it belonged to them), Philip offered in the letter either to give it to them (implicitly denying their claim to prior ownership) (2) or to submit the matter to arbitration (7).[6]

---

[4] This was a different letter from the one preserved as Dem. 12, which belongs to the year 340.

[5] It is debatable whether ancient Halonnesus is the same as the island now called Alonnisos: see MacDowell 2009: 343 n. 1.

[6] The issue was less petty than it might appear, since although Halonnesus itself was unimportant, the principle that Philip should give places back

Philip also proposed the establishment of bilateral judicial agreements between Macedonia and Athens (9–13) and suggested that he and the Athenians should undertake joint action to suppress piracy in the Aegean (14–15). He repeated the offer made by his envoy Python in 344/3 to negotiate a revision of the terms of the Peace of Philocrates (18–32),[7] made general protestations of goodwill towards Athens (33), and promised great benefits if the Athenians would trust him (34). He also undertook to refer territorial disputes to arbitration (36) and specifically addressed the disagreement about the location of the border between Athenian and Cardian territory in the Chersonese (39–44), promising to compel the Cardians to submit the dispute to arbitration.[8]

The speech does not include the reply to Philip that Hegesippus proposes to draft (46), but the likely nature of that reply is clear from the intransigent tone of the entire speech. Hegesippus rejects every overture that Philip makes and invariably attributes to him the most malign intentions towards Athens. For example, Philip is willing to give the island of Halonnesus to the Athenians only on terms that are humiliating to them (6); his offer to establish judicial agreements—usually an indication of amicable commercial relations—is intended to force the Athenians to admit that they have no quarrel with him over their former possession Potidaea (13). Hegesippus accuses Philip of backtracking on his offer to renegotiate the Peace of Philocrates to Athens' satisfaction, and he rejects any offer of arbitration as either insulting (7) or unnecessary, since the facts of the matter are clear (36). Philip's offer to force his ally Cardia to accept arbitration is also interpreted as an insult to the Athenians, since it implies that they are too weak to compel the Cardians themselves (44).

The tone of the speech is relentlessly scornful, with frequent use of irony and sarcasm: Philip's promised benefits will exist only in some new world, not the real world (35); he "truly" wishes the Greeks to be free and autonomous (35); even as he is building a fleet, he has no naval ambitions (16); his offer to force the

---

to the Athenians, implying that they belonged to Athens, could be applied to more important cities under his control such as Amphipolis.

[7] On this embassy, see the Introduction to Dem. 6.

[8] On relations between Athens and Cardia, see especially Dem. 8.

Cardians to enter into arbitration is a great favor to Athens (44); the Athenians should punish traitors among their leaders "if you carry your brains in your temples and not trampled down in your heels" (45).

Hegesippus clearly took the view that Philip was fundamentally ill disposed to Athens and that his various offers to improve relations were insincere. Whether or not this was the case, the truculent and intransigent tone of this response contributed to the continued deterioration of relations between Athens and Philip in the later 340s.

7. ON HALONNESUS

[1] There is no way, men of Athens, that Philip's accusations against those of us who speak up for your rights will prevent us from advising you where your interests lie. For it would be monstrous if the letters that he sends were to strip the speaker's platform of its freedom of speech. First, men of Athens, I wish to review the letters that Philip has sent; after that, we will address the speeches of his ambassadors.[9]

[2] Philip starts by saying that he is giving you Halonnesus, which is his, and that you are wrong to ask for its return.[10] For, he says, it was not yours when he took it, nor is it yours now that he possesses it. And when we went on an embassy to him, he told us that he had acquired the island by taking it from pirates and that it rightfully belongs to him.[11] [3] It is not difficult to refute this argument of his, since it is unjust. All pirates seize places that belong to other people; they fortify them and use them as bases from which to harm others. But it would surely be unreasonable for him to claim that just because he defeated and punished the pirates he is now the owner of property that belongs to others, of which the pirates had unjustly taken possession. [4] For if you agree with this argument, then if pirates should take some

---

[9]Ambassadors from Philip had both brought letters from him and addressed the Athenians.

[10]On Halonnesus, see the Speech Introduction. Little is known of its earlier history, and no city is attested on it in this period.

[11]This shows that the speaker was an ambassador to Philip in 343.

place in Attica, or in Lemnos or Imbros or Scyros,[12] and someone should expel those pirates, what is to prevent the place where
the pirates had been and which belongs to us from immediately
becoming the property of those who had punished the pirates?
[5] Philip is perfectly aware that what he says is unjust—he knows
it as well as anyone—but he thinks that you have been led astray
by those who have promised to manage things here in accordance
with his wishes, and who are now doing just that. And indeed he
is well aware that whichever term you use—whether you take it or
take it back—you will get the island. [6] So, what difference does
it make to him not to "return" it to you (to use the right word)
but to "give" it as a gift (to use the wrong word)? He insists on
this term not to gain credit for doing you a favor, since it would
be a ridiculous favor, but to demonstrate to all of Greece that the
Athenians are happy to receive places on the coast from the hands
of a Macedonian.[13] This, men of Athens, you must not do.

[7] Whenever he says that he wishes to submit these matters to arbitration,[14] he is simply mocking you, first in suppos-
ing that you, who are Athenians, should go to law with him, the
man from Pella,[15] over the islands, to determine whether they are
yours or his. For when your power, which liberated the Greeks, is
unable to preserve your maritime possessions, and so you entrust
the dispute to judges, who are masters of the ballot, who will preserve them for you, unless Philip bribes them, [8] if you follow
this policy, how will it not amount to an admission on your part
that you have abandoned the entire mainland of Greece,[16] and a

---

[12]The islands of Lemnos, Imbros, and Scyros in the northern Aegean
were Athenian possessions, settled by Athenian cleruchs (*clērouchoi*, lit. "al-
lotment holders"). Thus, an attack on any of them was tantamount to an attack on Attica itself.

[13]On the real significance of the distinction between giving and giving
back, see the Speech Introduction.

[14]It was common for interstate disputes to be referred by mutual agreement of the two parties to arbitration by a third party.

[15]Pella was the capital of the Macedonian kingdom.

[16]Hegesippus advances an a fortiori argument: if the Athenians will not
dispute with Philip over islands such as Halonnesus, they are even less likely
to do so over places on the mainland.

demonstration to everyone that you will not fight him for a single thing—if indeed you do not fight for the places on the sea, where you claim to be strong, but go to law instead?

[9] He also says that men have been sent to you to make judicial agreements, and that these will be valid, not when they are validated in your courts as the law requires but when they have been referred to him, which would make any judgment passed by you open to appeal to him.[17] For he wishes to get the advantage of you and establish it as agreed in the judicial agreements that you do not accuse him of wrongdoing as regards any of the wrongs he did at Potidaea, and that you confirm that he took it, and now possesses it, justly.[18] [10] And yet the Athenians who were living in Potidaea, at a time when there was no state of war between them and Philip, but rather an alliance, and when oaths had been sworn by Philip to the inhabitants of Potidaea, were deprived by him of their possessions. These are the unjust actions that he wishes you to ratify outright, by stating that you neither accuse him nor believe that he is wronging you.[19] [11] The Macedonians have no need of judicial agreements with the Athenians, as history shows: for neither Amyntas the father of Philip nor the other kings ever made judicial agreements with our city.[20] [12] And yet our dealings with each other were more numerous

---

[17]Judicial agreements (*symbola*) between states provided the citizens of each state with access to the courts of the other. The exact nature of Hegesippus' complaint is unclear.

[18]Philip captured the Athenian-controlled city of Potidaea in the Chalcidic peninsula in 356 and expelled the Athenian settlers there (see 1.9n).

[19]The connection between judicial agreements and the status of Potidaea is not explained. Perhaps Hegesippus' point is that a judicial agreement would be made only if there were no outstanding matters of dispute between the two parties (cf. 12.22, where Philip argues that when the Athenians made peace with him, they implicitly accepted his claim to Amphipolis).

[20]Amyntas III was king of Macedonia from ca. 393 to 370. In the 370s he made an alliance with Athens (Tod 1948: no. 129) and supplied the city with timber for shipbuilding. The claim that there were no previous judicial agreements between Athens and Macedonia is probably correct.

then than they are now. For Macedonia was under our control and paid us tribute,[21] and we made greater use of their markets and they of ours than is the case now, and there were no commercial suits every month as there are now, strict ones, which mean that people who are so distant from each other have no need of judicial agreements.[22] [13] Nevertheless, since there was no one like Philip then, there was no benefit in establishing judicial agreements, either for them sailing from Macedonia to Athens to receive judgment or for us sailing to Macedonia, but parties from each place received judgment, we in accordance with their laws, and they with ours.[23] So you must realize that the reason why these judicial agreements are being created is to force you to admit that you no longer have any legitimate claim to Potidaea.

[14] As for the pirates, he says that it is right for you and him to share in guarding against criminals at sea, but his sole purpose is for you to set him up as a sea power and to admit that without Philip, you are unable even to police the sea; [15] and, further, that he is free to sail around and launch attacks on the islands, on the pretext of guarding against pirates, and to destroy the islanders and detach them from you, and not only to have used your generals to convey the exiles to Thasos[24] but also to win over the other islands, sending men to accompany your generals on their voyages, on the ground that he is sharing in the policing of the sea.

---

[21] The kingdom of Macedonia never paid tribute to Athens, although many of the coastal cities of the region were tributary members of the fifth-century Athenian empire. See 3.24n for discussion of this untrue claim.

[22] Monthly suits (*dikai emmēnoi*) were introduced at Athens in the fourth century to expedite the handling of commercial disputes and thereby encourage trade. In what sense they were monthly is disputed: see *Ath. Pol.* 52.2, with the commentary of Rhodes 1981; Cohen 1973: 9–59.

[23] The proposed agreement would have required cases to be handled by the courts of the state to which the defendant belonged.

[24] According to the ancient commentary on the speech (Dilts 1983: 130.28–31), these were supporters of Philip who had been exiled from Thasos and were returned there at his request by the Athenian general Chares. The island of Thasos was a strategically important Athenian ally in the northern Aegean: see 4.32.

And yet some people deny that he has naval ambitions! [16] But this man who has no naval ambitions is building triremes, and constructing docks, and wishes to send out naval squadrons, and to incur considerable expense with regard to the dangers of the sea—in which he supposedly takes no interest.[25]

[17] Do you imagine, men of Athens, that Philip would expect you to make these concessions to him, if he did not despise you, and did not have confidence in those here whom he has chosen to make his friends? These men are not ashamed to live for Philip rather than for their own country, and when they receive gifts from him they think that they are bringing them home, when in reality it is their own homes that they are betraying.

[18] As for the revision of the peace,[26] which the ambassadors he sent offered to revise, and we proposed a revision—which is agreed by all mankind to be just—to the effect that each party should have what belongs to it,[27] he disputes that he made this offer or that his ambassadors said this to you, being quite simply persuaded by these men here, whom he treats as his friends, that you do not recall what was said in the Assembly.[28] [19] But this is one thing that you cannot forget, since it was at one and the same meeting of the Assembly that his ambassadors addressed you and the decree was proposed. Since the reading of the decree followed immediately after the speeches, it is impossible that you voted for a resolution that gave the lie to the ambassadors.[29] So it is not

---

[25] On Philip's generally small-scale naval ambitions, see 4.34n.

[26] Philip sent an embassy to Athens in 344/3, led by the orator Python of Byzantium (20), offering to negotiate revisions to the Peace of Philocrates. See the Introduction to Dem. 6, a speech that was probably delivered in response to this embassy.

[27] There is an important distinction between each side having what it *holds* (i.e., maintaining the status quo), which was the basis of the Peace of Philocrates, and the Athenians' wish that each side should have what *belongs* to it, which was intended to reopen their claim to such places as Amphipolis and Potidaea.

[28] It is not credible that Philip promised to accept any revision whatsoever that the Athenians might propose.

[29] Hegesippus argues (surely misleadingly) that the Athenian decree—to demand that each party have what belongs to it—must have been in con-

against me but against you that he has directed this allegation—
that you sent off your decision in response to something that you
had not even heard! [20] The ambassadors themselves, to whom
the decree gave the lie, when you read out your answer to them
and invited them to enjoy our hospitality,[30] did not dare to come
forward and say, "You are telling lies about us, men of Athens,
and are accusing us of saying something that we did not say." Instead, they went off in silence and departed. I want to remind
you, men of Athens, of the speeches made by Python, who was an
ambassador on that occasion and who was popular with you because of them.[31] I know that you remember them. [21] They were
very similar to the content of the letters that Philip has recently
sent. Python found fault with those of us who slander Philip and
also blamed you, claiming that Philip had set out to treat you
well and had chosen to make you more than any of the Greeks
his friends but that you were preventing this, and paying heed to
bringers of baseless accusations (sykophantai),[32] men who accuse
him of bribery and slander him; for (he says) when he hears it
said that he has a bad reputation, and that you endorse this view,
such reports cause him to change his policy, since he is distrusted
by those whom he has chosen to benefit. [22] He therefore urged
those who speak in the Assembly not to find fault with the peace,
saying that it is wrong to do away with a peace. But (he said)

---

formance with what Philip's ambassadors had just offered. See the previous note.

[30] Foreign ambassadors to Athens were offered hospitality in the Tholos,
a public building in the *agora* that also housed those fifty members of the
Council (the *prytaneis*) who served in an executive capacity for one tenth of
the year.

[31] Python of Byzantium was a famous orator, employed by Philip as a
diplomatic agent. See the Introduction to Dem. 6; Dem. 18.136.

[32] *Sykophantēs* was a term used to describe someone who made a habit
of bringing prosecutions for financial gain, either from the rewards that
were given to successful prosecutors or by threatening to prosecute wealthy
men unless they paid him: see *OCD*[3] s.v. sycophants. It is used here to describe those Athenian politicians who make accusations against (rather than
prosecute) Philip. Its meaning is therefore different from the English word
sycophant.

if any clause of it had been badly drafted, it should be revised, and he would do whatever you might vote.[33] Yet if any speakers should slander him, and make proposals that would fail to result in the preservation of the peace and an end to your mistrust of Philip, no attention should be paid to such men. [23] When you heard these words, you welcomed them and said that Python spoke justly. And so he did. He spoke as he did not in order to remove from the peace those terms that were advantageous to Philip, and for which Philip had spent a lot of money, but as a result of the briefing he had received from his instructors here, who thought that no one would make a proposal contrary to the decree of Philocrates, the one that lost Amphipolis.[34] [24] I did not dare to make an illegal proposal, men of Athens, but it was not illegal to make a proposal contrary to the decree of Philocrates, as I shall show. For the decree of Philocrates, by which you were deprived of Amphipolis, was itself contrary to the previous decrees by which you acquired this land.[35] [25] This decree—the one of Philocrates—was illegal, and the proposer of a lawful decree could not have proposed the same thing as an illegal decree. But I proposed the same decree as those previous decrees that are lawful and that preserve your land, a lawful decree, and convicted Philip of deceiving you and of wishing not to revise the peace but to undermine the credibility of those who speak in your interest. [26] You all know that he granted this revision but now denies it. He claims that Amphipolis is his, since you voted that it was his

---

[33]Although Philip may have promised to consider any Athenian proposal, it is inconceivable that he honestly bound himself in advance to agree to any amendment that the Athenians might propose. He may, however, have deceitfully said something to this effect.

[34]Philocrates is represented as being responsible for the "loss" of Amphipolis because of the peace of 346 that bore his name, which effectively ceded the city to Philip.

[35]Hegesippus is presumably referring to the fifth-century decree(s) that established Amphipolis as an Athenian settlement. He argues unconvincingly that Philocrates' decree moving the making of peace with Philip, and thereby ceding Amphipolis to him, was in conflict with those earlier decrees and therefore illegal.

when you voted that he should keep what he possesses.[36] You did indeed pass this decree, but you did not resolve that Amphipolis was his. For it is possible to possess things that belong to someone else, and not everyone who possesses something possesses his own property, since many people have acquired things that belong to someone else. So this clever argument of his is in fact stupid. [27] Moreover, he remembers the decree of Philocrates but has forgotten about the letter he sent you when he was besieging Amphipolis, in which he admitted that Amphipolis is yours. For he said that when he captured it he would return it to you, since it belonged to you rather than to those who were then in possession of it.[37] [28] And apparently the people who formerly lived in Amphipolis, before Philip took it, were in possession of Athenian territory; but now that he has taken it, it is not Athenian territory that he possesses but his own. Nor does he possess Olynthus or Apollonia or Pallene on the basis that they belong to someone else but on the basis that these too are part of his own territory.[38] [29] Do you think that he has carefully composed his whole letter to you so as to give the impression that he is doing and saying what everybody agrees to be just? Has he not rather completely despised you in claiming that the land, which the Greeks and the Persian King voted and agreed was yours, belongs to him rather than to you?[39]

[30] Concerning the other revision that you made to the peace,

---

[36] See 18n above. Cf. 5.25, where Demosthenes acknowledges in 346 that Athens has ceded Amphipolis to Philip.

[37] For Philip's alleged offer, see 2.6n. Whether or not Philip offered to give the city to Athens in 357, it is unlikely that he acknowledged Athens' right to it, as Hegesippus claims.

[38] These places were destroyed in 348. On Apollonia, see 9.26. Pallene is the westernmost of the three peninsulas of the Chalcidice, and contained a number of Greek cities that were sacked by Philip at the same time.

[39] It was believed by Athenian politicians that Athens' claim to Amphipolis had at some point been accepted by the Greeks and the Persian King (see also Dem. 19.253; Aes. 2.32); when this might have happened is unclear: perhaps the peace conference of 370/69 (thus Hammond and Griffith 1979: 232–233).

that the rest of the Greeks, who do not share in the peace, should be free and autonomous, and that, if anyone marches against them, the participants in the peace should help them, [31] you thought it both just and considerate that the peace should not be restricted to us and our allies and Philip and his allies, which would expose those who are neither our allies nor his to lie in the middle and be wronged by any who are stronger than they, but that they too should enjoy security on account of your peace, and that we should lay down our weapons and keep the peace in earnest.[40] [32] Although he agreed in his letter, as you have heard, that this revision was just and that he accepted it, he has deprived the Pheraeans of their city and installed a garrison on their citadel,[41] in order no doubt that they may be autonomous, and he is marching against Ambracia, and has ravaged the land of the three cities in Cassopia—Pandosia and Bouches and Elatcia, colonies of Elis—and has taken the cities by force and handed them over to Alexander his kinsman into slavery.[42] He certainly does want the Greeks to be free and autonomous, as his actions show!

[33] As regards the promises that he continues to make, that he will grant you great benefits, he says that I am lying and slandering him before the Greeks, since he claims that he has never yet promised you anything. That's how shameful he is: he has written in the letter that is now in the Council Chamber[43] that he would

---

[40]I.e., the Athenians proposed that the Peace of Philocrates be converted into a Common Peace to which all the Greeks could sign up. Even if Philip did accept that this revision was just, it was never enacted.

[41]On Philip's treatment of Pherae in Thessaly, see 8.65n.

[42]In early 342 Philip marched on Epirus, deposed its king Arybbas, and replaced him with his (Arybbas') nephew Alexander, whose sister Olympias was a wife of Philip and the mother of his son Alexander (the Great): see Diodorus 16.72.1. Arybbas fled to Athens, where he was granted asylum (see *IG* II² 226 = Rhodes and Osborne 2003: no. 70). Cassopia is a region in western Greece to the north of the Gulf of Ambracia. The three cities named were not places of great importance.

[43]The Athenian archives were at this period housed in a building in the Agora dedicated to the Mother Goddess (the *Mētrōon*). This building had

grant you as many benefits as would stop the mouths of those of us who speak against him, if peace should be made, and that he would already have put them in writing if he knew that peace would be made—as if the benefits, which we were to enjoy once peace was made, were ready to hand. [34] But once peace was made, all the benefits that we were going to enjoy vanished, while a destruction of the Greeks has taken place on such a scale as you all know about. In the present letter he promises that if you trust his friends who speak on his behalf, and punish us who slander him to you, he will grant you great benefits. [35] The benefits will be as follows: he will not give you your possessions back—for he says that they belong to him—nor will the gifts exist in the inhabited world, to avoid his getting a bad name with the Greeks,[44] but some other territory and place, it seems, will appear, where these gifts will be given to you.

[36] As for the places that you possessed and that he seized during a time of peace, in breach of the treaty and the peace,[45] since he has nothing to say but is clearly guilty of wrongdoing, he says that he is willing to refer the disputes over these places to a fair and public court. But concerning these places there is no need of referral, since a counting of the days is decisive. For we all know in which month and on what day the peace was made. [37] And just as we know that, so we know in which month and on what day Fort Serrium and Ergisce and the Sacred Mountain were taken.[46] Actions like these are certainly not invisible or in

---

previously been used as the Council Chamber, and it may be that Hegesippus is referring to it by its former name. It is hard to see why a letter of 346 or earlier should have been kept in the new Council Chamber.

[44]The gifts, i.e., places, would in this case come from some other city's territory, which would give Philip a bad name.

[45]These are not separate agreements: the Peace of Philocrates was both a peace and a treaty.

[46]Hegesippus complains about Philip's seizure of various places in Thrace in the period before he ratified the Peace of Philocrates: see 9.15n. In a later speech, Aeschines (3.82) mocks the obscurity of the places in Thrace about which Demosthenes and his supporters complained.

need of a court decision: everybody knows which month came first—the one in which the peace was made or the one in which these places were seized.[47]

[38] He claims that he gave back all our prisoners who had been taken during the war[48]—he who was so eager to do you a favor that the Carystian, the honorary consul of our city, on whose behalf you sent three envoys to ask for his return, he put to death and did not even permit his body to be taken away for burial.[49]

[39] As regards the Chersonese, what he writes to you deserves to be examined, and you should be aware of what he is doing. He has given the whole region beyond Agora[50] to Apollonides of Cardia to enjoy, on the ground that it is his and has nothing to do with you.[51] And yet the boundary of the Chersonese is not Agora but the altar of Zeus of Boundaries, which is between Pteleum and Leuce Acte,[52] where the cutting through of the Cher-

---

[47] Hegesippus does not provide dates, and his argument that "everyone knows" invites suspicion that he is lying. In fact, the Athenians agreed to the peace in the month Elaphebolion (March/April 346), but Philip did not swear to it until he had returned to Pella from his Thracian campaign, i.e., *after* the capture of these places. In any case, Hegesippus does not prove that any of these places belonged to Athens.

[48] Presumably the Athenian soldiers captured in the fall of Olynthus in 348 (Aes. 2.15).

[49] The Greek is ambiguous: either "the man from Carystus" (a city in Euboea) or a man called Carystius. An honorary consul (*proxenos*) was appointed by a foreign state to look after the interests of its citizens in his city. This episode is otherwise unknown.

[50] Agora ("Marketplace") lay slightly to the southwest of Cardia.

[51] Apollonides was presumably a prominent figure at Cardia, but nothing further is known of him. In speaking about the territory "beyond Agora," Hegesippus adopts the point of view of the Athenian settlers in the south of the peninsula, for whom the territory "beyond Agora" was to the north of it.

[52] Pteleum and Leuce Acte ("White Beach") were on the western and eastern coasts respectively, to the northeast of Cardia, at the narrow point of the peninsula. Hegesippus' point is that Philip has supported a Cardian encroachment into land that belongs to Athens. The Cardians presumably

sonese was going to be,[53] [40] as the epigram on the altar of Zeus of Boundaries shows. It reads as follows:

> They established this very beautiful altar to the god,
> placing it as a boundary at the midpoint between Leuce and Pteleum,
> the inhabitants, a sign of a place, that shares a border.
> The lord of the blest ones himself is in the middle, the son of Cronus.[54]

[41] Yet of this land, whose extent most of you know, he treats one part as his own property, and has given away another part as gifts to others, and is bringing all your possessions under his control. And not only is he alienating the land beyond Agora but in the present letter he tells you to go to arbitration with the Cardians who live on this side of Agora—with the Cardians who live in your territory—if you have any dispute with them.[55] [42] But they *are* in dispute with you—and see if it is over a small matter. They say that the land that they live on is their own, not yours, and that your holdings do not belong to you, since they are in others' land, whereas their possessions belong to them, since they are in their own land. And they say that a fellow-citizen of yours wrote this in a decree: Callippus of Paeania.[56] [43] About this at any rate they are telling the truth: he did write it. And

---

argued that this was their own land. It is not known where the borders of Cardian territory in fact lay.

[53] Philip had proposed cutting a canal across the Chersonese to provide security for the Athenian settlers there from Thracian incursion: see 6.30n.

[54] The text of the third line of this epigram is corrupt. The son of Cronus in the fourth line refers to Zeus, the king of the gods. The text of the epigram may mean that the altar marked the midpoint between Pteleum and Leuce Acte rather than, as Hegesippus claims, the border of the Chersonese.

[55] Clearly the Cardians laid claim to some land to the southwest of Agora that was currently in Athenian hands.

[56] This Athenian politician is not otherwise known. Hegesippus puts a brave face on Athens' acceptance of Cardia's claim to this land.

when I prosecuted him on a charge of proposing an illegal decree, you acquitted him.[57] As a result, he has made your ownership of the place open to dispute. When you venture to go to arbitration with the Cardians over whether the land is yours or theirs, why will the same right not also exist with regard to the other inhabitants of the Chersonese? [44] And Philip has treated you so insultingly that he says that if the Cardians refuse to go to arbitration, he will compel them, as if you would be quite unable to compel them to do so; since you are unable, he says that he will compel them: does he not seem to be doing you a great favor? [45] Some people say that this letter is well written: people whom you should hate even more than you hate Philip. He at any rate is acting against you in every way, after he has won for himself a good reputation and many assets. But all those Athenians who show goodwill not to their own country but to Philip are villains, and deserve to be destroyed most vilely by you—if, that is, you carry your brains in your temples and not trampled down in your heels.[58]

[46] It remains for me to draft a reply to this fine letter and to the speeches of the ambassadors, one which I think to be both just and advantageous to you.[59]

---

[57]Libanius reports that Hegesippus, not Demosthenes, prosecuted Callippus: see the Speech Introduction.

[58]This striking expression was regarded by Libanius as vulgar, and a sign that the speech is not the work of Demosthenes. See the Speech Introduction.

[59]Hegesippus' proposal is not preserved, but there is no doubt that it would have been intransigent.

8. ON THE CHERSONESE

INTRODUCTION

This speech, which is dated 342/1 by Dionysius of Halicarnassus, was delivered in spring 341.[1] Demosthenes' statement in it that Philip has been campaigning in Thrace for ten months (2) is consistent with this date, assuming that he started his campaign in summer 342, and the Etesian winds of summer for which Philip may wait (14) are therefore those of 341. At the time of the speech Philip was on campaign in the interior of Thrace: he is said to be in the Hellespont region with a large army (3, cf. 14) and to be currently capturing a number of obscure places in Thrace (44).

The Chersonese (modern Gallipoli) is a long peninsula running down the western side of the Hellespont (modern Dardanelles), the narrow straits separating Europe from Asia, and connecting the Aegean Sea and the Sea of Marmara. The Athenians had a long-standing interest in the Chersonese, because it controlled the sea route to the Black Sea region from which they imported large quantities of grain.[2] Already in the sixth century the Athenian aristocrat Miltiades established an Athenian settlement there, which was later recovered by his son of the same name (Herod. 6.34–41). Athens controlled the Chersonese in the fifth century but had lost it by the end of the Peloponnesian War. In

---

[1] *First Letter to Ammaeus* 10. The theory that this speech was revised by Demosthenes to incorporate material from the later *Fourth Philippic* (Dem. 10) is discussed in the Introduction to that speech.

[2] For Athens' dependence on grain from southern Russia, see, in detail, Moreno 2007.

353/2 the Athenian general Chares sailed to the Hellespont, captured the city of Sestos in the Chersonese, and entered into negotiations with Cersobleptes, who was ruler of the eastern part of Thrace. Wishing to gain Athens' support against Philip, Cersobleptes renounced his claim to the Chersonese, except for the city of Cardia at its northern end, whereupon Athenian cleruchs (*clērouchoi*, settlers) were sent out there (Diodorus 16.34.3; *IG* II² 1613 lines 297–298). The Cardians, however, refused to admit the Athenian settlers into their city (Diodorus 16.34.4).

Philip had ambitions to gain control of all Thrace, the large region extending eastwards from Macedonia to the western coast of the Black Sea. In 356 he had defeated Cetriporis, the ruler of western Thrace (Diodorus 16.22.3), and in the autumn of 352 he launched a campaign, apparently with the support of Amadocus, the ruler of central Thrace, against Cersobleptes.[3] During this campaign he besieged Fort Heraeum near Perinthus (3.4) and "evicted some kings and installed others" (1.13). In response to this threat, Athens prepared to send a large force to the north, but it was delayed and in the end called off on rumors that Philip was either ill or had died (3.4–5).

It was perhaps at this time that Philip made alliances with Byzantium (9.34; Dem. 18.87, 93) and Cardia (5.25; cf. 12.11). In the summer of 346 Philip was once more campaigning against Cersobleptes and rejected the Athenian attempt to bring him under the protection of the Peace of Philocrates. Philip finally dealt with Cersobleptes in 342–340, allegedly acting in defense of the Greek cities of the Hellespont. According to Diodorus (16.71.1–2), he defeated the Thracians, imposed a tithe on them, and "founded great cities" at key sites in the region.

Philip's military operations in eastern Thrace were viewed with alarm by the Athenians, who by 343/2[4] had sent additional cleruchs to the Chersonese led by the general Diopeithes (8.6, 9.15).[5]

---

[3]See Theopompus *FGH* 115 fragment 101 for Amadocus' support for Philip.

[4]The date is given by Philochorus *FGH* 328 fragment 158.

[5]The sources relating to his operations there are collected by Pritchett 1971–1991: 2.92–93.

There he acted aggressively to strengthen Athenian control of the peninsula.[6] In particular, he sought to impose Athenian settlers on Cardia; when the Cardians refused to accept them, he attacked their territory. The Cardians in turn appealed to their ally Philip, who wrote to Athens demanding that Diopeithes cease his activities and then sent a force of mercenaries to support Cardia. Meanwhile Diopeithes had raised his own mercenaries and was ravaging territory and forcing ships to put to land (see 9), as well as raiding places on the Thracian coast that belonged to Philip. As hostilities continued, Philip wrote again to the Athenians to complain of Diopeithes' actions; it was in response to this letter that Demosthenes delivered the speech *On the Chersonese*.

Demosthenes repeatedly insists in this speech that by his actions Philip has already broken the Peace of Philocrates and is at a state of (undeclared) war with Athens. He tells the Athenians that they "must fully acknowledge that Philip is at war with our city and has broken the peace" (39) and that Philip's aim is to destroy Athens (60). He is at war because he has seized many places claimed by Athens in breach of the peace (6). Of particular concern to Demosthenes is the campaign that Philip is waging in eastern Thrace, since both the Chersonese and Byzantium are under threat (14–17).

Consequently Demosthenes argues that Diopeithes, who is short of money and the object of criticism at Athens, should be supported both politically and with further resources. Diopeithes' shortage of funds was not unusual for Athenian generals in this period, and it forced him to take various measures of dubious legality: ravaging farmland, forcing cargo ships to put in to land, and extorting money from Athens' allies and others. Demosthenes concedes that Diopeithes should be recalled if his actions are in fact illegal (28–29), but he argues that Athens needs to maintain a standing force in the north (17–18), rather than rely on expeditionary forces sent from Athens (17, 47), and that this force needs to be funded somehow (21–27). He insists that criticism of

---

[6]The following narrative is provided by Libanius' *Introduction* to this speech, 2–3.

Diopeithes merely distracts from the real issue, which is Philip's aggression towards Athens (2–3).

The dominant tone of the speech is anger. Demosthenes is sharply critical of the policies and attitudes of the Athenians and their political leaders. The former refuse to pay taxes or campaign in person (21) and are more willing to hear criticism of their own leaders than of Philip (30). The latter have been in some cases bribed by Philip (61) and have enriched themselves at the city's expense (66); they are more interested in finding fault, with Diopeithes and with their political rivals, and winning popularity than in proposing effective measures. As a result, Athens has lost the moral authority to ask the rest of Greece to join it in resisting Philip (34–37). Demosthenes contrasts the corruption and incompetence of his political opponents with his own principled and patriotic leadership.

A substantial section of this speech is also found with some differences in the slightly later *Fourth Philippic* (38–51 ≈ 10.11–27, 52–67 ≈ 10.55–70). The implications of this are discussed in the Introduction to Dem. 10.

There is a text of this speech with commentary by Sandys 1900.

8. ON THE CHERSONESE

[1] Every speaker, men of Athens, ought to speak neither out of enmity nor to curry favor but to declare what he thinks is the best policy, especially in view of the great public interest of the matters you are discussing. But since there are some who are being induced to speak either out of rivalry or for some other reason, you the majority, men of Athens, must discount everything else, and vote and act in accordance with what you judge to be the interest of the city. [2] The trouble we face relates to events in the Chersonese and the campaign that Philip has been conducting for more than ten months in Thrace,[7] but most of the speeches

---

[7] Lit. "for the eleventh month." Philip began campaigning in summer 342 in eastern Thrace.

that have been made deal with what Diopeithes is doing and is going to do.⁸ Yet I think that you already have the power to investigate whatever accusations have been directed against any of these men⁹—whom you can punish according to the laws whenever you want, either now if you wish or later—and there is absolutely no need for me or anyone else to speak at length about them. [3] But all the places that an established enemy of our city, who is in the Hellespontine region¹⁰ accompanied by a large military force, is trying to seize before we can stop him, and which, if we are too late, we will no longer be able to save—about these I think that it is profitable for us to deliberate and to make our preparations as soon as possible and not to run away from them as a result of these irrelevant and rancorous accusations.¹¹

[4] I am amazed by many of the things that are regularly said to you, men of Athens, but I was astonished most of all at what I recently heard someone say in the Council,¹² that any advisor must advise you either to wage war openly or to keep the peace. [5] But the fact is, if Philip keeps quiet and neither possesses anything of ours in breach of the peace nor organizes everybody against us, there is no further need for speeches: all we have to do is keep the peace, and on your side I see that you are quite ready to do so. But if the texts of our oaths and the terms on which we made peace are available for inspection,¹³ [6] and it is evident that from the start, before the departure of Diopeithes and the cleruchs whom they now accuse of having caused war, Philip has illegally seized

---

⁸Diopeithes had been sent out as leader of Athenian cleruchs to the Chersonese in or before 343/2: see the Speech Introduction.

⁹Diopeithes and those under his command.

¹⁰Demosthenes implies that Philip's campaigning in Thrace is directed specifically at gaining control of the Hellespont.

¹¹I.e., the accusations against Diopeithes.

¹²The Council (boulē) of Athens had important executive and judicial powers and also prepared business for the Assembly. Demosthenes' words do not imply that he was a member of the Council in 342/1.

¹³The terms of the Peace of Philocrates were inscribed on a stone pillar (stēlē) and set up in a public place in Athens; copies will also have been available in the city's archive (on which see 7.33n).

many of our possessions, about which you complain in these decrees that remain in force,[14] and continues to seize the possessions of Greeks and foreigners alike, and is mobilizing against us, what do they mean by saying that we must either wage war or remain at peace? [7] We have no choice in the matter: all that is left for us is to take the most just and necessary course of action, which these men are happy to pass over. What is this action? To oppose the man who has started a war against us—unless indeed, by Zeus, they claim that so long as Philip keeps away from Attica and Piraeus, he is neither wronging the city nor waging war on it! [8] But if they define justice in these terms, and consider this to be peace, you can presumably all see that what they are saying is impious, intolerable, and dangerous for you. Moreover, their statements are logically inconsistent with the allegations that they direct against Diopeithes. Why on earth should we give Philip license to do whatever he wants so long as he keeps away from Attica, but not permit Diopeithes even to help the Thracians[15] without our claiming that he is waging war? [9] But, by Zeus, it might be said, although these men are wrong on this point, our mercenaries are wrong to ravage places in the Hellespont, and Diopeithes is acting unjustly in forcing ships to land, and we should not leave matters to him.[16] All right; so be it; I make no protest. [10] Yet if they are really offering this advice in good faith, I think that just as they are seeking to disband our city's existing force by slandering the man who commands it and provides money for it, they should likewise show how Philip's power will be broken if

---

[14]The texts of these decrees have not been preserved.

[15]Demosthenes here puts a favorable gloss on Diopeithes' raids on places on the coast of Thrace that now belong to Philip (see Libanius' *Introduction* 3). Philip complains about Diopeithes' activities in his letter to the Athenians of 340 (12.3–4).

[16]In addition to the Athenian cleruchs, Diopeithes evidently also had a force of mercenaries. Like most Athenian generals of the period, he received little money from the city (see 21–26 below) and was presumably forcing merchant ships to put in to land in order to confiscate or forcibly purchase their cargoes to feed his troops. Some of these ships may have been sailing from Macedonian-controlled ports.

you follow their advice. Otherwise, observe how they are simply directing the city towards the same behavior that caused the present disaster. [11] For you know, I suppose, that the most important way in which Philip has got control of everything is by being the first to take action. He has a standing army always with him and knows in advance what he wishes to do, and strikes suddenly against whomever he chooses; whereas we, whenever we hear that something is happening, are thrown into confusion and only then start to make our preparations. [12] The result, it seems to me, is that he gets possession of any place he is attacking with great ease, whereas we are too late, and all our expenditure is in vain, and we make a show of our hostility and of our desire to hinder him, but in acting too late we succeed only in incurring shame.[17]

[13] Please realize, men of Athens, that even now the rest[18] is just words and pretexts, but that Philip's actions and preparations have this as their aim—that while you remain at home and our city has no force abroad, he can make all his arrangements completely unhindered. First, look at what is going on at present. [14] Philip is currently spending his time with a large force in Thrace and is summoning many reinforcements from Macedonia and Thessaly,[19] according to eyewitnesses. If he waits for the Etesian winds,[20] marches against Byzantium and lays siege to it, do you suppose that the Byzantines will continue with the same folly that they show now and will decide neither to call for your help nor to help themselves?[21] [15] I do not think so, and imagine

---

[17]I.e., the Athenians look foolish in the eyes of the other Greeks. On shame as a motivating factor, see 51n. For the imagined criticism of Athens by the other Greeks, see 34–37.

[18]I.e., the decrees that the Athenians pass.

[19]As ruler of Thessaly (see 1.13n), Philip was able to exploit the military resources of the region, especially the strong Thessalian cavalry (on which see 6.14n).

[20]On the importance of the Etesian winds, i.e., the north winds of summer, see 4.31n.

[21]Byzantium had been a leader of the anti-Athenian revolt in the Social War of 357–355 (Diodorus 16.7.3); its "folly" consists of its continued hostility to Athens in the face of Philip's nearby campaigns in eastern Thrace. De-

that they would rather bring into their city even those whom they distrust more than us than hand it over to Philip, if he does not seize it first. Thus, if we are unable to put to sea from here, and there is no help at hand there, nothing will prevent their destruction. [16] "But, by Zeus, those people are possessed by an evil spirit and are exceedingly foolish." True indeed, but they must nevertheless be saved, since it is in our city's interest.[22] Indeed, it is not clear to us even that he will not attack the Chersonese, since according to the letter he sent you, he claims to be defending himself against those who are in the Chersonese.[23] [17] If the army that has already been formed remains in existence,[24] it will be able both to assist that place[25] and to damage some of his interests. But if it is ever disbanded, what will we do if he attacks the Chersonese? "We will put Diopeithes on trial, by Zeus." And how will that help? "We can provide a relief force ourselves from here." What if we are prevented by the winds?[26] "By Zeus, he will not attack." But who will guarantee this? [18] Are you aware, men of Athens, and do you take account of the coming season,[27] which some people think will force you to abandon the Hellespont and surrender it to Philip? What if he leaves Thrace and attacks neither the Chersonese nor Byzantium but (this too is something you should consider) advances against Chalcis[28] and

---

mosthenes provides no evidence in this speech of a breakdown of relations between Philip and Byzantium, but in the following year Philip in his letter to the Athenians (12.2) complains that their ally Thasos was providing assistance to Byzantium by admitting Byzantine warships into its harbor.

[22]Byzantium's site on the Bosporus meant that whoever possessed it would be able to control the grain trade from the Black Sea on which Athens depended.

[23]This letter has not survived, but in his slightly later *Letter* (12.16), Philip makes a similar claim: that the Athenian cleruchs in the Chersonese are waging war on him.

[24]I.e., the force under Diopeithes' command.

[25]The Chersonese.

[26]On the Etesian winds, see 14 above; 4.31n.

[27]I.e., the summer of 341, with reference to the Etesian winds.

[28]Chalcis on the west coast of Euboea and Megara (see next note) were neighbors of Athens. Chalcis had seceded from Athens in 348 but, under

Megara,[29] just as he recently did against Oreus:[30] is it better to resist him here and allow war to enter Attica, or to cause difficulties for him over there? The latter, I think.

[19] Since we all know this and base our deliberations on it, we must not, by Zeus, disparage or attempt to disband the force that Diopeithes is trying to organize for the city, but must prepare a further force ourselves, supplying him with money and in other respects joining the struggle as friends. [20] For if someone were to ask Philip, "Tell me, would you rather that these soldiers whom Diopeithes now commands, however poor they are," (I do not dispute it) "succeed and be held in high regard by the Athenians and be increased in number, and that the city of Athens join in the struggle, or that they be disbanded and destroyed, as a result of the slanders and accusations that certain men have brought against them?" I think that he would choose the latter option. But aren't some of us here doing the very things that Philip would pray to the gods that we do? And do you still ask how the affairs of our city have been totally ruined?

[21] I wish to provide a candid appraisal of our city's present predicament and to examine what we are currently doing to address it. We are not willing to raise taxes,[31] or to campaign in person, or to keep our hands off public funds,[32] nor do we provide Diopeithes with financial contributions, [22] or approve of the provisions that he makes for himself, but we disparage him and investigate the source of his funds and his intentions and the like; nor—for such is our nature—are we willing to mind our

---

the leadership of Callias, turned to Athens in 341 in fear of Macedonian and Theban intervention. See Aes. 3.85–105 for a long and hostile survey of Callias' dealings with Athens and with Demosthenes, especially 91–93 on the embassy from Chalcis of 341 and the alliance that resulted from it.

[29]Megara suffered from political upheaval in 343, and the oligarchs there turned to Philip for support. See 9.27n.

[30]For Macedonian intervention in Oreus, a city in northern Euboea, see 9.59–61.

[31]Demosthenes refers here to the wealth-tax (*eisphora*), an occasional tax levied on the rich. See further 14.26n.

[32]The reference is to distributions to Athenian citizens from the theoric fund, on which see the Introduction to Dem. 3.

own business, but in our speeches we praise those who speak worthily of the city, whereas in our actions we join with their opponents. [23] You are accustomed on each occasion to ask the speaker, "What are we to do?" but I want to ask you "What are *we* to say?" For if you will not raise taxes, or campaign in person, or keep away from public money, or provide allowances, or let him provide for himself, and refuse to take care of your own affairs, I have nothing to say. You already give so much freedom to those who wish to blame and slander that you listen to them accusing someone in advance for things that they say he is going to say—what can anyone say to you?

[24] Some of you need to be told what the consequence of this can be. I will speak candidly; I can do nothing else. All your generals who have ever set sail—and if I am wrong, I condemn myself to suffer any punishment at all—take money from the Chians and the Erythraeans and anyone else they can (I mean of those who live in Asia).[33] [25] Those with one or two ships take less; those with a larger force take more. And those who give to them, whether it is a small or a large sum, do so not for nothing—they are not so crazy as to do that—but to buy protection from ill treatment and plundering for the merchants who sail from their cities, and for the convoying of their own ships, and the like. They say that they are giving "goodwill payments," as these takings are called. [26] Now too it is quite clear that all these cities will give Diopeithes money, since he has an army. How else do you suppose that one who has received nothing from you, and has no other source of funds with which to pay wages, can supply his troops? From the sky? No: he lives off what he collects and begs and borrows. [27] Those who accuse him before you are simply announcing to everyone[34] that they should not give him any-

---

[33]The island of Chios in the eastern Aegean had been a member of the Second Athenian Confederacy and had played a prominent part in the revolt of 357 that precipitated the Social War. Erythrae, a Greek city on the coast of Asia Minor directly opposite Chios, remained a part of the Persian Empire, as did all other Greek cities in Asia Minor. Any Athenian interference in such cities was certain to antagonize the Persian King.

[34]I.e., to any city from which Diopeithes might try to get help.

thing, on the ground that he will be punished for what he is going to do, though he has not done or achieved anything. This
is the meaning of their statements that "he is planning a siege"
or "he is sacrificing the Greeks." Do any of these men care for
the Greeks who live in Asia? If they do, they obviously care more
for other people than they do for their own country![35] [28] And
this is the implication of sending another general to the Hellespont.[36] If Diopeithes is acting terribly and forcing ships to put in
to land,[37] a small tablet, men of Athens, just a small one, could
put a stop to all this—and the laws tell us to impeach those who
commit crimes of this nature, not to keep watch on our own people at such expense and with so many triremes.[38] That would be
the height of madness. [29] Against our enemies, who cannot be
arrested under the laws, we have no choice but to maintain troops
and send out ships and raise taxes; but against our own people, it
is decrees, impeachment, and the *Paralus* that are effective.[39] This
is how intelligent men behave, but these men act to disparage and
destroy our affairs. [30] And yet, terrible though it is that some
of these men are behaving like this, this is not the really terrible thing. Rather, you who sit here are already so disposed that if
someone were to come forward and say that it is Diopeithes who

---

[35]Demosthenes criticizes his opponents for making sweeping and unfounded allegations about Diopeithes' intentions and denies that they have
any real concern for the Greeks (of Asia Minor). His claim that they show
more concern for other cities than for their own is sarcastic.

[36]I.e., the purpose of sending another general to the region would be
to restrain Diopeithes rather than to augment his force and cooperate
with him.

[37]Cf. 9 above.

[38]I.e., a writing tablet, containing the text of an impeachment. This
would force Diopeithes to return to Athens to stand trial. Demosthenes
suggests that it is cheaper and more effective to recall him to stand trial
for misconduct than to send a second general to supervise him. On the impeachment (*eisangelia*) of generals, see 4.47n.

[39]The *Paralus* was a special ship of the Athenian navy used on diplomatic missions and to carry official messages, in this case, the text of a decree indicting Diopeithes. See 4.34n.

is responsible for all our troubles, or Chares,[40] or Aristophon,[41] or whichever citizen one might care to mention, you immediately agree and cry out that he is speaking the truth. [31] But if someone should come forward and tell the truth, that "you are deluded, Athenians: it is Philip who is responsible for all these evil circumstances, since if he were keeping quiet, our city would be in no trouble," you are unable to refute this claim, but you seem to be distressed, as if you think something of yours is being destroyed. [32] The reason for this is as follows—and, by the gods, please allow me to speak freely for your benefit! Some public speakers have prepared you to be fearsome and severe in your Assembly meetings, but lax and contemptible in your preparation for war. If you are told that the man who is responsible is one whom you know you can arrest from among your own number, you agree and are willing to do so; but if you are told that he is one whom you can punish only after you have defeated him in war, you do not know what to do, I think, and your bewilderment makes you angry. [33] Contrary to your present practice, men of Athens, the public speakers should all have trained you to be mild and considerate in the Assembly, since it is there that you discuss your rights and those of your allies, but to show yourselves fearsome and severe in your preparations for war, since there the struggle is against your enemies and rivals. [34] Instead, acting as demagogues towards you[42] and currying favor with you to an excessive

---

[40]Chares was a leading Athenian general, active from the 360s to the 330s. His aggressive conduct (see 4.24n, 13.6n) made him a plausible object of such criticism. On his career, see Pritchett 1971–1991: 2.77–85.

[41]Aristophon was a prominent and long-lived Athenian politician, whose earliest known political activity was in the fifth century. After the Social War, he prosecuted Chares' fellow-generals Iphicrates and Timotheus for treason in their conduct of the war (Arist. *Rhetoric* 1398a4–7; Din. 1.14; 3.17), and in 354 he supported a law proposed by Leptines (Dem. 20.147–149). If Demosthenes has any particular action of his in mind, it may be this prosecution of two of Athens' most experienced generals, of whom Timotheus was forced into exile.

[42]The Greek word *dēmagōgos* (lit. "leader of the people") was originally a neutral term, but it came to have negative connotations, especially when applied to populist politicians of the late fifth century who were accused by their critics of pandering to the Athenian lower class.

degree, they have made it so that in meetings of the Assembly, you are spoiled and easily flattered, listening to everything with an ear to your own pleasure, but your public affairs have come to the point that you are in deadly danger. Come now, by Zeus, if the Greeks were to ask you to give an account of the opportunities you have squandered due to your indolence, and if they were to ask of you: [35] "Athenians, do you not send us ambassadors on every occasion,[43] and say that Philip is plotting against us and all the Greeks, and that we must guard ourselves against the fellow, and the like?"—and we must agree and admit that this is what we do—"Then, you most useless of people, when that man had been absent for ten months and was prevented by disease and winter and wars from returning home, [36] you failed to liberate Euboea or recover any of your own possessions.[44] But while you stayed at home, in good health—if indeed those who behave like this can be said to enjoy good health—he set up two tyrants in Euboea, planting one like a fortress opposite Attica, the other over against Sciathos.[45] [37] Yet you did not rid yourselves even of these—if that was the limit of your ambitions—but permitted them, did you not? You have evidently given way before him and have made it clear that you will not stir yourselves one whit more, even if he dies ten times over. Why then do you come as ambassadors and make accusations and cause trouble for us?" If they ask this, what answer shall we give, Athenians, or what shall we have to say? I do not see what we can say.

[38] There are some men who think that they confute a speaker when they ask him, "So, what must we do?"[46] To them I give this most just and truthful answer: you must stop behaving as you do. But I will also address each point in detail and hope that they

---

[43]On Athenian embassies to the Peloponnese in this period, see 9.72n.

[44]The reference is primarily to Amphipolis in Thrace, on which see 4.12n.

[45]The two Euboean tyrants were respectively Clitarchus of Eretria (see 9.57–58) and Philistides of Oreus (see 9.59–62). Oreus, a city on the northern coast of Euboea, faced the small Athenian-controlled island of Sciathos, on which see 4.32n.

[46]38–51 is substantially repeated at 10.11–27. For discussion, see the Introduction to Dem. 10.

may be as eager to act as they are to ask questions. [39] First, men of Athens, you must fully acknowledge that Philip is at war with our city and has broken the peace—and please stop accusing each other about this—and is malignly hostile to the entire city down to its very foundation, [40] and, I should add, to all its inhabitants, including those who most think that they are doing him a favor. And if they do not believe me, let them consider the Olynthians Euthycrates and Lasthenes,[47] who seemed to be on terms of intimacy with him, but who, after they betrayed their city, suffered a worse fate than anyone. But it is against our constitution that he is most at war, and towards its overthrow that his plots and policies are above all directed. [41] And in a sense it is reasonable for him to do so. For he is well aware that even if he gets control of everyone else, he will be unable to possess anything securely, so long as you are a democracy; and if ever some slip occurs—and there are many slips that may befall a man—all those places that he has now forced into union will come and seek refuge with you. [42] You are not yourselves well suited to acquire or possess an empire. Rather, you are good at preventing another from taking places, and at recovering them from one who has got hold of them, and at generally obstructing those who wish to rule, and at liberating people. He does not wish freedom at your hands to be lying in wait on any moment of crisis for him— quite the contrary—and his calculation is sound and to the point. [43] First, you must understand that he is an inveterate enemy of our democratic constitution. If you are not fully convinced of this, you will not be willing to treat the situation seriously. Second, you must recognize clearly that all his policies and machinations are directed against our city, and that wherever anyone resists him, he does so on our behalf. [44] For there is no one so naive as to suppose that Philip has a positive desire for the evils of Thrace—what else can one call Drongilus and Cabyle and Mastira[48] and the places that he is now taking?—or that seizing

---

[47]These men were pro-Macedonian politicians at Olynthus. At 9.66 Lasthenes is identified as cavalry commander (*hipparchos*).

[48]These are all places in Thrace, no doubt chosen by Demosthenes for their obscurity.

these places is the reason why he endures toil and winters and the utmost dangers, [45] or to suppose that he has no desire for Athens' harbors and docks and triremes[49] and silver works[50] and vast revenues, but will allow you to keep these, and is spending the winter in the pit[51] for the sake of the millet and wheat[52] in the grain pits of Thrace. On the contrary, all his activities in Thrace and elsewhere are directed towards getting control of our possessions. [46] What then should sensible people do? They should understand and acknowledge the situation, and should put aside this excessive and incurable negligence of ours, and should raise taxes and require our allies to do so too,[53] and their policies and actions should be directed towards ensuring that this army that has been raised remains together, in order that, just as Philip has a force prepared to mistreat and enslave all of Greece, so you may have a force ready to save and provide assistance to everybody. [47] For you can never achieve anything that you need to by sending relief forces.[54] Instead, we must equip a force, and provide supplies for it and financial officers[55] and public clerks,[56] and take measures to ensure that the money is very closely guarded. Once we have done this, we should hold these men responsible for the money,

---

[49] The Athenian navy, based in the harbor town of Piraeus, was by far the largest in Greece. See Dem. 14.

[50] The extensive silver mines of the southern tip of Attica were an important source of revenue for Athens in the fifth century. Mining was seriously interrupted by the Peloponnesian War and seems to have resumed on a substantial scale only in the middle of the fourth century.

[51] At Athens the pit (*barathron*) was a chasm into which convicted criminals were thrown to their deaths. It is not clear whether the reference here is to this, but the general sense of being in an unpleasant place is clear.

[52] For the identification of the Greek word *olura* as emmer wheat, see Sallares 1991: 365–367.

[53] On the financial contributions of Athens' allies in the Second Athenian Confederacy, see 5.13n, 13.4n.

[54] The same complaint is made at 4.32.

[55] Financial officers (*tamiai*) regularly accompanied generals on campaign to assist them in keeping their accounts: see Dem. 49.10; Aes. 1.56; Pritchett 1971–1991: 2.38–39.

[56] Lit. "public men": publicly owned slaves who assisted the financial officers in a clerical capacity. See also 2.19n.

and the general responsible for his actions. If you take these measures, and are truly willing to pursue this policy, you will either force Philip to keep the peace as he should and to remain in his own territory—which would be the most beneficial outcome—or you will be waging war against him on an equal footing.

[48] If anyone thinks that these plans involve great expense and much toil and trouble, he is absolutely right; but if he reckons what will happen to the city if it refuses to take these measures, he will find that it is in our interest for us to do our duty with enthusiasm. [49] If you had some divine guarantor—since no human would suffice for a matter of such importance—that if you keep quiet and give up everything, Philip will not in the end advance against you, it would be shameful, by Zeus and all the gods, and unworthy of you and of what the city has and of your ancestors' achievements, to sacrifice all the other Greeks into slavery for the sake of your own indolence, and I at any rate would rather die than advocate this course. Nevertheless, if someone else speaks and persuades you otherwise, so be it: do not resist, throw everything away. [50] But if no one takes that view, but on the contrary we all already know that the more places we allow him to control, the more dangerous and the stronger an enemy we will have, where can we retreat to? Why do we delay? When, men of Athens, will we be willing to do our duty? [51] "By Zeus, when we are compelled to." But if we are speaking of the compulsion placed on a free man, that has already arrived, and indeed has long passed us by; and we can only pray never to suffer that of a slave. How do they differ? For a free man, the greatest compulsion is a sense of shame at what is happening—I do not think that anyone could imagine any greater compulsion than that[57]—but for a slave it consists of blows and outrage to the body. May that never happen to us! Indeed, one should not even talk about it.[58]

---

[57] The desire to avoid humiliation was an important motivating factor in the "shame culture" of ancient Greece.

[58] Slaves had no legal rights in Greece and could routinely be beaten, or threatened with beatings, by their owners. The prospect of the Athenians suffering enslavement is so terrible that it should not even be spoken. On the concept of *hybris* (here translated "outrage"), see 62n.

[52] I would gladly tell you about all the rest,[59] and show how certain men are ruining you by their policies, but I shall pass over other matters and say only this: that whenever any matter relating to Philip arises, someone immediately stands up and says how fine it is to keep the peace, and how difficult it is to maintain a large military force, and that certain people wish to plunder public funds,[60] and other remarks of this kind, and as a result, they put you off and give him time to act as he wishes. [53] In consequence, you are idle and do nothing at the right time—and I fear that you may later come to realize how much this has cost you—while they secure favors from Philip and payment for their services. I think that it is not you who need to be persuaded to keep the peace, since you sit there already believing it, but the one who is waging war. If he were to be persuaded, your side is quite ready to do so.[61] [54] The real difficulty, you should realize, is not what we may have to spend to ensure our safety but what we will suffer if we do not take these actions, and you should prevent the money being stolen by announcing the establishment of a guard to ensure its safety, not by refusing to do your duty. [55] I am also angry, men of Athens, that some of you are distressed at the prospect of public money being seized, when you have the power both to guard it and to punish those who break the law, but are not distressed that Philip is seizing all of Greece city by city, as he is doing, and moreover his actions are directed against you.

[56] What possible reason is there, men of Athens, why none of these men will admit that Philip is at war, when he is so openly campaigning and acting illegally and seizing cities, but they accuse those of us who are advising you to stand firm and not abandon these places of planning to go to war? Let me explain. [57] They wish to turn the anger that you reasonably feel if you suffer any reverse in war against those who are giving you the best advice, in order that you may put them on trial rather than re-

---

[59]The wording at 52–67 is reused with minor changes in the slightly later *Fourth Philippic* (10.55–70). For discussion, see the Introduction to Dem. 10.

[60]Demosthenes' opponents represent his policy of using public money to wage war on Philip as one of looting the treasury.

[61]Compare 5 above for the same thought.

sist Philip, and that they themselves may act as the accusers of these men rather than pay the penalty for their own actions. This is what they mean when they say that certain people here wish to bring about war, and this is what this dispute is about. [58] But I know for certain that, without any Athenian having yet made a proposal of war, Philip holds many of our city's possessions and has now sent help to Cardia.[62] If we are willing to pretend that he is not waging war on us, he would be an utter fool to refute us. [59] But when he marches against us, what shall we say then? He will deny that he is at war, as he did to the people of Oreus when his soldiers were in their territory,[63] as he did before that to the Pheraeans even as he attacked their walls,[64] and as he did at the outset to the Olynthians, until he was in their territory with an army![65] At that point shall we say that those who are telling you to defend yourselves are warmongers? The only remaining option is slavery—nothing else is possible if we do not defend ourselves and are not allowed to live at peace. [60] Indeed, you do not face the same danger as others do, since Philip's aim is not to subject your city but to destroy it utterly. He is well aware that you will not willingly be slaves, nor, if you were willing, would you know how to do so, since you are accustomed to rule, but you will be able to cause more trouble for him, if you take the opportunity to do so, than any other people can.

[61] And so you should recognize that the struggle will be for our very existence, and should hate and cudgel to death[66] those who have sold themselves to him. For it is impossible, impossi-

---

[62] On Philip's support of Cardia, see the Speech Introduction.

[63] On Macedonian intervention in the Euboean city of Oreus in 342, see 36 above; 9.12, 59–62.

[64] Pherae was the leading city of southern Thessaly. Philip intervened there in 344/3 in his role as ruler (see 1.13n) of Thessaly: see 65n below, 7.32, 9.12; Dem. 19.260; Diodorus 16.69.8.

[65] Philip had been allied to Olynthus, but relations deteriorated in the years leading up to the outbreak of war in 349: see the Introduction to Dem. 1–3.

[66] Demosthenes refers to a gruesome form of capital punishment (*apotympanismos*) that was used against traitors and slaves: see Todd 2001.

ble I say, to defeat your enemies outside the city until you have punished your enemies in the city itself. [62] Why do you suppose that he is treating you with contempt—for this is exactly what I think he is doing?[67] And why does he deceive others by doing them favors but threatens you outright? For example, he gave the Thessalians many benefits before he led them into their present slavery;[68] nor would anyone be able to say how much he deceived the wretched Olynthians, after he had previously given them Potidaea and much else besides;[69] [63] and he is now leading on the Thebans, after handing Boeotia over to them and relieving them of a long and difficult war.[70] After each of these cities enjoyed some benefit, some of them have already suffered a fate that is well known to everyone; the others will suffer at some time in the future. As for you, to say nothing of all the places you have recently been deprived of, how much were you tricked out of during the actual making of the peace?[71] [64] Phocis, Thermopylae,[72] the coast of Thrace, Doriscus, Serrium,[73] Cersobleptes him-

---

[67]Demosthenes accuses Philip of treating the Athenians with violent contempt (*hybris*). Such conduct was commonly attributed to the rich and powerful in their dealings with those poorer or weaker than themselves, and *hybris* was treated as a serious offense under Athenian law: see in general *OCD*[3] s.v. *hubris*; Fisher 1992.

[68]See 59 above on Philip's treatment of the Thessalian city of Pherae. Demosthenes uses the emotive language of slavery to describe the Macedonian domination of Thessaly.

[69]See 59 above. Philip made an alliance with Olynthus in 357/6 (see 2.1n) and handed over the city of Potidaea to it (see 2.7n, 6.20n).

[70]After the Third Sacred War was brought to an end in 346, Thebes' domination of the other cities of Boeotia was confirmed.

[71]Demosthenes refers to the making of the Peace of Philocrates between Athens and Philip in 346. For the episodes complained about here see the Introduction to Dem. 5. The manuscripts follow this question with "and of how much were you deprived?," but these words were probably inserted by a later copyist.

[72]Philip ended the war in 346 by gaining control of Thermopylae and destroying the cities of Phocis.

[73]Doriscus and Serrium, towns on the coast of Thrace, were captured by Philip in 346 before the peace was ratified. See also 9.15; 10.8, 65.

self?[74] Does he not now admit that he possesses Cardia?[75] Why then does he deal in this way with everyone else but not with you? Because only in your city are men allowed to speak on behalf of the enemy with impunity, and it is safe for a man who has received bribes to address you even though you have been deprived of what is yours. [65] It would not have been safe to plead Philip's cause in Olynthus, if the majority of the Olynthians had not profited from the enjoyment of Potidaea.[76] It would not have been safe to do so in Thessaly, if the majority of the Thessalians had not benefited from Philip expelling their tyrants[77] and handing the Pylaea over to them.[78] Nor was it safe to do so in Thebes, until he handed over Boeotia and destroyed Phocis.[79] [66] But at Athens, after Philip has not only deprived you of Amphipolis[80] and the territory of the Cardians[81] but is also establishing Euboea[82] as a fortress against you and is now advancing against Byzantium,[83] it is safe to speak on his behalf. Indeed, some of those who do

---

[74]Cersobleptes was the ruler of eastern Thrace. Since he was not a member of Athens' league, he was not protected by the Peace of Philocrates, and Philip was free to wage war on him. See further 12.8n.

[75]See the Speech Introduction for Philip's support for the city of Cardia in the Chersonese, with which he was allied.

[76]On Olynthus and Potidaea, see 62 above.

[77]Philip intervened in some of the cities of Thessaly in 344/3 (see 59n above). The "tyrants" whom he expelled were the rulers of Pherae in the south and perhaps also of Larissa in the north. See further Hammond and Griffith 1979: 523–526.

[78]The Pylaea was the council of the Delphic Amphictyony, which was now dominated by the Thessalians: see 5.23.

[79]See 63n.

[80]On Amphipolis, see 4.12n.

[81]The Athenians claimed Cardia as part of their more general claim to the Chersonese. See 58n and the Speech Introduction.

[82]On Philip's establishment of a power base in some of the cities of Euboea, see 36 above.

[83]Demosthenes does not elaborate on his (untrue) claim that Philip is marching against Byzantium. At 14 he merely raises the possibility of Philip attacking the city.

so were once poor but are now rapidly becoming rich, and were once without name or reputation but are now reputable and well known, whereas you suffer the reverse process: you used to have a good reputation but are now disreputable; you were rich but are now in need. For I think that the wealth of a city consists of its allies, and the trust and goodwill that it inspires—all of which you now lack. [67] Because you despised these advantages and allowed them to be carried off, Philip is wealthy and powerful and an object of fear to all, Greeks and foreigners, whereas you are abandoned and brought low, glorying in the abundant goods for sale in the marketplace, but a laughingstock when it comes to making appropriate preparations. I see some speakers taking one view about you and another about themselves: they say that you must keep quiet, even if someone wrongs you, but they are unable to keep quiet in your presence, even though no one is wronging them.

[68] Then someone or other of them comes forward and says to me: "Well, but you won't make a proposal, or take any risk, but are cowardly and soft." I am not arrogant or disgusting or shameless, and hope I may never become so, and I consider myself braver than the numerous men who participate so irresponsibly in public life. [69] For, men of Athens, anyone who brings prosecutions, who confiscates people's property and then gives it away, and who makes accusations, without regard to the city's interest, does not do these things out of bravery, but can be rash with impunity, since his safety is guaranteed by the fact that in speaking and taking part in public life he curries your favor. But anyone who frequently opposes your wishes for the sake of what is best, and who always speaks not to gain favor but to give the best advice, and who chooses a policy that owes more to chance than to calculation, yet accepts responsibility for both of these—[70] it is this man who is brave, and a useful citizen, not those who have destroyed our city's greatest assets for the sake of a short-lived popularity. I am so far from envying them or thinking them good citizens that, if anyone were to ask me, "Tell me, what good have you done our city?," although, men of Athens, I could mention the command of triremes and the sponsoring of choral produc-

tions and financial contributions and the ransoming of prisoners and other such acts of generosity,[84] I would not mention any of them. [71] Instead, I would say that my conduct of public affairs has nothing in common with theirs; and that, although I perhaps could, as others can, make accusations and do favors and confiscate property and do the other things that these men do, I have never yet taken up any of these positions, nor have I been motivated by profit or ambition, but I continue to say things which make me a lesser man than many in your eyes, but will make you greater, if you are persuaded by me—this much, perhaps, it is not invidious for me to say. [72] Nor do I think that I would be acting as a good citizen if I were to devise policies that will make me the first among you, but you the last among all people. Rather, the city must prosper through the policies proposed by its good citizens, and everyone must always advocate what is best, not what is easiest. Nature will move towards the latter of its own accord; towards the former, the good citizen must lead the way, teaching through his words.

[73] In the past I have heard it said that I always say what is best but that I produce nothing but words, whereas what the city needs is deeds and action. I shall tell you frankly my attitude towards these complaints: I think that the only action that is required of one who advises you is to say what is for the best, and I think that I can easily show that this is the case. [74] You doubtless know that the famous Timotheus once made a speech before you saying that you should assist and go to the rescue of the Euboeans when the Thebans were trying to enslave

---

[84]On the liturgical service imposed on wealthy Athenians to equip and command a ship of the Athenian navy, or sponsor a choral performance, see 4.36n. The financial contributions to which Demosthenes refers are the payment of the wealth-tax (*eisphora*): see 14.26n. Although these responsibilities were all obligatory, citizens were encouraged to show their patriotism by lavishly performing liturgies and by paying the wealth-tax promptly and in full: see Whitehead 1983. It was also regarded as public-spirited to ransom a fellow-citizen who had been captured by the enemy. Demosthenes' own expenditure on behalf of the city is analyzed by Davies 1971: 135–138.

them,[85] and that he said something like this: "Tell me, when you have the Thebans on an island, are you deliberating about how to treat them and what to do? Will you not fill the sea, men of Athens, with triremes? Will you not leap to your feet and proceed to Piraeus? Will you not launch your ships?" [75] Timotheus spoke these words, and you acted, but the success arose from these two things together: his words and your action. If he had given the best possible advice, as he did, but you had remained idle and paid no attention, would any of the things that then benefited the city have happened? They could not have. So too with what I say: you should seek action from yourselves, but the best advice from the man who steps up to speak.[86]

[76] I wish to summarize my proposal and then step down. I say that we must raise money, keep together our existing force, correcting any fault that is detected but not disbanding the whole because of any details that are open to criticism; we must send out ambassadors in every direction to instruct, warn, and act; and in addition we must punish those who are taking bribes in connection with public affairs and show our utter hatred of them, so that those who are moderate and upright may be seen, by themselves and others, to have given the right advice. [77] If you handle matters in this way and stop belittling everything, perhaps, perhaps even now our situation may yet improve. But if you remain in your seats, serious only about heckling or cheering, but shrinking back if anything needs to be done, I do not see how any speech will be able to save the city, if you refuse to do your duty.

---

[85] In 357. See also 1.8, 4.17; Dem. 21.174; Aes. 3.85; Diodorus 16.7.2. Aeschines reports that within thirty days, Athens had taken control of the island. The inscription recording the subsequent alliance between Athens and the Euboean city of Carystus has been preserved: *IG* II²124 = Rhodes and Osborne 2003: no. 48. On Timotheus, see 13.22n.

[86] The Greek text is corrupt, but the meaning is clear.

9. THIRD PHILIPPIC

〰〰

INTRODUCTION

The *Third Philippic* was delivered in spring 341, at about the same time as Dem. 8.[1] Certainly the two speeches paint a similar picture of the situation in Thrace and the Chersonese. In the present speech, Demosthenes claims that Philip has set out against the Hellespont (27), is marching on Byzantium (34), and has sent mercenaries into the Chersonese, that is, to support his ally Cardia (16). Both Byzantium and the Chersonese are in such grave danger that the Athenians must take immediate action (19) and send funds to those in the Chersonese (73), by which he means the Athenian force there commanded by Diopeithes.[2]

This speech differs from Dem. 8, however, in being concerned with the rest of Greece as much as with Athens. Demosthenes accuses Philip of intervening in the affairs of numerous Greek states (Megara, Elis, Pherae, Ambracia, and the Euboean cities of Eretria and Oreus), of seizing Echinus in central Greece, and of threatening Byzantium and the Chersonese. He also has much to say about the reaction of the Greeks: they have given Philip more freedom to dominate Greece than they ever allowed Athens or Sparta (22–25); they are demoralized and disunited (28); their love of liberty, shown in their resistance to the Persian inva-

---

[1]It is dated 342/1 by Dionysius of Halicarnassus (*First Letter to Ammaeus* 10).

[2]On Diopeithes and the Chersonese in the late 340s, see the Introduction to Dem. 8.

sion of Greece in 480–479, has now vanished (36–40). Demosthenes introduces a historical example: the Athenian decision in the
fifth century to outlaw Arthmius of Zeleia, an agent of the Persian King, as proof of the concern that the Athenians of that time
showed for the welfare of Greece as a whole (41–45).

By contrast, he attacks Philip in a famous passage as a *barbaros* (i.e., non-Greek, but with implications of barbarity; 30–32):
he is "a wretched Macedonian, from a land from which you could
not previously have bought even a decent slave" (31), and it is disgraceful that such an interloper should "administer the Pythian
festival [at Delphi], the shared competition of the Greeks" (32).
This xenophobic attack on Philip is of a piece with the Panhellenic[3] tone of the speech as a whole. Demosthenes argues that the
cities of Greece need to unite to resist Philip: he criticizes their
failure to communicate with each other by means of ambassadors
(28), praises an Athenian embassy to the Peloponnese of which he
had been a member (72), and demands that the Athenians send
out further embassies in every direction (71). Athens must take
the lead (74) but cannot defeat Philip alone.

A central purpose of this speech is to convince the Athenians
that a state of undeclared war with Philip already exists. Demosthenes insists repeatedly that although the Peace of Philocrates
(negotiated between Athens and Philip in 346) is still nominally
in force, in practice Philip is at war with Athens and indeed has
been ever since the destruction of Phocis in 346 (19). He argues
that Philip, who claims to wish to remain at peace with Athens, must be judged by his actions rather than by his words, and
that he acts as if he is already at war with Athens (15). But it is in
Philip's interest to pretend to be keeping the peace, since the example of other Greek cities (Olynthus and Phocis: 11) shows that
he uses such claims to lull his victims into a false sense of security. Demosthenes lists a series of Philip's alleged interventions in
the affairs of other Greek cities that, he argues, are breaches of

---

[3]Panhellenism was the belief that the Greeks should set aside their differences and unite against a common external foe (typically the Persians).
See in general Flower 2002; Mitchell 2007.

the Peace of Philocrates and thus acts of war against Athens (17). The Athenians must learn from the fates of others and wake up to the deadly threat of Philip.

Demosthenes' other main theme is that the Athenians are prevented from recognizing that Philip is at war with them, or from taking effective action against him, by the influence of certain politicians who have, he alleges, been bribed by Philip. These men (whom he does not name) seek to persuade the Athenians that they should keep the peace and that Philip's intentions towards them are friendly, and they accuse patriotic leaders such as himself of warmongering (53–55). He provides examples from elsewhere in Greece of cities that have been deceived by politicians in the pay of Philip and have in consequence now lost their freedom (56–68) and argues that Athens risks suffering the same fate.

Demosthenes' specific policy proposals are to support Byzantium (19) and the Athenian force in the Chersonese (19, 73), to conduct the war in the north with vigor to keep Philip at a safe distance from Athens (51), to engage him in a naval campaign rather than risk pitched battle with his powerful army (52), to make appropriate military preparations (70), and to try to rally support from the rest of Greece (71).

Two slightly different versions of this speech are found in the manuscripts of Demosthenes, one longer and one shorter.[4] The longer version contains a number of brief passages, ranging in length from a few words to several sentences, which do not appear in the shorter one. These passages, which are italicized in this translation, appear to have been written by Demosthenes and are not later interpolations. On the other hand, it is difficult to see why anyone involved in the later transmission of the speech would have excised these passages to create a slightly shorter text, and it therefore seems likely that two different versions in some way go back to Demosthenes' time. One possible explanation is that Demosthenes edited the longer version of the speech after he

---

[4]The shorter version is found in the oldest medieval manuscript of Demosthenes, conventionally labeled S (= Paris Bibliothèque Nationale de France ms. Gr. 2934). See Dilts 2002: xvi.

had spoken it, removing material that was more suited to delivery or was likely to appeal only to an Athenian audience, with a view to circulating it elsewhere in Greece.[5] An alternative, and in my view more likely, explanation is that Demosthenes crossed these passages out in his text of his speech and that whoever first published the speech after his death was uncertain whether or not to include them.[6]

There is a text of this speech with commentary by Sandys 1900.

9. THIRD PHILIPPIC

[1] Many speeches are made, men of Athens, at almost every meeting of the Assembly, about the wrongs that Philip has been doing, from the moment that he concluded the Peace,[7] not only against you but also against the others, and I am sure that everyone would say—even if they do not act accordingly—that all our words and actions should have as their aim to put an end to his arrogance and make him pay the penalty; but I see that all our advantages have been so undermined and thrown away that—I fear it is ill omened to say, but it is true—if all the regular speakers wished to speak, and you wished to vote, in such a way as to make your situation as bad as possible, I do not think that things could be any worse than they are now. [2] There are no doubt many reasons for this, and matters did not reach their present state from one or two causes only. But most of all, if you examine the matter closely, you will find that it is due to those men who choose to curry favor rather than to give the best advice—some of whom, men of Athens, cherish the things that give them

---

[5] Thus, most recently, Wooten 2008: 167–173. It should be noted, however, that the editor of the text that is followed in this translation (Dilts 2002) regards the omission of the longest such passage (6–7) from manuscript S as due to a copyist's error (see 6n). I am in any case not convinced that the shorter version is significantly better suited for publication than the longer one.

[6] Thus, MacDowell 2009: 353.

[7] I.e., the Peace of Philocrates between Athens and Philip of 346.

a good reputation and power, and take no thought for the future, *and do not think that you need do so either*; others blame and slander those who participate in public life and do nothing other than cause the city to be preoccupied with punishing itself, whereas Philip is able to speak and act as he wishes. [3] Such policies are habitual to you and are the cause of your troubles. I ask you, men of Athens, not to be at all angry with me if I speak freely in telling the truth. Look at it like this: You believe so strongly that in other areas freedom of speech should be granted to all inhabitants of the city that you have allowed foreigners and slaves to share in it,[8] and many slaves here can be seen saying whatever they like with greater freedom than is enjoyed by the citizens of some other states, but you have entirely banished freedom of speech when it comes to the giving of advice. [4] The result is that in meetings of the Assembly, you are spoiled and easily flattered, and listen to everything with an ear to your own pleasure, but in your public policy and in the reality of the situation, you are already in deadly danger. If this is your disposition even now, there is nothing I can say to you. But if you wish to hear what is to your advantage, without any flattery, I am ready to speak. Even if our situation is desperate and much has been squandered, nevertheless it is still possible to set matters right, if you are willing to do what is needed. [5] What I am about to say to you may be paradoxical, but it is the truth: the worst aspect of what has happened holds out the best hope for the future. What do I refer to? To the fact that your affairs are in a bad state even though you are doing none of the things, small or large, that you should be doing; for, if things were as they are, and you were doing all that you should, there would be no hope of improvement.[9] As it is, Philip has got

---

[8]There was no absolute right to free speech in Athens (see MacDowell 1978: 126–129 on the laws relating to slander), and it is very unlikely that the foreigners and slaves had any legally defined rights in this area, but, in general, restrictions on public speech were few. For the comparative freedom of slaves at Athens, see the complaints of Pseudo-Xen. *Athenian Constitution* 1.10.

[9]The section "the worst aspect . . . improvement" is taken over almost word for word from 4.2.

the better of your idleness and negligence, but he has not got the better of the city. You have not been defeated: you have not even been aroused!

[6] If we were all in agreement that Philip is at war with our city and is breaking the peace, anyone who comes forward to speak would need to advise us only how to resist him most securely and most easily.[10] But in fact some men have such an absurd attitude that, at a time when Philip is seizing cities and possesses many places that belong to you and is wronging everybody, they tolerate certain people repeatedly saying in the Assembly that it is some of us[11] who are making war; since this is the case we must be on our guard and must correct the situation. [7] For there is a danger that anyone who proposes and advises that we defend ourselves will be accused of warmongering. I assert this principle first of all: that it is up to us to determine whether we should keep the peace or go to war. [8] If, then, it is possible for our city to remain at peace, and if this is in our hands—to start from this point—I say that we must indeed keep the peace, and I think that anyone who agrees should make proposals and take action to that effect and not try to deceive us. Yet if someone who has weapons in his hands and a great army around him offers you the name of peace but by his actions is waging war, what is left for us to do but to defend ourselves? But if you wish to say that he is keeping the peace, as he claims, I have no quarrel. [9] If anyone regards as peace a situation in which Philip, after he has captured every other place, will then attack us, first of all, he is insane; and sec-

---

[10]Sections 6 and 7 are omitted in manuscript S. This manuscript contains a text of this speech that omits a number of short passages that are to be found in other manuscripts (see the Speech Introduction). Dilts 2002, whose Greek text is followed in this translation, regards the omission of 6–7 as accidental. He notes that 6 and 8 both start with the same three words in Greek (*ei men oun*), and he suggests that a scribe's eye mistakenly jumped from the beginning of 6 to the beginning of 8, causing him to leave out the intervening text.

[11]This was directed primarily at anti-Macedonian politicians such as Demosthenes, but also at Diopeithes and the Athenian settlers in the Chersonese (see Dem. 8).

ond, what he describes is your being at peace with him, not his being at peace with you. This is what Philip has bought with all his lavish expenditure: that he is at war with you, but you are not at war with him!

[10] If we wait until he admits that he is at war with us, we will be utter fools. For even if he marches against Attica itself and Piraeus, he will not admit that he is doing so, to judge from his treatment of others. [11] This is what he said to the Olynthians, when he was forty stades[12] from their city: that there were two alternatives—either they should stop living in Olynthus or he should stop living in Macedonia—although for the whole time up until then he got angry and sent ambassadors to defend himself, if anyone should accuse him of having any such intention.[13] And he marched to Phocis as if towards an ally, and was accompanied by Phocian ambassadors as he went, and most speakers here insisted that his arrival would not benefit the Thebans.[14] [12] Moreover, he has recently seized and is now in possession of Pherae, after entering Thessaly as a friend and ally.[15] And last, he offered these wretched men of Oreus the pretext that the troops had been sent as friendly observers.[16] For, he said, he saw that they were suffer-

---

[12]About eight kilometers (five miles). A stade was the length of the *stadion* footrace, 200 yards.

[13]Demosthenes is wrong to imply that relations between Philip and Olynthus had been friendly up to the outbreak of war in 349. In fact, they had been deteriorating since 352 (see the Introduction to Dem. 1–3 and 1.7n).

[14]In 346 Philip marched south into central Greece to bring an end to the war between Thebes and Phocis, accompanied by ambassadors from many Greek cities, not just Phocis. The speakers referred to are Aeschines and Philocrates: see 5.10n.

[15]On Philip's expulsion of the rulers of the Thessalian city of Pherae in 344/3, see 8.59n. Philip was not merely an ally of the Thessalians but had previously been elected chief magistrate (*archōn*) of Thessaly: see 1.13n. Presumably his intervention in the affairs of Pherae was in fact sanctioned by the Thessalian League, the body that nominally governed the country.

[16]On Macedonian involvement in the affairs of Oreus on Euboea, see 33, 59–62 below.

ing from factionalism, and it is the duty of allies and true friends to assist in such situations. [13] Do you suppose that he chose to deceive these people, who would have done him no wrong, although they would perhaps have defended themselves from attack, rather than declare war on them, but that he will go to war with you only after declaring it, so long as you are willing to be deceived? [14] Of course not. Philip would be a complete fool if, when you make no complaint about the harm he is doing you but instead blame some of your own citizens, he were to put an end to your internal strife and rivalry, and announce that you should direct them against him instead, and deprive those who are in his pay of the argument by means of which they put you off: that Philip is not at war with the city.

[15] Is there anyone, by Zeus, in his right mind who would decide who was at peace with him and who at war by their words rather than by their actions? Of course not. Yet Philip, from the start, as soon as the peace had been made, at a time when Diopeithes was not yet a general and those who are now in the Chersonese had not yet been sent out,[17] set about seizing Serrium and Doriscus[18] and expelling from Fort Serrium and the Sacred Mountain the troops whom your general had stationed there.[19] [16] In taking these actions, what was he doing? It was peace he had sworn! And let no one say, "What are these places?" or "How does this concern the city?" For whether these places were small, or whether any of them concerned you, are different matters. Piety and justice are equally important, whether someone transgresses over a small or a large matter. Very well then, when he sends mercenaries into the Chersonese,[20] which the King and all the Greeks

---

[17]The Athenian general Diopeithes was sent out with a force of Athenian settlers to the Chersonese in or before 343/2: see 8.2n.

[18]See also 8.64. These places in Thrace were captured by Philip in 346.

[19]Fort Serrium (Serriou Teichos) and the Sacred Mountain (Hieron Oros) were sites in Thrace on the north shore of the Sea of Marmara: see 7.37n. They are also mentioned by Aeschines (3.82), who mocks their insignificance. These activities also date to 346.

[20]Demosthenes here refers to Philip sending troops to aid his ally Cardia, a city in the north of the Chersonese, against the Athenian settlers in

have recognized as yours,[21] and admits that he is providing help and sends a letter to this effect,[22] what is he doing? [17] He says that he is not at war. But I so completely disagree that, by these actions, he is keeping the peace with you, that I make this assertion: by seizing Megara for himself and establishing a tyranny in Euboea and now entering Thrace and intriguing in the Peloponnese and doing all that he is doing by force, he is in breach of the peace and is at war with you[23]—unless you will claim that even those who have set up siege engines are keeping the peace, until they bring them up to the city walls! But you will not say this, since anyone whose actions and preparations are aimed at seizing me is at war with me, even if he has not yet started throwing missiles or shooting at me. [18] What dangers would you face, if war should break out? The loss of the Hellespont, your enemy gaining control of Megara and Euboea, the Peloponnesians going over to his side.[24] Am I then supposed to say that the man who has set up this engine against our city is at peace with you? [19] Absolutely not! I define him as having been at war with us from the day he destroyed Phocis.[25] And I say that if you are sensible, you will de-

---

the south of the peninsula. The Athenians claimed ownership of the entire Chersonese. See the Introduction to Dem. 8.

[21] When this happened is unknown: perhaps in the negotiation of a Common Peace in 366/5 (see Cawkwell 1961b: 80–82). Cf. 7.29n for the parallel assertion that the Greeks and the King had at some point recognized Athens' claim to Amphipolis. Demosthenes clearly wishes the Athenians to suppose that the Persians and other Greeks had expressly recognized Athens' claim to the Chersonese, but this may not have been the case.

[22] Philip admits sending help to Cardia in his later letter to the Athenians, preserved as Dem. 12 (12.11), but he claims that he was perfectly entitled to do so, since Cardia was his ally.

[23] Philip intervened in the affairs of Megara in 343: see 8.18n. Events on the island of Euboea are narrated in 57–62 below. On Philip's Thracian campaign of 342–340, see 8.44–45; Diodorus 16.71–72; Hammond and Griffith 1979: 554–566. On his intriguing in the Peloponnese, see 6.9 and 15 (Argos and Messene) and 27 below (Elis).

[24] The Hellespont was a vital stage of the grain route from the Black Sea to Athens; Megara and Euboea were Athens' immediate neighbors to the west and east respectively.

[25] In 346.

fend yourselves; but if you give him free rein, you will not be able to do even this when you wish to. I see the situation so differently than your other advisors, men of Athens, that at this point I think you shouldn't be deliberating about even the Chersonese or Byzantium;[26] [20] instead, you should be assisting their inhabitants and on your guard to ensure that they do not suffer any harm, and should be taking counsel on behalf of all the Greeks, since they are in such great danger. I wish to tell you why the situation alarms me, in order that, if my assessment is correct, you may share it and take precautions for yourselves at least, even if you refuse to do so for the other Greeks. But if you think that I am talking nonsense and have been struck senseless, you should conclude that I am not in my right mind and pay no attention to me, either now or in the future.

[21] That Philip has grown great from small and humble beginnings, and that the Greeks are distrustful and quarrelsome towards each other, and that it was much more surprising that he should have become so great from his previous condition than that now, when he has taken so many places already, he should be bringing the rest under his control as well, and all such topics that I could discuss, I shall leave to one side. [22] But I see that everyone, starting with you, has conceded to him the one thing that has been the cause of every single previous Greek war. What is this? It is the right to do what he wants, and to plunder and rob each of the Greeks in turn, and to attack and enslave their cities. [23] And yet you were the leaders of Greece for seventy-three years,[27] and the Spartans were leaders for twenty-nine.[28] The The-

---

[26]Demosthenes' point is that these two places are already directly threatened by Philip and that there is no point in the Athenians discussing whether they are in danger.

[27]Demosthenes appears to be counting inclusively from 476 to 404, the year of Athens' defeat by Sparta in the Peloponnesian War. The Delian League, the anti-Persian alliance led by Athens, was in fact founded in winter 478/7.

[28]Apparently counting from the end of the Peloponnesian War in 404 (see the previous note) to Sparta's defeat by Athens in the sea battle of Naxos in 376. Sparta's domination of Greece is more generally reckoned to have ended with its defeat by Thebes at the battle of Leuctra in 371.

bans also became quite powerful in recent times, after the battle at Leuctra.[29] Nevertheless, men of Athens, the Greeks have never yet conceded to you or the Thebans or the Spartans the right to do whatever you wish—far from it! [24] But first, since you—or rather the Athenians of the time—were thought to be treating some people unfairly, everyone, even those who had no complaint to make of them, thought that they had to go to war with them in support of those who had been wronged.[30] Again, after the Spartans had become the masters and attained the same supremacy as yours, when they tried to encroach and were disturbing the status quo beyond what was reasonable everyone declared war on them, even those who had no complaint against them.[31] [25] What need is there to speak of the others? Both we and the Spartans, although at first we had virtually no wrongs to complain of at each other's hands, nevertheless felt driven to go to war because of the injustice that we saw others suffering.[32] And yet all the wrongs that were done by the Spartans in those thirty years, and by our

---

[29]The Theban "hegemony" of Greece is generally held to have lasted from the battle of Leuctra in 371 (see the previous note) to the indecisive battle of Mantinea in 362, at which the leading Theban general Epaminondas was killed.

[30]Demosthenes sees the history of Greece in the fifth and early fourth centuries through distinctly rose-tinted glasses. Although in starting the Peloponnesian war in 431 Sparta claimed to be liberating the subject cities of Athens' empire (Thuc. 2.8.4), the war was fundamentally caused by the rising alarm felt by Sparta and its allies at the growth of Athenian power, as Thucydides makes clear (most explicitly at 1.23.6), and was waged exclusively by the cities of Sparta's Peloponnesian League.

[31]Demosthenes refers to the Corinthian War of 395–386, fought by an anti-Spartan alliance consisting of Athens, Thebes, Corinth, and Argos. All four cities in fact had their own complaints against Sparta: Athens had been stripped of its empire by Sparta and had been forced to accept an oligarchy and the destruction of its walls; Argos was an inveterate enemy of Sparta; Thebes thought that its contribution to the defeat of Athens was insufficiently appreciated by Sparta and feared the growth of Spartan power; Corinth, whose motivation is not entirely clear, was perhaps concerned by Spartan involvement in Sicily (see Hornblower 2002: 215–217).

[32]This is the opposite of the truth. See previous notes.

ancestors in seventy, are fewer, men of Athens, than the wrongs that Philip has done to Greece in the fewer than thirteen years since he emerged from obscurity.[33] Or rather, they are scarcely a fraction of them. [26] *And this is easily shown from a brief account.*[34] I say nothing about Olynthus and Methone and Apollonia and the thirty-two cities on the coast of Thrace, all of which he destroyed with such cruelty that it would be hard for a visitor to tell whether they had ever been inhabited.[35] I also pass over in silence the destruction of the Phocian nation, which was so populous.[36] But what of Thessaly? Did he not remove their constitutions and cities and establish tetrarchies, so that they might be slaves not only by city but also by region?[37] [27] Are not tyrants now in control of the cities of Euboea, an island that is close to both Thebes and Athens?[38] Does he not expressly write in his letters: "I am at peace with those who wish to give heed to me"? Nor does he fail to put what he has written into effect. For he has set out against the Hellespont,[39] previously he marched against Am-

---

[33]Philip became king in 359. Thirteen years (counting inclusively) before the date of this speech is 353, the year in which he first campaigned in Thessaly against the Phocians (Diodorus 16.35.1–2). Demosthenes presumably thought that this campaign marked Philip's entry onto the Greek stage, although he had been at war with Athens since 357.

[34]This and other italicized passages are omitted in some manuscripts; see the Speech Introduction.

[35]Methone was captured by Philip in 354 (see 1.9n). Apollonia, a city in the Chalcidic peninsula, was sacked in 349 or 348; in the same campaign Olynthus and the thirty-two cities of the Chalcidic League were razed to the ground.

[36]In 346; see 19n. The Phocians were resettled in villages, and some went into exile.

[37]In 344 Philip reinstated, in name at least, an earlier regional system of political organization, with four magistrates called tetrarchs administering the four regions of Thessaly. One of the tetrarchs, Thrasydaeus, is described by Theopompus as a tyrant (*FGH* 115 fragment 209), but an inscription gives him the official title "tetrarch of the Thessalians" (*SIG*[3] 274.VIII).

[38]On events in Euboea in the late 340s, see 57–62 below.

[39]Philip's campaign in eastern Thrace brought him within striking distance of the Hellespont, for the strategic significance of which see 18n.

bracia,[40] he possesses a city as great as Elis in the Peloponnese,[41] and he has recently plotted against Megara.[42] Neither Greece nor the rest of the world can contain the man's greed. [28] We Greeks all see and hear these things happening, but we do not send ambassadors about them to each other and get angry; we are in such poor condition and are so entrenched in our separate cities that right up to the present day, we have been unable to take any advantageous or necessary step, or to unite, or to form an association for mutual aid and friendship. [29] We overlook his growing power, and though each of us recognizes that Philip profits from the opportunities that others squander, or so it seems to me, none of us deliberates or acts to save Greece. Yet we all know that, like the periodic return or the sudden onset of a fever or some other evil, he visits even those who seem to have kept far away from him. [30] You also know that all the wrongs that the Greeks suffered at the hands of the Spartans or of ourselves were injustices committed by genuine Greeks at least, and one should treat this in the same way as if a legitimate son, after coming into a great fortune, manages it badly and unjustly: such a person deserves blame and censure for his actions, but it cannot be denied that despite his behavior, he is still a kinsman and heir. [31] But if a slave or a changeling[43] wasted and spoiled what did not belong to him, by Heracles, how much more terrible and deserving of anger would everyone have said this was. And yet they do not take this

---

[40]See 72n below.

[41]Elis was a city of the northwestern Peloponnese. In 343 its democratic constitution was overthrown and an oligarchy set up. Demosthenes claims that Philip was involved in this coup: see 10.10; Dem. 19.260, 294; Pausanias 4.28.4, 5.4.9.

[42]In a speech delivered in 343 (Dem. 19), Demosthenes refers to recent unrest in Athens' western neighbor Megara: 19.204, 294–295, 326, 334. Its leaders were two pro-Macedonians, Ptoeodorus and Perillas, of whom the latter is said to have brought soldiers from Philip (19.295). Demosthenes' remarks indicate that Megara was threatened (19.204) and nearly came under foreign control (19.334).

[43]Demosthenes refers to a boy who has been substituted as a baby for a legitimate son.

attitude towards Philip and his actions—he who is not only not Greek and in no way related to the Greeks, nor even a foreigner from a land to which it is honorable to say that one belongs, but a wretched Macedonian, from a land from which in the past you could not even have bought a decent slave.[44]

[32] How is this not the height of insolence? In addition to his destruction of the cities, does he not administer the Pythian festival, the shared competition of the Greeks, and, if he himself is absent, does he not send his slaves to preside at the games?[45] *Is he not master of Thermopylae and the entranceways into Greece, and does he not occupy these places with garrisons and mercenaries?*[46] *Does he not have the right of pre-audience at the oracle, thrusting us aside together with the Thessalians and the Dorians and the other Amphictyons—a right that not even every Greek enjoys?*[47] [33] Does he not

---

[44]The ethnic identity of the Macedonians has been disputed since antiquity. Greek writers of the classical period generally draw a distinction between the Macedonian kings and people. Herodotus records a story that the royal family came originally from Argos in Greece (8.137.1; see also Thuc. 2.99), and the contemporary rhetorician Isocrates, in a speech that seeks to flatter Philip, describes him as a Greek ruling over barbarians (5.107–108). This tradition of a separate origin for the ruling family is, however, implausible. Greek sources also mention a Macedonian language that was not comprehensible to Greeks (Plut. *Alexander* 51.6). Personal names within the Macedonian elite are often obviously Greek (e.g., Philip, Alexander), although it is hard to know how far this is the result of their deliberate adoption of aspects of Greek culture (see *OCD*³ s.v. Hellenism, Hellenization). On Greek attitudes towards the Macedonians, see Badian 1982.

[45]The Pythian Festival was celebrated at Delphi every four years in honor of the god Apollo. It was a Panhellenic festival (i.e., one that was open to all Greeks) and included athletic, musical and poetic competitions. Demosthenes affects to view all the subjects of Philip, including the undoubtedly high-ranking deputy who presided over the festival in 342 when the king was absent on campaign in Thrace, as his "slaves"; cf. 43 on Arthmius of Zeleia as a "slave" of the King of Persia.

[46]Philip gained control of the strategically vital pass of Thermopylae, which controls passage between northern and central Greece, in 346.

[47]Philip was granted the privilege of being allowed to consult the Delphic oracle before others. The Delphic Amphictyony comprised twelve "peo-

write to the Thessalians telling them what form of political organization to have?[48] Is he not sending out mercenaries—some to
Porthmus to expel the Eretrian people, others to Oreus to establish Philistides as tyrant?[49] But even though they see these things,
the Greeks put up with them. They seem to me to watch them
happening in the same way as one might watch a hailstorm, each
praying that it does not strike him, but none trying to avoid it.
[34] No one retaliates for his insults towards Greece, or even for
the wrongs that he does to each individually. The worst is already
here. Has he not advanced against Corinthian Ambracia and Leucas?[50] Has he not sworn to hand over Achaean Naupactus to the
Aetolians?[51] Has he not deprived the Thebans of Echinus?[52] Is he
not now marching against his allies the Byzantines?[53] [35] As for
our own possessions—leaving aside those of others—does he not
hold Cardia, the greatest city of the Chersonese?[54] This is how
we are treated, yet we all delay, and are weak, and cast suspicious

---

ples," each of which sent two representatives to the Amphictyonic council.
The Thessalians and the Dorians each formed one "people," while Athens
contributed one of the two representatives from the Ionian "people." Members of the Amphictyony were permitted to consult the oracle before other
Greeks. See Dem. 5 on Philip's control of Delphi.

[48]See 26n above.

[49]On Macedonian intervention in the Euboean cities of Eretria and
Oreus, see 57–62 below.

[50]On Ambracia in western Greece, see 72n below. The island of Leucas
off the western coast of Greece was an ally of Athens, against Philip, in 338:
see Dem. 18.237.

[51]Naupactus, on the northern coast of the Gulf of Corinth, had been acquired by the Achaeans of the Peloponnese by 367 (Diodorus 15.75.2). The
Aetolians, who bordered Naupactus to the north, had longstanding designs
on the city (see Xen. *Hellenica* 4.6.14).

[52]Echinus was a small city in Malis in central Greece. Nothing further
is known of its history in this period.

[53]The Greek does not specify whose ally Byzantium was, and it is possible that it should be translated "their [i.e., the Thebans'] ally." In a later
speech, however, Demosthenes identifies the Byzantines as allies of Philip
(Dem. 18.87).

[54]On Cardia, see 16n above and in general Dem. 8.

glances at our neighbors, distrusting each other rather than the man who is wronging us all. But when he treats us collectively with such brutality, what do you suppose he will do when he becomes master of each of us separately?

[36] What is the explanation for this state of affairs? It is not without reason or just cause that the Greeks were so enthusiastic for liberty in the past, but for slavery now. There was something then, there really was, men of Athens, in the spirit of the people, which is now absent, which overcame the wealth of Persia and led Greece to freedom, and was undefeated in battle on sea and land—but now it has been lost, ruining everything and turning Greece upside down. [37] What was this thing? It was the fact that everyone hated any person who took money from those who were seeking to dominate or destroy Greece: it was most dreadful to be convicted of taking bribes, and such a man was punished with the severest penalty. [38] Neither the crucial opportunity in each situation—an opportunity that fortune often grants even to the careless against the attentive—nor the mutual concord that existed, nor the distrust of tyrants and barbarians, nor in brief any such thing could be bought from the politicians and generals. [39] But now all these things are exported as if from the marketplace, and in exchange we import things that cause Greece's sickness and ruin. What are these? Envy of anyone who has taken a bribe; laughter, if he admits it; *pity, for those who are convicted*; hatred of anyone who rebukes this conduct; and everything else relating to the taking of bribes. [40] Now we possess triremes and men and money and abundant military equipment, and whatever else serves to demonstrate the strength of a city, in far greater quantities than we did then, but these are rendered useless, ineffectual, and unprofitable by those who are selling us out.

[41] That this is the case at present you see for yourselves, I presume, and have no need of me as a further witness. Yet in previous times the opposite was the case, as I shall show not in my own words but from a document of your ancestors that they inscribed on a bronze pillar and deposited on the Acropolis—*not because it would be useful to them, since even without it they had a strong sense of duty, but to leave you reminders and examples of how seriously such offenses should be treated.* [42] *What then does the document*

say? It reads: "Arthmius the son of Pythonax of Zeleia is to be an outlaw and enemy of the Athenian people and its allies, himself and his descendants." After that is written the explanation: "because he brought the gold from the Medes into the Peloponnese." This is the document.[55] [43] Consider, by the gods, what was the purpose and resolve of the Athenians of that time in taking this action. They wrote that a man of Zeleia, Arthmius, a slave of the King (for Zeleia is in Asia), because in the service of his master he had brought money to the Peloponnese—not to Athens—should be declared their and their allies' enemy, himself and his descendants, and that they should be outlaws. [44] And this is not the form of outlawry that people commonly speak of—for what would it matter to a Zeleian to be forbidden to participate in Athenian public life?[56] *But that is not what its means*; rather, it is written in the laws of homicide, with regard to cases where prosecutions for homicide may not be brought, *but one may kill without pollution*: "and let the outlaw be killed." This law means that anyone who has killed such a man shall be free from pollution.[57] [45] These men thus thought it their duty to ensure the safety of all of Greece. For they would not have been concerned if someone

---

[55]The decree outlawing Arthmius of Zeleia, a city in northwestern Asia Minor, is referred to in several texts of this period (Dem. 19.271; Aes. 3.258; Din. 2.24–25). Meiggs (1972: 508–512) discusses the decree in detail, and suggests that it dates to the early 460s, and may have been proposed by the leading politician and general Cimon (on whom see 13.29n). The Greeks commonly conflated the Persians and the Medes (i.e., inhabitants of Media, in northern Iran), the two peoples who together formed the ruling class of the Persian Empire.

[56]In the sixth and early fifth centuries the Greek word *atimos* meant "outlaw" in Athenian law, but by the fourth century it came to have the meaning of "disfranchised." Such disfranchisement was imposed on citizens as a legal penalty for various offenses and involved the loss of some of the rights of a citizen to participate in the public life of the city. See MacDowell 1978: 73–75.

[57]On Athenian homicide law, see MacDowell 1978: 109–122. Pollution (*miasma*) was thought by some to spread from a killer to the community at large unless he was brought to justice, but a justifiable homicide did not give rise to it.

was bribing and corrupting other people in the Peloponnese, unless they held this opinion; they sought to punish and take vengeance on those whom they detected, and thus they posted their names on a pillar. As a result, it is not surprising that the Greeks inspired fear in the foreigner, rather than the other way round. But this is not the case now, since you do not have the same attitude either towards such offenses or towards others. What then is your attitude? [46] *You know for yourselves—what need is there to criticize you over every detail? And all the other Greeks have a similar attitude and are no better than you. As a result, I assert that the present situation requires great energy and good counsel. What is my advice?* Do you ask me to speak? And do you promise not to be angry with me?[58]

[47] There is a foolish argument put about by those who wish to reassure the city, which goes as follows: "Philip is not yet as strong as the Spartans once were, when they ruled the sea and all the land, and had the Persian King as their ally, and were irresistible.[59] Nevertheless our city resisted them and was not swept away." But in my opinion, although virtually all aspects of life have advanced considerably, and everything nowadays is quite different from how it was in the past, nothing has changed or progressed as much as the conduct of war. [48] First, I am told that at that time both the Spartans and everyone else would invade and ravage their enemies' land for four or five months, during the summer, with hoplites and citizen armies, and then withdraw back home—so old fashioned were they, or rather so like true citizens, that they did not buy anything from anybody, but war was fought according to custom and in the open. [49] Now, however, I dare say you see how most places are destroyed by traitors and how nothing results from the drawing up of armies in pitched

---

[58]At this point the text notes that a document was read, but this is probably a mistake. Some description of Athenian behavior may have dropped out.

[59]Demosthenes refers either to the immediate aftermath of the Peloponnesian War at the end of the fifth century or to the years following the King's Peace of 386. In both periods Sparta enjoyed Persian support and dominated Greece.

battle; and you hear how Philip goes wherever he wishes not by leading a phalanx of hoplites but by providing himself with light infantry, cavalry, archers, mercenaries, and other similar troops.[60] [50] In addition to these advantages, he attacks those who are sick from internal dissension, and no one is willing to go out to defend their territory on account of their mutual distrust, and so he sets up his siege engines and lays siege to them—to say nothing of the fact that he makes no distinction between summer and winter and that there is no off season, when he leaves off fighting. [51] In full knowledge of these factors and taking due account of them, we must all prevent war from approaching our land, and must avoid being thrown to the ground through contemplation of the simplicity of our previous war against the Spartans. Instead, we must defend ourselves from as great a distance as possible, by our actions and by our preparations, and be on watch in case he stirs from his home, and must avoid grappling with him in a decisive engagement. [52] We have many natural advantages, men of Athens, for waging war—so long as we are willing to do our duty: the nature of his territory, much of which can be ravaged and damaged, and a host of others, but he is better suited than we are to the fighting of battles.[61]

[53] We must not only acknowledge this, and resist him through acts of war, but we must also make it our policy and be resolved to detest those who speak to you on his behalf, keeping in mind that it is not possible to defeat our city's enemies until

---

[60]The contrast between Philip's army and Greek armies of the fifth century is exaggerated. The Macedonian army contained numerous infantry who fought in a phalanx formation similar to that of Greek hoplites, although they differed in being less well protected and in being armed with a long pike (*sarissa*) rather than the shorter hoplite spear. Moreover, Greek armies of the fifth century certainly included both light infantry and cavalry. This passage is discussed by van Wees (2004: 115–117), who concludes that "Demosthenes was peddling a nostalgic myth" (115). On the Macedonian army, see Hammond and Griffith 1979: 405–449.

[61]In an earlier speech (14.9–10), Demosthenes makes precisely the opposite point about the Persians: they are superior to the Athenians in waging war but inferior in battle.

you punish those in the city itself who are their servants. [54] But this, by Zeus and the other gods, is something that you will be unable to do, since you have reached such a state of foolishness or madness or I do not know what to call it—I have often come to fear that some demon is driving our affairs—that out of a spirit of quarrelsomeness or envy, or for a joke, or for any other reason that might occur to you, you urge hired men to speak, some of whom would not even deny that they are hired, and you laugh if anyone attacks them. [55] And this is not the really terrible thing, terrible though it is. For you have also permitted these men to participate in public life with more security than you give to those who speak in your interest. But observe how many disasters arise from a willingness to listen to such men. I shall tell you about events that will be familiar to you all.

[56] Of those who took part in public life at Olynthus, some supported Philip and served him in all things, whereas others desired what was best for their city and acted to prevent the enslavement of their fellow-citizens. Which of these destroyed their native land? Which of them betrayed the cavalry, leading to the destruction of Olynthus?[62] It was the men who supported Philip, who, while the city was still in existence, slandered and brought malicious prosecutions against those who were offering the best advice, as a result of which the Olynthian people were persuaded to exile Apollonides.[63]

[57] Nor is it the case that this habit of mind caused all sorts of evils only for these people and had no effect anywhere else. On the contrary, in Eretria, after Plutarchus and his mercenaries had been expelled, and the people held both the city and Porthmus, some of them wished to side with you and others with Philip.[64] The wretched and unfortunate Eretrians listened to the latter for the most part, or rather entirely, and were finally persuaded

---

[62]The fall of Olynthus is narrated at Diodorus 16.52.2–3. See the Introduction to Dem. 1–3.

[63]Apollonides was the leader of the pro-Athenian party at Olynthus. After his exile, probably in 351, he fled to Athens, where he received a (short-lived) grant of Athenian citizenship: see Dem. 59.91; Osborne 1983: T61.

[64]Plutarchus was expelled by the Athenians in 348: see 5.5n.

to exile those who were speaking in their interests. [58] For in fact their ally Philip, after sending Hipponicus with a thousand mercenaries, demolished the walls of Porthmus and set up three men as tyrants: Hipparchus, Automedon and Clitarchus.[65] Since then he has twice already exiled from the territory of Eretria people who wanted to be saved, *first by sending the mercenaries under Eurylochus, and then by sending those under Parmenion.*[66]

[59] What need is there to speak at length? At Oreus Philistides, Menippus, Socrates, Thoas, and Agapaeus acted for Philip;[67] these men now possess the city, as everyone knew they would, but a man named Euphraeus, who once lived here among us, acted to try to ensure that they would be free and slaves to nobody.[68] [60] This man—and much could be said about the other ways in which he was insulted and treated with contempt by the people—in the year before the city fell charged[69] Philistides and his supporters with treason, since he saw what they were up to. But many men banded together, with Philip as paymaster and con-

---

[65]Porthmus was the harbor of Eretria. Hipponicus' mission probably took place in 343, since in a speech of that year Demosthenes claims (19.204) that Philip has troops in Euboea (see Hammond and Griffith 1979: 502–503). A number of slingshots bearing the name Hipponicus that were found in the excavations of Olynthus suggest that he was involved in the siege of the city in 348.

[66]These two Macedonian interventions occurred in 342. Eurylochus and Parmenion were prominent Macedonians: both men served (with Antipater) as ambassadors to Athens in 346, and Parmenion was Philip's most trusted general and a leading figure in the reign of his son Alexander. See Heckel 2005, s.v. Eurylochus [1] and Parmenion.

[67]Oreus was a city in northern Euboea. This passage is the principal account of Macedonian intervention there. See also 8.18, 59; 10.9, 61. On the volatile history of Euboea in this period, the details of which are much debated, see Brunt 1969; Sealey 1993: 259–264.

[68]Euphraeus of Oreus had been a pupil of the philosopher Plato and spent some time at the court of Philip's predecessor Perdiccas III in the second half of the 360s.

[69]Demosthenes refers to the legal procedure of *endeixis*, literally the "pointing out" of an alleged wrongdoer to the magistrates so that they can arrest him.

troller, and took Euphraeus off to prison, claiming that he was throwing the city into disorder. [61] When they saw this, the people of Oreus, instead of helping the one and cudgeling the others to death,[70] did not get angry with them, but said that Euphraeus deserved his suffering, and were glad about it. Later one party began to act with perfect freedom to ensure that the city would be seized, and started to arrange the deed; and any member of the majority who noticed what was happening kept silent and was intimidated, recalling what kinds of things Euphraeus had suffered. They were in such a wretched condition that no one dared speak out, as such an evil drew near, until their enemies had equipped themselves and approached the city walls. At that point some resisted, but others turned traitor. [62] After the city was captured in this shameful and evil way, the one group has been ruling it as tyrants, after exiling some and killing others of the men who at that time had been prepared to protect them and to do all manner of harm to Euphraeus, while the admirable Euphraeus killed himself, thereby demonstrating that he had resisted Philip, acting with justice and honesty, on behalf of his fellow-citizens.

[63] Perhaps you are wondering what possible reason induced the people of Olynthus and Eretria and Oreus to pay more attention to those who were speaking in Philip's interest than to those who were speaking in their own. This is the case with you too: those who advocate the best policy are not always able to win your favor, even if they want to, since they are obliged to examine affairs of state and how to provide security; whereas the others are collaborating with Philip through the very things by which they win your favor. [64] The one group urged them to raise taxes, others said there was no need; one group told them to wage war and be on their guard, others told them to keep the peace—until they were ensnared. I think that other matters all went the same way, so I will not mention every instance. One group said what would make themselves popular; the other said what would lead to safety. But many things, including the last, were approved by the majority not so much as a favor or out of ig-

---

[70]On this brutal form of capital punishment, see 8.61n.

norance but out of resignation, since they believed that they were being utterly defeated. [65] This, by Zeus and Apollo, is just what I fear may happen to you, if when you consider the matter, you conclude that there is nothing left for you to do. I pray, men of Athens, that our affairs never reach that state! But in any event it is better to die ten thousand times than to do anything out of flattery of Philip, *or to abandon any of those who speak in your interest.*[71] It is a fine return that the majority at Oreus have received, for entrusting themselves to the friends of Philip and exiling Euphraeus! [66] Equally fine is the return for the people of Eretria, who drove away your ambassadors and entrusted themselves to Clitarchus: now they are slaves, subject to whippings and killings! How nobly did Philip spare the Olynthians who elected Lasthenes cavalry commander and exiled Apollonides![72] [67] It was folly and wickedness to cherish such hopes, as it is for those who follow bad advice and are utterly unwilling to do their duty, but pay attention to those who speak in their enemies' interests, to imagine that the city they inhabit is so great that it cannot suffer any disaster at all. [68] This at any rate is shameful, to say after the event: "Who would have thought that such things could happen? We should have done this thing or that, and not the other." The Olynthians could tell you many things now: if they had known them at the time, they would not have been destroyed. There are many things too that the people of Oreus could tell you, and the Phocians, and the people of every city that has been destroyed. [69] But what good is this to them now? While the boat can still be saved, whether it is a large or a small one, that is the time for the sailor and the steersman and everyone on board to be energetic, and to be on their guard to prevent anyone, wittingly or unwittingly, from capsizing it. Once the sea overwhelms it, their effort is useless. [70] In the same way, what are we to do, men of Athens, while we are still safe and have a very

---

[71]The italicized words, which appear in the longer version of the speech (see the Speech Introduction), are deleted by Dilts 2002 in his edition as a later intrusion.

[72]On Lasthenes, see also 8.40; on Apollonides, see 56n above.

great city, with many assets and an excellent reputation? Perhaps someone who has long been sitting here would like to ask that question. By Zeus, I will tell you, and I shall propose a resolution on which you will be able to vote, if you so desire. First, I say, we must defend ourselves and make our preparations in person, with triremes and money and troops. Even if everyone else submits to be enslaved, we at least must fight for liberty! [71] After making all these preparations in person and in the open, let us then call upon the others, and send out ambassadors to instruct people in every direction—*to the Peloponnese, to Rhodes, to Chios, and to the King, since it is in his interest not to allow this man to overturn everything*[73]—so that if you succeed in persuading them you will have people to share both the risks and the costs, if you need anything; and even if you do not succeed, you may at any rate delay his plans. [72] Since this war is against a man rather than a strong and united city, even this initiative is useful, as were those recent embassies around the Peloponnese[74] and the accusations that I and that excellent man Polyeuctus[75] and Hegesippus[76] and the other ambassadors went around making, as a result of which we forced Philip to stop and prevented him from attacking Ambracia

---

[73]On Athenian embassies to the Peloponnese, see 72n below; for diplomatic contact with the Persian King, see 10.31–34. It is odd that Demosthenes should advocate sending embassies to Chios and Rhodes if, as is generally believed, they were both still ruled by Carian-backed oligarchies (see Dem. 15 on Rhodes, 15.19 on Chios).

[74]The ancient commentary on Aes. 3.83 refers to Athenian embassies to the Peloponnese in 343/2 that resulted in the securing of several alliances. For an earlier Athenian embassy to Messenia and Argos in the Peloponnese, see 6.19–26.

[75]Polyeuctus was an anti-Macedonian Athenian politician.

[76]On Hegesippus, see the Introduction to Dem. 7. Some manuscripts of the speech add after Hegesippus the names Clitomachus and Lycurgus. The former is otherwise unknown, but Lycurgus was an important politician who dominated Athenian politics during the period after the battle of Chaeronea in 338. Pseudo-Plut., *Lives of the Ten Orators* 841e, also claims that Lycurgus went on an embassy to the Peloponnese with Demosthenes and Polyeuctus.

or invading the Peloponnese.[77] [73] I do not urge you to summon others, when you are unwilling to take any necessary steps yourselves, since it would be foolish to claim to care for other people's affairs when you neglect your own; or to overlook your present predicament and worry about what others may do in the future. That is not what I urge. But I do say that you should send funds to those who are in the Chersonese[78] and should do whatever else they ask, and make your own preparations, and summon, gather, inform, and warn the other Greeks: this is the duty of a city with as great a reputation as ours. [74] But if you think that the Chalcideans will rescue Greece, or the Megarians, while you run away from the situation, you are mistaken.[79] Each of these cities will be content if they are saved themselves. It is up to you to act: your ancestors won this prize, having faced many great dangers in doing so, and bequeathed it to you. [75] But if every one of you sits around following his own desires and trying to avoid having to do anything himself, first he will never find anyone who will take action, and then I fear that we may be forced to take every kind of undesirable measure, all at the same time.

[76] This then is my speech; these are my proposals. If they are put into effect, I believe that even now our fortunes may be restored. If anyone has anything better to say, let him speak and offer his advice. But whatever you decide—all you gods!—may it be to our advantage!

---

[77]In early 342 Philip threatened the Corinthian colony of Ambracia in northwestern Greece: see 34, 7.32, 10.10. In response Athens sent troops to nearby Acarnania: see Dem. 48.24–26, which dates this expedition to 343/2.

[78]On the Athenian force in the Chersonese, see Dem. 8.

[79]Chalcis on the island of Euboea and Megara were neighbors of Athens to the east and west respectively. Both were very much smaller cites than Athens.

10. FOURTH PHILIPPIC

INTRODUCTION

The authenticity of the *Fourth Philippic* has in the past been denied, but it is now generally accepted as a genuine speech of Demosthenes. Scholars in antiquity expressed no doubts on this score: Dionysius of Halicarnassus treats it as genuine,[1] and Libanius makes no mention of its authorship. Moreover, the Hellenistic scholar Didymus included it in his commentary on Demosthenes' deliberative speeches, without any discussion of its authorship, which strongly suggests that he and his contemporaries did not regard it as a matter of controversy.[2]

The speech's authenticity came to be doubted in the nineteenth century, before the discovery of Didymus' commentary, on a number of grounds. First, two long passages of it are also to be found with minor differences in Dem. 8 (10.11–27 ≈ 8.38–51 and 10.55–70 ≈ 8.52–67). Since the latter speech is universally accepted as genuine, and since it was thought unlikely that Demosthenes would have published or even delivered the same material twice, it was concluded that Dem. 10 is probably a later pastiche. As a result of the discovery of Didymus' commentary, however, it has generally been accepted that Dem. 10 is by Demosthenes, and the overlap with Dem. 8 must therefore be explained differently (see below).[3]

---

[1] *First Letter to Ammaeus* 10.

[2] On Didymus, see Harding 2006.

[3] The speech's authenticity is defended by Hajdú 2002. See too Mac-Dowell 2009: 354–355.

The second argument against the speech's authenticity is that Demosthenes' attitude in it to the theoric fund, which earlier had been very critical (see 3.10–11, 19), is here much milder (36). But this is only a problem if we believe that Demosthenes cannot have changed his mind over the course of almost a decade or altered his policies to respond to changing circumstances.[4] This seems more likely than that a forger should have attributed to Demosthenes a statement that went against his previous policy on this issue.

The third argument relates to the attack on the politician Aristomedes at 70–74. This passage is unique in Demosthenes' deliberative speeches, where his regular practice is to refer to his rivals and opponents anonymously. Since Plutarch claims that the *Philippics* contain no personal abuse (*Moralia* 810d), its presence here has been taken as an indication that he regarded the speech as spurious. This argument is weak, since Plutarch may easily have forgotten about this passage and made a remark that is otherwise true.

It remains to consider the relationship of this speech to Dem. 8 (see above). The fullest discussion of this issue is by Daitz (1957), who argues that the common passages fit better in, and were written for, Dem. 10 (which is a later speech than Dem. 8). To explain this paradox, he proposes that Demosthenes delivered Dem. 10 to the Assembly but did not circulate it. He then incorporated certain passages into the text of an earlier speech on the Chersonese, which he published as Dem. 8. This solution cannot be disproved, but simpler (and in my view more plausible) ones can be proposed. First, it is not impossible that both speeches were delivered as they stand and that the repetition was not regarded as troubling. Another possibility is that Dem. 8 was written but (for whatever reason) not delivered, and so the common material was heard for the first time when Demosthenes delivered Dem. 10. In either case, if these passages do indeed fit better in Dem. 10, it does not follow that they must have been written for it: they could have been

---

[4]Both the increase in Athens' revenues and the prospect of support from Persia were significant changes. It has also been argued that Demosthenes and his supporters had by now gotten control of the theoric commission: see Cawkwell 1963b: 135–136.

used first in Dem. 8, and then reused—and better integrated—in Dem. 10.[5]

The speech was delivered in 341, although scholars in antiquity disagreed about whether to place it in the Athenian archon year 342/1 or 341/0.[6] Dionysius of Halicarnassus dates it to 341/0.[7] In his commentary Didymus gives the same date (col. 1.30) but reports that other scholars place it a year earlier (col. 2.2–3). It is probably the last of the triad Dem. 8, 9, and 10, as the traditional order suggests. Certainly, comparison of the parallel passages 8.44 (where it is reported that Philip is now taking various obscure places in Thrace) and 10.15 (where he is said now to possess them) suggests that it is later than Dem. 8. The speech twice refers to Philip's gaining control of the Euboean city of Oreus (9, 61), without noting its recapture by Athens in the last month of 342/1.[8] This has been taken to indicate that the speech must have been delivered before that event, that is, in 342/1. It is certainly possible that Dionysius dated the speech a year too late, but these passages do not in my view prove it, since Demosthenes' concern in them is with the fact and manner of Philip's seizure of Oreus, not its current status.[9]

The general situation that the speech addresses is similar to that of the slightly earlier speeches Dem. 8 and 9: Philip is still on campaign in eastern Thrace (15–17), and both Byzantium and the Hellespont are in danger. One significant new element is the emergence of the Persian King as a potential ally for Athens (31–34). In his earlier deliberative speeches, Demosthenes regarded Persia as a threat (Dem. 14 and 15), but here he relates two new,

---

[5] Hajdú 2002 discusses the matter in detail, and finds it hard to reach a firm conclusion. See too MacDowell 2009: 354–355.

[6] If the speech was delivered around the end of the year, i.e., midsummer, it was probably very difficult for ancient scholars to determine to which year it should be assigned.

[7] *First Letter to Ammaeus* 10.

[8] The recapture of Oreus is referred to and dated by Philochorus *FGH* 328 fragment 159, cited by Didymus, col. 1.13–18.

[9] Thus, Cawkwell (1963b: 134–135), who also regards the evidence insufficient to choose between these two years.

and welcome, developments. The first is that the King's trusted "benefactors" are now at war with Philip (31); the second is the arrest by the Persians of an agent of Philip who is privy to Philip's plans against the Persian King (32). Demosthenes is referring here to Persian military support to the cities of Perinthus and Byzantium and to the seizure of Hermias, the dynast of Atarneus in western Asia Minor (see notes ad loc.). Evidently the Persians had come to regard Philip's campaign in Thrace as a threat to their interests and security.[10] Demosthenes, seeing this as a heaven-sent opportunity to join forces with the powerful Persian Empire against Philip, urges the Athenians to put aside their existing hostility to the King and send an embassy to him (33–34).

Much of the speech recycles, often with little alteration (see above), themes that are familiar from Demosthenes' earlier speeches, especially Dem. 8 and 9. The Athenians, he says, must wake up to the reality of the danger that Philip poses (in a memorable simile, 6, he likens them to people who are drugged). Philip is in reality already at war with Athens, and all his actions are directed towards its overthrow. Demosthenes criticizes the Athenians for their idleness and irresponsibility and directs sharp words at his fellow politicians, who are corrupt and self-seeking, singling out a certain Aristomedes for particular blame (70–74).

A new element is the lengthy discussion of the payments made to poorer Athenians from the theoric fund (35–45). Demosthenes' earlier view had been that these payments were a waste of money and that the money could better be used to fund military operations against Philip (see Dem. 3). Here, however, he argues that the rich should not begrudge the poor the handouts on which they depend, and in return the poor should not resent or seek to expropriate the private wealth of the rich. This apparent change of policy is explained in part by an improvement in Athens' public finances: Demosthenes claims that the city's annual revenue has risen in recent years, for reasons that are not entirely clear to us, from 130 to 400 talents (37–38). He no doubt also hoped that the

---

[10]It is likely that by 341 Philip already had plans to attack the Persian Empire (which he did in 337), though this cannot be proved.

anticipated rapprochement between Athens and Persia (see above) would soon put an end to Athenian financial concerns. But it was not simply a matter of money: Demosthenes is seeking to heal a rift within Athenian society between rich and poor and to create a spirit of civic unity—under the leadership of men such as himself—in the face of the threat posed by Philip.

There is a detailed commentary on this speech in German by Hajdú 2002.[11]

IO. FOURTH PHILIPPIC

[1] In my opinion, men of Athens, the matters under discussion are both serious and of vital importance to the city, and I will try to tell you what measures you can usefully take. Quite a number of errors have been committed over a period of time, and as a result our situation is bad. And yet none of these errors, men of Athens, is more distressing for the present than your giving up your resolve for action and your paying attention only so long as you are seated listening, or when some piece of news is being announced. After that, each of you goes away and not only gives no thought to the issues but does not even remember them. [2] The wanton violence and greed with which Philip acts towards everyone are as great as you have been told. You all know, I imagine, from reports or from speeches in the Assembly, that he is unable to refrain from such conduct. And if anyone is unable to understand this in any other way, let him think about it like this: whenever we have been required to speak about justice, we have never yet been beaten or seemed to be in the wrong, but we defeat all comers and win the argument. [3] And yet has this resulted in the deterioration of his situation and the improvement of ours? Far from it. For when he takes up arms and marches out, willing to risk all that he has, while we are seated—some after delivering speeches about justice, others after listening to them—it is

---

[11] Hajdú's commentary is helpfully reviewed by D. M. MacDowell, *Classical Review* 53 (2003): 301–302.

quite natural, I suppose, that actions outstrip words, and that everyone pays attention not to the righteous speeches that we made in the past, or could make now, but to our actions. Yet these cannot save any of the victims of injustice, and it is pointless to say anything more about them. [4] Accordingly, at a time when the inhabitants of the cities of Greece are divided into two groups—those who wish neither to rule anybody else by force nor to be enslaved to another but to manage their city in peace and in accordance with the laws, on terms of equality, and those who desire to rule over their fellow-citizens, submitting to anyone who they imagine will allow them to do so—those who are of his persuasion, men who desire tyrannies and dictatorships, are everywhere victorious, and I cannot think of a single securely democratic city apart from our own.[12] [5] And those who allow him to control their government are successful by means of all the things that get things done: first and foremost by having someone who will give money on their behalf to those who are willing to take it; and second—though no less important—by the existence of a power that can subdue their opponents whenever they ask. [6] Nor is it only in these ways that we are being left behind, men of Athens: we cannot even wake ourselves up but are like people who have drunk mandrake juice[13] or some other such drug. And then, I think—for in my view one should speak the truth—we have consequently been so slandered and despised that of those who are in real danger, some dispute with us about leadership, others quarrel about where we should hold our Council meetings,[14] and others yet have decided to defend themselves on their own rather than with us.

---

[12]Despite Philip's general support for oligarchies, there certainly were other democracies in Greece, though perhaps none of them was as securely democratic as Athens: see, e.g., 17.10 on the democratic cities of Achaea in the 330s. Demosthenes made a similar claim, that virtually every city is an oligarchy, at 15.19.

[13]Mandrake (*Mandragora officinarum*) is a poisonous plant of the nightshade family. It was used in antiquity as a narcotic.

[14]The reference here is probably to meetings of the Council (*synhedrion*) of the Second Athenian Confederacy, on which see Cargill 1981: 115–128.

[7] Why am I going into detail about these matters? It is not, by Zeus and all the gods, that I want to make myself an object of hatred to you. My aim is rather to make all of you, men of Athens, understand that just as in our private lives, so in the case of cities, day-to-day nonchalance and slackness are not immediately detectable in the individual details that are being neglected but are seen in the overall situation. [8] Look at Serrium and Doriscus. In the immediate aftermath of the peace, these places, which many of you have perhaps not even heard of, were regarded as unimportant. But later, after they had been left alone and disregarded, they brought about the destruction of Thrace and of your ally Cersobleptes.[15] Next, seeing that they were being neglected and were receiving no assistance from you, Philip demolished Porthmus and planted a tyranny in Euboea against you, like a fortress opposite Attica.[16] [9] And while you were paying no attention to this, Megara was almost taken.[17] You paid no thought or attention to any of these places, nor did you show that you would prevent him from acting in this way, and so he bought up Antrones and soon afterwards took control of affairs in Oreus.[18] [10] There are many places that I pass over—Pherae, the route to Ambracia, the massacres in Elis[19]—and countless others! I have recounted these events not in order to enumerate how many people have suffered violence and injustice at the hands of Philip but to demon-

[15]Serrium and Doriscus were places in Thrace that were captured by Philip in 346: see 8.64n. Cersobleptes was the ruler of eastern Thrace; an ally of Athens, he was excluded from the Peace of Philocrates in 346 and defeated by Philip in the late 340s.

[16]On Porthmus, the harbor of Eretria on Euboea, see 9.57–58nn; cf. 8.36 and 66.

[17]On Philip's involvement in the affairs of Athens' neighbor Megara in 343, see 8.18n.

[18]Antrones (also called Antron) was a small city in Phthiotic Achaea in central Greece. On Macedonian interference in the northern Euboean city of Oreus, see 9.59–62nn.

[19]Philip captured the city of Pherae in southern Thessaly in 344: see 8.59n. On his threat to Ambracia in western Greece in 342, see 9.72n; on events in Elis, see 9.27n.

strate to you that he will continue to wrong everybody, and bring everything under his control, unless someone stops him.

[11] There are those who, even before they listen to speeches about our affairs, immediately ask, "What then must we do?"[20] Their aim is not to listen first and then take action—which would make them the most useful of all citizens—but to be rid of the speaker. Nevertheless, it *is* necessary to tell you what you should do. First, men of Athens, you must clearly acknowledge that Philip is waging war on our city and has broken the peace, and is ill disposed and hostile to our city down to its very foundations, and to the gods of the city as well—may they destroy him! He is quite frankly waging war and plotting against our constitution, and his overriding aim is to dissolve it.[21] [12] And it is in a sense inevitable that he is doing this now. Think about it: he wishes to rule and has formed the view that you are the only people who will oppose his doing this. For a long time now he has been acting unjustly, and he knows very well that it is through his possession of the places that belong to you that all his other acquisitions are secure, since if he were to abandon Amphipolis and Potidaea, he would not be secure even in Macedonia.[22] [13] He is quite deliberately plotting against you and knows that you know it. And on the assumption that you have your wits about you, he believes that you hate him. Besides these important considerations, he is well aware that even if he gets control of everything, he will be unable to possess any of it securely so long as you govern yourselves democratically. For if ever any slip should befall him—and many things can happen to a man—all the places that he has taken by force will come and seek refuge with you. [14] You are not yourselves well suited to acquire or possess an empire. Rather, you are good at preventing another from taking places, and at recovering them from one who has got hold of them, and at gener-

---

[20]Sections 11–27 are very similar to 8.38–51: see the Speech Introduction.

[21]Philip and Athens were still formally at peace at the time of the speech. When Philip defeated the Greek alliance in 338 he did not in fact overthrow Athens' democracy: see 62n below.

[22]Section 12 is almost identical to 6.17.

ally obstructing those who wish to rule, and at liberating people. He does not wish freedom at your hands to be lying in wait on any moment of crisis for him—and his calculation is sound and to the point. [15] First, then, you must accept that Philip is an irreconcilable enemy of constitutional government and democracy. Second, you must acknowledge that all his plans and machinations are directed against our city. For none of you is so naive as to suppose that Philip is desirous of the evils of Thrace—for what else would one call Drongilus and Cabyle and Mastira and the places he is now said to possess?[23]—or that seizing these places is the reason why he endures toil and winters and the utmost dangers, [16] or to suppose that he has no desire for Athens' harbors and docks and triremes, or our territory and reputation—may neither he nor anyone else get the better of our city and become master of them!—or that he will allow you to keep these, but passes the winter in the pit for the sake of the millet and wheat in the grain silos of Thrace.[24] [17] On the contrary, all his activities in Thrace and elsewhere are directed towards getting control of our possessions.

Although every one of you should appreciate and understand these arguments, you should not, by Zeus, urge one who is giving the best and most just advice[25] to propose that we declare war. That would be the act of people who are looking for someone to go to war with instead of benefiting the city! [18] Look: if as a result of Philip's first breach of the peace, or his second or third—for there is a whole series of them—someone had proposed that we declare war on him, and he, just as he is doing now when none of you is proposing to declare war, had assisted the Cardians, would the proposer not have been ruined, and would everyone not have accused him of being responsible for the support that Philip was giving to the Cardians? [19] So do not look for someone else to hate for Philip's wrongdoings, nor hand that person over to be torn apart by those who have been bribed by

[23]On these obscure places in Thrace, see 8.44n.
[24]On "in the pit" and "wheat," see 8.45nn.
[25]I.e., Demosthenes and his supporters.

Philip; and do not vote for war and then fight among yourselves over whether or not you did the right thing. Instead, you should imitate the way in which he makes war: by providing money and whatever else is needed to those who are already resisting him, and by raising taxes, men of Athens, and by preparing an army, fast triremes,[26] cavalry, horse transports, and everything else that is needed for war. [20] People now laugh at the way we manage our affairs and, by the gods, I think that you are doing exactly what Philip would pray for you to do: you are too late, you waste money, you look for others to entrust your affairs to, you complain, you blame each other. But I shall explain to you both how this situation came about and how to put a stop to it.

[21] From the beginning, men of Athens, you have never once entered upon or prepared for any undertaking properly, but you always react to events, and when you are late, you stop. Then if something else should happen, you make your preparations and are thrown into uproar. [22] This is wrong. You can never do anything that you need to do by means of relief forces. Instead, you must equip a force and provide it with supplies and financial officers and public slaves, and make sure to keep a very close guard of the money; and require these men to provide an account of the money, and the general to provide an account of his actions, and leave him no excuse for sailing elsewhere or doing something else. [23] If you do this really wholeheartedly, you will either compel Philip to keep the peace in accordance with justice and to remain where he is or you will be at war with him on terms of equality. And maybe, just maybe, just as now you learn by hearsay what Philip is doing and where he is marching to, so he may come to worry about where the city's forces are sailing for and where they will appear.

[24] If anyone thinks that these proposals require substantial expenditure and much toil and upheaval, he is quite right. But if he calculates what the consequence will be for the city, if it is un-

---

[26]Athenian triremes were divided into classes according to their sailing qualities: see 14.18n. Demosthenes is probably calling for ships of either the "select" or "first" class.

willing to take action, he will find that it is in our interest to do
what is needed with a good will. For even if some god were to
guarantee—and no human would serve for a matter of this importance—that if you keep quiet and give up everything, Philip
will not in the end attack you, [25] it would be shameful, by Zeus
and all the gods, and unworthy of you and the city and the deeds
of your ancestors, to sacrifice the rest of the Greeks into slavery
for the sake of our private comfort, and I for one would rather
die than make such a proposal. [26] Nevertheless, if some other
speaker persuades you differently, so be it: do not resist; throw everything away. But if no one takes such a view, but on the contrary we all already know that the more we allow him to get control of, the more dangerous and the stronger an enemy we shall
have, where do we shrink back to? Why do we delay? When, men
of Athens, will we be willing to do our duty? [27] "Whenever, by
Zeus, we are compelled to." But if we are speaking of the compulsion placed on free men, that has already arrived and indeed has
long passed us by; the compulsion for slaves we must surely hope
to avoid. How do they differ? For a free man the greatest compulsion is a sense of shame at what is happening—I do not know
what compulsion could be greater than that—but for a slave it
consists of blows and outrage to the body. May that never happen
to us! Indeed, one should not even talk about it.

[28] Your reluctance, men of Athens, to undertake the public
services that each of you should perform, both in person and by
means of his wealth, is quite wrong, but nevertheless some excuse
can be made for it, whereas your refusal even to listen to what you
ought to hear and deliberate about deserves every kind of criticism. [29] You habitually fail either to pay attention until, as now,
events are upon you, or to deliberate about any matter when you
have the time to do so. Whenever he makes his preparations, you
fail to follow suit and prepare yourselves in return, and are lazy,
and, if anyone says anything about this, you eject him. It is only
when you learn that some place has been destroyed or is being besieged that you pay attention and make preparations. [30] The
time for listening and deliberating was in the past, but you were
unwilling to do so then; now, when you are listening, is the time
when you should be taking action and making use of the prepara-

tions that you made previously. As a result of such habits, you behave in the opposite way to anyone else in the world: other people are in the habit of deliberating before they act, but you do so afterwards.

[31] What is left for us to do, and has long been necessary, and even now is not too late, I shall explain to you. What our city needs more than anything for the coming troubles is money, and there have occurred some strokes of good fortune, which, if we use them well, may bring about what is needed. In the first place, the men whom the King trusts and considers his Benefactors hate Philip and are at war with him.[27] [32] Second, the agent who is privy to all of Philip's preparations against the King has been arrested,[28] and the King will hear everything that has been done not from accusations laid by us—whom he would suppose to be speaking with a view to our own advantage—but from the agent and manager himself, so that he will believe them, and our ambassadors will only have to make a speech that the King will be

---

[27] King's Benefactor was an honorific title within the Persian Empire (see Briant 2002: 303–304). The reference here is to the satraps of western Asia Minor who were operating in support of Perinthus and to Mentor of Rhodes (see the next note). This sentence is discussed by Didymus (col. 4.1–15, with Harding 2006: 117–123).

[28] The reference is to Hermias, the ruler of the two cities of Atarneus and Assus in northwestern Asia Minor. Hermias combined political ambition with philosophical interests. A pupil of Plato's Academy, he welcomed philosophers to his kingdom, most notably Aristotle, who married his niece. Hermias kept his kingdom independent of the Persians until 341, when the King's general Mentor of Rhodes captured Atarneus and arrested him. This passage is the subject of a long note by Didymus (cols. 4.59–6.62, on which see Harding 2006: 124–162). Demosthenes implies both that Philip is already planning to attack the Persian Empire and that Hermias had been co-operating with him, and some historians believe that he wished to use Hermias' kingdom as a bridgehead for an invasion of Asia. Be this as it may, Hermias' independence from Persian rule will have been sufficient reason for the Persians to seek to have him suppressed; it should not be assumed that Demosthenes had reliable information about the relationship between Hermias and Philip.

delighted to hear.[29] [33] They should say to him that we ought to join in punishing the man who is harming both of us, and that Philip will be much more frightening to the King if he attacks us first, since if we are abandoned and defeated Philip will move against him with impunity. I think that you should send an embassy to hold discussions with the King about all these matters[30] and should abandon that fatuous slogan, which has often proved damaging to you, "the foreigner, and common enemy of all,"[31] and the like. [34] For whenever I see anyone who is afraid of the man in Susa and Ecbatana[32] and claims that he is ill disposed to our city, although he previously helped to restore our affairs[33] and recently has offered to do so again[34]—and it is not his fault

---

[29] It is not clear why Demosthenes does not name Hermias or Mentor. Perhaps, as MacDowell suggests (2009: 356), this was very recent news about which most Athenians would already be aware.

[30] Athens and Persia did cooperate in 340 in helping Perinthus and Byzantium: see 11.5–6, 12.6.

[31] This phrase was applied to the Persian King (on the word *barbaros*, "foreigner," see 3.16n). It was the central tenet of Panhellenism (see the Introduction to Dem. 9) that the Greeks should set aside their differences and unite to wage a war of both revenge and territorial conquest against the Persian Empire. It is instructive to compare Demosthenes' earlier statement in a speech of the mid 350s (14.3): "I believe that the King is the common enemy of all the Greeks."

[32] The Persian court moved between a number of cities, including Susa in Persia and Ecbatana in Media.

[33] Having fallen out with the Spartans over their support for his brother Cyrus (see 15.24n), in 395 the Persian king Artaxerxes supported an anti-Spartan Greek alliance that included Athens. A Persian fleet commanded by the exiled Athenian general Conon defeated the Spartans in the sea battle of Cnidos in 394 and then restored the walls of Athens that the Spartans had demolished after their victory in the Peloponnesian War. See Didymus cols. 6.67–8.2.

[34] According to Didymus (col. 8.2–32, with Harding 2006: 185–192), this refers to a Persian embassy to Athens in 344/3 asking for the continuation of friendly relations. The context was probably the Persian campaign to recapture Egypt. Didymus quotes the historian Philochorus (*FGH* 328 frag-

that you did not accept this offer but voted against it—but who says something quite different about the man at our gates, close at hand as he is, and growing powerful in the midst of Greece, the brigand of the Greeks—I am amazed, and I for one fear such a man, whoever he may be, since he does not fear Philip.

[35] There is also another matter that gives rise to unjust calumny and unhelpful speeches, and damages our city and gives an excuse to those who are reluctant to pursue any policy that is correct; and you will find that the blame for all our deficiencies—since they must have *some* cause—is referred to it. This matter causes me very great anxiety, but nevertheless I shall address it,[35] [36] in the belief that I can say what is just and in the public interest, speaking both to the well-off on behalf of the poor and to the needy on behalf of the rich. We could make no greater improvement to our affairs than to do away both with the unfair criticisms that certain men make of the theoric fund and with the fear that stopping it[36] will have disastrous consequences, nor is there anything that would more strengthen the entire city collectively. [37] Look at it like this: First, I shall speak from the point of view of those who are clearly in need. There was a time, not long ago, when the city's annual revenues were no more than one hundred and thirty talents,[37] and yet none of those who were able

---

ment 157) for the date and the sharp tone of the Athenian reply: "The King would continue to have their friendship, so long as he not attack the cities of Greece."

[35]For Demosthenes' earlier reluctance to speak frankly about the theoric fund, see 1.19n.

[36]I.e., that payments will stop being made for such purposes as festival attendance.

[37]This and the following figure are discussed by Didymus (cols. 8.44–9.9, with Harding 2006: 194–197). He guesses that the (annual) figure of 130 talents relates to the final years of the Peloponnesian War, but the reference is more likely to be to the recent financial crisis of the mid 350s, in the aftermath of the Social War. The figure of 400 talents is supported by a fragment of Theopompus (*FGH* 115 fragment 166) in which the Athenian politician Aristophon (see 8.30n) is quoted as claiming in a speech, whose dramatic date is probably 346, that Athens has revenues of almost 400 talents.

to serve as trierarchs or pay the wealth-tax thought that he should not do his duty in person, on the ground that there was a shortage of money, but instead triremes sailed and money was found and we all did what was required. [38] Subsequently, fortune has smiled on us and increased our collective revenues, and our income is now four hundred talents instead of one hundred,[38] without a single one of the rich being fined[39]—indeed, they also receive something, since the well-off all have a share of this wealth and are doing well. [39] Why then do we reproach each other over this and use it as an excuse for doing nothing, unless we begrudge the assistance that fortune has provided to the destitute? I certainly would not blame these people or approve of anyone else blaming them. [40] Even in private homes I do not see any man in the prime of life who is so ill disposed towards his elders, or so senseless or idiotic, as to refuse to lift a finger because they do not do as much as he does.[40] Indeed, such conduct would make him liable for prosecution under the laws of ill treatment.[41] For in my opinion it is only proper that we take on and willingly discharge for our parents a debt of gratitude, which is doubly required, both by nature and by law.[42] [41] Just as each one of us has a parent, so we should think of all the citizens as the collective parents of the whole city. Far from depriving them of whatever the city gives

---

[38] Demosthenes gives a lower figure for Athens' previous revenues here than he does at 37, presumably to exaggerate the improvement in Athenian finances.

[39] I.e., the increase in revenue is not the result of public prosecutions (*graphai*) being brought against the rich, who if convicted would have to pay substantial fines into the public treasury.

[40] Just as in a family, Athenians should contribute according to their means and not expect the same contribution from everybody.

[41] Under Athenian law, a son could be prosecuted for maltreatment of his parents (*kakōsis goneōn*), including failure to provide them with food and shelter. See MacDowell 1978: 92.

[42] The Greek word translated as debt of gratitude (*eranos*) means an interest-free loan raised by contributions. Demosthenes' point is that the care that young children freely receive from their parents is like an *eranos*, which they should repay by looking after them when they are old.

them, we should consider, if they receive nothing, what other sources we can use to ensure that they have whatever they need.

[42] I think that if the wealthy take this view, they will be doing both what is just and what is to their advantage, since to deprive anyone of the necessities of life will produce in people a common sense of discontent. At the same time, I would advise the needy to get rid of the thing that causes the rich distress and about which they rightly complain. [43] I shall now examine the matter, in the same way as before, from the point of view of the well-off, and I shall not shrink from telling the truth. For it seems to me that no Athenian, at any rate, is so miserably hard-hearted as to be distressed at the sight of those who are poor and in need of the necessities of life receiving these payments. [44] Why then are people irritated and annoyed? It is when they see certain people transferring an attitude towards public money to the treatment of private wealth,[43] and when they see a speaker being regarded by you as great, indeed as immortal because of the security that he enjoys,[44] and when they see that the votes cast in secret differ from what people had indicated in public by their clamoring.[45] [45] These things cause distrust and anger, men of Athens, since we must share the commonwealth with each other in an equitable manner. The wealthy should be confident that their possessions are safe, and not be afraid for them; but when danger threatens, they should share their wealth for the sake of our collective security. The rest[46] should take the view that what is pub-

---

[43]This section is unclear: Demosthenes is alluding to behavior of which his audience would presumably be aware. Here he may be suggesting that the Athenians' tight control over public money has led to the malign practice of prosecuting wealthy Athenians to raise revenues through the imposition of fines: see 38n.

[44]The security that such politicians enjoy is provided not by bodyguards but by their popularity, which allows them to speak freely without fear of prosecution, since they feel confident that they will not be convicted by a jury.

[45]Demosthenes' point is apparently that the Athenians publicly express their solidarity with the rich in the Assembly, but as jurors cast their (secret) ballot to convict them when they are put on trial.

[46]I.e., the poor.

lic is public, and should have their fair share of it; but they must understand that each man's private property belongs to its owner. This is how a small state becomes great, and a great state is secure. As far as describing what is required on each side, these remarks are perhaps sufficient; but putting them into practice requires regulation by law.[47]

[46] The present disordered state of our affairs has many long-standing causes, which I am prepared to explain to you if you are willing to listen. Men of Athens, you have abandoned the policy you inherited from your ancestors, and have been persuaded by speakers who think it an unnecessary and pointless expense to champion the Greeks and use a well-organized force to help all who are victims of injustice. You supposed that living a quiet life and neglecting your duty, but instead abandoning every place one after another and allowing others to take them, provided you with wonderful happiness and great security. [47] As a result, another man[48] has come forward to the post that you should have occupied and has become wealthy and powerful and the ruler of many. And this is quite understandable, since something great and honorable and glorious,[49] over which all the leading states have for a very long time disputed among themselves, has, as a result of Sparta's misfortune[50] and Thebes' involvement in the war with Phocis[51] and our neglect, been carried off by this man by default. [48] As a result, he has emerged as an object of fear to others, in possession of many allies and a great army, whereas the Greeks are now surrounded by so many serious problems that it is difficult even to offer advice about what to do.

[49] The present situation, in my judgment, is alarming to

---

[47] For the need to appoint Law-Givers to change the laws relating to the theoric fund, see 3.10–11nn.

[48] Philip.

[49] Demosthenes here refers to the somewhat nebulous concept of the leadership of Greece. See also 52n below and 9.23.

[50] The battle of Leuctra in 371, at which Sparta was decisively defeated by Thebes. As a result, it was stripped of Messenia and lost its ability to dominate even the Peloponnese.

[51] The Third Sacred War of 356–346. Thebes' resources were sapped by this long-running war against Phocis.

everyone, men of Athens, but no one is in greater danger than you, not only because it is against you in particular that Philip is plotting but also because you are the idlest people of all. If the sight of numerous goods for sale and the wealth of the market-place has beguiled you into believing that the city's plight is not serious, your judgment of the situation is inappropriate and incorrect. [50] That might be a sound basis for determining whether or not a market or a festival is well organized,[52] but the one city that anyone who wishes to rule Greece understands will oppose him single-handedly and will be a champion of freedom for all, such a city must be evaluated not, by Zeus, on the basis of what is for sale there but on whether it enjoys the goodwill of allies and is militarily strong—these are the aspects of the city that one must examine, and in your case these things are all precarious and wholly unsound. [51] It may help you to understand the situation by looking at it in this way: At what time have the affairs of Greece been in the greatest confusion? Everyone would agree that it is right now, since previously all Greece was divided between two sides, the Spartans and us,[53] with some of the other Greeks loyal to us and others to them. The King in himself was viewed with equal distrust by both sides, but, by taking the side of those who were getting the worse of the war, he was trusted by them until he made them the equals of the others, whereupon those whom he had saved came to hate him just as much as did those who were his enemies at the outset.[54] [52] But now, first of all, the King is on friendly terms with all the Greeks, though least of all

---

[52]The Athenians closely supervised commercial activity in the market-place: see *Ath. Pol.* 51, with the commentary of Rhodes 1981. On the efficient organization of Athens' religious festivals, see 4.35–36.

[53]This statement is true of much of the fifth century, and of the fourth century until the battle of Leuctra. Thereafter Athens aligned itself with Sparta against Thebes.

[54]Persian policy towards the Greeks was driven largely by the desire to prevent the emergence of a dominant power in Greece that might threaten its interests, in particular its control of Asia Minor. Demosthenes' point is most clearly illustrated by the switches in Persian support (for Sparta, then Athens, then Sparta again) in the period 411–386.

with us, unless we bring about some improvement in our relations with him.[55] Next, many forms of domination are coming into existence, and everyone lays claim to the primacy of Greece,[56] although in practice they have abandoned it, and envy and distrust each other, rather than those whom they should, and everyone is isolated—the Argives, the Thebans, the Spartans, the Corinthians, the Arcadians, and us. [53] Nevertheless, at a time when Greece is split into so many factions and tyrannies, the candid truth is that there is no city whose magistrates' office and Council Chamber take less interest in the affairs of Greece than ours—as indeed one might expect, since no one is motivated by affection or trust or fear to speak to us. [54] There is no single explanation for this situation, men of Athens—if there were, it would be easy for you to change it—but numerous errors of various kinds have been made over a long period. Passing over their individual details, I shall tell you where they are heading—and I ask you not to be annoyed with me if I speak the truth frankly. Whenever an opportunity has arisen, our advantage has been sold, and you have accepted in return leisure and tranquility, which bewitch you so that you do not feel bitter toward those who are injuring you, and others take the honors. [55] There is no point examining other matters now;[57] but whenever Philip attacks anywhere, someone immediately stands up and says that no one should talk nonsense or make a proposal of war, adding immediately that it is good to keep the peace, and that it is difficult to maintain a large force,

---

[55]The Persian King is described as well disposed towards the Greeks because he has been seeking their assistance in his bid to regain Egypt (see 34n above; Isoc. 12.160; Diodorus 16.44). Demosthenes claims that he is least well disposed towards Athens in part because the Athenians were most inclined to interfere in Asia Minor (see 8.24n on Erythrae; 4.24n on Chares and Artabazus), and in part because of their response to his recent embassy (see 34n above).

[56]Demosthenes exaggerates the number of cities that had a realistic claim to the leadership of Greece: only Athens and Thebes (and arguably Sparta) were major powers.

[57]Sections 55–70 are very similar to 8.52–67: see the Speech Introduction.

and that certain people wish to steal our money, and they provide other reasons that are as close to the truth as they can get.[58] [56] It is not you who need to be persuaded to keep the peace, since you sit there already persuaded, but rather the man who is waging war. If he should be persuaded to keep the peace, you are already quite prepared to do so. You must understand that the hardship for us is not the amount of money we will have to spend to ensure our safety but what we will suffer if we refuse to take these measures; and you should prevent money being stolen[59] by creating a guard to protect it, not by abandoning our interests. [57] This too makes me angry: the fact that some of you are upset at the prospect of our money being plundered, when you are able to guard it and to punish any wrongdoers,[60] but are not upset at Philip plundering all of Greece, one city after another, as he is doing, especially since his plundering is directed against you.

[58] Why, men of Athens, has none of these men yet admitted that Philip, whose seizing of cities is so clearly unjust, is acting illegally and is at war, but instead they say that those who advise you not to give way and not to abandon these places want to be at war? Because they wish to pass the blame for the unpleasant consequences of the war—for many distressing things inevitably, yes, inevitably happen in war—on to those who regularly give you the best advice. [59] They believe that if you all agree to resist Philip with one mind, you will defeat him, and they will no longer be able to work for hire; but if from the first alarm you are diverted towards bringing charges against certain men[61] and putting them on trial, they, by accusing these men, will have it both ways, winning your esteem and receiving money from him, while you will inflict on those who have spoken in your interests the punishments that should be inflicted on them. [60] These are their hopes, and this is why they contrive to accuse some people of warmongering. But I know very well that without any Athe-

---

[58]That is to say, they are completely untrue.

[59]Demosthenes refers to the allegations of his opponents that money allocated to military operations will be misappropriated. See also 8.52–54.

[60]Specifically, anyone who attempts to steal the money.

[61]Anti-Macedonian politicians such as Demosthenes.

nian proposing a declaration of war, Philip holds many of our possessions and now has sent help to Cardia.[62] If we are willing to pretend that he is not waging war on us, he would be an utter fool to refute us: for when the victims deny they are being wronged, why should the wrongdoer be concerned? [61] But when he attacks us, what shall we say then? For he will deny that he is at war, as he did to the people of Oreus when his soldiers were in the place, as he did previously to the Pheraeans as he attacked their walls, and as he did at the outset to the Olynthians, until he was actually present in their territory with an army.[63] Or shall we say, even then, that those who are urging you to defend yourselves are warmongering? It remains then for us to be slaves—there is no alternative.

[62] Indeed, the danger is greater for you than for anyone else, since what Philip wishes is not to make your city subject to him, no, but wholly to destroy it. For he knows well that you will refuse to be slaves, and, even if you do not refuse, you will not know how to be slaves, since you are accustomed to rule, but you will be able to cause more trouble for him, if you get the opportunity, than any other people. For these reasons he will not spare you, if he gets control of you.[64] [63] You should recognize that the struggle will be for our very existence, and you should publicly cudgel to death[65] those who have sold themselves to him. For it is impossible, yes, impossible, to defeat your enemies abroad until you have punished your enemies within the city; but if you

---

[62] On Philip's assistance to Cardia at the northern end of the Chersonese, see 8.58n.

[63] See 8.59nn.

[64] In fact, Philip treated Athens mildly after his victory over the Greeks at the battle of Chaeronea in 338. The reason was twofold. First, he wished to be able to represent himself as the champion of Greece in his planned war against the Persians (Athens had been a leader of the Greek resistance to Persia in the fifth century and had indeed been sacked by the Persian army in 480). Second, he planned to use Athens' powerful navy to take on the Persians at sea.

[65] On the brutal form of capital punishment called *apotympanismos*, see 8.61n.

trip up against the barrier posed by the latter, you will inevitably be too late to deal with the former. [64] Why do you think that he is outraging[66] you—for this is exactly what he seems to me to be doing—and, though he deceives the rest by at least doing them favors, threatens you outright? For example, he gave many things to the Thessalians before he led them into their present slavery, nor would anyone be able to say how much he deceived the wretched Olynthians, after previously giving them Potidaea and many other places; and he is now leading the Thebans down after handing Boeotia over to them and relieving them of a long and difficult war.[67] [65] As a result, of all these cities that have enjoyed some benefit from him, some have already suffered as they have; the rest will do so at some point in the future. As for you, I say nothing about the places of which you have been deprived, but how often were you deceived in the very making of peace, and how much was taken from you! Have you not lost Phocis? Thermopylae? The Thracian coast? Doriscus? Serrium? Cersobleptes himself? Does he not now admit that he holds Cardia?[68] [66] Why then does he treat the others in this way, but treats you differently? Because in your city, alone of all the cities, it is possible to speak on behalf of the enemy with impunity, and it is safe for a man who has been bribed to address you, even if you have been deprived of what is yours. [67] It would not have been safe to plead Philip's cause in Olynthus, if the Olynthian majority had not profited from their enjoyment of Potidaea. It would not have been safe to speak for him in Thessaly, if the majority of the Thessalians had not benefited from Philip's expulsion of the tyrants and his handing over the Pylaea to them. It would not have been safe to do so in Thebes, before he handed over Boeotia and destroyed Phocis.[69] [68] But at Athens, when Philip has not only deprived you of Amphipolis and the territory of the Cardians but is also establishing Euboea as a fortress against you and is now advancing against Byzantium, it is safe to speak on Philip's behalf. Indeed, some of those who do so are rapidly becoming

---

[66]On the concept of outrage (Greek *hybris*), see 8.62n.

[67]See 8.62nn.

[68]See 8.64nn for this list of Philip's wrongdoings.

[69]See 8.65nn.

rich, after being poor, and reputable and well known, after being without name or reputation, whereas you suffer the reverse: you were reputable and now are disreputable; you were rich and are now poor.[70] [69] For I believe that the wealth of a city consists of its allies, and the trust and goodwill that it inspires—in all of which you are deficient. Because you despise these things and have allowed them to be carried off in this manner, he is wealthy and powerful and an object of fear to all, Greeks and foreigners alike, whereas you are abandoned and brought low, glorying in the prosperity of the marketplace, but laughable when it comes to making appropriate preparations.

[70] I see that some speakers do not themselves follow the advice that they give you, since they say that you must keep quiet, even if someone wrongs you, but they are unable to keep quiet in your presence, even though no one is wronging them. And yet, if anyone should ask politely, "Tell me, Aristomedes[71] (for no one is ignorant of these matters),[72] why exactly, when the life of a private citizen is safe and free from trouble and risk, whereas the life of a politician is exposed to criticism and full of daily struggles and perils, do you choose the dangerous rather than the quiet life?" how would you reply? [71] If you were able to give the most creditable reply, we would accept that you are telling the truth in claiming to do all these things out of love of honor and glory; but I wonder why you think that you must toil and run risks in order to do all these things, but advise the city to abandon them in idleness. You would surely not claim that you ought to be seen as a person of note in the city but that our city need not be worth anything among the Greeks! [72] Indeed, I do not see how the city

---

[70]Compare 38, where Demosthenes speaks about Athens' improved public finances.

[71]The identity of this opponent of Demosthenes is discussed by Didymus (cols. 9.38–10.11, with the commentary of Harding 2006: 199–208), who identifies him as an Athenian politician nicknamed "the Brazen" (signifying either cheapness or toughness) and satirized on the comic stage as a thief. This is the only place in his deliberative speeches where Demosthenes names a rival politician: see the Speech Introduction.

[72]I.e., Aristomedes' (alleged) misconduct is a matter of public knowledge.

will be safe if it keeps to itself, or how you will be in danger if you are no busier than anyone else. On the contrary, the greatest dangers for you arise from your activities and officiousness, whereas for the city they arise from idleness. [73] But, by Zeus, perhaps you have inherited a good reputation from your grandfather and father, which it would be shameful for you to squander, whereas the deeds of our city's ancestors are obscure and trivial? But that is not the case. Your father was a thief, if he was like you, whereas our city's ancestors, as all the Greeks know, saved them from the greatest dangers.[73] [74] Indeed, there are certain men here who do not engage in political life for themselves in the same way that they do for the city, or as befits a citizen. For how is it reasonable for some of them, who have come from the prison, to forget their former selves,[74] whereas our city, which recently was the leader of Greece and held a position of primacy, is now utterly humbled and has lost its good name?

[75] Although I have much more to say on many topics, I shall stop, since it is not lack of words, either now or at any other time, that in my view has caused our fortunes to deteriorate. Rather, it is when you have heard everything that is required, and agree that it was well said, but then sit listening with equal attention to those who wish to defile and distort these things, not out of ignorance—for as soon as you see them you know well who is speaking for hire and takes part in public life in Philip's interest, and who is truly speaking for the best—but in order that by accusing the latter and reducing the matter to ridicule and abuse, you may avoid doing any of the things that you need to do. [76] That is the candid truth. I have offered the best advice in a spirit of goodwill, instead of a flattering speech full of harm and deception, which will make money for its speaker but will surrender the affairs of the city to our enemies. Either you must abandon these habits or you will have no one to blame but yourselves for our utter failure.

---

[73]The reference is to Athens' role in defending Greece during the Persian Wars of 490–479.

[74]Athens' prison contained men who had been arrested and were awaiting trial, men who had been convicted and awaited execution (a famous example is the philosopher Socrates), and public debtors. It is unknown to whom (if anyone) Demosthenes is specifically referring.

11. RESPONSE TO THE LETTER OF PHILIP

~~~~~~

INTRODUCTION

The authenticity of this short speech[1] is open to doubt, and the majority opinion among scholars is that it is spurious, even though ancient critics generally accepted it as genuine.[2] Dionysius of Halicarnassus regards it as authentic, "the last of the speeches against Philip."[3] It is also included by Didymus in his commentary on the deliberative speeches of Demosthenes (cols. 10.13–13.12). He apparently accepts it as genuine, though he writes that it is "cobbled together" from some of Demosthenes' previous speeches on the same issues (col. 11.7–10). This statement is clearly true, since part of the speech is closely adapted from the *Second Olynthiac* (8–17 ≈ 2.14–23), and there are echoes of other speeches too.[4]

---

[1] As MacDowell (2009: 360) has correctly pointed out, it is misleading to translate the title of the speech (literally *To the Letter of Philip*) as Answer or Reply to Philip's letter, since the speech is directed not to Philip but to the Athenian Assembly.

[2] Sealey (1993: 239) denies that it is a work of Demosthenes, and Hammond and Griffith (1979: 714) are skeptical of its authenticity. On the other hand, Harding (2006: 217) is open to the possibility that it is authentic, and MacDowell (2009: 360–363) is inclined to accept it as genuine.

[3] *First Letter to Ammaeus* 10.

[4] The speech clearly purports to be by Demosthenes and is thus different from Dem. 7 and 17, which are genuine speeches of the period misattributed to him.

Didymus also addresses two other matters relating to the speech's authorship. First, he reports the view of unnamed scholars that it was the work of the fourth-century BC historian Anaximenes of Lampsacus and was to be found in almost the same words in the seventh book of the latter's *Philippic History* (col. 11.10–14).[5] He does not comment on the actual degree of similarity between this speech and the one in Anaximenes' (now lost) history. But even if the two speeches were very similar, it does not follow that Dem. 11 was *written* by Anaximenes and then wrongly inserted into the collection of Demosthenes' speeches, since Anaximenes may equally well have taken a speech of Demosthenes and inserted it, perhaps after some adaptation, into his history.

Second, Didymus records the view of some ancient critics that elements of the speech's vocabulary are not Demosthenic (col. 11.14–26). The particular word singled out for criticism is *orrōdein* ("to shudder in fear": see 2), which was thought to be vulgar and unworthy of Demosthenes. Didymus discusses the meaning and use of this word, but he does not directly offer an opinion about its propriety. In fact, the word is not stylistically inappropriate and was regularly used by fourth-century writers.[6] On the other hand, technical analysis of the speech's prose rhythm suggests that it is of doubtful authenticity.[7]

Most scholars have judged that the speech's lack of detail and borrowings from earlier works of Demosthenes make it more likely to be a later pastiche than a genuine work.[8] But these arguments are subjective, and the most recent discussions of the speech have concluded that there is no compelling reason to deny that Demosthenes wrote it. In particular, since Demosthenes often reworks material from his earlier speeches, the reuse of mate-

---

[5] The Greek text of Didymus is damaged at this point, and there is some doubt about what exactly he is saying.

[6] See Harding 2006: 221–224.

[7] McCabe 1981: 170–171.

[8] As noted above (p. 201 n. 4), it cannot be a genuine speech of the period misattributed to Demosthenes.

rial from Dem. 2 in this speech constitutes a very weak argument against its authenticity.[9] I am therefore inclined to agree that the speech is quite likely genuine.

The date (dramatic or actual) of the speech is summer or autumn 340. Dionysius of Halicarnassus dates it 340/339, after the outbreak of war with Philip.[10] Its date and context are also discussed by Didymus, who agrees that "war had obviously already broken out" (col. 10.20–21). Certainly 11 seems to indicate that war has just been declared or is at any rate imminent.

There are various accounts of the sequence of events leading to the outbreak of war between Athens and Philip. Dionysius of Halicarnassus quotes the historian Philochorus (relating events in early 340/339) to the effect that after he had laid siege to Perinthus and Byzantium, Philip wrote a letter to the Athenians making a series of complaints against them, and that in response to this letter, Demosthenes persuaded the Athenians to declare war, and that as a result, they tore down the pillar recording the Peace of Philocrates and prepared for war.[11]

Didymus gives a different account. He quotes Philochorus and Theopompus in support of the view that war broke out because of Philip's seizure of a fleet of grain ships bound for Athens that was anchored at Hieron, on the Asiatic side of the Bosporus.[12] This is consistent with Demosthenes' later claim (in 330) that it was the seizure of the ships that broke the peace (18.73). The ancient commentary on Dem. 11.1 adds more detail: Philip alleged that these ships were being sent to relieve the city of Selymbria, which he was besieging, and sent a letter of complaint to the

---

[9]Thus Harding 2006: 217–218. See too MacDowell (2009: 360–363), who correctly points out the material has been reworked to fit the context (as Demosthenes does on other occasions).

[10]See p. 201 n. 3 above. Dionysius evidently placed it later than Dem. 10.

[11]Dionysius of Halicarnassus, *First Letter to Ammaeus* 11 quoting Philochorus *FGH* 328 fragments 53–55a. See too Diodorus 16.77.2. For tearing down the pillar on which a treaty is recorded as a public repudiation of it, see 16.27n.

[12]Didymus cols. 10.34–11.5, quoting Philochorus *FGH* 328 fragment 162 and Theopompus *FGH* 115 fragment 292.

Athenians, accusing them of breaking the peace.[13] It was in response to this letter, the commentator claims, that this speech was delivered.

Turning to the speech itself, the speaker claims that Philip's letter acknowledges the reality of the claim (of anti-Macedonian politicians at Athens) that he has been waging war on Athens for a long time (1); that he wishes to attack Perinthus and Byzantium (3); that Persian support to Perinthus has prevented its capture; and that the Persians will be in great danger if Byzantium is defeated (5). If the speech is genuine, it probably does belong to the debate that led to the declaration of war, although it is curious in that case that Demosthenes neither states explicitly that Byzantium is already under siege nor mentions Philip's seizure of the grain ships. Perhaps he did not need to because these events were all too familiar to the Athenians. If this is the case, then this speech may have been delivered in response to the letter of Philip preserved as Dem. 12, if (as some scholars believe) that is the letter that led the Athenians to declare war (see the Introduction to Dem. 12). If, on the other hand, the speech is spurious, its author may not have known (or cared) about the precise sequence of events of that summer.

The speech argues that Philip's position is not as strong as it might appear. His deceitful conduct has made him an object of suspicion in Greece, even to his allies (3–4); the Persians are now acting against him (5–6); Macedonia is not united behind him (8–14). Philip prospers because he is active (17) and has bribed some of the politicians (18). The Athenians have been disgracefully idle but must now take action (19–23).

11. RESPONSE TO THE LETTER OF PHILIP

[1] It is now clear to all of you, men of Athens, that Philip did not make peace with you[14] but merely postponed war. For by

---

[13]Dilts 1983: 158.3–11. The siege of Selymbria (on the city see 15.26n) is not mentioned by any contemporary source, but its historicity is argued for in detail by Hammond and Griffith 1979: 574 n. 2.

[14]The Peace of Philocrates of 346.

handing Halus over to the Thessalians[15] and administering the affairs of the Phocians[16] and overturning all of Thrace,[17] fabricating nonexistent reasons and discovering unjust excuses, he has in reality been waging war against our city for a long time, and now he acknowledges it in the letter he has sent.[18] [2] I shall try to explain to you why you should neither shudder at[19] his power nor face him in an ignoble fashion, but should set out for the war with your persons and money and ships and—to speak simply—without sparing anything. For, first, it is reasonable to suppose that you have as allies and helpers the supreme gods, since he overlooked his pledges and transgressed his oaths to them when he unjustly broke the peace.[20] [3] Next, the means by which in the past he grew strong, always cheating someone and announcing that he would do them great benefits, have all now been exhausted, and the Perinthians and the Byzantines and their allies all recognize that he wishes to attack them just as he previously attacked the Olynthians.[21] [4] He is known by the Thessalians to be a despot and not the elected leader of an alliance.[22] He is an object of

---

[15]The city of Halus in Phthiotic Achaea in northern Greece was captured by Philip's general Parmenion in 346 (Dem. 19.163) and its territory handed over to the Thessalian city of Pharsalus (Dem. 19.36). The Athenians had tried unsuccessfully to save Halus in the negotiations leading to the Peace of Philocrates by having it included among their allies.

[16]On the harshness of Philip's settlement of Phocis after the end of the Third Sacred War in 346, see Diodorus 16.60.1–2.

[17]Philip's campaign against Cersobleptes and Teres in eastern Thrace from 342 to 340 brought him into conflict with the Greek cities Perinthus and Byzantium and eventually with Athens.

[18]The only surviving letter of Philip to the Athenians is preserved as Dem. 12: on its date and authorship, see the Introduction to Dem. 12.

[19]See the Speech Introduction on the use of this word.

[20]The gods were regularly invoked as guarantors of treaties.

[21]The important cities of Perinthus on the northern coast of the Sea of Marmara and Byzantium on the Bosporus were threatened by Philip's campaign in eastern Thrace. Olynthus had been besieged and captured by him in 348 (see the Introduction to Dem. 1–3).

[22]Philip had been elected by the Thessalians as chief magistrate (*archōn*) for life: see 1.13n. For his heavy-handed treatment of Thessaly in the later 340s, see 6.22 and 9.12, 26.

suspicion to the Thebans since he holds Nicaea[23] with a garrison, and has wormed his way into the Amphictyony,[24] and leads the embassies from the Peloponnese to himself and detaches them from their alliance.[25] Consequently some of his former friends are now irreconcilably at war with him, others are no longer willing accomplices, and all are treated with suspicion and slandered by him. [5] Furthermore—and this is no small matter—those who have been appointed as satraps in Asia have recently sent mercenaries and prevented Perinthus being taken by siege.[26] Now that their hatred is implacable and the danger to them is close at hand, if Byzantium should be defeated,[27] not only will they eagerly join in the war [6] but they will urge the King, who is richer than anyone else, to supply us with money.[28] He has such power to influ-

---

[23]On Nicaea in eastern Locris, see 6.22n. See also Didymus col. 11.26–52, with Harding 2006: 224–228.

[24]In 346 Philip received the two seats on the Amphictyonic council that had belonged to Phocis, and as ruler of Thessaly, he effectively controlled a majority of the votes on it. See further the Introduction to Dem. 5.

[25]Several anti-Spartan states of the Peloponnese (Argos, Messenia, Arcadia in particular) received support from Philip during the second half of the 340s. The alliance from which they were being detached was with Thebes, which had been responsible for breaking Spartan control of the Peloponnese in the aftermath of the battle of Leuctra in 371. (On Thebes' alliance with the Arcadian city Megalopolis, see Dem. 16.) Events in the Peloponnese in this period form much of the subject matter of Dem. 6.

[26]Philip laid siege to Perinthus in or about July 340 (narrated by Diodorus 16.74.2–76.3). The Persians had by now realized the threat that Philip represented to them, and they sent support to the city: see Diodorus 16.75.1–2, claiming plausibly that the order came from the Persian King. See also Pausanias 1.29.10; Arrian *Anabasis* 2.14.5. Cf. 10.34–35 for Demosthenes' hope (in 341) that Persia would join the anti-Macedonian cause; also 12.6–7 for Philip's complaints about Athens' diplomatic contact with Persia.

[27]Byzantium was of obvious strategic importance, both for its control of the Bosporus and as a place from which to invade Asia Minor. Philip laid siege to the city in ca. September 340.

[28]The Greeks believed (correctly) that the Persian King was enormously wealthy. The Persians more commonly intervened in Greek affairs in the fourth century by financial than by military means.

ence events in Greece that previously, when we were at war with Sparta, he caused whichever side he supported to prevail over the other.[29] So now, if he joins us, he will easily defeat the power of Philip.

[7] Despite these weighty advantages, I shall not deny that he has used the peace to deprive us of many places and harbors and other assets that are useful for war,[30] but I see that whenever all the participants in a war are held together by goodwill and a common interest, they remain securely united; but when they are held down by plotting and greed, as a result of deception and violence, as they are now by this man, a small pretext and a chance slip will swiftly shake them up and dissolve them.[31] [8] And often, men of Athens, when I consider the matter I find not only that Philip's alliances have declined into suspicion and hostility but that even his own kingdom is neither cohesive nor friendly to him nor as people imagine it to be. For, all in all, the power of Macedonia has a certain influence and value as a supplement, but on its own it is weak and contemptible in relation to so great a mass of affairs. [9] Moreover, his wars and expeditions, and all the things by which one might think him great, have made his kingdom less secure for him. For you should not suppose, men of Athens, that Philip and his subjects take pleasure in the same things. Instead, you should realize that he desires glory, whereas they want security, and that he cannot get glory without risk, whereas they have no wish to leave their children, parents, and wives at home and to be destroyed and to take daily risks on his account. [10] From these considerations it can be seen how the majority of the Macedonians feel about Philip: you will find that both the Companions[32]

---

[29]The speaker refers to the period from 411 to 386. During the final stage of the Peloponnesian War (411–404), Persia supported Sparta against Athens, and in the early years of the Corinthian War (395–386), it backed Athens and its allies against Sparta.

[30]The following section (8–17) is closely adapted from the *Second Olynthiac* of 349/8: cf. 2.14–23. See the Speech Introduction for discussion of the implications of this borrowing for this speech's authorship.

[31]This sentence is adapted from 2.9.

[32]On the Companions, see 2.10n.

who accompany him and his mercenary commanders have a reputation for bravery but in fact live in greater fear than those who live in obscurity. For the latter face only the risk of fighting the enemy, whereas the former are more frightened of the flatterers and slanderers than they are of battle. [11] The people fight alongside everyone else against their enemies, but the Companions not only have a substantial share of the evils of war but also individually are in fear of the moods of the king. Moreover, if one of the people does something wrong, he is punished as he deserves; but whenever the Companions are most successful, then most of all they are treated with contempt and are undeservedly trampled down.[33] [12] Nor would any sensible person find these things unbelievable; for according to those who have spent time with him, Philip is so ambitious that he claims every great achievement for himself and is more distressed at those generals and leaders who have done something praiseworthy than at those who have utterly failed. [13] Why then, if all this is true, have these men remained loyally by his side for so long? Because at present, men of Athens, his success obscures all such concerns. For success is good at hiding or obscuring men's errors. But if he stumbles at all, all these problems will be clearly uncovered. It is the same with our bodies: [14] whenever a man is strong, he notices no individual weakness, but when he is unwell, everything comes out, whether it be a break or a sprain or some other existing condition that is not completely healthy. So in the case of kingdoms and tyrannies, for as long as they are successful in war, their weaknesses are invisible to most people, but when they suffer some reverse, such as that man is now likely to suffer, by taking too heavy a burden upon himself, all his difficulties become evident to everyone.

[15] If any of you, men of Athens, is led by the sight of Philip's good fortune to think him fearsome and hard to fight against, he shows good sense. For fortune has great influence, or rather is everything, in all the affairs of men: yet in many ways our fortune is preferable to his. [16] We have inherited from our ancestors over a considerable period of time not only his fortune but,

---

[33]See also 2.18 on Philip's temperamental nature.

in short, that of every king of Macedonia, since they paid tribute to Athens,[34] whereas our city has not yet paid tribute to any of them. Furthermore, because we continue to act with greater piety and justice than he does, we have greater access to the goodwill of the gods. [17] Why then was he more successful than us in the previous war? Because, men of Athens, (for I shall speak freely to you) he campaigns in person and endures hardships and is present when there is danger, and neither lets any opportunity pass nor leaves any season of the year aside, whereas we, if the truth be told, sit around here doing nothing, always delaying and taking votes and asking in the marketplace if there is any news. And yet what could be bigger news than that a Macedonian despises the Athenians and dares to send letters such as you heard a while ago?[35] [18] He possesses hired men: both soldiers and also—by god!—some of your politicians, who think it right to take home gifts from him, and shamelessly live for Philip, and fail to realize that they are selling both their city and themselves for a small sum. And yet we fail to prepare ourselves to throw his affairs into disorder, and are unwilling to hire mercenaries, and lack the courage to go on campaign. [19] What is strange, then, is not that he has gained some advantage over us during the previous war but that we imagine that we, even though we do none of the things that men who are at war should do, will defeat someone who does everything that a man who means to get the upper hand has to do.

[20] If we recognize this, men of Athens, and accept that it is not open to us to say that we are keeping the peace—for he has already declared war in advance and has demonstrated it by his actions—we must spare nothing either in public or in private, and must go on campaign, if the occasion arises, all of us willingly, and must employ better generals than previously. [21] Let none of you suppose that the same things that caused our situation to deteriorate will also lead to its recovery and improvement. Nor should you suppose that while you are remiss, as you were

---

[34] This claim is untrue: see 3.24n.
[35] This sentence is modeled on 4.10.

before, others will struggle on your behalf. Instead you should reflect that it is shameful that your fathers endured much toil and great dangers when they were at war with Sparta, [22] but you are unwilling to offer vigorous resistance even for the things that they rightfully acquired and handed on to you. Instead, whereas the man who is setting out from Macedonia so loves danger that he has suffered wounds[36] over his whole body while fighting his enemies in order to increase the size of his empire, the Athenians, whose ancestral custom is to obey no one else and to be universally victorious in war, because of their idleness or softness are abandoning both the achievements of their ancestors and their country's advantage.

[23] Not to speak at length, I say that we must prepare ourselves for war and must summon the Greeks to an alliance with us, not by words but by deeds, since all words are pointless if they are not accompanied by action, and this applies most of all to us, since we seem more ready than the other Greeks to use them.

---

[36]On this passage see Didymus cols. 12.37–13.12, with Harding 2006: 233–242. Philip was shot in the eye during the siege of Methone, and also suffered wounds to his collarbone and thigh.

12. LETTER OF PHILIP

INTRODUCTION

The *Letter of Philip* to the Athenians, whether genuine or not, clearly does not properly belong in a collection of Demosthenes' deliberative speeches, but ancient editors presumably included it because they believed (perhaps correctly) that it was the letter to which Dem. 11 responds.

The *Letter* is found in only some of the manuscripts of Demosthenes (FY, not SA) and is not discussed by the ancient commentators. Didymus, however, quotes (col. 10.24–30) the closing sentences from a "letter of Philip" that are very close to, and in some cases identical with, the closing words of this letter. It is unclear whether he is quoting this letter from memory, referring to a different letter of Philip whose conclusion was nevertheless very similar, or confusing two different letters. The fact that Didymus elsewhere (col. 9.45–47) reports that in "the letter to the Athenians" Philip writes about a mercenary commander named Aristomedes of Pherae, whom he does not mention in this letter, perhaps suggests that he knew only one, different, letter of Philip. But the matter is unclear.

There is no doubt that Philip communicated on more than one occasion with the Athenians by letter, as he did with other states. In addition to the letter(s) referred to by Didymus, and the letter to which Dem. 11 responds, there are references to letters at Dem. 7.1 (a letter of 342), 8.16 (a letter in which Philip claimed to be defending himself against the Athenians in the Chersonese), 9.16 (a letter in which he admits that he has sent soldiers into the Chersonese), and 9.27 (letters in which he states that he is at peace with those who are willing to heed him). How many different letters are involved is hard to assess, and there may well have been others of which we know nothing. All such letters would have been preserved in the Athenian archives and accessible to interested parties. It is thus not implausible that a genuine letter of Philip should have been preserved among the speeches of Demosthenes.

The date of the letter has to be determined on internal grounds. It is clearly earlier than the outbreak of war between Athens and Macedon in late summer 340 (5). There is continued friction over the Chersonese (at 11 Philip admits to helping Cardia), and Philip is still on campaign in Thrace (at 8 he complains that the Athenians are ordering him to allow Cersobleptes and Teres to rule). Specific new points are:

1. The Athenian general Callias is seizing cities in the Gulf of Pherae (5).

2. An Athenian embassy has been sent to the Persian King (6) to persuade him to wage war on Philip.

3. A very recent incident has taken place relating to the island of Peparethos (12).

4. The Macedonians have made an incursion into the Chersonese, prompted by Philip's desire to send ships to the Hellespont (16).

Of these, the first and third cannot be dated. The fourth probably relates to Philip's desire to move ships into the Sea of Marmara to blockade Perinthus, the siege of which began in summer 340. Athenian overtures to Persia also belong to the same period, since we know that the Persians sent help to Perinthus and cooperated with Athenian forces on the spot. All of this points to a date in summer or perhaps autumn 340. On the relationship between this letter and Dem. 11, see below.

The letter seems well informed about the situation in Greece and about relations between Athens and Macedonia, and it contains details not found elsewhere. The one apparent error is at 9, where two different Thracian rulers seem to be confused (see the note). The arguments are vigorously expressed and strong, especially over the disputed city of Amphipolis, to which Philip contends that the Athenian claim is weaker than his (20–23). He makes numerous complaints against the Athenians, both about specific actions and about their relentlessly hostile attitude to him (1). He accuses them of seizing a herald and an ambassador, of raiding his and his allies' territory, of negotiating with the Persian King against him, and of refusing to accept his offers either to put their disputes to arbitration or to renegotiate the Peace of Philocrates. He also defends himself against Athenian allegations that he has been sending help to Cardia and that he illegally sent troops into the Athenian-controlled Chersonese. Many of these complaints appear, from a different point of view, in the speeches of the late 340s of Demosthenes and Hegesippus (Dem. 6–10).

The language and style of the letter are consistent with a fourth-century date, and there seems no good reason to deny that it is a genuine letter sent by Philip to the Athenians. Whether it was written by Philip himself is impossible to say, since we have no genuine writings of his with which to compare it. In any case, we do not know whether he wrote official letters in person or relied on Greek writers to do so for him. Certain rather undiplomatically blunt features of the letter have been thought more likely the work of Philip himself than of a Greek. These include the ominously vague final sentence, the poor taste of his criticism of Athens' democracy, and the tactless boast that he could buy up those Athenian politicians who opposed him if he chose (20). But absolute certainty is impossible.

It remains to consider the relationship of this letter to the Athenian declaration of war against Philip in 340 and to Dem. 11. We know (see the Introduction to Dem. 11) that the Athenians declared war against Philip in response to a letter from him that made a series of complaints against them and that in some way acknowledged that a state of war existed between him and them. Although this letter is generally dated somewhat earlier in 340, it is possible that it is in fact the same letter.[1] In particular, its

---

[1] The matter is well discussed by MacDowell (2009: 363–366), who tentatively concludes that this is the letter that precipitated war. Other scholars, however, believe that this letter was sent earlier in the summer of 340 and that the letter that led to war has not survived: see, e.g., Sealey 1993: 187.

peremptory and threatening final words—"I will defend myself with justice . . . and will deal with your case"—could have been interpreted at Athens as tantamount to a declaration of war.

The letter is helpfully discussed by Hammond and Griffith 1979: 714–716.

12. LETTER OF PHILIP

[1] Philip, to the Athenian Council and People, greetings. Since you have paid no attention to the many ambassadors I have sent to you to ensure that we abide by our oaths and agreements, I thought it necessary to send you a letter about the wrongs that I believe you are doing me. Do not be surprised by the length of the letter: I have many complaints, and it is necessary to give a clear demonstration of all of them.

[2] First, when Nicias the herald was snatched from my territory, not only did you fail to punish the culprits but you detained the victim for ten months, and you read out from the speaker's platform the letters from us that he was carrying.[2] Then, when the Thasians were admitting the Byzantine triremes and any pirate who wished to land there, you took no notice of it, although the agreement expressly states that those who do this are to be enemies.[3] [3] Moreover, at about the same time, Diopeithes,[4] after

---

[2]Heralds were by convention regarded as inviolable: see, e.g., Rhodes and Osborne 2003: no. 35 (an Athenian protest of the 360s against the arrest of Athenian heralds by the Aetolians).

[3]The Peace of Philocrates contained a clause forbidding either party or its allies to harbor pirates (see also 7.14). Thasos in the northern Aegean was an ally of Athens and as such bound by the terms of the peace (cf. 4.32, 7.15). Philip's complaint as regards Byzantium would be justifiable, since he and Byzantium were by now at war with each other. It is also possible that Byzantium had, as earlier, been forcing merchant ships to put in to land (see 5.25n) and that Philip chose to interpret this as piratical behavior. As de Souza notes (1999: 36), in this period "the difference between legitimate warfare and piracy was often only a matter of opinion and interpretation."

[4]Diopeithes was the commander of the Athenian settlers in the Chersonese: see the Introduction to Dem. 8.

attacking my territory, enslaved Crobyle and Tiristasis, ravaged the adjoining part of Thrace,[5] and finally went so far in lawlessness that he arrested Amphilochus who had come as an ambassador about the prisoners, and, after subjecting him to the harshest of constraints, ransomed him for nine talents: and he did these things with the approval of the Athenian people.[6] [4] Yet the illegal treatment of a herald and of ambassadors is viewed as impious by everyone else—and most of all by you! At any rate, when the Megarians killed Anthemocritus,[7] your people went so far as to bar them from the Mysteries, and set up a statue before the gates as a memorial of this act of injustice.[8] Yet is it not strange that you are now openly doing the very things for which, when you suffered them, you so hated the perpetrators? [5] Moreover, your general Callias[9] seized all the inhabited cities on the Gulf of

---

[5]Crobyle and Tiristasis were towns in eastern Thrace. They had previously belonged to the Thracian king Cersobleptes but were now subject to Philip.

[6]Philip's ambassador Amphilochus is not otherwise known.

[7]The killing of the Athenian ambassador Anthemocritus probably occurred in 432/1, during the period of tension between Megara and Athens preceding the outbreak of the Peloponnesian War (see de Ste. Croix 1972: 246–251). An alternative view places his death much later, in the context of the dispute over the area of sacred land called the Hiera Orgas on the border between Athens and Megara in ca. 350: see Connor 1962. On the latter episode, see also 13.32n.

[8]The Mysteries were a religious ceremony celebrated at Eleusis in Attica in honor of the two goddesses Demeter and Persephone: see 3.5n. A decree proposed by one Charinus banned the Megarians from setting foot in Attica on pain of death and arranged for Anthemocritus' burial near Athens' Dipylon Gate (Plut. *Pericles* 30.3).

[9]This man is generally identified as Callias of the Euboean city Chalcis, who was by now collaborating with Demosthenes in his opposition to Philip and to whose career Aeschines devotes a lengthy passage of his speech *Against Ctesiphon* of 330 (3.85–104). On Demosthenes' proposal, he was granted Athenian citizenship, though the date of this grant is uncertain: see Osborne 1983: T73. If he was in fact serving as one of Athens' ten generals in 341/0, he must have already received Athenian citizenship, though Philip may simply mean that he is commanding a force fighting on Athens' side. On relations between Chalcis and Athens in this period, see 8.18n.

Pagasae, which were bound by oath to you but allied to me,[10] and sold into slavery all those who were sailing to Macedonia, judging them to be your enemies. And you praised him in your decrees for these actions! Consequently I cannot say that it would be anything new if you were to admit that you are at war with me: for indeed, at the time when we were openly at war with each other, you sent out privateers, sold those who were sailing to us into slavery, gave help to my enemies, and did damage to my territory.[11]

[6] Besides, you have reached such a degree of lawlessness and hostility that you have even sent ambassadors to the Persian King to persuade him to wage war on me.[12] This in particular might be thought extraordinary, since before his conquest of Egypt and Phoenicia, you voted to summon me and all the other Greeks alike against him, if he should stir up any trouble.[13] [7] But now your hatred of me is so excessive that you are holding talks with him about a defensive alliance. And yet long ago your ancestors, I learn, censured the sons of Peisistratus for inviting the Persian against the Greeks, but you feel no shame in doing the very things for which you always found fault with the tyrants![14]

---

[10]It has been thought surprising that Callias should have been able to capture all these cities, including Pagasae, without meeting effective Macedonian opposition. It is possible either that the text is corrupt or that Philip is exaggerating and that in either case Callias only attacked the cities. On this point, see the discussion of Hammond and Griffith 1979: 553–554. The nature of the oaths between these cities and Athens is unknown.

[11]This refers to the period before the Peace of Philocrates of 346.

[12]On Athenian diplomatic contact with Persia, see 10.34–35, 11.5–6. By summer 340 the Persians had come to see Philip as a threat to themselves and had joined Athens in sending help to the besieged cities of Perinthus and Byzantium.

[13]The context may be the sharp reply that Athens gave to the Persian King in 344/3 (see 10.34n). For earlier Athenian fear of Persia, see Dem. 14. Philip here implicitly identifies himself as Greek: see 9.31n.

[14]On the sons of Peisistratus, see 17.3n. Hippias and Hipparchus ruled Athens as tyrants after the death of their father in 528/7. Hipparchus died in 514, and Hippias was exiled in 510. In 490 the Persian King Darius attempted to restore Hippias as pro-Persian ruler of Athens, but the Persian invasion of Attica was defeated at the battle of Marathon. The Athenians

[8] On top of everything else, you order me in your decrees to allow Teres and Cersobleptes to rule Thrace, on the ground that they are Athenian citizens.[15] But I know that these men neither shared with you in the agreements about the peace[16] nor are recorded in the pillars[17] nor are Athenian; rather, Teres marches with me against you, and Cersobleptes told my ambassadors in private that he had been keen to swear the oaths but was prevented by your generals who declared him to be an enemy of Athens.[18] [9] And yet how is it fair or just for you to say that Cersobleptes is your enemy when it suits you, but to declare that he is an Athenian citizen whenever you wish to make malicious allegations against me? Or, straight after the death of Sitalces, to whom you gave citizenship, for you to grant friendship to his killer, and to choose to go to war against us on Cersobleptes' behalf?[19] And

---

thus had no opportunity to censure the one surviving Peisistratid, Hippias, who probably died soon thereafter.

[15] Teres and Cersobleptes were rulers in central and eastern Thrace respectively and had been driven out of their kingdoms by Philip in 342 (Diodorus 16.71.1–2). The Athenians often made grants of citizenship to foreign rulers whom they wished to cultivate. See Osborne 1983: T54 (Cersobleptes) and T65 (Teres).

[16] I.e., the Peace of Philocrates.

[17] Treaties were published at Athens by being inscribed on stone pillars (*stēlai*).

[18] Cersobleptes was not included among Athens' allies to be protected by the terms of the Peace of Philocrates. Demosthenes and Aeschines later wrangled about which of them was responsible for this (Dem. 19.174, 334–335; Aes. 2.81–93, 3.73–75), but his inclusion would in any case have been unacceptable to Philip, who was on campaign against him in Thrace at the time.

[19] The allusion here is uncertain. Sitalces was a Thracian king of the fifth century, but he is not known to have received Athenian citizenship and in any case died in battle. Also, the context shows that more recent events are meant. It has been proposed that Sitalces is a slip for the fourth-century Thracian king Cotys, who had been an ally of Athens and was murdered in 358 by two Greeks from Aenus, who were honored for their action by the Athenians. But the letter refers to one killer, and we are told that these men received Athenian citizenship rather than "friendship" (Dem. 23.119, 127),

you act like this even though you know very well that nobody who receives such gifts from you pays any attention to your laws or decrees! [10] Nevertheless, to leave everything else to one side and speak briefly, you made grants of citizenship to Evagoras of Cyprus[20] and Dionysius of Syracuse[21] and their descendants. If you can persuade those who exiled each of these men to give the exile his kingdom back, *then* you may recover from me as much of Thrace as Teres and Cersobleptes ruled. But if you do not see fit to offer even a mild reproach to those who defeated these men, and yet get angry with me, how is it wrong for me to defend myself against you?

[11] I have many more just claims to make about these matters, but I choose to pass over them. As for the Cardians, I admit that I am helping them, since I became their ally before the peace, but you are unwilling to submit the matter to judgment, although I have often requested it, as have they on a number of occasions.[22]

---

a term that in any case suggests a relationship with a foreign ruler rather than with private citizens. Alternatively, an otherwise unknown Thracian ruler named Sitalces may be meant. See Osborne 1983: T36 (Cotys), T52 and T53 (the killers), and X3 (Sitalces). The suggestion that this (apparent) error means that this cannot be a genuine letter of Philip is baseless.

[20]Evagoras was the ruler of the Cypriote city of Salamis in the late fifth and early fourth century. He was granted Athenian citizenship at an uncertain date (see Isoc. 9.54; Osborne 1983: D3). He is only known to have been exiled in his youth, i.e., before he became ruler.

[21]Dionysius I of Syracuse ruled much of Sicily from 405 to 367. He and his descendants were granted Athenian citizenship in 368 (see *IG* II² 103 = Rhodes and Osborne 2003: no. 33; Osborne 1983: D10). It was his son, Dionysius II, who was (twice) exiled, and ended his life at Corinth. In both this and the previous case, the author's grasp of earlier fourth-century Greek history seems to be somewhat inexact.

[22]The independent city of Cardia in the northern Chersonese, which in 340 was in conflict with Athens, had become an ally of Philip by 346, the year of the Peace of Philocrates. The Athenians claimed Cardia for themselves, on the ground that it formed part of the Chersonese (for the recognition by the Greeks and the Persian King of Athens' claim to which, see 9.16n), but this is not a matter that either the Cardians or Philip would have considered negotiable. The dispute to which Philip refers is presumably that

Would it not be despicable of me to desert my allies and take more thought for you, who criticize every aspect of my behavior, than for those who have always remained my staunch friends?

[12] Since I must address this matter too, you have become so overbearing that whereas previously you merely criticized me for the things mentioned above, most recently, when the Peparethians were claiming to have suffered terribly, you ordered your general to punish me on their behalf, although I had punished them less than they deserved.[23] And the Peparethians, at a time when there was peace, seized Halonnesus and refused to surrender either the place or its garrison, though I often sent ambassadors about them.[24] [13] You failed to denounce a single one of the wrongs that the Peparethians did to me but instead criticized my punishment of them, even though you knew the details of the case. And yet it was neither they nor you from whom I took the island, but the pirate Sostratus.[25] So if you claim that you had handed it over to Sostratus, you are admitting that you dispatched pirates; but if he controlled it against your wishes, what terrible loss have you suffered as a result of my taking it and making the place safe for sailors? [14] Although I was showing such concern for your city, and offering you the island, the politicians did not allow you to take it; they wanted you to take it back, thereby admitting that I possessed an island that belonged to someone else; or else, if I did not surrender the place, I would become an object of suspi-

---

over the location of the border between Cardian and Athenian territory in the Chersonese, on which see 7.39–44. On Cardia and the Chersonese, see in general Dem. 8.

[23]The Aegean island of Peparethus was a member of the Second Athenian Confederacy. In response to the Peparethians seizing the island of Halonnesus from him, probably in 341, Philip sacked their city in 340: see Dem. 18.70. The general mentioned is probably Chares, on whom see 8.30n.

[24]On the earlier diplomatic wrangling between Philip and Athens over Halonnesus, see Dem. 7: evidently Philip's offer to give the island to Athens on that occasion had been rejected, since the Peparethians subsequently took it from him (see also 15 below).

[25]The leader of the pirates who had seized Halonnesus and from whom Philip had in turn taken it. He is not named in Dem. 7.

cion to the people.[26] Recognizing this, I challenged you to submit these matters to arbitration, in order that if it was determined to be mine, I would give the place to you, but if it was determined to be yours, then I would give it back to the Athenian people.[27] [15] I made these requests often, but you paid no attention, and then the Peparethians seized the island. What was I supposed to do? Fail to punish those who had broken their oaths? Or fail to avenge myself on those who were behaving with such brazen arrogance? For indeed if the island belonged to the Peparethians, what business was it of you Athenians to demand it back? But if it was yours, why are you not angry with them for taking what was not theirs?

[16] Our hostility toward each other has gone so far that when I wished to get through to the Hellespont with ships, I was compelled to send them by way of the Chersonese with my army, since the cleruchs were waging war on me in accordance with the decree of Polycrates, and you were voting similar measures, and the general was summoning the people of Byzantium and announcing to everyone that you were ordering him to wage war if the occasion should arise.[28] Although I was suffering such wrongs, I nevertheless left your city and ships and territory alone, though I could have taken most or all of them, and have continued to invite you to submit the allegations that we make against each other to judgment. [17] Yet consider whether it is nobler to resolve a dispute by fighting or by talking, whether we are our own arbitrators or persuade others to do so; and consider how absurd it is for you Athenians to compel the people of Thasos and Maroneia to

---

[26]These speakers included Hegesippus, whose speech on Halonnesus (= Dem. 7) makes precisely this argument.

[27]The referral of an interstate dispute to a third party for arbitration required the agreement of both parties. See 7.7n.

[28]Philip claims that he sent troops into the Chersonese only to protect the passage of his ships through the Hellespont into the Sea of Marmara, where he presumably intended to use them against Perinthus and Byzantium. The general he refers to is Chares, who commanded an Athenian fleet operating in the region. See Hammond and Griffith (1979: 570–571), whose reconstruction of the episode is here followed.

resolve their dispute over Stryme by negotiation[29] but to refuse to resolve your disputes with me in the same way, especially when you know that if you lose, you will give up nothing, while if you win, you will take for yourselves what is now in my hands.

[18] The most unreasonable thing of all, in my opinion, is that when I sent ambassadors from my whole alliance, in order to have witnesses, and tried to reach a fair agreement with you for the sake of the Greeks, you did not even listen to what my ambassadors had to say about these matters, when it was possible for you either to allay the fears of those who suspected foul play on our part or to convict me openly of being the most worthless of men.[30] [19] This course of action was in the interest of your people but was unprofitable to the speakers. For those who have experience of your form of government say that to them peace is war, and war is peace: whether by cooperating with the generals or by bringing malicious prosecutions against them, they always take something from them; moreover, by abusing the most distinguished citizens and the most esteemed foreigners from the speakers' platform, they gain the reputation in the eyes of the majority of being friends of the people.[31]

[20] It is easy for me to put a stop to their abuse by paying them a tiny sum of money, and make them utter panegyrics of us instead.[32] But I would be ashamed to be seen to buy your goodwill from these men, who on top of everything else are so impu-

---

[29]Stryme was an outpost of Thasos on the northern coast of the Aegean close to the territory of Maroneia and had been a bone of contention between the two cities since the seventh century. See Dem. 50.20–22 for Athenian intervention in their dispute in 361/0.

[30]See the Introduction to Dem. 6 on Philip's embassy to Athens in 344/3 offering to renegotiate the Peace of Philocrates. Cf. 7.18–32 for a repeat of this offer in the following year.

[31]Ironically, Philip's accusation is similar to Demosthenes' recurring complaint that his fellow Athenian politicians curry favor with the people. See Dem. 7 for Hegesippus' intransigent response to Philip's overtures.

[32]Demosthenes regularly accuses Philip of bribing politicians in Athens and elsewhere. Philip counters that he could, if he wished, easily bribe violently anti-Macedonian politicians to change their tune.

dent as to try to wrangle with us over Amphipolis[33]—a place to which I think I have a much stronger claim than anyone else. [21] For if it belongs to those who originally conquered it, how can it be wrong for us to possess it, since it was our ancestor Alexander who first held the place, and from it he set up a gold statue at Delphi as first fruit for the Median prisoners?[34] If anyone wishes to dispute this, and thinks that it should belong to those who acquired it later, here too justice is on my side: for I besieged those who had expelled you and had been settled there by the Spartans, and took the place.[35] [22] The cities that we all inhabit have been either inherited from our ancestors or acquired in war. Yet you lay claim to Amphipolis, although you were not the first to acquire it, do not now possess it, and spent the shortest time in it. What is more, you have added a decisive proof on my behalf: for I often wrote about it in my letters to you, and you recognized that we possess it justly, at one point making peace while I held the city, and later making an alliance on the same terms.[36] [23] But how could any possession be more firmly based than this—of a city that was originally acquired for us by our ancestors, that later became mine in war, and that has been conceded by you, who are accustomed to dispute even about things that do not belong to you?

These are my complaints against you. Since you are the ag-

---

[33]Athens had effectively ceded their former colony of Amphipolis in Thrace to Philip in 346 (cf. 5.25), but some Athenian politicians wished to re-open the question: see esp. 7.23–29.

[34]Alexander I was king of Macedonia at the time of the Persian King Xerxes' invasion of Greece in 480: see also 6.11n, 13.25n. Greek writers commonly used Median (from the Iranian region of Media) as a synonym for Persian: see 9.42n. The reference here is to prisoners taken from the retreating Persian armies in the region of Amphipolis in either 480 or 479. The gold statue of Alexander at Delphi is mentioned by Herodotus (8.121).

[35]Amphipolis was won over by the Spartan general Brasidas in winter 424/3 (Thuc. 4.102–106) and captured by Philip in 357.

[36]Philip had told the Athenians in 348/7 that he wanted to make peace: see Aes. 2.12–15. The Peace of Philocrates of 346 was both a peace and an alliance.

gressors and are taking advantage of my caution to attack my interests and do as much harm as you can, I will defend myself with justice, and, making the gods my witnesses, I will deal with your case.[37]

---

[37] Philip's leaving it unclear how exactly he will deal with the Athenians makes his threat all the more menacing. On the difficulty of translating the final words of the letter, see Hammond and Griffith 1979: 715 n.2. See the Speech Introduction for the possibility that the Athenians interpreted the letter as tantamount to a declaration of war.

13. ON ORGANIZATION

INTRODUCTION

The date and authorship of this speech are both disputed. It was accepted as genuine both by Libanius in his *Introduction* to it and by Didymus, who included it in his commentary on the deliberative speeches of Demosthenes (cols. 13.14–15.10). It is, however, uniquely among the surviving deliberative speeches, not included among the speeches for which Dionysius of Halicarnassus provides dates.[1] This, among other arguments, has prompted some scholars to deny its authenticity.[2] In my view, the speech is in fact genuine, for the following reasons.[3]

First, Dionysius' omission of the speech does not prove that he judged it to be spurious; he may simply have been uncertain about its date and excluded it for that reason.[4] It is worth noting in this regard both that Didymus was aware of two different dates that had been proposed for the speech and that the author of the ancient commentary on the speech writes that it does not have a

---

[1] Dates for Demosthenes' earlier deliberative speeches are given at *First Letter to Ammaeus* 4.

[2] See Sealey 1967, 1993: 235–237.

[3] See more fully Trevett 1994; also MacDowell 2009: 226–227.

[4] It is important to appreciate that Dionysius gives the dates of the speeches not for their own sake (in which case the omission of this speech would be significant) but to prove that Aristotle's *Rhetoric* was written later than Demosthenes' deliberative speeches. The omission of a single, relatively early, speech would not materially affect his argument. It is also possible that Dionysius omitted to mention the speech by mistake.

clear date, and so evidently its dating was a matter of debate in antiquity (see further below).

Other arguments that the speech is spurious are not cogent. For example, there are two lengthy passages towards the end of the speech that are very similar to passages in other speeches (13.21–24 ≈ 23.196–200; 13.25–31 ≈ 3.23–32). This does not in itself show that the speech is spurious, since a similar reuse of material can also be observed in the two genuine speeches Dem. 8 and 10 and elsewhere in Demosthenes' oratory. It has, however, been argued that differences of detail between the parallel passages indicate that Demosthenes cannot have written both and that therefore Dem. 13 is spurious.[5] Yet it is hard to see why a forger would have wished to introduce minor changes into passages that he otherwise copied out almost word for word.

Demosthenes, by contrast, certainly did have a motive to make changes: to make his historical examples fit his argument. This may strike modern readers as a dubious procedure, but it is not uncommon for Attic orators to rework historical examples in this way.[6] It has also been found suspicious that only in this speech does Demosthenes refer to himself by name (12).[7] But there is no compelling reason to see this as a sign of spuriousness, and in any case Demosthenes clearly alludes to his own name in a speech that is certainly genuine (3.21). In addition, technical analysis of the prose rhythm of the speech shows that it is fully consistent with Demosthenic authorship.[8]

The date of the speech was debated even in antiquity. The author of the ancient commentary found it hard to determine and guessed that the speech preceded the "Philippics" (i.e., the se-

---

[5]See 23n and 24n for the details.

[6]Thus Harding 1987: 34, noting that the audience was unlikely to know (or greatly care) whether such examples were correct, and was in any case unable to check them: "An orator could . . . distort a reference to suit his point, sometimes even invent one altogether. As long as it sounded reasonable, it was likely to be accepted."

[7]The suggestion is that a forger introduced Demosthenes' name to make it clear who the supposed author was.

[8]See McCabe 1981.

quence of speeches dealing with Philip starting with Dem. 4).[9] Didymus discusses the matter at some length and proposes 349/8, on the basis of the reference at 32 to an Athenian vote to march out against Megara, since he knew of conflict between the two cities in 350/49 (cols. 13.40–14.2). But he wrongly assumes that the speech came after the conflict, whereas it probably preceded it.[10] Insofar as the speech makes no mention of Philip,[11] it has been argued that it belongs before Dem. 4 (see above), which was written most probably in 351.[12] But the matter is uncertain, and it is difficult to give a more precise date than the end of the 350s.[13]

The subject matter of the speech is Athenian public finances, which in this period were in a parlous state. The key text is 10.37 (of 340), where Demosthenes claims that "not long ago," Athens' annual revenue amounted to no more than one hundred and thirty talents. This claim is generally taken to relate to the aftermath of the Social War, that is, approximately the time of the present speech (see note ad loc.). The effects of this shortage of money are felt throughout Demosthenes' deliberative speeches, for example, in the reforms to naval finances proposed in Dem. 14 or the obvious problems he has explaining in Dem. 4 how a permanent naval force in the North Aegean will be paid for. In his desire to find money for military operations, Demosthenes looked towards the theoric fund (on which see the Introduction to Dem. 3). This fund was used in the first instance to subsidize citizens' attendance at theatrical performances but came to

---

[9] Dilts 1983: 163.2–7.

[10] Note, however, that Lewis (1997: 245–246) is reluctant to reject the testimony of Didymus on this point.

[11] Ancient critics debated whether the speech should be characterized as a "Philippic" (see Didymus col. 13.16–25; Libanius' *Introduction*). Since Philip's absence from the speech is obvious, the point at issue was probably one of chronology, i.e., whether the speech belongs within the sequence that begins with Dem. 4.

[12] Thus, Lane Fox 1997: 191–195. In terms of subject matter (i.e., military and financial reform), it is close to Dem. 14, which was probably delivered in 354/3.

[13] The speech's date is fully discussed by MacDowell (2009: 227–229), who argues for 350 as the approximately correct date.

be used for other nonmilitary expenditure as well. The use of this fund was hotly disputed: anti-Macedonian politicians such as Demosthenes wished it to be transferred to the military fund; those who opposed war with Philip wished it to remain in the theoric fund.

In this speech Demosthenes claims to be neutral on the issue of the theoric fund (2), and indeed he does not directly refer to it (although the reference to festivals in 2 makes it clear what he means), but he criticizes the expectation that citizens will receive public money for doing nothing. In its place he argues for a new system under which they will be paid only for service to the state, either as soldiers or as administrators (4). He wishes the Athenians to serve on expeditions in person, rather than use mercenaries (5), and alludes to a previous speech that he gave on the subject of army reform (9). That speech was ill received, and apparently it was the issue of two-obol payments (presumably a proposal to abolish some such daily payment to civilians, although the details are unclear: see 10n) that proved unpalatable to the Athenians. Demosthenes argues that his new system will have several benefits: the allies will be better treated (6), and the armed forces will be able to mobilize more quickly (11).

Beyond this rather sketchy proposal, Demosthenes uses the speech to survey many of Athens' deficiencies. The Athenians, he claims, are badly advised by their political leaders, who disparage Demosthenes, subvert the democracy, and deal in empty clichés (12–16); they are also ill led by their generals, who are driven by greed and ambition (19). Between them, the politicians and generals are exploiting the current system for their own advantage, at the expense of the people (20, 31). As a result, the Athenians squander money on civilian expenditure (30) but are culpably negligent in their foreign policy (32–33). Demosthenes draws a contrast with Athens' heyday in the fifth century, when its leaders were personally modest but oversaw a period of great success (21–31).

13. ON ORGANIZATION

[1] Regarding the money that is at issue and the reasons for this assembly, men of Athens, it seems to me easy either to criti-

cize those who distribute and pay out public money, and thereby win the approval of those who think that such payments harm the city, or to argue in support of these payments, and thereby win the favor of those who are most in need of receiving them. Each side praises or criticizes the institution not with a view to the interests of the city but depending on whether they themselves are needy or well off.[14] [2] I would neither argue in favor of people receiving payments nor oppose them as being unnecessary. I do advise you, however, to look and see that the amount of money under discussion is trivial but that the habit of mind that goes with it is not.[15] If you are prepared to combine the receipt of public money with doing your duty, you will not only do no harm but will in fact perform the greatest benefit both to the city and to yourselves. But if every single festival serves as an excuse for taking money,[16] and you refuse even to listen to discussions about what else you must do, you should beware lest you later come to judge that the practice of which you now approve was gravely mistaken. [3] In my opinion—and do not heckle me for what I am going to say, but listen and then make up your minds—just as we are devoting an assembly to the receipt of public money, so we should devote one to organization and military preparation, and each of us should be prepared not only to listen willingly but also to take action, men of Athens, in order that you may hold your hopes of success in your own hands, rather than inquiring what this or that man is doing.[17] [4] Of all the city's in-

---

[14]Demosthenes represents the rich as being opposed to theoric distributions and the poor as in favor of them. Insofar as only rich Athenians paid the wealth-tax (*eisphora*), whereas payments were made to the poor, this is a plausible claim. See also 10.35–45. On the theoric fund, see the Introduction to Dem. 3.

[15]It is not known how much money was paid out as theoric distributions.

[16]Money from the theoric fund was used in the first instance to subsidize the attendance of poorer citizens at theatrical performances put on at religious festivals; it is unlikely that payments were made for every festival.

[17]Demosthenes here refers to Athens' generals.

come, both what you now squander to no purpose from your own funds and all that comes from the allies,[18] I say that you should each take an equal share—those in the prime of life as military pay, those who are too old for military service[19] as auditors' pay[20] or whatever else one might call it—and should campaign in person and not leave this task to someone else. [5] Our city's armed forces should be our own, equipped from these sources, so that you can both be prosperous and do your duty;[21] and the general should command these forces, men of Athens, so as to prevent what happens now. For whenever you put the generals on trial,[22] the only result is that "So-and-so son of so-and-so impeached so-and-so," and nothing else.[23] [6] What then should you do? First, your allies should be made well disposed to you not by the imposition of garrisons but by the existence of common interests.[24] Next, the generals should stop using mercenaries to ravage the

[18]Athens' allies in the Second Athenian Confederacy paid "contributions" (syntaxeis) to help defray the cost of its operations, but very little is known about how much they contributed. See Cargill 1981: 124–127.

[19]Lit. "those over [the age to be included in] the list." Athenian citizens were liable for military service up to the age of 59, and a list (katalogos) was kept of those who could be called on to serve as hoplites (heavy infantry). On the conscription of hoplites, see Christ 2001.

[20]Auditors (exetastai) are mentioned twice by Aeschines (1.113, 2.177), but they do not appear in documentary texts of the period. They clearly had some financial role in military matters.

[21]That is to say, individual Athenians will be to some degree prosperous as a result of drawing state pay.

[22]Athenian generals on campaign were liable to impeachment (eisangelia), which would result in their being recalled to stand trial: see 4.47n.

[23]Demosthenes' point is not that these prosecutions never result in convictions (which they often did) but that even successful prosecutions will do nothing to correct the underlying problem.

[24]When the Second Athenian Confederacy was established Athens undertook not to impose garrisons on member-states, which had been one of the abuses of its fifth-century empire: see IG II² 43 (= Rhodes and Osborne 2003: no. 22) lines 21–22. Such garrisons are, however, securely attested in the 350s: see IG XII.7.5 (= Rhodes and Osborne 2003: no. 51) and IG II² 123 (= Rhodes and Osborne 2003: no. 52); Cargill 1981: 150–160.

territory of our allies,[25] without even laying eyes on our enemies, with the result that they keep the profits for themselves, but the city as a whole incurs the ill will and accusations that this behavior gives rise to. Instead, they should be accompanied by citizens and should do to our enemies what they are now doing to our friends. [7] Apart from these, many other matters require your attention. Leaving aside the fact that it is to your advantage to use your own forces against your own enemies, it is also necessary for you to do so, for other reasons. If you were content to be at peace and not meddle in the affairs in Greece, it would be a different story; [8] but as things are, you aspire to be in first place and to provide justice to others, yet you have not yet organized, nor are now organizing, a force that is capable of overseeing and securing these aspirations. You were enjoying your leisure and isolation when the democracy of Mytilene was overthrown.[26] You were also at leisure when the democracy of Rhodes was overthrown.[27] "But the latter at any rate were your enemies," someone might say.[28] But you, men of Athens, ought to be more opposed to oligarchies for their choice of constitution than to democracies for any reason whatsoever. [9] To return to my subject, I say that you should get yourselves organized[29] and have a single system both for getting paid and for doing your duty. I spoke to you about this on a previous occasion, when I set out how you might organize yourselves—hoplites and cavalry and others—and how we might

---

[25]By way of example, Diodorus records that in 361/0 the Athenian general Chares precipitated a violent civil war on the allied island of Corcyra and that his actions brought discredit on Athens (15.95.3).

[26]On the overthrow of democracy at Mytilene on the island of Lesbos at some point in the second half of the 350s, see 15.19n.

[27]Rhodes' democracy was also overthrown, probably at about the same time, and replaced by an oligarchy with the involvement of Mausolus, the satrap (i.e., governor) of Caria, a province of the Persian Empire in southwestern Asia Minor. See the Introduction to Dem. 15.

[28]Rhodes had been one of the leaders of the allied revolt from Athens in 357 that precipitated the Social War: see Diodorus 16.7.3 and the Introduction to Dem. 15.

[29]It is from this passage that the speech gets it title.

all enjoy a measure of prosperity.[30] [10] Let me tell you candidly what depressed me most of all: it is that no one remembers anything about these many excellent and ambitious plans except "the two obols"—*that* you all remember.[31] And yet two obols can only ever be worth two obols, whereas the other things that I spoke of are worth the entire fortune of the King,[32] namely, that a city that has so many hoplites and triremes and cavalrymen and so great an income should be organized and well prepared.

[11] Why do I mention this now? Since some of you are opposed to universal public pay, but you all reckon that it is useful to be well organized and prepared, I insist that we start with this matter and allow anyone who wishes to make a proposal to do so. The crux of the matter is as follows. If you are persuaded that now is the time to organize your armed forces, they will be in a state of readiness whenever you need them; but if you think that now is the wrong time and do nothing, you will find that you still need to organize yourselves whenever you do need to use them.

[12] But perhaps someone has already spoken like this, men of Athens—not one of you the majority, but one of those who burst with anger at the prospect of these plans being put into effect: "What good have the speeches of Demosthenes done us? He comes forward whenever he likes, fills our ears with words, disparages the present situation and praises our ancestors, and after inflating your hopes and puffing you up, steps down from the platform." [13] As for me, if I could persuade you of any of my arguments, I would think that I was doing the city such great ser-

---

[30]The speech to which Demosthenes refers was probably similar in theme and close in date to the surviving speech *On the Symmories* (Dem. 14), which is concerned with the navy rather than the army.

[31]A payment of two obols (the *diōbelia*) had been introduced in 410, probably as a dole to poorer Athenians, at the instigation of the politician Cleophon: see *Ath. Pol.* 28.3, with the commentary of Rhodes 1981. This was, however, almost certainly a temporary measure, and so Demosthenes must have been referring to a different payment. Probably he proposed canceling or curtailing this payment, which may have been related to (or identical with) the theoric distributions that he elsewhere criticizes (see 3.10–11).

[32]Here as elsewhere, the Persian King is meant.

vices that if I were to try to describe them, many people would reject them as being exaggerated. Nevertheless, I think that it would be a considerable benefit to you if I were simply to accustom you to hearing the best advice. For, men of Athens, anyone who wants to benefit our city must first heal your ears, which have been ruined, so accustomed have you become to hearing lies and indeed anything but the best advice. [14] To give an example—and please do not interrupt me before I have finished—apparently some men recently broke into the Opisthodomos.³³ All those who came forward to speak about it said that democracy had been undermined, and that the laws were no longer in force, and the like. And yet, men of Athens—and see whether I speak the truth—although the perpetrators' actions deserved death, they did not lead to the undermining of the democracy. Or again, someone stole some oars.³⁴ All those who spoke called for whippings and tortures and said that democracy was being undermined. What do I say? That the man who stole the oars did something that deserves death, as did the men whom I recently mentioned, but this does not undermine the democracy. [15] And yet our democracy is being undermined, although this is a matter about which no one talks freely. But I shall tell you. It is undermined whenever you, men of Athens, are badly led, many of you without resources or weapons, and are at cross-purposes, and no general or anyone else pays attention to your votes, and no one is willing to address these matters or correct them, or acts to prevent them happening—and they now always do happen. [16] And by Zeus, men of Athens, there are other mendacious claims that have slipped by you and that do much harm to the constitution, such as that "your salvation lies in the courts" and that "you must guard the constitution

---

³³The Opisthodomos was the rear room of the chamber of the Parthenon, the main temple to Athena on the Acropolis of Athens, and was used as a treasury. In another speech, Demosthenes refers to an allegation that the Treasurers of Athena had burned down the Opisthodomos in an attempt to conceal their misappropriation of money from it (see Dem. 24.136, with the ancient commentary on the passage).

³⁴Oars and other equipment for the triremes of the Athenian navy were public property. Cf. 14.21n. See Gabrielsen 1994: 146–169.

with your vote." I know that the courts have authority in disputes between ourselves, but it is by force of arms that we must defeat our enemies, and in our armed forces that the safety of the constitution lies. [17] For voting will not bring victory to men who are under arms. Rather, it is those who have defeated the enemy by force of arms who will enable you to vote or to do anything else you like without fear. We should be formidable when we are under arms but benevolent when we are in court.[35]

[18] If anyone thinks that I am making speeches that are beyond my capacity, he is quite right. Any speech about so great a city and about matters of such importance must always seem beyond the capacity of any individual speaker; such speeches should aspire to your level of distinction rather than to that of the speaker. I shall now explain why none of the men whom you honor speaks in this way. [19] Those who come forward to speak with an eye on the election of magistrates[36] and the holding of office go around as slaves of your favor, which they need in order to be elected, each one eager to be initiated[37] as general but unwilling to do any part of a man's work. As things are now, if anyone is capable of achieving anything, he takes the reputation and good name of the city as his capital, profits from the lack of anyone to oppose him, holds out to you nothing but hopes, and thinks that he will inherit all your wealth, which is indeed what happens. But if you do every individual thing yourselves, such a man will have to take his fair share along with the others both of the toil and of its rewards. [20] The politicians, and those who concern themselves with political matters, have stopped looking out for your interests and have gone over to these men.[38] Previously you paid taxes by symmory, but now you engage in politics by symmory, each with a speaker as leader, a general beneath him, and three hundred as-

---

[35]Demosthenes' desire for antithesis results in the curious claim that Athenian lawcourts are characterized by benevolence (*philanthrōpia*).

[36]Most magistrates were chosen by lot (from those citizens who put their names forward), but the ten generals were elected.

[37]Demosthenes makes metaphorical use of the language of initiatory cults such as the Mysteries at Eleusis: see 3.5n.

[38]The generals mentioned above.

sistants; the rest of you are assigned, some to one group and some to another.[39] As a result, one man receives a bronze statue,[40] one or two others get rich at the city's expense, while the rest of you sit around witnessing their good fortune, handing over your own considerable good fortune to them by your daily idleness.

[21] But consider how things were in the time of your ancestors, so that you may learn, by means of examples from here rather than from elsewhere, what you should be doing.[41] Your ancestors did not set up bronze statues of Themistocles, who was general at the sea battle of Salamis,[42] or of Miltiades, who led them at Marathon,[43] or of the many others whose exploits were greater than those of our present-day generals. Instead they honored them as being in no way superior to themselves. [22] As a result, men of Athens, they deprived themselves of none of the credit for their exploits at that time, and everyone would agree that it was the Athenians who won the sea battle of Salamis, not Themistocles, and that the city won the battle of Marathon, not Miltiades. But now many people say that Timotheus captured Corcyra and that Iphicrates cut the Spartan regiment to pieces and that Chabrias won the sea battle off Naxos.[44] You seem to have renounced your claim to these achievements, to judge by the extravagant honors you have given to each of these men for them.[45] [23] And so your

---

[39]This simile is also used at 2.29: see the note there.

[40]Bronze statues were erected in the Athenian Agora in honor of the fourth-century Athenian generals Conon (Dem. 20.70), Timotheus, Iphicrates, and Chabrias (Aes. 3.243). On the last three, see 22n below.

[41]Sections 21–24 are very similar to Dem. 23.196–200.

[42]Themistocles, an Athenian general, led the Athenian contingent at the sea battle of Salamis in 480 (see 14.29n).

[43]Miltiades, an Athenian general, was prominently involved in the Athenian victory at the battle of Marathon in 490.

[44]All three men were important fourth-century Athenian generals. Timotheus, the son of Conon (see n. 40 above), captured the island of Corcyra in spring 375 in the course of naval operations against the Spartans. Iphicrates commanded a force of light-armed peltasts in the Corinthian War and defeated a Spartan regiment at Lechaeum, the port of Corinth, in 390. Chabrias defeated the Spartans in a sea battle off the island of Naxos in 376/5.

[45]See 20n on statues erected in honor of these three generals.

ancestors rewarded their own citizens appropriately, but you do not. What about foreigners? Menon of Pharsalus, who gave twelve talents of silver for the war for Eion near Amphipolis, and contributed two hundred of his own serfs as cavalrymen, was rewarded not with citizenship but merely with immunity from taxation.[46] [24] And earlier, in the case of Perdiccas, the king of Macedonia at the time of the barbarian invasion, who destroyed the barbarians who were retreating after the defeat at Plataea and brought about the King's final defeat, they voted to grant him only immunity from taxation, not citizenship, in the belief that their own native land was too great and valuable and sacred to permit such a gift.[47] But now, men of Athens, you make citizens of pestilential

---

[46] Eion on the river Strymon in Thrace was captured from the Persians by the Athenians and their allies in 476/5 (Thuc. 1.98.1; Herod. 7.107); Amphipolis was a later Athenian settlement nearby, but at the time of this speech, it was in the hands of Philip of Macedon. Menon belonged to an aristocratic family from the city of Pharsalus in Thessaly in northern Greece: a man of the same name, probably his grandson, led a Pharsalian force allied to Athens in the Peloponnesian War (Thuc. 2.22.3). The serfs (*penestai*) of Thessaly were nonchattel, dependent workers, comparable in some respects to the helots of Messenia and Laconia who were dependent on the Spartans. This passage is almost identical to Dem. 23.199; in the latter passage, however, it is claimed that the number of serfs Menon contributed was 300 and that he was granted Athenian citizenship. See further Osborne 1983: T1. See the Speech Introduction for a rejection of the view that this discrepancy shows that this speech is not the work of Demosthenes.

[47] It is clear that rather than Perdiccas II (king of Macedonia ca. 454–413), it is his predecessor Alexander I who is meant. The latter was king at the time of the Persian invasion of Greece in 480 and had been honored by Athens at some time in the 480s, perhaps for making Macedonian timber available for shipbuilding (see Herod. 8.136.1). Alexander in fact fought on the Persian side (cf. 6.11), although it is reported that he offered secret support to the Greeks. After the battle at Plataea in 479 the Persian army retreated overland back to Asia and had heavy casualties inflicted on it. On this episode, see 12.21 (Philip writes that "our ancestor Alexander . . . first held the place [Amphipolis], and from it he set up a gold statue at Delphi as first fruit for the Median [i.e., Persian] prisoners"); cf. Herod. 8.99, though he names the Thracians not the Macedonians. This passage is almost identical to Dem. 23.200, where, however, it is claimed, perhaps correctly, that

fellows, slaves born of slave parents, taking a price as you would for any other goods for sale.[48] [25] You do these things not because you are naturally inferior to your ancestors but because they happened to have a high opinion of themselves, whereas you, men of Athens, have been stripped of this quality.[49] In my view, it is never possible for those whose actions are small and trivial to have a great and vigorous spirit, just as those whose actions are glorious and fine cannot have petty or humble thoughts. For men's spirits must conform to their habitual behavior.

[26] Look at how the situation might be summarized, listening to an account both of their achievements and of yours, to see whether you are perhaps capable of improving yourselves, from their example if not from your own. They ruled the Greeks as willing subjects for forty-five years, carried up more than ten thousand talents to the Acropolis, and after fighting on both land and sea, erected many fine trophies, on which even now we pride ourselves.[50] And yet you should consider that they erected them not for us to gaze on in admiration but for us to imitate the virtues of the men who set them up. [27] This is what they achieved, but we—and you can all see how much of a free hand we have—do we behave in a similar way? Have we not spent more than fifteen hundred talents in vain on the poor of Greece,[51] and have we

---

"Perdiccas" (i.e., Alexander) was granted citizenship. See Osborne 1983: PT124; and see the previous note.

[48]Slaves were not permitted to become citizens, but a small number of former slaves are known to have received grants of Athenian citizenship in the fourth century. Of these, the best known are the bankers Pasion (Dem. 59.2) and Phormion (Dem. 46.13). In the case of Pasion, we know that he donated military equipment to the city (Dem. 45.85), a contribution that could have been misrepresented by a hostile observer as buying citizenship. But since Pasion was the father of Demosthenes' political supporter Apollodorus, it is unlikely that a reference to him is meant here. On the family, see Trevett 1992.

[49]Sections 25–31 are very similar to 3.23–32. See the Speech Introduction.

[50]These claims are also made at 3.24: see the notes there.

[51]The reference is to the hiring of mercenaries, who were often regarded as enlisting to escape extreme poverty. See 3.28n, 14.31n.

not exhausted the resources of every private house and the common funds of the city and the money from the allies, whom we acquired during the war, and whom these men have lost during the peace?[52] [28] "But by god," it might be objected, "these are the only things that were better then than now; everything else was worse." This is far from the truth, but let us examine whatever point you want. As regards buildings and the adornment of the city, they left so many and such splendid shrines and harbors and the like that none of their successors can surpass them—I refer to the Propylaea, the docks, the colonnades,[53] and the other buildings, with which they adorned the city and handed it on to us. [29] But the private houses of those who were in power were so moderate and so in conformance with the name of the constitution[54] that if any of you knows the house of Themistocles or Cimon or Aristides or other men of distinction of that time,[55] he sees that it is no grander than its neighbor. [30] But now, men of Athens, in public our city is happy to build roads

---

[52]Athens' allies were mostly acquired during war with Sparta in the 370s, when the Second Athenian Confederacy was set up. Its members paid financial "contributions" (*syntaxeis*) to Athens: see 4n above. Several of the most important of these broke away from Athens in 357 in the Social War: see the Introduction to Dem. 15.

[53]The Propylaea was the massive ceremonial gateway to the Acropolis, built between 436 and 422 as part of Pericles' building program. The dockyards of Piraeus were built in the fifth century to accommodate Athens' navy, which was based there. Colonnades (stoas) such as the Royal Stoa and the Painted Stoa were built around the Agora in the same period. In addition, many other civic and religious buildings were erected in the fifth century, both in Athens and elsewhere in Attica. It is striking to the modern reader that Demosthenes names the Propylaea but not the Parthenon, the temple of Athena that was built on the Acropolis in the same period.

[54]Demosthenes suggests that in a democracy housing should be egalitarian.

[55]The same idea is expressed, with a slightly different list of fifth-century Athenians, at 3.26. On Aristides, see 3.26n. On Themistocles, see 21 above. Cimon, the son of Miltiades (on whom see 3.26n), was a prominent political and military leader in the period after the Persian Wars: he was one of the architects of Athens' fifth-century empire, but his pro-Spartan policies resulted in his ostracism (i.e., temporary exile) in 461. See 9.42n.

and fountains and apply whitewash and such nonsense—and I put the blame not on the proposers of this expenditure, far from it, but on you, if you think that this is good enough. But in private some of those who hold positions of public responsibility have made their houses not only more extravagant than most others but also grander than public buildings, while others have purchased more farmland than they ever dreamed of.[56] [31] The reason for all these differences is that in the past the people were lord and master of all, and each leader[57] was happy to receive honors and magistracies and other benefits from them, but now the opposite is true. These men control every benefit, and all business is conducted through them, while the people play the part of servant and appendage, and you are grateful to receive whatever they offer you. [32] As a result, the city is in such a bad way that no one who reads your resolutions and reviews your actions would believe that both are the work of the same people. For example, when the accursed Megarians were ravaging the Orgas, you voted to march out, to prevent them, and not to give in.[58] And when the Phliasians were recently exiled, you voted to help them, to stand up to the murderers, and to summon volunteers from the Peloponnese.[59] [33] All this, men of Athens, was noble and just and

---

[56]For the same thought, see 3.29. Demosthenes' claim that some politicians have bought up large areas of farmland is probably a substantial exaggeration, since there was limited land available in Attica, and even the richest Athenians seem not to have owned large estates.

[57]Lit. "each of the others," drawing a contrast between the masses and the political elite.

[58]Megara was a Greek city whose territory bordered Attica to the west. The Megarians and the Athenians were often in dispute over the Hiera Orgas ("Sacred Land"), a strip of border territory sacred to the two goddesses, Demeter and Persephone, who were worshipped at nearby Eleusis in southwestern Attica: see also 12.4n. The Megarians are called "accursed" because of their encroachment on this sacred land. Demosthenes here refers to very recent events: see Didymus cols. 13.40–15.10, with Harding 2006: 245–255; *IG* II² 204* = Rhodes and Osborne 2003: no. 58 with full commentary. See the Speech Introduction for the relevance of this reference to the dating of the speech.

[59]Phlius was a city of the Argolid in the northern Peloponnese. Along with Arcadia, Achaea, and Elis, it made an alliance with Athens in 362/1

worthy of the city, but your subsequent actions achieved nothing. And so you incur hatred because of your decisions but fail to accomplish anything. You pass decrees on the basis of our city's good reputation but lack the force that would correspond to your votes. [34] I would advise you—and please do not get angry with me—either to lower your ambitions and be content to mind your own affairs or to organize a larger force. If I knew you to be Siphnians or Cythnians or some other such people,[60] I would advise you to lower your ambitions. But since you are Athenians, my advice to you is to make military preparations. For it would be shameful, men of Athens, truly shameful, to abandon the resolute spirit that your ancestors handed down to you. [35] Moreover, it is not possible for you, even if you wish to, to withdraw from the affairs of Greece. You have achieved many things throughout your history, and it is shameful to sacrifice your existing friends, and impossible to trust your existing enemies and allow them to become great. In short, you are faced with the same fate as your political leaders, who cannot stop whenever they want.[61] For you are the political leaders of Greece. [36] To sum up everything I have said, men of Athens: the speakers never make you bad or good; it is you who make them so, according to your wishes. You do not aim at what they want; they aim at what they think you desire. And so you should desire whatever is best, and if you do so all will be well. For in that case, either no speaker will say anything ignoble, or, if any of them does, he will get nowhere, since no one will listen to him.

(*IG* II² 112 = Rhodes and Osborne 2003: no. 41). It emerges from the text of the alliance (line 30) that at that time Phlius was a democracy.

[60]Siphnos and Cythnos are islands in the Aegean. In the sixth century, Siphnos had prospered from the mining of gold and silver, but by the fourth century both islands were evidently regarded as utterly insignificant.

[61]Demosthenes' point appears to be, if his analogy holds, that a sense of responsibility makes it impossible for politicians to abandon political life, though he may be thinking that their personal ambition or pressure from their supporters makes them reluctant to do so.

14. ON THE SYMMORIES

INTRODUCTION

On the Symmories is the earliest surviving deliberative speech of Demosthenes. It is dated 354/3 by Dionysius of Halicarnassus, and this date has been generally accepted.[1] According to Libanius' *Introduction*, the occasion of the speech was a rumor that the Persian King was planning to attack Greece. Apparently some politicians at Athens had argued for an aggressive response (1), but Demosthenes advocates restraint: the Athenians should resist if they are attacked but not provoke war with Persia. At the same time, he argues that they should improve their readiness for war by reforming the financial organization of their navy.

Demosthenes refers back to this speech a year or two later, in his speech *On the Freedom of the Rhodians* (15.6), a passage that makes it clear that this speech was actually delivered:

> I imagine that some of you recall that at the time when you were deliberating about relations with the King, I came for-

---

[1]Dionysius of Halicarnassus *First Letter to Ammaeus* 4. See in general Lane Fox 1997: 177–181. The speech discusses the possibility that the Thebans will help the Persians (33), but it shows no awareness of the help that the Theban general Pammenes provided the rebel satrap Artabazus (on whom see below) *against* the forces of the Persian King. This is dated 353/2 by Diodorus (16.34.1), after the withdrawal of the Athenian commander Chares (see the next note). This speech is probably therefore earlier than Pammenes' expedition. See also MacDowell (2009: 142–143), who is agnostic on the date.

ward and was the first to advise you—I think that I spoke alone, or perhaps there was one other—and said that it was not sensible to use your hatred of him as an excuse for military preparation, but that you should prepare yourselves to fight your existing enemies, and defend yourselves against him only if he tried to wrong you. Nor did you think that I spoke wrongly, but on the contrary my advice was pleasing to you.

In the years after the King's Peace of 386, Persian policy towards Greece was directed towards deterring Greek, and in particular Athenian, interference on the mainland of Asia Minor, territory that the King claimed as his own and that had been ceded to him by the peace. The main means by which this was achieved was diplomacy: there was substantial Persian involvement in the series of peace conferences of the 370s and 360s. The Persian priority in the West (from their perspective) was not Greece but the recovery of the rich province of Egypt, which had been in revolt since the end of the fifth century. The Persian Empire was also destabilized by a series of satrapal revolts (i.e., revolts by provincial governors) in the middle years of the century, though Artaxerxes III Ochus, who came to the throne in 358, did much to restore stability.

There had, however, been recent friction between Athens and Persia, in addition to the support that Mausolus, satrap of Caria, gave to the anti-Athenian rebels in the Social War of 357–355 (see Dem. 15). In 355 the Athenian general Chares, who was short of money for prosecuting the Social War, had taken service with the rebel satrap Artabazus and had (on his own account) defeated a Persian army.[2] Artaxerxes reacted by demanding that the Athenians recall Chares, under threat of sending a large fleet to assist their enemies (Diodorus 16.22), and the Athenians backed down. The present speech makes no mention of Chares, Artabazus, or the Social War and was probably therefore delivered later than this crisis (see above).

Why then were there rumors of a planned Persian attack not just on Athens but apparently on Greece as a whole (see esp. 7)?

---

[2] For other sources, see Harding 1985: no. 72.

Part of the explanation is probably Athenian nervousness after the threats that Artaxerxes made against them in 355. But it may also be that the large fleet being built in such places as Cyprus and Phoenicia for the planned Persian invasion of Egypt (Diodorus 16.40.3, 44) was misinterpreted in Greece. In any case, the rumors were unfounded, since Persian policy was focused on Egypt (see 31 for the collection of Greek and other mercenaries for the same campaign). If there really was pressure at Athens to declare war—and Demosthenes may be exaggerating it—he was surely right to resist it.[3]

Demosthenes' specific advice is that since the Greeks are disunited, it would be the height of folly for the Athenians to go to war alone against Persia and risk much of Greece taking the Persian side against them. It would be better to wait on events: if the rumors are well founded, and the Persians do attack, the rest of Greece can be expected to rally to their side (3–14).

Demosthenes later described this speech as a contribution to the debate about relations with the Persian King (15.6, quoted above). But as the title it was given in antiquity suggests,[4] it is largely concerned with the symmory system, that is, with the system for funding the operations of Athens' navy. The Athenian navy was a large and complex organization, which was paid for in part with public money and in part by wealthy citizens, who were required to contribute to the equipping and operation of its ships. In the fifth century, rich Athenians were selected for annual performance of the trierarchy, that is, service as a trierarch (*triērarchos*, trireme commander).[5] Each trierarch was responsible for a single ship, and the system encouraged him to spend his own money freely and thereby be seen to be doing his patriotic duty. Later in the century the financial burden of taking responsibility for a whole ship became too much for many individ-

---

[3]Cf. 15.5, referring to those politicians at Athens who "advise the city to oppose the King for the sake of the Egyptians."

[4]There is no reason to believe that any of the speeches were given their traditional titles by Demosthenes himself.

[5]This form of service, whereby a rich man was required to spend his own money to perform a specified task for the benefit of the city, was called a liturgy (*leitourgeia*): on the term, see 4.36n.

uals to bear, and trierarchies started to be shared. In time this too became too onerous a burden, and under a law proposed by Periandros (see Dem. 47.21), probably in 358/7, the Athenians introduced a new system that transferred the expense to a much larger pool of wealthier Athenians (the "Twelve Hundred"), who were distributed into twenty contribution groups, each called a symmory (*symmoria*; see further the notes on 16–21).[6]

In this speech Demosthenes proposes further reforms to the system. He wishes to increase the number of those liable to contribution from twelve hundred to two thousand, to take account of exemptions (16). Although the number of symmories is to stay the same, they are to be subdivided into sections, with a fixed number of ships assigned to each section (17–18). The taxable value of Athens (its taxation base) is to be distributed over the symmories in such a way that each has roughly the same total worth (19–20). Demosthenes next discusses the provision of naval equipment (21) and the recruiting of rowers (22–23). He also addresses the problem of the rich evading their responsibilities by concealing the extent of their wealth, and he concludes that it is best to do nothing about this until some real crisis occurs, when (he optimistically predicts) a sense of self-preservation will make them willing to contribute (24–28).

Why Demosthenes proposed tinkering with Periandros' system so soon after it was established is not entirely clear. It may be that the new system had simply not worked well in its first few years of operation: the details of his proposal suggest specifically that the number of exemptions was causing problems (16). Moreover, Athens' military failure in the Social War, together with the lack of resources that drove Chares to enlist with Artabazus, may have convinced some Athenians that the system needed to be reformed again.[7]

---

[6]This system was modeled on, and may in fact have been identical with, the system of symmories established in 378/7 for the payment of the wealth-tax (*eisphora*), although the details are controversial. See MacDowell 1986; Gabrielsen 1994: 182–199 (and passim on the financing of Athens' fleet). The title of this speech is sometimes translated as *On the Navy Boards*.

[7]Contemporary sources, Demosthenes included, complain about various inefficiencies in the operation of the navy, some of which are attribut-

Although the speech may have received a favorable reception (thus 15.6, quoted above, but we only have Demosthenes' word for it), and although the attack on warmongering against Persia was effective, the specific reforms were not accepted. Demosthenes, however, had an abiding interest in organizational reform (see also Dem. 13, and the speech on army reform mentioned at 13.9) and successfully introduced reform of naval finances in 340/339 (Dem. 18.102–108).

14. ON THE SYMMORIES

[1] Those who praise your ancestors,[8] men of Athens, seem to me to have chosen to deliver speeches that will find favor with you but do no benefit to those whom they praise. For in seeking to speak about achievements to which no one could do justice, they win for themselves the reputation of being able speakers but leave their audience with a lesser opinion of those men's excellence. In my opinion, the highest praise of your ancestors is conferred by the passage of time. For, although much time has passed, no one has yet been able to surpass their achievements. [2] I, by contrast, will seek to explain how I think you can best prepare yourselves. The situation is as follows: Even if all of us who wish to address you were to show ourselves to be skilled speakers, I am certain that this would not lead to any improvement in your affairs. But if every one, whoever he is, who comes up to speak can tell you convincingly what kind of preparation will benefit our city, and on what scale it should be and how it should be paid for, the current panic would be wholly defused. This is what I shall try to do, if I can, after I have briefly told you what I think about our relations with the King.[9]

---

able to Athens' lack of money to fund the system, and part to the city being a democracy: in particular, there were problems with getting ships ready on time and with equipping them. Some of these complaints were probably exaggerated: see Cawkwell 1984.

[8]Demosthenes is referring to Athens' heyday in the first half of the fifth century: the time of the Persian Wars and of the acquisition of Athens' empire.

[9]I.e., the king of Persia.

[3] Although I believe that the King is the common enemy of all the Greeks,[10] I would certainly not advise you on that account to wage war against him on your own, independently of the others. For I see that the Greeks are not even all on good terms with each other, and indeed some of them put more trust in the King than they do in certain of their fellow Greeks. For such reasons I think that it is in your interest to ensure that any war that breaks out is on equal terms and just, and to make all the appropriate preparations, and for this to be the basis of your policy. [4] In my opinion, men of Athens, if it becomes absolutely clear that the King is attacking them, the Greeks will form an alliance and will be most grateful to those who are resisting him on their behalf and by their side. But if we go to war before this is clear, men of Athens, I fear that we may be forced to fight not only against the King but also against those very Greeks whose interests we are seeking to protect. [5] For in that event he will stop what he has started, if indeed he has decided to attack the Greeks, and will offer some of them money and friendship; and they, in their determination to win their own wars,[11] will disregard the collective security of Greece. I advise you not to plunge our city into such confusion and madness. [6] Moreover, I observe that you do not make your decisions about the King on the same basis as do the other Greeks. Many of them, I think, may pursue their private interests and neglect the rest of Greece, whereas you, even if you have suffered some wrong,[12] consider it ignoble to pun-

---

[10]Demosthenes here seeks to avoid any suspicion that he is pro-Persian. For similar concern that politicians should not be partisan supporters of another state, see 15.15, 16.1–2. It is interesting to contrast this passage with Demosthenes' later rejection of such anti-Persian slogans (10.33), at a time when Athens and Persia were cooperating against Philip.

[11]Demosthenes presumably has two conflicts in mind: the Third Sacred War between Thebes and Phocis and fighting in the Peloponnese between Sparta and its enemies, on which see Diodorus 16.34.3 (war between Sparta and Argos, dated to 353/2) and 16.39.1–7 (war between Sparta and an alliance of Megalopolis, Argos, Messene, Sicyon, and Thebes, dated to 352/1).

[12]I.e., if the Athenians are wronged by fellow Greeks. This claim is wishful thinking: Athens had been quite prepared to accept Persian support in the Corinthian War against Sparta earlier in the fourth century.

246   DEMOSTHENES

ish your wrongdoers if that would result in their subjection to the foreigner (*barbaros*).[13] [7] Since this is the case, we must consider how to ensure both that we are not at a disadvantage in any war and that the man[14] whom we suspect of plotting against the Greeks does not get credit for his apparent friendship with them. How can we achieve this? By making it clear to everybody that we have reviewed our armed forces and are well prepared and that our policies are based upon the principle of justice.

[8] To those speakers who are overconfident and who too readily encourage you to go to war, I have this to say: It is not hard to get the reputation for being brave when deliberation is called for or to seem a clever speaker when danger is at hand. What is hard is also our duty: to show bravery when faced with danger but to offer the most sensible advice when engaged in deliberation. [9] In my opinion, men of Athens, it would be hard for our city to wage war on the King, but the actual fighting that a war would involve would be easy. How is this so? Because, I believe, any war inevitably requires ships and money and the control of strategic positions, all of which I see that he has in greater quantity than we do. Fighting, on the other hand, requires brave men more than anything else, and I am confident that we and those who share the danger with us have more of these. [10] I therefore advise you on no account to start a war but to make appropriate preparations to fight. If fighting against Greeks and fighting against foreigners called for different types of force, we might perhaps reasonably show ourselves to be making our preparations against him;[15] [11] but since all military preparation takes the same form, and every force has the same basic purpose—to be able to resist one's enemies, to help one's allies, and to preserve one's existing assets—why, when we have acknowledged enemies,[16] should we go

---

[13]On the connotation of the Greek word *barbaros*, see 3.16n.

[14]The Persian King. For the nature of his suspected plotting, see the Speech Introduction.

[15]I.e., if the Athenians had to choose to prepare for war either against their enemies in Greece or against the King, it would be reasonable for them to choose the latter.

[16]Athens' list of enemies included Thebes, whose enemy Phocis enjoyed Athenian support; some of its former allies, who had revolted in the Social

looking for others? So, let us make our preparations against our existing enemies and defend ourselves against the King, if he tries to wrong us. [12] You are now calling on the Greeks to join you. But if you do not do as they bid,[17] how can you expect any of them, some of whom are not well disposed towards you, to comply? "Because, by Zeus, we will tell them that the King is plotting against them." But in Zeus' name, do you suppose that they do not see this for themselves? I am sure that they do, but their fear of him does not yet outweigh their disagreements both with you and, in the case of some of them, with one another. If we do that, our ambassadors will simply go round giving empty recitations.[18] [13] Later, however, if our current expectation is well founded, I do not suppose that any of the Greeks is so confident in his own power that he will not come begging to you at the sight of your thousand cavalrymen, as many hoplites as anyone might want, and your three hundred ships,[19] in the belief that these will guarantee his survival. Consequently, if you call on the Greeks now, you will do so as suppliants, and if you are unsuccessful, you will have failed outright. But if you make your preparations and then wait, you will be able to save them when they ask, and you may be certain that they will all come to you for help.

War (see 15.3n); Mausolus the satrap of Caria (see 15.3n); and Philip of Macedon (see 15.24n).

[17]The reference is unclear, and Demosthenes may not have anything specific in mind beyond the general difficulty of getting all the Greeks to cooperate with each other.

[18]The allusion is to rhapsodes, who gave professional recitations of (especially epic) poetry and whose performances were intended to entertain their audience rather than persuade them to take action.

[19]One thousand was the nominal strength of the Athenian cavalry throughout the classical period (see Thuc. 2.13.8). Demosthenes is vague about the number of hoplites, and in fact the number of Athenians who were liable for hoplite service varied over time. He gives a round figure for the number of ships in the Athenian navy: inscribed naval accounts indicate that Athens had more than 300 ships in this period (349 in 353/2: *IG* II² 1613, lines 284–292), although not all were serviceable. In any case, the Athenians would have found it impossible to put all their ships to sea at once. See Gabrielsen 1994: 126–129.

[14] For these and similar reasons, men of Athens, I have tried to make my speech neither rash nor longer than it need be, but I have taken great pains to work out how we can make our preparations as quickly and effectively as possible.[20] I request that you listen to my proposal and, if it pleases you, vote in favor of it. The first and biggest step, men of Athens, in making our preparations is for you to resolve that you will be ready and willing to do whatever is required in person. [15] For as you know, men of Athens, whenever you have all set your heart on anything, and as a result have each felt obliged to take action, you have always achieved your aim. But whenever you have formed some desire, but have then looked to one another, each refusing to do anything himself but expecting his neighbor to act, you have never yet accomplished anything. [16] If you do have such a keen and resolute attitude, I say that you should increase the Twelve Hundred to two thousand, by assigning an additional eight hundred people.[21] For if you designate this number, once heiresses, orphans, the property of cleruchs and associations, and invalids have been removed, you will have twelve hundred remaining.[22] [17] From

---

[20]Demosthenes contrasts his summary analysis of relations with Persia with his detailed financial proposals.

[21]At this time the number of wealthy Athenians liable to contribute financially to the running of the navy was fixed at 1,200 (see the Speech Introduction).

[22]Various categories of property owners were exempt from active service as trierarch (commander of a trireme): heiresses, orphans (i.e., boys whose fathers had died), and invalids were all deemed to be incapable of holding military command. Cleruchs were Athenian citizens who lived in Athenian settlements overseas, and who would have been unavailable by reason of absence. By associations are meant corporate bodies such as demes and phratries. Demosthenes wishes the 1,200 to consist entirely of men capable of active service. The interpretation of the Greek word here translated as "invalid" (*adynatos*, lit. "unable") is disputed. Alternative views are that Demosthenes is referring to men who were too poor (i.e., financially unable) to contribute, or to those who were exempt because they were already performing, or had recently performed, another liturgy. See in general Gabrielsen 1994: 85–102 (though I disagree with his proposal that these exemptions were granted by the Athenian state as privileges).

these I suggest that you create twenty symmories, as there are currently, each containing sixty members, and that you divide each symmory into five sections of twelve, in each case including the poorest to match the richest. This is how I think the personnel should be organized; I will explain my reasons after you have heard about the system as a whole. [18] What about the triremes? My proposal is that you designate a total of three hundred ships, and from these create twenty squadrons of fifteen ships, assigning to each squadron five of the first hundred, five of the second hundred, and five of the third hundred; then that you allot a squadron of fifteen ships to each symmory, and three triremes to each section of a symmory.[23] [19] Once these arrangements have been made, I make the following proposal for the reorganization of your finances. Since the taxable value of our land is six thousand talents,[24] you should divide this sum into one hundred lots of sixty talents, and then allot five lots of sixty talents to each of the twenty large symmories,[25] and each symmory should assign one lot of sixty talents to each of its sections. [20] As a result, if you need one hundred ships, sixty talents of property value will be taxed to provide the sum needed for each ship,[26] which will

---

[23]The ships are divided into three groups, each of 100, according to their age and sailing quality. At this period ships in the Athenian navy were rated as "first," "second," "third," or "select," the last being particularly fast ships. See Gabrielsen 1994: 129–131.

[24]The figure of 6,000 talents probably represents the most recent valuation of the total wealth of those liable for paying the wealth-tax (*eisphora*) (on which see 26n), rather than the total wealth of all Athenians: see 27 below, where Demosthenes uses the same figure of 6,000 talents to calculate how much money could be raised from the *eisphora*. In 378/7 the comparable figure (in the context of the *eisphora*) was 5,750 talents, according to the Hellenistic historian Polybius (2.62.6–7). On the process of self-assessment by which the rich probably declared their wealth, see Christ 2007.

[25]Demosthenes refers to the 100 proposed sections as (small) symmories, from which the symmories as such need to be distinguished.

[26]Demosthenes' words have been expanded a little in the translation to make his point clear. If the Athenians need 100 ships, each section (constituting 1 percent of the 1,200 and worth 1 percent of the tax base) will provide one ship, and so on.

have twelve trierarchs.[27] If you need two hundred ships, thirty talents will provide the sum needed for each ship, which will have six trierarchs. And if you need three hundred ships, twenty talents will provide the sum needed, and four people will be trierarchs. [21] In the same way, I propose that you value the naval equipment that is currently on loan according to the inventory[28] and divide this sum into twenty parts, and that you allot one share of the debt to each of the large symmories;[29] and each symmory should allot an equal share to each of its sections; and the twelve men in each section should recover what is owed, and each should put the triremes that are assigned to them into a state of readiness. [22] This, I think, is the best way for the money and the ships and the trierarchs and the collection of equipment to be funded and organized. Next, I shall describe a clear and straightforward system for providing crews for the ships. I propose that the generals[30] should divide the docks[31] into ten areas, after they have considered how to organize the berths into sets of thirty, as close as possible to each other.[32] In doing so, they should assign two symmories and thirty triremes to each of these areas and

---

[27]Here the 1,200 symmory members are all described as trierarchs, although in practice no more than one or two of them will have commanded each of the ships for which they were collectively responsible.

[28]The equipment (masts, oars, ropes, and other gear) for Athens' triremes belonged to the city and was lent to the trierarchs for the duration of their service. In practice, much of this equipment was not returned, as is clear from the partially surviving records kept by the Superintendents of the Dockyards (*IG* II[2] 1604–1632). This caused problems for incoming trierarchs (as, e.g., the speaker of Dem. 47). See in general Gabrielsen 1994: 146–169.

[29]The redundant reference to the symmories as "large" reinforces the distinction between them and the sections into which they were divided (cf. 19n).

[30]The board of ten annually elected generals were responsible for Athens' navy as well as its army.

[31]In Piraeus. On the "naval zone" of Piraeus, see briefly Garland 2001: 95–100.

[32]I.e., all thirty berths within each set are to be close to each other, so that there is a defined area for the ships assigned to each set.

then distribute the tribes[33] among the areas by lot. [23] Each taxi-arch[34] should divide the part of the docks that is allocated to his tribe into three areas, and the ships likewise, and then distribute the Thirds[35] by lot, so that each tribe has one part of the entire docks, and each Third has a third of each part. And so if you need anything, you will know where each tribe has been assigned, and each Third, and which trierarchs and triremes there are. If you start in this way, then if we omit anything now—and it is undeniably hard to think of everything—the system will find it out for itself, and there will be a single system both for the navy as a whole and for its constituent parts.

[24] As regards the source of funds, what I am about to say is paradoxical, I admit, but I shall say it nevertheless. For I am confident that on a correct assessment of the matter, I alone will be seen to have spoken the truth and to have anticipated what will happen in the future. I say that we do not need to talk about money now, since you have a source of funds, if you need it, that is great and fine and honorable. But if we look for it now, we shall reach the conclusion that it will not exist for us even in the future—so far short will we fall of making provision for the present. If on the other hand we leave it alone now, it will be there for us later. What is it that does not exist now but will exist in the future? It is like a riddle—which I shall now explain. [25] Look at this whole city of ours, men of Athens. It contains wealth that is almost equal to that of all other cities. But the owners of this

---

[33]The Athenian citizen body was divided for various civic and military purposes into ten units called "tribes" (*phylai*), of roughly equal size. Specifically, the heavy infantry (hoplites) of the Athenian army were organized into ten regiments (*taxeis*), one from each tribe.

[34]The ten annually elected taxiarchs (*taxiarchoi*) were military commanders, each of whom commanded the hoplite regiment (*taxis*: see the previous note) of his own tribe: see 4.26n.

[35]There were three "Thirds" (*trittyes*, singular *trittys*) in each tribe. Each Third was made up of a number of demes (communities) from one of the three regions into which Attica was arbitrarily divided, thus ensuring that the tribes were geographically diverse in their composition. See (briefly) Hansen 1991: 46–49.

wealth are so minded that if all the speakers were to raise the alarm that the King is coming, that he is here, that it cannot possibly be otherwise, and if together with the speakers an equal number of men were to deliver oracles to the same effect,[36] they would not only not contribute but they would not even reveal their wealth or give the appearance of being rich.[37] [26] But if they were to see the things that they are now frightened to hear about actually taking place, none of them is so stupid that he would withhold his money and not be the first to pay the wealth-tax.[38] For who would rather lose his life and his possessions than contribute a share of his wealth to save both himself and the rest of his property? And so I declare that the money will be available when it is really needed but not before. Consequently I do not advise you even to look for it now, since what you could provide now, if you choose to look for it, would provoke more laughter than if you were to provide nothing at all. [27] Look, what would happen if someone were to propose a wealth-tax of one hundredth? We would raise sixty talents.[39] What about one fiftieth, double that? We would raise one hundred and twenty talents. What is this against the twelve hundred camels that, so these men say, transport the King's money? Even if you wanted us to pay a wealth-tax of one twelfth, raising five hundred talents—you would not tolerate it nor, even if you did pay it, would the money be enough

---

[36]Oracle mongers, who peddled the texts of prophecies and oracular responses, were particularly active at times of crisis such as when war threatened. See Flower 2008: 60–65.

[37]Demosthenes alludes here to "invisible wealth," i.e., wealth held in forms such as cash, bank deposits or loans, that were not easily detectable, as opposed to visible wealth such as land, property, and slaves. Some rich Athenians sought to keep much of their wealth "invisible" to evade taxes and liturgies. See Gabrielsen 1986; Christ 1990.

[38]The wealth-tax (*eisphora*) was an occasional tax on wealth, levied by a vote of the Assembly as a proportion (see 27) of the assessed wealth of those rich enough to be liable to pay it. It was the main way in which the Athenians could raise extra money for military expenditure. The symmory system was also used for collecting *eisphora*: see the Speech Introduction.

[39]Demosthenes here uses, in the context of the *eisphora*, the same figure for the total value of Attica (6,000 talents) that he earlier used in the context of the naval symmories (see 19). Evidently there was only one valuation.

for the conduct of the war. [28] You must then prepare yourselves in other respects but allow those who have money to keep it for the present—and there is no finer city in which to keep it! But if ever the opportunity arises, you should take it, and they will willingly contribute. This course of action is both feasible, men of Athens, and honorable and expedient; it also sends the King an appropriate message about you, which would cause him no little concern. [29] He knows that with two hundred ships, of which we provided one hundred, our ancestors destroyed one thousand of his,[40] and he will hear that we ourselves now have three hundred ships prepared. So he would not think it at all a light matter, even if he were utterly mad, to make our city his enemy. But if he should think to pride himself on his wealth, he will find that here too his capital is less substantial than yours. [30] He is bringing much gold, they say. But if he distributes this, he will have to seek more. For fountains and wells must fail, if much is drawn from them at one time, whereas he will learn that the value of our territory is our capital. And we defend it against invaders, as those of his ancestors who were at Marathon would know best.[41] So long as we are victorious it is, I believe, impossible for our wealth to run out.[42]

[31] What some people fear, that he will use his money to collect a large force of mercenaries, seems to me implausible. For I think that although many Greeks would be willing to take pay from him to fight against Egypt[43] or Orontes[44] or some other for-

---

[40]Demosthenes refers to the battle of Salamis in 480. In a later speech (18.238) he claims that Athens contributed 200 out of a total of 300 ships, which is closer to the figures provided by Herodotus (8.42–48: 180 out of 366 ships were Athenian).

[41]On the battle of Marathon in northeastern Attica in 490, see 13.21n.

[42]Demosthenes is perhaps thinking here that the Athenians will be able to levy the *eisphora* indefinitely on the land of Attica.

[43]Egypt revolted from Persian rule at the start of the fourth century, and the Persians made several attempts to regain it before they finally succeeded in 343/2. Greek mercenaries were employed in large numbers on both sides of the conflict. See Parke 1933: 165–169.

[44]Orontes, the satrap (i.e., Persian governor) of Mysia in northwestern Asia Minor, was a leader of a revolt involving several of the western satraps

eigner, not out of a desire to help him capture any of them but each hoping to achieve a measure of individual prosperity and thereby escape his existing poverty,[45] I do not think that any Greek would march against Greece—where would he turn to afterwards? Will he go to be a slave in Phrygia?[46] [32] Since war against foreigners is about nothing less than the preservation of our territory and lives and customs and freedom and the like, who is so misguided as to wish to sacrifice himself, his parents, family tombs, and fatherland for the sake of a short-lived profit? No one, surely. Nor indeed is it in the King's interest to conquer the Greeks with mercenaries. For once they have defeated us, they in turn will be stronger than him, and he does not want to destroy you only to be in the power of others. What he would like best is to rule everyone; but if he cannot do that, to rule the slaves[47] that he already has.

[33] If anyone imagines that the Thebans will join him,[48] it is difficult to speak to you about them, since your hatred of them makes you unwilling to hear anything good about them, even if it is true.[49] Nevertheless, those who are deliberating about mat-

---

against the Persian King in the 360s and 350s. On this revolt, see Briant 2002: 656–675.

[45] It was assumed by Greek writers of the period that most mercenaries had enlisted to escape poverty at home. Others will have been political exiles, and some perhaps became mercenaries out of a desire for adventure.

[46] Phrygia was a Persian satrapy of western central Asia Minor and also a significant source of slaves for Greek cities such as Athens.

[47] Demosthenes uses the word slave to refer pejoratively to any subject of the Persian King: see 15.23n.

[48] The Thebans had (albeit reluctantly) joined the Persians during their invasion of Greece in 480, and thereafter it was easy for Athenians and others who were ill disposed to them to impute pro-Persian sympathies to them. More recently, at a peace conference held at Susa in 367, the Persian King had supported Thebes, to the disgust of the contemporary Athenian historian Xenophon (*Hellenica* 7.1.33–40).

[49] Athens and Thebes were rivals for the hegemony of Greece. In the 360s they had clashed in the Peloponnese, where Athens supported Sparta; in northern Greece; and in the Aegean, where Thebes made overtures to some of Athens' disaffected allies. At the time of the speech, Athens was also providing (mainly moral) support to Phocis in its war against Thebes.

ters of importance must not neglect any calculation that is to our advantage, for any reason. My view is that the Thebans are so far from ever joining him against the Greeks [34] that they would pay a lot of money, if they had it to give, for the chance to redeem their previous crimes against Greece.[50] But if anyone thinks that the Thebans are by nature utterly unregenerate, I imagine that you all realize this—that if they side with the King, their enemies must take the side of the Greeks.

[35] I think that justice is on our side and that those who are on it will be stronger than the traitors and the foreigner[51] in any situation. And so I say that we should not be afraid without good reason nor be induced to start a war. Indeed, I do not think that any of the other Greeks could reasonably dread such a war. [36] For who of them is unaware that so long as they accepted that he[52] was their common enemy, they were in accord with one another and were secure in their prosperity, but when they thought that he was their supporter in their disagreements with each other, they suffered more evils than could be devised by someone putting a curse on them? Are we then to fear the man whom fortune and the god show to be a useless friend but a useful enemy? Certainly not! But let us not act unjustly, both for our own sake and because of the disturbed condition and unreliability of the rest of Greece. [37] If we unanimously agreed to attack him, I would not consider it wrong for us to wrong him. But since that is not the case, I say that we should be on our guard not to offer the King any excuse to seek justice on behalf of the other Greeks. For if you remain at peace, such an action would make him suspect; but if you go to war, he could reasonably represent himself, because of their hatred for you, as a friend of the others. [38] Do not then put the evils of Greece to the test, by summoning the Greeks when they will refuse to come and by fighting a war that you will be unable to win. Instead, you should remain at peace, be confident and prepare yourselves, and hope that it is reported

---

[50]I.e., their going over to the Persians in 480: see 33n.

[51]Referring to the Thebans, as traitors to Greece in 480, and the Persian King respectively.

[52]The Persian King.

about you to the King, not by Zeus that you are all confused or alarmed or in a state of uproar—far from it—[39] but that if lying and perjury were not as shameful to the Greeks as they are admirable to him, you would long ago have marched against him. As things are, you would not take this action on your own account, but should pray to all the gods that the same madness may overtake him as once overtook his ancestors. And if it occurs to him to think about this, he will realize that your plans are not to be scorned. [40] He knows that it was from the wars against his ancestors that this city became rich and powerful, whereas from the peace that it once kept[53] it surpassed none of the Greek cities by as much as it does now. Indeed, he sees that the Greeks are in need of someone who will, wittingly or unwittingly, reconcile them to each other, and knows that he would be doing exactly that, if he were to stir up war. And so the news that he will receive will be both familiar to him and credible.

[41] I do not wish to irritate you, men of Athens, by speaking at too great a length, and so I shall summarize my advice and then depart. I recommend that you make preparations against your existing enemies, and I declare that you should resist the King and anyone else if they try to wrong you, with this same force, but should not take the first step in either speaking or acting unjustly; and you should consider how our actions, not the speeches from this platform, may be worthy of our ancestors. If you do this, you will be doing what is in the interest both of yourselves and of those who are trying to persuade you of the opposite course, since you will not get angry with them later because of any mistake you make now!

---

[53]Demosthenes is referring to the period before the Persian Wars, when Athens was not (as he implies) always at peace but was indeed not yet a dominant power in Greece.

15. ON THE FREEDOM OF THE RHODIANS

〰〰〰

INTRODUCTION

The date of this speech is open to some doubt. Dionysius of Halicarnassus places it in 351/0, although we do not know how he or his source arrived at this date.[1] It was clearly delivered after the death of Mausolus, ruler of Caria, and during the rule of his sister and widow Artemisia (e.g., 27). Mausolus died in 353/2 (Diodorus 16.36.2), and Artemisia died in 351/0 (Diodorus 16.45.7), and so the speech must belong within those years. Demosthenes reports rumors that the Persian campaign to regain Egypt is failing (12), but the dates of this campaign are not exactly known.[2]

A possible obstacle to accepting Dionysius' date lies in the passage (24) in which Demosthenes claims that some Athenians despise Philip of Macedon as being of no consequence. Since in summer 352 Philip had secured a decisive victory over the Phocians at the battle of the Crocus Field and thereby gained control of all Thessaly, and in winter 352/1 was campaigning successfully in Thrace, it is unlikely that many Athenians regarded him as inconsequential in 351/0. It is also hard to believe that Demosthenes

---

[1] *First Letter to Ammaeus* 4.

[2] Diodorus' confused account of the eventual Persian conquest of Egypt (in the 340s, but misdated by him) refers in vague terms to earlier failures (16.40.3–5; cf. 16.44.1 and 48.1). Isocrates (5.101) also refers in 346 to an embarrassing Persian failure. There seems no evidence that Artaxerxes' failed campaign started as late as 351/0, as it is often dated, except for the desire to synchronize it with the presumed date of this speech. See Lane Fox 1997: 187–191.

advocated sending a force to the southeastern corner of the Aegean at the same time as, or even after, he delivered the *First Philippic* (Dem. 4), in which he argued that Philip posed a very serious threat to Athens. From this point of view, a more likely date would be 353/2, shortly after the death of Mausolus, whenever in the year that occurred, and after the defeat of Philip by the Phocian army in summer 353 (Diodorus 16.35.2), an event that may have led observers at Athens to regard his threat as exaggerated.[3] On the other hand, 24 may relate to the rumors that Philip was ill (or even dead) at the time of his Thracian campaign of 352/1 (see 4.10), which might explain why some Athenians had started to discount him as a threat.[4] On this view, Dionysius' date could be correct.

The context of the speech is an appeal to Athens by the exiled democrats of Rhodes for help in restoring them to their city. The island of Rhodes in the southeastern Aegean was a founding member of the Second Athenian Confederacy (as it is generally called) or League.[5] This was created in the early 370s under Athens' leadership as an anti-Spartan alliance. Its constitution sought to prevent many of the abuses that had made Athens' fifth-century empire unpopular with its subjects, and it was initially very successful in recruiting members. Over time, however, a number of allies became increasingly disaffected. They resented Athens' imperialistic policies of the 360s and early 350s, such as the establishment of an Athenian cleruchy (i.e., settlement) on the Aegean island of Samos (see 9n) and the diversion of the league's resources to attempts to recover Athens' former possessions in the north Aegean, especially Amphipolis and the Chersonese.

They also resented Athens' breaches of the league's constitu-

---

[3] See Lane Fox (see the previous note).

[4] The text of 24 contains a particle (*ara*) that has the sense "after all," i.e., that Philip is after all of no consequence. This might indicate that some specific event had happened to cause people to downplay the threat he posed to Athens.

[5] *IG* II[2] 43 = Rhodes and Osborne 2003: no. 22 (an inscription recording the establishment of the confederacy and listing its members), line 82. See in general Cargill 1981.

tion, such as the imposition of garrisons and demands for money, and its failure to adequately police the Aegean.[6] This culminated in 357 when a number of prominent members of the league—Rhodes, Chios, and Byzantium—led a revolt against Athens (3n). The resulting war (known as the Social War)[7] was a disaster for the Athenians: their fleet was defeated by the rebels, and they were forced to acquiesce in their secession. The mood at Athens in the aftermath of the war was understandably gloomy: its foreign policy had failed, public finances were weak, and the navy had suffered a humiliating reverse (for Demosthenes' concern with naval reform, see Dem. 14).

According to Demosthenes in this speech, the catalyst for the revolt of Rhodes was Mausolus, the satrap (i.e., Persian-appointed governor) of Caria, a province of the Persian Empire in southwestern Asia Minor (3n).[8] Mausolus, who was a native Carian, ruled his homeland from 377/6 to 353/2. Although appointed by the Persian King, he took advantage of the remote location of Caria, and of a degree of political disorder within the Persian Empire, to act in a quasi-autonomous manner, especially in his foreign policy. The King's Peace of 386 had limited Persian territorial claims to the mainland of Asia Minor, but Mausolus sought to extend his authority over several of the offshore Greek islands of the southeastern Aegean (see 27, naming Cos). In particular, he had supported the Rhodian oligarchs, who overthrew the democracy on Rhodes and exiled their democratic opponents (14–15). After his death the oligarchs continued to enjoy the support of his successor Artemisia. Many of the exiled democrats came to Athens, where they lobbied for the Athenians to restore them and reestablish democracy.

In speaking in support of their appeal, Demosthenes tries to persuade the Athenians that it is both right and in Athens' inter-

---

[6]See Dem. 50.4 and Diodorus 15.95 for raids on the territory of Athens and its allies by Alexander, ruler of the Thessalian city of Pherae, in the late 360s.

[7]I.e., a war between or against allies, from the Latin word *socius*, "ally."

[8]On Mausolus, see the detailed treatment of Hornblower 1982; more briefly the same author's entry "Mausolus" in *OCD*[3].

est to try to restore democracy on Rhodes. The opposing view was clearly that the Rhodians deserved no help, because of their role in the Social War, and that it was dangerous for Athens to risk hostilities with Artemisia, especially because this might also lead to conflict with her master, the Persian King (6). As regards the Rhodians, Demosthenes admits that they do not deserve Athens' help, but he argues that it is in Athens' interest to help them nevertheless: both because they will be chastened and therefore loyal in the future (15–16) and because it will signal Athens' policy of supporting democracy throughout Greece (4). He claims that oligarchy is the inveterate enemy of democracy and that it is in Athens' interest to support those who are on the same side of this ideological divide (17–21).

Demosthenes addresses the likely reaction of Artemisia and the Persian King to an Athenian-backed restoration of democracy on Rhodes as follows: The King did nothing when the Athenians previously expelled a Persian garrison from the island of Samos (9–10), and hence he is unlikely to do anything different in the case of Rhodes, although Demosthenes is aware that any Persian claim to the island would alter the situation (13). Moreover, Artemisia would rather that Athens control Rhodes than that it fall into the hands of the King, if he should fail to conquer Egypt, since in that eventuality he would use the island against her (11–12). If the Athenians were to try to restore democracy, any intervention on her part would be half-hearted at best (12). Demosthenes seems to believe—not wholly implausibly—that relations between Caria and Persia are tense, and he wishes to take opportunistic advantage of it.

A further aspect to the speech is a desire that Athens redeem itself after the dark years that culminated in the outbreak of the Social War. There is a tension in it between the cynicism of 28—since no one else's actions are motivated by justice, it would be naïve of the Athenians to do otherwise—and the prominent assertion that they need to dispel the slanders to which their actions have given rise (2). For Demosthenes, the support of freedom and democracy was Athens' duty.

Demosthenes failed to persuade the Athenians on this occa-

sion.[9] His idealistic approach was probably regarded by many
Athenians as foolish, especially his belief that Artemisia would
not strenuously oppose Athenian interference on an island that
she controlled. In view of Athenian fear of Persia in this period
(see Dem. 14), Demosthenes' lack of concern about the possibility
of Persian retaliation may have seemed reckless; others may have
taken the view that Athens lacked the financial resources to engage in such adventurism, which would bring with it few tangi-
ble benefits.[10]

There is a detailed German commentary on this speech by Radicke 1995.

15. ON THE FREEDOM OF THE RHODIANS

[1] In my opinion, men of Athens, those who are deliberating
about matters of such importance should allow each of their advisors to speak freely. And until now my difficulty has never been
to advise you what is the best policy to pursue—to tell the truth,
I think that you all already know what it is—but to persuade you
to do so. For whenever a policy is approved and voted on, you remain as far from taking action as you were before. [2] There is,
however, one thing for which I think you owe a debt of gratitude
to the gods: the fact that the only hope of rescue for those who,
through their own arrogance, recently went to war with you[11]
now lies in your hands. You ought to be delighted by the present opportunity, since if you make the right decision, you will
dispel the slanders of those who criticize the city and will also
win for yourselves a glorious reputation. [3] The Chians, Byzan-

---

[9] *Prologue* 24 apparently belongs to the same affair, and is interpreted by
MacDowell (2009: 222–223) as being written in response to a subsequent
embassy to Athens from the Rhodian oligarchs.

[10] The Athenian politician most closely associated with this cautious
view was Eubulus, on whom see the Introduction to Dem. 3.

[11] The Rhodians, who had taken a leading part in the Social War against
Athens of 357–355 (see the Speech Introduction).

tines, and Rhodians accused us of plotting against them, and as a result combined against us in this most recent war,[12] but it will emerge that the man who engineered this and persuaded them was Mausolus, who claimed to be the Rhodians' friend, but instead deprived them of their freedom.[13] The Chians and Byzantines declared themselves their allies but provided no help to them in their misfortune. [4] You, however, whom they used to fear, will now be single-handedly responsible for rescuing them. If you make this clear to everybody, you will cause the majority in every city to regard friendship with you as a guarantee of their own freedom.[14] There is no greater benefit you could secure than the willing and trusting goodwill of all.

[5] I am amazed to see that the same men advise the city to oppose the King[15] for the sake of the Egyptians,[16] but are too frightened of him to take action on behalf of the Rhodian people. And yet everyone knows that the latter are Greek, whereas the former are part of his empire.[17] [6] I imagine some of you recall that at the time when you were deliberating about relations with the King, I came forward and was the first to advise you—I think that I spoke alone, or perhaps there was one other—and said that

---

[12]The mention of Athenian plotting possibly refers to the actions of the Athenian general Chares, who was notorious for taking a hard line with the allies: see 8.30n.

[13]On Mausolus, see the Speech Introduction. Demosthenes alleges that he was responsible for Rhodes' revolt from Athens. There may be some truth in this, but Demosthenes, who is seeking to persuade the Athenians to help their recent enemies the Rhodians, has a clear motive to transfer the blame for the secession of Rhodes as far as possible from them to Mausolus.

[14]The majority (*hoi polloi*) in every city are the poorer citizens, who naturally support the constitution that gives them a share in political power (i.e., democracy), and thus have an affinity with democratic Athens.

[15]I.e., the Persian King.

[16]Egypt was in revolt from Persian rule throughout the first half of the fourth century. During this period the native Egyptians received help from various Greek cities, including Athens. In the late 350s Artaxerxes III made an unsuccessful attempt to recapture Egypt (see the Speech Introduction).

[17]Egypt was annexed by the Persian King Cambyses in the late sixth century, when it became part of the Persian Empire.

it was not sensible to use your hatred of him as an excuse for military preparation, but that you should prepare yourselves to fight your existing enemies, and defend yourselves against him only if he tried to wrong you. Nor did you think that I spoke wrongly, but on the contrary my advice was pleasing to you.[18] [7] My present speech follows on from what I said on that occasion. For my part, if the King were to summon me to his side as his advisor, I would give him the same advice that I give you—to fight for his own possessions if any of the Greeks should oppose him but to make no claim to rule what does not belong to him.[19] [8] If you have made up your minds, men of Athens, to cede to the King every place that he has acquired by stealing a march or by deceiving some of its inhabitants, in my opinion you are wrong. But if you are resolved even to go to war in the cause of justice, if need be, and to suffer whatever you believe you must, then the more you are resolved to resist, the less you will need to fight, and in addition your policy will be acknowledged to be the correct one.

[9] To show that I am saying nothing new now in encouraging you to liberate the Rhodians, and that you will be doing nothing new if you follow my advice, I shall remind you of some events that proved advantageous to you. Men of Athens, you once sent Timotheus to help Ariobarzanes, adding to the decree the condition that he was not to break the treaty with the King.[20] When

---

[18]Demosthenes here refers to his earlier speech *On the Symmories* (Dem. 14). The claim that his advice was pleasing to the Athenians does not imply that his proposal to reform the financing of the navy was approved by the Assembly (it was not). The speech did, however, succeed in dissuading the Athenians from taking military action against the King.

[19]By "his own possessions" Demosthenes means the mainland of Asia Minor, to which the Persians laid claim in accordance with the King's Peace of 386. The Persians had no rightful claim to any of the other offshore islands, including Rhodes.

[20]Demosthenes refers to events of 366/5. Ariobarzanes, satrap of Hellespontine Phrygia in northwestern Asia Minor, refused an order from the Persian King to surrender his satrapy and called on Sparta and Athens for help. The Athenians sent their general Timotheus with orders to assist him, so long as he did not breach the King's Peace.

Timotheus saw that Ariobarzanes was clearly in revolt from the King,[21] but that Samos was garrisoned by Cyprothemis, who had been appointed by the King's hyparch Tigranes, he decided not to help Ariobarzanes but instead went to the assistance of Samos, laid siege to it, and liberated it.[22] [10] And this has not yet up to the present day resulted in the outbreak of war. For no one would go to war for the sake of making a profit in the same way as he would for the sake of his own property, but everyone fights as hard as he can to hold onto things that someone else is trying to deprive him of. When it comes to making a profit, the situation is quite different: men aim at it, if they have the chance; but if they are prevented, they do not think that their opponents have done them an injustice.

[11] I do not believe that even Artemisia would be opposed to our taking this action, if the city is fully committed to it.[23] As for my reasoning, listen for a moment and judge whether or not it is correct. In my view, if the King were being quite as success-ful in Egypt as he hopes to be, Artemisia would have tried very hard to make Rhodes over to him, not out of goodwill towards the King but from a wish to do him a considerable favor, since he is in the vicinity, in order to induce him to treat her as amicably as possible.[24] [12] But if he is doing as is rumored, and has failed

---

[21] Ariobarzanes was prominently involved in the so-called Great Satraps' Revolt of the late 360s, on which see Diodorus 15.90–92; Briant 2002: 656–675.

[22] Neither Athens nor Persia had any claim to the island of Samos, but Timotheus took advantage of the disorder in the western Persian Empire to expel a Persian garrison that had been installed there. Demosthenes implies that Tigranes (an Armenian by name) was acting as an agent of the King, but the circumstances in which the island had come under Persian control are obscure. After a ten-month siege (see Isoc. 15.111) Samos was captured, but its "liberation" consisted of the expulsion of the native Samians and the establishment of an Athenian cleruchy (i.e., settlement). The exiled Samians received refuge in various Greek cities, and Athens' action was a source of considerable resentment and anxiety to its allies (see 3n).

[23] Artemisia succeeded her husband (and brother) Mausolus as satrap of Caria on the latter's death in 353/2.

[24] Demosthenes refers to the Persian campaign to reconquer Egypt, led by the new King Artaxerxes III. Wherever exactly Artaxerxes was based—

in his undertaking, she thinks that this island, as is the case, has no other use to the King at present than as an obstacle to prevent her making any move at all.[25] And so in my view she would rather that you have it, as long as she does not surrender it to you publicly, than that he take it.[26] I do not even think that she would help; but if she did, she would do so in a cursory and ineffective way.[27] [13] As regards the King, I certainly cannot confidently predict what he will do, but I do maintain that it is in the city's interest to clarify whether or not he will lay claim to the city of the Rhodians. For if he does lay claim to it, we will be obliged to take counsel not only for the Rhodians but also for ourselves and for the rest of Greece.

[14] Nor indeed would I have advised you to support those Rhodians who now occupy the city, even if they held it without assistance from others or promised to do everything for you.[28] For I observe that at first they recruited some of their fellow-citizens to overthrow the democracy, but when they had achieved their goal, they turned around and exiled them. I do not see how men who have acted in bad faith towards both parties could be reliable allies of yours.[29] [15] Nor would I have ever spoken as I

---

perhaps in Phoenicia—he was much nearer to Caria than he would have been at court in Persia. On the role of benefactions in the Persian court, see 10.31n.

[25] This Persian expedition did in fact fail (Isoc. 5.101), although Egypt was recovered in the 340s. Demosthenes argues that direct Persian control of Rhodes would limit the hegemonic ambitions of the satrap of Caria.

[26] Persia had no claim to Rhodes (see 7n above), but the King might interpret the handing over of the island to Athens as a rebellious, or at any rate unfriendly, action on the part of Artemisia. Although Demosthenes is arguing for the liberation of Rhodes, it is revealing that he speaks of Athens "having" it (see MacDowell 2009: 220).

[27] The Greek text provides no object for the verb "help." The object to be supplied is either the Persian King (if he should try to annex Rhodes) or the Rhodian oligarchs (if Athens should try to liberate the island).

[28] Demosthenes here refers to the Rhodian oligarchs.

[29] These people were presumably (on the model of the oligarchic coup at Athens in 411) "moderate" oligarchs whose support was needed to overthrow the democratic constitution but who were promptly discarded when a narrowly based oligarchy was set up in its place. The two parties to whom

have if I thought that I was doing so only in the interest of the Rhodian people. For I am not their honorary consul nor is any of them a personal guest-friend of mine.[30] But even if both these were the case, I would certainly not have spoken as I did unless I thought it to be in your interest, since as regards the Rhodians— if it is possible for one who is advising their rescue to say so—I rejoice at what has happened to them. For by grudging you the recovery of your possessions, they have lost their own liberty.[31] And although they had the chance of being allied on equal terms with Greeks and with their superiors,[32] they have become the slaves of foreigners and slaves, whom they admitted into their citadels. [16] I might almost go so far as to say that if you are willing to help them, this affair will have done them good. For if they had prospered, I do not know whether they would ever have come to their senses, since they are Rhodians;[33] but now that they have learned by experience that folly is the cause of much misfortune

---

the oligarchs showed bad faith were thus these men and the mass of the people.

[30] An honorary consul (*proxenos*) was a man appointed by a foreign city to look after the interests of its citizens in his own city. This was a position of considerable prestige, especially in the case of the larger cities. Demosthenes implies that a *proxenos* might not give impartial advice concerning the city that he represented, and it is known that sometimes they were appointed for reasons of political sympathy. A guest-friend (*xenos*) was a foreigner with whom personal ties of hospitality and friendship had been established. On the need for Athens' political leaders to avoid partiality towards other states, see 16.1–2.

[31] The possessions to which Demosthenes refers are primarily Amphipolis and the Chersonese, which Athens had sought to regain during the 360s. Athens' allies had resented being required to serve on campaigns that benefited only the Athenians, and this proved a contributory factor to the outbreak of the Social War.

[32] The manuscripts add the word "you," making Demosthenes' point explicit. It is deleted by Dilts 2002.

[33] Demosthenes represents the Rhodian people's revolt from their alliance with Athens as an act of folly; it has taken the overthrow of democracy and foreign invasion to bring them back to their senses. He depicts the Rhodians as congenitally inferior to the Athenians (cf. 15).

for many people, they are likely to be more sensible in the future, if they win your help. This I consider to be no small benefit to them. I therefore declare that we ought to try to rescue them, and not bear a grudge against them, bearing in mind that you too have been greatly deceived by men who plotted against you—and you would not say that you ought to be punished for what happened then.[34]

[17] Consider too, men of Athens, that you have fought many wars against both democracies and oligarchies. That much you know, but perhaps none of you has thought about what you were fighting for in each case. For what, then? Against democracies you were fighting either over private claims, which you could not resolve in public, or over the division of land or border disputes or out of rivalry or over leadership. But against oligarchies you fought not over any of these things but for a form of government and for freedom.[35] [18] And so I would say, without hesitation, that in my opinion it would be better for all the Greeks to be at war with you, so long as they are democrats, than for them to be friendly to you and oligarchs. For I believe that you would have no difficulty in making peace with free men, whenever you wish, but with oligarchs I do not think that even friendship can be secure, since there is no way that the few can be well disposed to the many, or that those who seek to rule others can be well disposed to those who have chosen to live on terms of political equality.

[19] I am surprised if none of you sees that, with Chios and Mytilene ruled by oligarchies,[36] and now Rhodes and almost the

---

[34]The reference is probably to the oligarchic revolution of 411, when the Athenians were persuaded to suspend their democratic constitution, and perhaps also to the establishment of the oligarchic "Thirty Tyrants" in 404 (on whom see 22n).

[35]This sweeping claim reflects Demosthenes' view of interstate relations but has no basis in fact.

[36]On Chios, see 3 and 27. It is possible that Mausolus had some role in its change to oligarchy, the date of which is uncertain. Mytilene, the largest city on the island of Lesbos, was a democracy in the first half of the fourth century and a founding member of the Second Athenian Confederacy, but it had complained in the early 360s about the direction of Athenian foreign

whole world reduced to this form of slavery, our own constitution is also at some risk; or that if oligarchies are set up everywhere else, they will surely not allow us to retain our democracy. For they know that no one but us will act to restore freedom, and so they will wish to destroy the one place that they expect to cause them trouble. [20] Other wrongdoers should be deemed to be the enemies only of those whom they have wronged, but I urge you to regard anyone who overthrows constitutional forms of government and changes them to oligarchy to be the common enemy of all who desire freedom.[37] [21] And so it is right, men of Athens, that you who are democrats should be seen to adopt a similar attitude towards democrats who are in trouble as you would expect others to adopt towards you, if ever—may it never happen—you should suffer something similar yourselves. Indeed if anyone were to say that the Rhodians have got their just desserts, this is not the moment to gloat. Those who enjoy good fortune must always be seen to look after those in trouble, since the future is uncertain for all men.

[22] I often hear it said here in the Assembly that when our democracy was in trouble, certain men made plans to rescue it; of these, I shall confine myself to reminding you briefly about the Argives. For I would not want you, who have the reputation of always rescuing those who are in trouble, to appear inferior to the Argives in this respect. These men, who are the Spartans' neighbors and saw them ruling on land and sea, showed no fear or hesitation in demonstrating their support for you; and when envoys came from Sparta, it is said, demanding the surrender of some of your exiles, they voted to treat the envoys as enemies, unless they

---

policy (see *IG* II² 107 = Rhodes and Osborne 2003: no. 31). On the establishment of an oligarchy in the 350s, see 13.8; Isoc. *Letter* 8 (a letter of advice to the new oligarchic rulers of the city). Shortly after the delivery of this speech, the city was ruled by a tyrant named Cammys (Dem. 40.37), but by 346 democracy had been restored: see *IG* II² 213, an Athenian decree renewing Athens' alliance with the Mytilenean people (i.e., with the democratic government of Mytilene).

[37] In Demosthenes' view only democracy counts as constitutional government. For democrats' desire for and affinity with freedom, see 18 above.

left by nightfall.[38] [23] Is it not disgraceful, men of Athens, that in the past the Argive people did not fear the imperial might of Sparta, but that you, who are Athenian, are now afraid of a foreigner—and a woman at that?[39] Moreover, the Argives could adduce that they had often been defeated by the Spartans,[40] whereas you have often been victorious over the King and have never been defeated either by his slaves[41] or by the man himself. For if in any way the King has got the better of our city, he has only done so by bribing the most despicable Greek traitors.[42] [24] Even this, however, did him no good, since you will find that even as he was using the Spartans to weaken our city, he was in danger of losing his own kingdom to Clearchus and Cyrus.[43] And so he has never openly defeated us, nor has it benefited him to plot against us. I

---

[38]After the installation of the "Thirty Tyrants" in 404 Athenian democratic exiles were harbored by various cities, including democratic Argos (Diodorus 14.6.2).

[39]Artemisia.

[40]Most notably, the Argives suffered a shattering defeat at the hands of the Spartans at the battle of Sepeia in 494 (Herod. 6.77–80).

[41]The men whom Demosthenes refers to as slaves were (in fact) high-ranking Persian generals, whom the Greeks nevertheless liked to describe as the slaves of the King.

[42]Demosthenes is alluding to Sparta's victory over Athens in the Peloponnesian War, which was made possible by Persian financial support. Although he does not name the men he has in mind, the chief "traitor" will presumably have been the Spartan general Lysander, who was responsible for liaising with Sparta's Persian paymasters. By "the King" Demosthenes means not just the current King (Artaxerxes III) but any of his predecessors.

[43]The Persian prince Cyrus unsuccessfully contested the Persian throne with his brother Artaxerxes (II) in 401, after the death of their father Darius II. He raised a Greek mercenary force in Asia Minor, of which Clearchus the Spartan was the leading general, and marched into the heart of the Persian Empire. At the battle of Cunaxa near Babylon, Cyrus was killed, and shortly afterwards the mercenaries' commanders, including Clearchus, were treacherously seized by the Persians and put to death. An eyewitness account of this campaign is provided by the Athenian writer Xenophon in his *Anabasis*.

see that some of you frequently despise Philip as being of no consequence[44] but are afraid of the King on the ground that he is a formidable enemy to whomever he chooses. But if we are to take no measures against the former on the ground that he is insignificant, and are to yield in every respect to the latter on the ground that he is formidable, against whom, men of Athens, are we to take the field?

[25] There are some men here, men of Athens, who are very clever at telling you the rights of others with respect to you. I would give them just one piece of advice: they should seek to tell you your rights with respect to others, if they wish to be seen to be doing the right thing, since it is absurd for anyone to lecture you about justice who is not himself acting justly, and it is wrong for a citizen to have considered the arguments against you but not those for you.[45] [26] In the name of the gods, consider why there is no one at Byzantium to forbid the Byzantines to seize Chalcedon, which belongs to the King, was once yours, and has nothing to do with them.[46] Or to forbid them to make Selymbria, a

---

[44]It is, to say the least, striking that this oblique allusion is the only mention of Philip of Macedon in Demosthenes' three earliest deliberative speeches (Dem. 14–16), even though by the time of the present speech Philip had annexed many places on the north Aegean littoral that were claimed by Athens and had already started to intervene in central Greece. Demosthenes certainly does not endorse the view that Philip is no danger to Athens, but his proposing an expeditionary force to the southeastern Aegean shows that he had not yet come to believe that Philip was a uniquely serious threat to Athens (as he soon saw him to be). See the Speech Introduction.

[45]In the aftermath of the Social War there were those at Athens who regarded their city's aggressive self-interest (e.g., towards its allies, in the establishing of a cleruchy on Samos) as the root cause of the disaster. For example, sharp criticism of Athenian imperialism is to be found in Isocrates' work On the Peace of 355. Demosthenes probably also has in mind Eubulus, whose policy of avoiding expensive campaigning abroad could be represented as one of abandoning Athens' strategic interests. On Eubulus, see the Introduction to Dem. 3.

[46]Byzantium controlled passage from the Sea of Marmara into the Black Sea. Chalcedon, on the mainland of Asia Minor opposite it, belonged to Persia by virtue of the King's Peace of 386 and had previously been a mem-

city that was once allied to you, pay contributions to them.[47] Or
to forbid them to redefine the land of the Selymbrians as belonging to Byzantium in breach of the oaths and treaty, in which it is
written that the cities should be autonomous.[48] [27] Nor was there
anyone to forbid Mausolus while he was alive, or Artemisia after
his death, to seize Cos[49] and Rhodes and various other Greek cities, of which his master the King had deprived the Greeks in the
treaty, and for whose sake the Greeks in those days faced many
dangers and engaged in glorious struggles.[50] Even if there is someone to forbid either of them, it seems that they are not minded to
obey. [28] I believe that it is right to restore the Rhodian people.
But even if it were not, whenever I see what these men[51] are doing I think it right to advise you to restore them. Why? Because,
men of Athens, if everyone were set on acting justly, it would in
my view be shameful for us to be the only ones to refuse to do so;
but when everyone else is preparing to do wrong, I consider it not
justice but cowardice for us alone to offer justice without getting
anything in return. For I see everyone claiming their just desserts

---

ber of Athens' fifth-century empire. Demosthenes' point is that, when other
states pursue their own interest unapologetically, the Athenians are handi-
capping themselves if they do not do likewise.

[47] Selymbria, on the north shore of the Sea of Marmara to the west of
Byzantium, had also been a member of Athens' fifth-century empire.

[48] The King's Peace was the first of a series of "common peaces" (*koinai
eirēnai*) that guaranteed the freedom and autonomy of participating cities.

[49] On Mausolus and Artemisia, see 12n. It is unclear how Mausolus got
control of Cos, an island of the southeastern Aegean. Demosthenes implies
forcible seizure, but it is possible that the Coans turned to him in fear of
Athens after the establishment of the Athenian settlement on Samos in 365
(on which see 9).

[50] Demosthenes refers to the situation of the Greek cities on the mainland of Asia, which by the terms of the King's Peace were agreed to form
part of the Persian Empire. He does not name the cities of which Mausolus got control (see the discussion of Hornblower 1982: 107–137). The "glorious struggles" of the past were the military operations in the eastern Aegean conducted, on the whole successfully, by Athens and its allies against
the Persians in the middle years of the fifth century.

[51] His Athenian political opponents.

in accordance with their present strength. [29] I can provide an example of this that will be familiar to all of you. There are two treaties between the Greeks and the King, the one which your city made, of which everyone approves,[52] and the later one which the Spartans made, which they criticize.[53] In these the two parties have unequal rights. For as regards individual justice in constitutionally governed states, the laws give an equal share to the weak and the strong alike, but in disputes between the states of Greece, the strong lay down the law to the weak.

[30] Since you have decided to do what is right,[54] we must determine how you will be able to achieve this. You will do so by undertaking to be the champions of freedom for all. It seems to me that there is a good reason why you find it very difficult to do what you should. For all other people face a single struggle, against their declared enemies: if they defeat them, there is nothing to prevent them getting control of their assets. [31] You, however, men of Athens, face two struggles, both the one that others face, and another that is prior to and greater than it. For when you deliberate, you must overcome those among you who have chosen to act against the interests of the city.[55] So, whenever they

---

[52]Demosthenes refers to the Peace of Callias of the early 440s between Athens and the Persian King. Athens and its allies had remained at war with the Persians after the repulse of the Persian invasion of Greece in 479. The peace, which takes its name from the main Athenian negotiator, represented a backing down by the Persians. Some historians believe that the Peace of Callias is a fourth-century fabrication, on the ground that it is not mentioned by any fifth-century source, but see Badian 1987, who argues convincingly for its historical reality. At any rate, Demosthenes believed in its historicity.

[53]The King's Peace, also known as the Peace of Antalcidas after its Spartan negotiator. Although it was a "common peace," and guaranteed autonomy to states that signed up to it, it was in reality used as a tool for the Spartans to dominate Greece with Persian backing.

[54]MacDowell 2009: 219 observes that this seems to show that the Athenians have already agreed in principle to help the Rhodians.

[55]See 25n on the identity of these men.

make it difficult to take any necessary measure, you naturally miss many opportunities. [32] Although perhaps the main reason why many men get away with such behavior is the help that they receive from their pay masters,[56] you too deserve some of the blame. For, men of Athens, you should have the same attitude towards constitutional discipline as you have towards military discipline. What do I mean? You think that a man who deserts the position assigned to him by the general should be deprived of his civic rights and allowed no share in the community.[57] [33] In the same way, those who desert the constitutional position handed down to them by their ancestors, and whose political conduct is oligarchic, should be deprived of the civic right to offer you advice. As it is, you consider those of your allies who have sworn to have the same enemies and friends as you to be best disposed to you, but of the politicians it is those whom you know to have committed themselves to the enemies of our city in whom you put the greatest trust.

[34] It is not difficult to find allegations with which to charge these men, or to rebuke you. But to find the right kind of words or action to set right what is now awry—that is a task indeed. Perhaps the present moment is not the right time to address every issue. But if you are able to confirm the decision that you take by some beneficial action, then these other things too may gradually improve. [35] You must apply yourselves vigorously to the present situation and act in a manner that is worthy of the city, keeping in mind the delight you feel whenever anyone praises your ancestors and recounts their achievements and praises their victory trophies.[58] You should reflect that your ancestors erected these trophies not for you to gaze on in admiration but to encourage you to imitate the virtues of the men who set them up.

---

[56] Here, as often, Demosthenes treats those politicians who disagree with him as traitors in the pay of a foreign power.

[57] Demosthenes refers to the offense of desertion (*lipotaxion*), on which see briefly MacDowell 1978: 160.

[58] This passage is repeated almost word for word at 13.26. On trophies, see 3.24n.

16. FOR THE MEGALOPOLITANS

〜〜

INTRODUCTION

Dionysius of Halicarnassus states that this speech was delivered in 353/2.[1] This date is consistent with the recording by the historian Diodorus Siculus (16.39) of a Spartan attack on Megalopolis in the following year, 352/1, although Diodorus' chronology is often faulty and cannot be relied on.

By the middle of the fourth century the three major powers of mainland Greece—Sparta, Thebes, and Athens—were all in a considerably weakened state. Sparta, which had dominated Greece since the end of the Peloponnesian War, had been decisively defeated by Thebes at the battle of Leuctra in 371. As a result of Theban intervention in the Peloponnese, Sparta lost its grip on the peninsula. The Thebans liberated Messenia, which had been a Spartan possession since the seventh century and whose inhabitants had been reduced to the status of publicly owned slaves ("helots") of the Spartans. A new city of Messene was founded there, and an independent and staunchly anti-Spartan Messenian state created. Also in the early 360s Megalopolis (literally "great city") was founded in Arcadia in the central Peloponnese; it became the leader of a new Arcadian Confederation, which looked to Thebes to protect it against Sparta. The Spartans resented both of these developments, and during the 360s and 350s they sought, with little success, to regain their former hegemony of the Peloponnese.

---

[1] *First Letter to Ammaeus* 4. Dionysius gives the speech a slightly different title: *On Aid for the Megalopolitans*. None of the traditional titles of Demosthenes' speeches are original.

Thebes had in turn dominated the years after Leuctra, and remained the most powerful land power in Greece. But it found it increasingly difficult in the 360s to retain control of its allies in the Peloponnese and became overstretched by involvements in central and northern Greece and in the Aegean region. Then in 356 it got dragged into a draining war (the Third Sacred War) with its neighbor Phocis. The Phocians seized the wealthy sanctuary of Delphi, from which the war took its name, and used its treasures to pay for large numbers of mercenaries.

Athens had been an ally of Sparta since 370, when the two states were united in fear of the growing power of Thebes. But Athenian foreign policy was directed mainly towards the maintenance of its naval alliance, to the recovery of its former possessions in the north (Amphipolis and the Chersonese above all), and to the security of its grain route from the Black Sea. Moreover, the Athenians had recently suffered a humiliating defeat at the hands of disaffected allies, in the Social War of 357–355, and were hampered by a lack of money to pay for military operations.[2]

In 353/2 Sparta sought to take advantage of Thebes' entanglement in the Sacred War to reassert itself in the Peloponnese. Its initial aggression was directed against Arcadia and Megalopolis. Megalopolis was allied to Thebes, but it could expect little help from that quarter and so appealed to Athens for support. The Spartans also sent ambassadors to Athens (see 1), either to ask for Athenian support, as Libanius states in his *Introduction* to the speech, although Sparta's alliance with Athens was a defensive one only, or to ask them not to get involved.

Demosthenes argues in this speech that the Athenians should accept the appeal of the Megalopolitans, on condition that they repudiate their alliance with Thebes (28). In doing so, he is seeking to persuade the Athenians to alter their established policy of support for Sparta and opposition to Thebes. His central claim is that it is in Athens' interest for Megalopolis to remain independent, since if the Spartans conquer it, they will next move against Messene and thereby regain control of the Peloponnese. This, he

---

[2]See the Introductions to Dem. 14 and 15.

argues, would make Sparta dangerously powerful; he even suggests that Athens and Thebes would be in danger (20–21). He denies that accepting the Megalopolitan appeal will provoke a showdown with the Spartans, on the ground that the latter are still allies of the Athenians, and also owe them a debt of gratitude for their support against the Thebans in the 360s.

Athenian policy towards Thebes was directed in general towards reducing its power (4–5). Specifically, Athens sought to regain the border town of Oropus, control of which it disputed with Thebes, and to secure the restoration of a number of cities of Boeotia, above all Plataea, that the Thebans had destroyed (4). Against the argument that the Athenians need Spartan support to press their claim to Oropus, Demosthenes first denies that the Spartans will withdraw their support (13) and then asserts that the freedom of the Peloponnese is more important to Athens than control of Oropus (18). As regards the cities of Boeotia, he proposes nothing more concrete than encouraging others to help secure their restoration (25).

This clever speech makes interesting use of the concept of the balance of power, but Demosthenes does not convincingly explain how his policy will avoid creating a rift with Sparta while doing nothing to improve relations with Thebes. It is also clear from hindsight that he exaggerates the residual power of Sparta, which proved wholly unable to regain control of the Peloponnese. It is not surprising, therefore, that his advice was rejected by the Assembly. The Spartans went on to attack the Megalopolitans, who appealed to their allies and received help both from various Peloponnesian states and from Thebes (Diodorus 16.39; cf. Pausanias 8.27.9–10).

16. FOR THE MEGALOPOLITANS

[1] Both groups—those speaking in support of the Arcadians and those speaking in support of the Spartans—seem to me to be wrong, men of Athens. For they accuse and slander each other, as if they had come here from one or other of these cities, rather than being your fellow-citizens and the recipients of these embassies. Their behavior would be appropriate if they were foreign-

ers; but those who propose to offer you advice should be discussing the situation impartially and considering in an amicable spirit what is best for you. [2] As it is, if I did not know these men and if they were not speaking Attic,[3] I think that many people would suppose some of them to be Arcadian and the others, Spartan. For my part, I certainly see that it is difficult to give you the best advice, since at a time when you have all been deceived, with some people wanting one thing and others another, if any speaker tries to offer a compromise, but you refuse to stay and learn from him, he will win the favor of neither side but will be slandered by both. [3] Nevertheless, I would rather be thought to be talking nonsense, if indeed such is my fate, than allow certain men to deceive you, against what I believe are the city's interests. I will talk about the other matters later, if you wish, but will start from what is generally agreed, since in my opinion this is the best way to offer advice.

[4] Not a single person, I take it, would deny that it is in our interest for both the Spartans and these Thebans here to be weak.[4] Yet the situation at the moment is as follows, to judge from the speeches that are often made to you: the Thebans will be weakened if Orchomenus and Thespiae and Plataea are resettled,[5] and

---

[3] There were various regional dialects of Greek, and both Spartans and Arcadians would have spoken with a Doric dialect, as opposed to the Attic dialect of the Athenians.

[4] Demosthenes refers to "these Thebans here" because Boeotia, the region of which Thebes was the leading city, was Athens' neighbor to the north. It is also possible that Theban ambassadors were present in Athens.

[5] These three Boeotian cities had been destroyed by Thebes in the course of establishing its control of the rest of Boeotia: Plataea and Thespiae in 373 (Diodorus 15.46.6; Pausanias 9.1.4–8); Orchomenus in 364 following a revolt (Diodorus 15.79.3–6). The Athenians supported their restoration (see also 5.10; 6.30). Athens had particularly close ties with Plataea, which was the only city to fight alongside the Athenians at the battle of Marathon in 490 (on which see 13.21–22, 14.30n), and which had been a loyal ally in the Peloponnesian War. When the city was captured after a long siege in 427, Plataean refugees in Athens were given Athenian citizenship (Dem. 59.104). After its destruction in 373, the Plataeans were again given refuge in

the Spartans will recover their power if they make the Arcadians their subjects and destroy Megalopolis. [5] We must therefore ensure that we do not allow Sparta to become fearsome and powerful until Thebes is weakened, nor allow Spartan power to grow so much, without our noticing, that it outweighs the reduction in Theban power that our interest demands.[6] For we would not claim to wish to exchange the Spartans for the Thebans as our enemies, nor is that our intention. Rather, our aim is to ensure that neither city is able to do us any harm, since in this way we would have least ground for fear.

[6] And yet, by Zeus, we may agree that this is how things should be, but we will also say that it is terrible to choose as allies those against whom we fought at the battle of Mantinea, and to help them against those who shared the danger with us on that occasion.[7] I agree, but only on condition that the others[8] are willing to do what is right. [7] So if everyone is willing to keep the peace, we shall not help the Megalopolitans, since there will be no need for us to do so. And as a result, we will have absolutely no quarrel with those who fought beside us. One party is already allied to us, so they say, and the other will shortly become so:[9] what more could we wish for? [8] But suppose that the Spartans act unjustly and decide to go to war. In that case, if all we had to decide was whether or not to let them have Megalopolis, I concede that we should abandon it, even though it is wrong to do so, and not oppose our former comrades-in-arms. But since you all realize that if the Spartans take Megalopolis, they will next attack Messene, will someone who now takes a hard line towards

---

Athens (cf. 5.18) and the earlier grant of citizenship was revived (Diodorus 15.46.6). For Athenian support for the restoration of Plataea, see also Isoc. 14 *Plataicus*.

[6]The thought is a little convoluted. Demosthenes claims that it is in Athens' interest for Theban power to decline somewhat, but not at the cost of a major increase in Spartan power.

[7]At the inconclusive battle of Mantinea in 362, the Athenians fought alongside the Spartans against the Arcadians and Thebans.

[8]I.e., the Spartans.

[9]The Spartans and Megalopolitans respectively. On the alliance with Sparta, see 12n.

Megalopolis tell me what he will advise us to do in that eventuality? No one will have anything to say. [9] Indeed, you are all aware, whether these men advise it or not, that we are bound to help the Messenians, both because of the oaths that we swore to them and because it is in our interest for their city to be saved.[10] Ask yourselves, is it better and more honorable for us to begin our resistance to Spartan wrongdoing by supporting Megalopolis or by supporting Messene? [10] In the former case, you will be seen both to be helping the Arcadians and to be intent on maintaining the peace, for which you risked battle.[11] But in the latter case, everybody will see that you desire the survival of Messene not from a sense of justice but out of fear of Sparta. You should always determine what is right and do it—but at the same time you should ensure that this coincides with your own interests!

[11] Those who speak on the other side, however, say something like this: that we must try to recover Oropus and that if we make enemies of those who might now help us to do so, we will be bereft of allies.[12] I agree that we should try to recover Oropus. And yet, the claim that the Spartans will become our enemies, if we make allies of those Arcadians who want to be our friends, is one that those who persuaded us to help the Spartans when they were in danger have absolutely no right to make. [12] For this is not what they said when they persuaded you, at a time when all the Peloponnesians had come to you and demanded that you attack Sparta, to turn them away—so that they had no choice but to turn to the Thebans—and to contribute money and risk your lives for the safety of the Spartans.[13] I presume that you would

---

[10] According to Pausanias, Athens promised to help Messene if it was attacked by Sparta (4.28.2). He dates this alliance to the time of the Third Sacred War (i.e., in or after 356).

[11] Demosthenes refers again to the battle of Mantinea in 362 (see 6n).

[12] On Oropus, see the Speech Introduction. Demosthenes addresses the argument that Athens needs to maintain friendly relations with Sparta to ensure its support in regaining Oropus. Although Athens had other allies, most of these were islanders, and it would have needed Spartan help to take on the powerful Theban army.

[13] In 370 the Arcadians, together with their allies in the Peloponnese, appealed to Athens for help against Sparta. The Athenians turned them

not have been willing to save the Spartans if they had told you beforehand that once they had been rescued, if you did not allow them to do as they pleased once more and to act unjustly, they would have no gratitude to you for rescuing them. [13] And even if an alliance between us and the Arcadians is wholly contrary to the Spartans' plans, I imagine that their gratitude to us for saving them in their hour of greatest danger should outweigh their anger with us at stopping them acting unjustly now. How then can they fail to help us over Oropus, when the alternative is to reveal themselves to be the most despicable of men? By the gods, I do not see how they can.

[14] I am, however, surprised by those who claim that if we make an alliance with the Arcadians and then act in accordance with it, we will give the impression that we are changing course and are wholly unreliable. I take the opposite view, men of Athens. Why? Because I do not think that anyone would deny that when our city rescued the Spartans, and before that the Thebans, and most recently the Euboeans, it always had one and the same purpose in doing so.[14] [15] What was that purpose? It was to save those who were being wronged. Since that is the case, it would not be we who are changing course but those who are unwilling to abide by what is just. And it will be clear that although the course of affairs is always being altered by those who seek to get more for themselves, our city does not change.

[16] The Spartans seem to me to be engaging in sharp prac-

---

down, since they did not wish to oppose Sparta, and as a result the Arcadians turned to Thebes (Diodorus 15.62.3; Xen. *Hellenica* 6.5.19). Athens in turn allied itself with Sparta in 369 (see 7n). The expense and risk that the Athenians incurred relate to their military support for Sparta in the Mantinea campaign of 362 (see 6).

[14]Demosthenes' first reference is to Athens' alliance with Sparta in 369 (see 7n); the second is to Athens' consistent support for Thebes against Sparta from the 390s to the 370s. Specifically, the Athenians gave sanctuary to Theban exiles after the Spartan seizure of the citadel of Thebes in 382 and also contributed to the liberation of the city in winter 379/8. The third is to Athenian intervention on the island of Euboea in 357 to counter Theban activity there, on which see 8.74n.

tice, since the reason why they now say that the Eleans should recover part of Triphylia, and the Phliasians should recover Tricaranon, and some other Arcadians should regain their own land, and we should recover Oropus is not so that they can see each of us in possession of our own territory.[15] Far from it—it is too late for them to become so charitable! [17] Rather, their purpose is to give everyone the impression that they are being cooperative in allowing each of these cities to recover the territory to which it lays claim, in order that when they in turn move against Messene, these others will all march with them and be eager to help them, rather than be seen to wrong those who had supported them over the places to which each of them laid claim, if they should fail to return the favor. [18] But I think that whether or not some of the Arcadians are subjected by the Spartans, our city can recover Oropus, with the help both of the Spartans, if they are prepared to act justly, and of those other cities that oppose the Thebans' possession of other people's territory.[16] But if it were to become clear to you that we cannot take Oropus unless we allow the Spartans to conquer the Peloponnese, I think that it would be preferable, if I may say so, to leave Oropus alone than to abandon the Messenians and the Peloponnese to the Spartans. For I do not suppose that our reckoning with them would be over this alone—I shall pass over what I was going to say, but I think that we would be in all sorts of danger.[17]

[19] And yet it is absurd to direct recriminations against the

---

[15]Triphylia, the central coastal region of the western Peloponnese between Elis to the north and Messenia to the south, had revolted from Elis and joined the Arcadian League in the early 360s (Xen. *Hellenica* 7.1.26). Control of Tricaranon in the central-eastern Peloponnese was disputed by Phlius and Argos (Xen. *Hellenica* 7.4.11). In each case, Sparta was supporting the territorial claim of its enemy's enemy. On Oropus, see 11n.

[16]It is not clear whether Demosthenes has any particular cities in mind. If he does, he is perhaps thinking of Phocis, which was already at war with Thebes.

[17]Demosthenes is reluctant to express openly the possibility that Athens itself would be in danger if the Spartans were to succeed in conquering Arcadia and Messene.

Megalopolitans for their previous support of Thebes against you, now that they want to become our friends and help us instead, or to find fault and think of ways to prevent this alliance, and not to recognize that the more loyal these men[18] show the Megalopolitans to have been towards Thebes, the more anger you should feel towards them for depriving the city of such allies, when the Arcadians approached you before they approached the Thebans.[19] [20] This, I think, is the behavior of men whose aim is to make the Megalopolitans the allies of others for a second time. I know, as far as one can calculate the future—and I think that most of you would agree—that if the Spartans capture Megalopolis, Messene will be in danger; and if they capture Messene, I predict that we will find ourselves allied to Thebes.[20] [21] It is both much more honorable, and more to our advantage, to take over the Thebans' alliance ourselves and resist Spartan greed than to shrink from helping Thebes' allies and abandon them, and later be forced to rescue the Thebans, as well as putting ourselves in danger. [22] For I believe that we would not be unconcerned if the Spartans were to capture Megalopolis and become great again. I see that even now they choose to make war not to avoid some evil but to recover their former power. The extent of their ambitions when they had that power you perhaps know better than I, and you would be right to be alarmed about it.[21]

---

[18]Those Athenian politicians who argued against helping the Megalopolitans in part on the ground that they were still bound by their alliance with (Athens' enemy) Thebes.

[19]In 370: see 12n.

[20]Demosthenes predicts that a revival in Spartan power will drive Athens and Thebes into each other's arms, as happened in the aftermath of the Peloponnesian War. Such a rapprochement in fact occurred in different circumstances in 339, when Athens and Thebes laid aside their differences and made an alliance to oppose Philip of Macedon.

[21]This refers to the period of the Spartan domination of Greece, 404–371. Specific Spartan outrages included the overthrow of democracy and the establishment of an oligarchy at Athens in 404, the seizure of the citadel of Thebes in 382 (above, 14n), and a planned raid on Athens' port of Piraeus in 378. Many in the audience would be old enough to recall some of these events.

[23] I would like to hear from those speakers who claim to hate the Thebans or the Spartans, whether they hate them out of concern for you and your interests or whether they hate the Thebans out of concern for Sparta, and the Spartans out of concern for Thebes. If the latter is the case, you should listen to neither group, since they are both insane. But if they say that they hate one of these cities out of concern for you, why do they unduly elevate the other?[22] [24] For it is possible, it really is, to humble Thebes without making Sparta strong—and much easier. How? I shall try to explain. We all know that everyone is ashamed not to do what is right, at least up to a point, even if they do so reluctantly, and that they are openly opposed to those who act unjustly, especially if it results in people being harmed. And we will find that what ruins everything and is the root of all evils is simply the reluctance to behave justly. [25] Thus, to prevent this alliance from obstructing the reduction of Theban power, let us declare that Thespiae and Orchomenus and Plataea must be restored, and let us collaborate with them, and let us encourage others to help, for it is noble and just to prevent the destruction of long-established cities.[23] But let us not sacrifice Megalopolis and Messene to those who are engaged in wrongdoing, nor use Plataea and Thespiae as an excuse to allow existing cities, which are still inhabited, to be destroyed.[24] [26] If this policy is made clear, everybody will wish to prevent the Thebans possessing what does not belong to them.[25] But if we do otherwise, these people[26] will oppose our plans— and reasonably so, considering that the resettlement of the cities of Boeotia will bring ruin on them, and we will have endless troubles. For in truth how will it ever end if we keep on allowing existing cities to be destroyed and demanding that ruined cities be resettled?

---

[22]I.e., he asks why the Athenian opponents of Thebes support Sparta so strongly, and vice versa.

[23]On these three cities, see 4 above. Demosthenes encourages the Athenians to collaborate with their exiled inhabitants, of whom the Plataeans had received sanctuary at Athens.

[24]I.e., Megalopolis and Messene.

[25]Oropus and the Boeotian cities that Thebes had destroyed.

[26]The Thebans.

[27] Those who seem to speak with most justice say that the Megalopolitans should take down the inscribed pillars relating to Thebes, if they are to be our firm allies.[27] The Megalopolitans, however, express the view that it is not inscribed pillars but mutual advantage that make friendship, and they think that those who help them are their allies. If that is their opinion, here is mine. I say that they should decide to take down the pillars and that at the same time the Spartans should keep the peace. And if either side refuses, then we should immediately take the side of those who are willing to do so. [28] For if, while remaining at peace, the Megalopolitans retain their alliance with Thebes, it will be clear to everybody that they prefer Theban greed to the claims of justice. But if they make an honest alliance with us, and the Spartans refuse to keep the peace, I presume that it will be clear to everybody that the Spartans are exerting themselves not to secure the resettlement of Thespiae[28] but in order to subject the Peloponnese to themselves, at a time when the Thebans are engaged in war.[29] [29] I am surprised that some people are afraid to see the enemies of Sparta become allies of Thebes, but think there is nothing to be feared in the destruction of those same cities by the Spartans, considering that we know from experience that the Thebans always use them as allies against the Spartans,[30] whereas the Spartans, when they had them, used them against us.[31]

---

[27] The texts of alliances were commonly inscribed on stone or bronze pillars (*stēlai*) and erected in public places. Taking down the pillars recording their alliance with Thebes would demonstrate that the Megalopolitans had repudiated it.

[28] Thespiae is perhaps singled out for the sake of example, although it may be that Sparta demanded its restoration in particular: elsewhere in the speech Demosthenes regards its situation as comparable to that of Orchomenus and Plataea (see §4 and 25).

[29] The Third Sacred War (356–346) against Phocis; see the Speech Introduction.

[30] During the 360s Thebes had sought to use the Arcadians as a counterweight to Sparta in the Peloponnese (see 4n).

[31] During the fifth and early fourth centuries most of the cities of Arcadia were allied to Sparta and contributed troops to the Spartan army. Al-

[30] I think that you should also consider what will happen if you reject the Megalopolitans. If they are defeated and forced to live in villages,[32] the Spartans will immediately have grown stronger, whereas if they are saved, as has unexpectedly happened to some extent already, they will rightly become firm allies of the Thebans. But if you do accept them, they will owe their salvation directly to you. As for the consequences of doing so, let us examine them by assessing the risks for the Thebans and the Spartans. [31] If the Thebans are defeated, as they deserve,[33] the Spartans will be no greater than they should be, since to balance this they will have these Arcadians, their neighbors, as opponents. But if in fact the Thebans recover and are saved, they will nevertheless be weaker, since these people[34] will have become our allies and will owe their salvation to us. So from every point of view, it is in our interest that we do not abandon the Megalopolitans and that they are seen to owe their survival, if indeed they survive, not to their own efforts or to others but to you.

[32] By the gods, men of Athens, I have spoken not because of any private friendship for or dislike of either party, but from my assessment of what is to your advantage. My advice to you is not to give up the Megalopolitans, nor, in general, to abandon any weaker state to a stronger one.

---

though in the fifth century, Sparta had indeed used its allies against Athens, during the fourth century, and especially in the 370s, its campaigning on land was directed primarily against Thebes rather than against Athens.

[32] Demosthenes refers to the practice of dioecism (*dioikismos*), used in particular by Sparta to subjugate and control a defeated enemy. This involved the destruction of an enemy's towns and the dispersal of its population into unfortified villages. For the Spartans' use of it against Mantinea in 385, see Xen. *Hellenica* 5.2.1–7.

[33] I.e., in the Third Sacred War against Phocis (see 28n). It was politic for Demosthenes to tell his Athenian audience that the Thebans should be defeated in the war because Athens supported their enemy Phocis, albeit without much direct involvement.

[34] The Megalopolitans.

17. ON THE AGREEMENT WITH ALEXANDER

〜〜〜〜〜〜〜〜〜〜〜〜〜〜〜〜〜〜〜〜〜〜〜〜〜〜〜〜〜〜〜〜〜〜

INTRODUCTION

This speech is certainly later than any of the other speeches in this volume, since it belongs to the reign of Philip's son Alexander. After the defeat of an anti-Macedonian Greek coalition, led by Athens and Thebes, at the battle of Chaeronea in 338, Greece fell under Macedonian domination. Philip imposed on the Greeks a common peace and established an alliance known by modern historians as the League of Corinth (from the Greek city where its Council met).[1] The league served both as an instrument of Macedonian domination and as a legitimization of Philip's leadership of Greece in the planned war against the Persians. Its Greek members sent representatives to the Council (*synhedrion*), and Philip was appointed its leader (*hēgemōn*). After the assassination of Philip in 336, his son Alexander succeeded him both as king of Macedon and as leader of the league.

Our knowledge of the league's constitution derives from two main sources. The first is a fragmentary inscription from Athens (*IG* II² 236 = Rhodes and Osborne 2003: no. 76) containing part of the oath that the Greek members of the league swore to Philip. The second is this speech, which alludes to a number of clauses in the agreement that, the speaker alleges, the Macedonians have breached.

---

[1] On common peaces, see *OCD*³ s.v. Common Peace. On Philip's diplomatic dealings with the Greeks and the setting up of the League of Corinth, see Hammond and Griffith 1979: 604–646.

Although Demosthenes was politically active during Alexander's reign, this speech is almost certainly not his work.[2] Analysis has shown that in its handling of prose rhythm, it differs from the genuine speeches of Demosthenes,[3] and its overall style is also quite different. Its authenticity was also generally denied in antiquity: Dionysius of Halicarnassus regarded it as spurious (*Demosthenes* 57), and Libanius in his *Introduction* to the speech suggests that it is closer in character to those of Demosthenes' contemporary and political ally Hyperides. Some scholars are in fact inclined to attribute the speech to Hyperides, but this is uncertain.[4] Other scholars in antiquity[5] attributed the speech to the anti-Macedonian politician Hegesippus, who is generally agreed to be the author of the speech *On Halonnesus*, wrongly attributed to Demosthenes (Dem. 7). Certainly the two speeches share a legalistic attitude and extreme belligerence towards Macedon. On the available evidence, however, all that can safely be said is that this speech, if a genuine product of Alexander's reign (see below), was written by an Athenian politician who was strongly opposed to the Macedonian domination of Greece.

It has been argued that the speech is not in fact a genuine work of Alexander's reign, on the ground that it focuses so narrowly on Alexander's alleged breaches of his agreement with the Greeks (see below) and is silent about matters that one might expect to find in a speech advocating that Athens declare war. Instead, it is suggested, it was written in the early third century, per-

---

[2]MacDowell 2009: 380–381 concludes that it cannot be proved that Demosthenes did not write it but that it is more likely to be by someone else.

[3]McCabe 1981.

[4]Libanius singles out two words in the speech (see 11n, 23n) as more characteristic of Hyperides than of Demosthenes. The attribution to Hyperides is accepted by Bosworth (1988: 190), even though Libanius does not directly suggest that the speech is by him. It has also been observed that the bellicose tone of the speech does not accord with an ancient description of the style of Hyperides' deliberative speeches as colorless, though this is not a particularly strong argument: see Whitehead 2001: 7 n. 26.

[5]The ancient commentary reports that "some people" attribute it to Hegesippus (Dilts 1983: 195.2–7).

haps by Demosthenes' nephew Demochares, who is believed to have played a role in the compilation and publication of his uncle's speeches.[6] This view has attracted some support[7] but is in my opinion implausible.[8]

No ancient scholar discusses the date or context of the speech, and so we must rely on internal evidence.[9] The speaker lists a series of alleged Macedonian breaches of the constitution of the League of Corinth but gives no information about the specific circumstances that prompted its delivery. It seems likely that the speech, with its invitation to the Athenians to declare war on Alexander (30), was spoken at a time of crisis, when the possibility of war was in the air. At the same time the reference to the expulsion of the tyrants of Eresus on the island of Lesbos (see 7n) suggests that the speech was written no earlier than 332. The most likely context is the anti-Macedonian revolt of Sparta, led by its King Agis III, in 331, but certainty is impossible.[10]

Although Philip had generally supported the smaller cities of the Peloponnese against the threat of Spartan aggrandizement, Sparta had not participated in the anti-Macedonian Greek alliance that was defeated at the battle of Chaeronea, nor did it become a member of the League of Corinth. Nevertheless it too resented the Macedonian domination of Greece, and, after several years of disaffection and increasing collaboration with the Persian generals operating in the Aegean, Sparta went to war in the first half of 331.[11] Its revolt was joined by "most of the Pelopon-

---

[6] Thus Culasso Gastaldi 1984: 159–183. On Demochares, see the Introduction to this volume, p. 19.

[7] E.g., by Ehrhard 2001.

[8] The speech's narrow focus may be due to a division of labor among the advocates of war, with other speakers in the debate concentrating on other aspects.

[9] The ancient commentary states in its introduction to the speech, without any discussion (or likelihood of being correct), that it belongs "at the beginning of Alexander's reign" (Dilts 1983: 196.18).

[10] See Cawkwell 1961a. Cf. Will 1982, arguing for 333.

[11] Alexander heard of trouble in the Peloponnese while he was at Tyre in Phoenicia in early summer 331 (Arrian *Anabasis* 3.6.3).

nesians and some of the northern Greeks" (Diodorus 17.62.7), and overtures were made to Athens, the only other significant military power in Greece (Thebes had been sacked in 335). There was a vigorous debate at Athens over whether to join the Spartans, and it is to this debate that the current speech was perhaps a contribution. The Athenians, mindful of the fate of Thebes and with a number of their citizens held prisoner by Alexander (Diodorus 17.22.3), decided not to intervene. The revolt was eventually crushed by Antipater, Alexander's governor in Greece, and Agis was killed.[12]

The speech consists of a series of complaints about Macedonian breaches of the agreement with the Greeks. Some of these relate to Athens: the forcing of grain ships en route from the Black Sea to Athens to put in to land (19–22) and the sailing of a Macedonian warship into Athens' harbor of Piraeus (26–28). Others relate to other cities in Greece: the restoration of the sons of Philiadas to power at Messene (4–7); the overthrow of democracy at Pellene (10–11); and the return of exiles to various places, including Sicyon (15–16). The speaker argues that the terms of the agreement not only permit but require the Athenians to react to these (alleged) breaches, and the speech ends with an abrupt proposal that they declare war against the transgressor.

It is likely that the clauses of the agreement are reasonably accurately reported, but the speaker's interpretation of Macedonian actions is probably tendentious. For example, it has been argued that the grain ships may have been forced to put in to land as a security measure, in view of intense Persian naval activity in the Aegean.[13] Again, the word "tyrant" (*tyrannos*), applied to the sons of Philiadas, was often bandied about in this period and meant little more than an oligarchic leader. It is also unlikely that individual cities such as Athens had the right to take action against alleged infractions without involving the league's Council. Other complaints, such as the sailing of a single ship into Piraeus, were relatively trivial. This is not to say that the Macedonians always

---

[12]On the revolt, see Diodorus 16.62–63; Curtius Rufus 6.1; Badian 1967; Bosworth 1988: 198–204.

[13]See Cawkwell 1961a.

followed the letter of the agreement or showed sensitivity for Greek feelings, but the sum total of complaints that the speaker can muster are not very impressive. Although many Athenians resented Macedonian domination, as is shown by their attempt to regain their freedom after the death of Alexander, they also enjoyed a striking measure of renewed prosperity in this period and were doubtless deterred by the example of Thebes from taking premature military action against Macedonia. If it was in fact delivered, the speech clearly failed to persuade its audience.

17. ON THE AGREEMENT WITH ALEXANDER

[1] It is absolutely right, men of Athens, to agree with those who urge you to abide by your oaths and agreements[14]—so long as they mean what they say![15] For in my view nothing is more appropriate for those who live in a democracy than to have a serious concern for fairness and justice. But those who go too far in exhorting you in that direction should stop making a nuisance of themselves with their speeches while their actions are anything but just, and should now face the test, and either convince you of their arguments, or step aside and allow you to be advised by speakers who know more about justice, [2] in order that you may either willingly endure being wronged, as a favor to the man who is wronging you, or choose to set most store by what is right and, without reproaching anyone, consult your own interest with no further delay. From the actual agreements and oaths relating to the Common Peace, it is possible for anyone who examines them to see who are the transgressors. Although these are matters of great importance, I shall speak briefly.

[3] If anyone were to ask, men of Athens, what you would be most angry to be forced to tolerate, I think that if the sons of Pei-

---

[14]The speaker refers to the oaths and agreements that were first sworn in making the common peace of 338/7 (the League of Corinth: see the Speech Introduction) and renewed with Alexander.

[15]The speaker's point is that strict adherence to the oaths and agreements will (in his opinion) require the Athenians not to keep the peace, as these men argue, but to go to war.

sistratus[16] were alive today and someone were trying to restore them by force, you would snatch up your arms and endure any danger rather than accept them. For if you were persuaded to do so, you would be just as much slaves as those who are bought, especially since no one would deliberately kill his own slave,[17] whereas we see those who live under a tyranny being executed without trial and their children and wives assaulted.[18] [4] Did Alexander[19] give any thought to justice when he restored the sons of Philiadas to Messene[20] as tyrants contrary to the oaths and agreements recorded in the Common Peace, or did he follow his own tyrannical nature and give scant thought to you or to the common agreement? [5] You ought not get angry if someone treats you with such violence, yet fail to prevent such things happening elsewhere in breach of the oaths that were sworn to you; and certain men here ought not tell us to abide by the oaths, while giving license to others who have so conspicuously broken them. [6] But

---

[16]I.e., Hipparchus and Hippias, the sons of the sixth-century Athenian tyrant Peisistratus, who succeeded their father after his death in 527. Hipparchus was murdered in 514, and thereafter Hippias ruled alone until he was forced into exile in 510. Subsequently both the Spartans and later the Persians tried to reinstate Hippias to rule Athens in their interests. Cf. 12.7.

[17]Since slaves were valuable assets, it was against their owner's economic interest to kill them. Although in Athenian law it may have been illegal for an owner to kill his own slave, it is difficult to see who would have prosecuted him for doing so. See MacDowell 1963: 21–22.

[18]Such abusive behavior formed part of the standard Greek characterization of the tyrant. See, e.g., Herodotus' portrait of the sixth-century Corinthian tyrant Periander (5.92).

[19]Alexander III, "the Great," king of Macedonia and leader of the League of Corinth. See the Speech Introduction.

[20]On Messene in the southwestern Peloponnese, see 16.8n. As the bitter enemy of Sparta, it had looked towards Philip of Macedon for protection from Spartan aggression in the 340s: see 6.9, 15. Neon and Thrasybulus, the sons of Philiadas, appear in a list of Greek "traitors" in a later speech of Demosthenes (Dem. 18.295); Neon is described by the historian Theopompus as a friend of Philip (FGH 115 fragment 41). The Hellenistic historian Polybius defends the brothers' integrity (18.41), arguing that they had acted in what they perceived to be the interests of their city.

this cannot be the case, if you are willing to do what is right. For it is further written in the agreement that anyone who does what Alexander is doing shall, himself and his city, be the enemy of all the participants in the peace and that everyone should march against him. So if we are to act in accordance with the agreement, we should treat the one who restored the tyrants as an enemy.[21] [7] These supporters of tyranny might argue that the sons of Philiadas were tyrants of Messene before the agreement was made,[22] and that this is why Alexander restored them. But it is ridiculous to claim that he expelled the tyrants from Lesbos—from Antissa and Eresus—men who were tyrants before the agreement was made, on the ground that the form of government is unjust,[23] but to suppose that in Messenia, where the same harsh conduct exists, it is a matter of indifference. [8] Next, the agreement states right

---

[21] The agreement stipulated that cities be governed by the form of constitution in effect at the time that they swore to accept it (see also *IG* II² 236 = Rhodes and Osborne 2003: no. 76: fragment *a*, lines 12–14). On the face of it, the speaker's complaint about Alexander's intervention in the affairs of Messene is justified. It is, however, unlikely that individual cities were allowed to take the law into their own hands if they believed the agreement had been breached, without referring the matter to the Council (on which see 15n).

[22] I.e., that they held power at the time that the agreement was made. If this was the case, their restoration was in accord with the agreement. It is not known when or under what circumstances the "tyrants" (a rhetorically loaded term: see the Speech Introduction) were expelled from Messene.

[23] Antissa and Eresus were cities on the large eastern Aegean island of Lesbos. The complex political history of Eresus in this period is illuminated by a dossier of inscriptions that deal with the various tyrants who ruled the city during the reigns of Philip and Alexander (*IG* XII.2.526 = Rhodes and Osborne 2003: no. 83). The tyrants referred to here were probably Eurysilaus and Agonippus, who were installed as pro-Persian rulers of Eresus in the course of the Persian naval counter-attack in the Aegean in 333; upon the recovery of the island by the Macedonians in 332 they were tried and executed by the new democracy. If this is correct, the tyrants who were executed were not in power at the time the agreement was made; in any case, they had forfeited any rights they might have had by their support for the Persians. Nothing further is known about events in Antissa.

at its start that the Greeks are to be free and autonomous.[24] How then is it not the height of absurdity, when the clause about freedom and autonomy heads the agreement, that you do not think that one who has enslaved people has acted in breach of the common agreement? We are therefore obliged, men of Athens, if we are to abide by the agreement and the oaths and do what is right, to do as the oaths bid you and take up arms and march against those who have transgressed them, together with whoever is willing to join you.[25] [9] Or do you suppose that opportunity is sometimes strong enough to lead people to do what is in their interest even if it is wrong, but that now, when justice and opportunity and self-interest coincide, we should wait for some different occasion to seize our freedom and that of the other Greeks?

[10] I turn now to another rightful claim, in accordance with the agreement in which it is written that any people who overthrow whatever form of government was in force in a state at the time when it swore the oaths about the peace are to be the enemies of all who share in the peace. But consider, men of Athens: the Achaeans in the Peloponnese were democrats, but the democracy in Pellene has been abolished by the Macedonian, who expelled most of the citizens, gave their property to their slaves, and installed Chaeron the wrestler as tyrant.[26] [11] Yet we are partici-

---

[24]Freedom and autonomy were paired as standard elements in Greek political thought and in the various common peaces of the fourth century. Insofar as there was a significant distinction between them, freedom relates to the conduct of an independent foreign policy and autonomy relates to internal self-government.

[25]On the speaker's confident (but almost certainly mistaken) belief that the Athenians had the right to act on their own initiative against alleged breaches of the agreement, without referring their complaint to the Council, see 6n.

[26]The region of Achaea is in the northern Peloponnese, along the coast of the Gulf of Corinth. Nothing is known of the history of Pellene in the period before the installation of Chaeron as its pro-Macedonian ruler. As a wrestler, Chaeron was twice a winner at the Isthmian Games and four times a winner at the Olympic Games (Pausanias 7.27.7). See also Cawkwell 1961a: 76–77.

pants in the peace, which stipulates that those who do such things are to be treated as enemies. Since this is the case, are we to obey the common ordinances and treat these people as enemies, or will someone make the disgusting claim[27] that we should not—one of these men who take bribes from the Macedonian, and who have enriched themselves at your expense? [12] None of these things has escaped their notice. Instead, they have reached such a height of insolence that, escorted by the tyrant's army,[28] they tell you to abide by oaths that have already been broken, as if that man has "full powers"[29] to perjure himself too, but force you to repeal your own laws, and have released those who have been convicted in your courts,[30] and violently break the law in many other similar ways. [13] And yet it is reasonable for them to do so, since men who have sold themselves to oppose their country's interests are incapable of being concerned about laws or oaths: they pay lip service to the words, and deceive those whose attendance at meetings of the Assembly here is cursory and uncritical, and who think that the securing of a quiet life now will never lead to catastrophic trouble in the future. [14] But I do urge you, as I said at the beginning, to obey these men when they say that we should abide by the common agreements—unless they suppose that when they tell us to abide by the oaths, those oaths do not forbid wrongdoing; or unless they think that no one will notice that tyrannies are being set up in place of democracies, and constitutional governments are being overthrown!

[15] And here is something even more ridiculous: the treaty states that the members of the Council[31] and those who are in

---

[27] The Greek word *bdelureusetai* ("will be disgusting") is regarded by Libanius as unworthy of Demosthenes: see the Speech Introduction.

[28] The Greek supporters of Alexander ("the tyrant") are represented as requiring armed protection because of their unpopularity with their fellow-citizens.

[29] The speaker makes ironic allusion to Alexander's appointment by the League of Corinth as "general with full powers" (*stratēgos autokratōr*) for the war against Persia (Diodorus 17.4.9).

[30] It is not known what event(s) are alluded to here.

[31] The League of Corinth had a Council (*synhedrion*) to which its Greek members sent delegates, apparently in accordance with a system of propor-

charge of collective security[32] should ensure that in those cities that share in the peace no one is to be killed or exiled contrary to the city's existing laws, nor is any property to be confiscated, or land redistributed, or debts cancelled, or slaves set free with a view to revolution.[33] Yet they are so far from preventing any of these things that they actually help to organize them! How do they not deserve to be put to death, these men who devise disasters of such magnitude in the cities—disasters that they themselves, in all their greatness, are under orders to investigate because of their gravity!

[16] I shall now demonstrate yet another breach of the treaty. For it is written in it that exiles are not permitted to set out from cities that share in the peace, bearing arms with a view to war, against any city that shares in the peace. If they do so, the city from which they set out is to be expelled from the agreement.[34] But the Macedonian was so eager to be under arms that he never once put them down, and he still goes around armed as much as he can, now even more than before, insofar as he has used an edict to restore different people to different places, including the physical trainer to Sicyon.[35] [17] If then we are obliged to abide

---

tional representation, since the inscription from Athens containing the text of the oath sworn by the Greeks (*IG* II² 236 = Rhodes and Osborne 2003: no. 76) also includes, as fragment *b*, a partial list of members each followed by a numeral.

[32] The role and identity of these officials is unclear, but they were probably responsible for the maintenance of security in Greece during the absence of the league's leader, i.e., Alexander, who at the time of the speech was on campaign in Asia. See Hammond and Griffith 1979: 639–646.

[33] All these prohibitions were intended to ensure the political stability of the Greek cities of the league. Cancellation of debt and the redistribution of land were common demands of the poor against the rich and (in an oligarchy) were elements of a democratic revolutionary program. Slaves could be offered their freedom, or even citizenship, in return for their active support in overthrowing the existing constitution.

[34] In the factionalism (*stasis*) between oligarchs and democrats that was widespread in Greece in this period, an exiled faction often sought to recapture its own city and establish itself in power.

[35] Sicyon was a city of the northeastern Peloponnese, and in the late 350s it had been at war with Sparta (see 14.5n). Like other Peloponnesian ene-

by the common agreements, as these men say, then the cities that have acted in these ways are in breach of their treaty with us. If we must conceal the truth, we must avoid mentioning that the cities are Macedonian.[36] But if those who serve the Macedonian against your interests keep on telling you to obey the common agreements, let us do so, since what they say is right, and, just as the oath requires, let us declare them to be in breach of the agreement, and let us deliberate about how to treat those who behave in a tyrannical and insolent manner, and who are always plotting here, and giving orders there, and laughing at the Common Peace. [18] What objection will these men make to this conclusion? Will they treat any agreement that is against the interest of our city as binding, but reject one that saves it? Is this just? And will they always insist that any item in the sworn agreement is valid if it favors our enemies and is against the interest of the city, but think it their duty to be unremittingly opposed if in any respect justice and advantage are on our side against them?

[19] To make it clearer to you that no Greeks will ever reproach you for breaching any of the common agreements, but will instead be grateful that you alone convicted those who are doing so, I shall touch on a few of the many points that might be made. It says in the agreement, I believe, that those who participate in the peace are to be permitted to sail the seas, and no one is to prevent them or force a ship belonging to any of them to put in to land; and if anyone breaks this agreement, he is to be treated as an enemy by all who participate in the peace.[37] [20] You have very clearly seen, men of Athens, that this is just what the Mace-

---

mies of Sparta in this period, it looked to Macedonia for support: see 4n on Messene. Demosthenes in a speech of 330 includes Aristratus and Epichares of Sicyon in a lengthy list of "traitors" to Greece (Dem. 18.295; cf. 18.48, where Aristratus alone is named): i.e., they were pro-Macedonian rulers of the city. The identity of the man dismissively identified only by his humble occupation as a physical trainer (*paidotribēs*) is unknown (Cawkwell 1961a: 76 n. 19 presumes that it is Aristratus).

[36]I.e., if we are obliged to tell the truth, we must say that these cities are Macedonian (in the sense that they are effectively controlled by Alexander).

[37]For examples of states forcing merchant ships to put in to land, see 5.25n; Dem. 50.6, 17–19.

donians have done. They have reached such a height of insolence that they forced all the ships from the Black Sea to put in at Tenedos, and did not stop this villainous behavior until you voted to man one hundred triremes and launch them right away, and appointed Menestheus as general in charge of them.[38] [21] Is it not absurd that so many great wrongs have been committed by others, and yet their friends here do not deter the transgressors, but instead advise you to abide by an agreement that they so despise? It is as if a clause has been added to the effect that some people are allowed to offend, but others cannot even defend themselves! [22] How were these men not simultaneously breaking the law and acting stupidly, when they broke an oath of such importance that they came very close to being rightly stripped of their command of the sea?[39] And now they have indisputably handed us the right to do so, whenever we wish to act. For the fact that they have stopped doing wrong does not make their breach of the common agreement any less serious. [23] But they are fortunate, because they take advantage of your indolence—you who do not even choose to enjoy your rights. What is most insolent is this: that although the other Greeks and non-Greeks are all afraid of incurring your hatred, these *nouveaux riches*[40] alone compel you to despise yourselves, sometimes by persuasion, sometimes by

---

[38]Merchant ships transported grain from the Black Sea to the cities of Greece, in particular to Athens. The island of Tenedos lies off the coast of Asia Minor to the south of the Hellespont and was on the grain route south. Menestheus was the son of the famous Athenian general Iphicrates, on whom see 4.24n, 8.30n, 13.20n. The sending of such a large squadron indicates how seriously the Athenians took this incident. Cawkwell (1961a) discusses this episode and dates it to 332. He argues that the writer has misrepresented the issue and that the Macedonians probably required Athens to provide an escort for its grain ships, since the activities of Persian naval forces in the Aegean and the lack of Macedonian naval capacity made them vulnerable to attack without adequate protection.

[39]I.e., by Athens, on whose naval superiority, see 25n below.

[40]The speaker turns rather abruptly from the Macedonians to those Athenian politicians whom he accuses of having been bribed by them (cf. 11). The Greek word translated as *nouveaux riches*, *neoploutoi*, is regarded by Libanius as untypical of Demosthenes: see the Speech Introduction.

force, as if they were dealing with men of Abdera or Maroneia,[41] not Athens. [24] Moreover, at the same time as they weaken you and strengthen your enemies, they unwittingly admit that your country is invincible, since they unjustly order you to abide by what is just, as though if you chose instead to look to your own advantage you could easily defeat your enemies! [25] And it is reasonable for them to do so, since as long as we are able even on our own to have undisputed naval superiority,[42] we will be able to find ourselves other stronger defenses on land in addition to our existing forces, especially since fortune has put a stop to those men who went around escorted by the tyrant's troops—some of whom have been destroyed, and others shown to be worthless.[43]

[26] In addition to the points I have already made about shipping, the Macedonian has also committed a major breach of the peace. For the most arrogant and contemptuous action of the Macedonians took place recently: they dared to sail into Piraeus contrary to the common agreements that we have with them.[44] This, men of Athens, must be interpreted not as a trivial matter, on the ground that it was a single trireme, but as a trial—to see if we would overlook it—to allow them to do it with more ships, and as proof that they paid no more heed to the common decisions than they paid to those I have previously mentioned. [27] That this was an encroachment by degrees and an attempt to

---

[41] Abdera and Maroneia were two cities on the northern coast of the Aegean, both at this time subject to Macedonian rule. On Maroneia, cf. 12.17. For a similar thought (naming two different cities), see 13.34.

[42] By the middle of the fourth century the total number of ships in Athens' navy was over 300 (see 14.13n), which was considerably more than either Macedonia or any other Greek city possessed. Moreover, during the period of the Macedonian ascendancy Athenian public finances had revived to a remarkable extent, and under the leadership of Lycurgus, Athens invested heavily in its armed forces, including the construction of new shipsheds. See Bosworth 1988: 204–211.

[43] See 10n.

[44] As Cawkwell (1961a: 75–76) has observed, if this relatively trivial breach of the agreement was really "the most arrogant and contemptuous action," the speaker does not have much of a case against Alexander.

make us used to tolerating such incursions is clear from the following considerations. Does not the fact that the captain of the ship—whom you should have immediately done away with along with his ship—asked permission to build small boats in your harbors make it clear that rather than sailing in, they were plotting directly to be inside the harbor?[45] And if we accept light vessels, a little later it will be triremes. And if at first we admit a few, soon afterwards it will be many. [28] For it cannot be claimed that Athens has a plentiful supply of timber for shipbuilding, when it is imported with difficulty and from far away, but that there is a shortage of it in Macedonia, which has arranged a very cheap supply even for others who want it.[46] But they thought that at the same time they would build ships here and crew them in our harbor, although it is stated in the common agreements that nothing of the kind is permitted, and would be able to continue to do so to an ever greater extent. [29] So in every way they treat the city with contempt, thanks to their teachers here who tell them what to do. With their help they have discovered that our city suffers from some indescribable feebleness and slackness, that it takes no thought for the future, and that it pays no attention to the way in which the tyrant is treating the common agreements.

[30] I urge you to abide by these agreements, men of Athens, in the way that I instructed you to, and I would claim, with all the authority of my age, that in doing so we will at the same time be

---

[45] The speaker's point seems to be that the specific request to build boats in Piraeus shows that the Macedonian ship put in there with this intention, rather than by chance (e.g., because it was damaged or to escape bad weather).

[46] The mountains of Macedonia were a very important source for the fir trees that were needed to build triremes, particularly for Athens, which had a very large navy and no suitable timber of its own, and Macedonian kings had for a long time used access to this timber as a diplomatic tool: see 7.11n on Amyntas III; 13.24n on "Perdiccas" (probably a slip for Alexander I). Access to timber also contributed to Athenian imperial ambitions on the Macedonian and Thracian coasts, most notably the fifth-century foundation of Amphipolis (on which see Thuc. 4.108.1, referring to access to shipbuilding timber).

doing what is right, without exposing ourselves to criticism, and be making use of the opportunities that work to our advantage, without incurring danger. For the agreement also includes the clause "if we wish to share in the common peace." The words "if we wish" also imply their opposite,[47] or else we must never stop following others disgracefully, but . . .[48] nor recall with any sense of ambition those qualities that from ancient times we have possessed in much greater quantity than any other people. And so, if you bid me do so, men of Athens, I shall move a proposal, just as the agreement requires, that we wage war on the transgressors.

---

[47] I.e., the Athenians can choose whether or not they wish to participate in the peace.

[48] The syntax of this sentence is debated, and Dilts 2002 in his edition accepts the suggestion that some words have dropped out of the Greek text.

BIBLIOGRAPHY FOR THIS VOLUME

ABBREVIATIONS

FGH = F. Jacoby, *Die Fragmente der griechischen Historiker.* Leiden. 1923–.

IG = *Inscriptiones Graecae.* Berlin. 1873–.

OCD³ = S. Hornblower and A. Spawforth (eds.), *The Oxford Classical Dictionary.* 3rd ed. Oxford. 1996.

SIG³ = W. Dittenberger, *Sylloge Inscriptionum Graecarum.* 3rd ed. Leipzig. 1915–1924.

Badian, E., 1967: "Agis III," *Hermes* 95: 170–192.

Badian, E., 1982: "Greeks and Macedonians," in B. Barr-Sharrar and E. Borza (ed.), *Macedonia and Greece in Late Classical and Early Hellenistic Times.* Washington, DC: 33–51.

Badian, E., 1987: "The Peace of Callias," *Journal of Hellenic Studies* 107: 1–39.

Badian, E., 1995: "The Ghost of Empire: Reflections on Athenian Foreign Policy in the Fourth Century BC," in W. Eder (ed.), *Die Athenische Demokratie im 4. Jhdt. v. Chr.* Stuttgart: 79–106.

Bers, V., 1985: "Dikastic Thorubos," in P. Cartledge and D. Harvey (eds.), *Crux: Essays in Greek History Presented to G. E. M. de Ste. Croix.* London: 1–15.

Borza, E. N., 1990: *In the Shadow of Olympus: The Emergence of Macedon.* Princeton.

Bosworth, A. B., 1988: *Conquest and Empire.* Cambridge.

Briant, P., 2002: *From Cyrus to Alexander: A History of the Persian Empire,* tr. P. T. Daniels. Winona Lake, IN.

Brunt, P. A., 1969: "Euboea in the Time of Philip II," *Classical Quarterly* 19: 245–265.

Buckler, J., 1989: *Philip II and the Sacred War*. Leiden.

Cahill, N., 2002: *Household and City Organization at Olynthus*. New Haven.

Calhoun, G. M., 1933: "Demosthenes' Second Philippic," *Transactions of the American Philological Association* 64: 1–17.

Carey, C., 2000: *Aeschines* (The Oratory of Classical Greece, vol. 3). Austin.

Cargill, J., 1981: *The Second Athenian League: Empire or Free Alliance?* Berkeley.

Carlier, P., 1990: *Démosthène*. Paris.

Cawkwell, G. L., 1961a: "A Note on Ps. Demosthenes 17.20," *Phoenix* 15: 74–78.

Cawkwell, G. L., 1961b: "Notes on the Common Peace of 366–365 BC," *Classical Quarterly* 11: 80–86.

Cawkwell, G. L., 1962a: "The Defence of Olynthus," *Classical Quarterly* 12: 122–140.

Cawkwell, G. L., 1962b: "Demosthenes and the Stratiotic Fund," *Mnemosyne*, 4th ser. 15: 377–383.

Cawkwell, G. L., 1963a: "Eubulus," *Journal of Hellenic Studies* 83: 47–67.

Cawkwell, G. L., 1963b: "Demosthenes' Policy after the Peace of Philocrates," *Classical Quarterly* 13: 120–138, 200–213.

Cawkwell, G. L., 1978: *Philip of Macedon*. London.

Cawkwell, G. L., 1984: "Athenian Naval Power in the Fourth Century," *Classical Quarterly* 34: 334–345.

Christ, M. R., 1990: "Liturgical Avoidance and the Antidosis in Classical Athens," *Transactions of the American Philological Association* 120: 13–28.

Christ, M. R., 2001: "Conscription of Hoplites in Classical Athens," *Classical Quarterly* 51: 398–422.

Christ, M. R., 2007: "The Evolution of the *eisphora* in Classical Athens," *Classical Quarterly* 57: 53–69.

Cohen, E., 1973: *Ancient Athenian Maritime Courts*. Princeton.

Connor, W. R., 1962: "Charinus' Megarian Decree," *American Journal of Philology* 83: 236–237.

Culasso Gastaldi, E., 1984: *Sul trattato con Alessandro: Polis, monarchia macedone e memoria demostenica*. Padua.

Daitz, S. G., 1957: "The Relationship of the *De Chersoneso* and the *Philippica Quarta* of Demosthenes," *Classical Philology* 52: 145–162.

Davies, J. K., 1971: *Athenian Propertied Families, 600–300 BC.* Oxford.

de Ste. Croix, G. E. M., 1963: "The Alleged Secret Pact between Athens and Philip II concerning Amphipolis and Pydna," *Classical Quarterly* 13: 110–119.

de Ste. Croix, G. E. M., 1972: *The Origins of the Peloponnesian War.* London.

de Souza, P., 1999: *Piracy in the Graeco-Roman World.* Cambridge.

Dickey, E., 2007: *Ancient Greek Scholarship.* Oxford.

Dilts, M. R., 1983: *Scholia Demosthenica*, vol. I. Leipzig.

Dilts, M. R., 2002: *Demosthenis Orationes*, vol. I. Oxford.

Ehrhardt, C., 2001: Review of C. W. Blackwell, *In the Absence of Alexander: Harpalus and the Failure of Macedonian Authority. Bryn Mawr Classical Review* 2001.05.21. http://bmcr.brynmawr.edu/2001/2001-05-21.html.

Ellis, J. R., 1967: "The Order of the Olynthiacs," *Historia* 16: 108–111.

Ellis, J. R., 1976: *Philip II and Macedonian Imperialism.* London.

Ellis, J. R., and R. D. Milns, 1970: *The Spectre of Philip.* Sydney.

Fisher, N. R. E., 1992: *Hybris: A Study of the Values of Honour and Shame in Ancient Greece.* Warminster.

Flower, M. A., 1997: *Theopompus of Chios: History and Rhetoric in the Fourth Century BC.* Oxford.

Flower, M. A., 2002: "Alexander the Great and Panhellenism," in A. B. Bosworth and E. J. Baynham (eds.), *Alexander the Great in Fact and Fiction.* Oxford: 96–135.

Flower, M. A., 2008: *The Seer in Ancient Greece.* Berkeley.

Gabrielsen, V., 1986: "*Phanera* and *aphanes ousia* in Classical Athens," *Classica et Mediaevalia* 36: 99–114.

Gabrielsen, V., 1994: *Financing the Athenian Fleet: Public Taxation and Social Relations.* Baltimore.

Garland, R., 2001: *The Piraeus from the Fifth to the First Century BC^2.* London.

Gibson, C. A., 2002: *Interpreting a Classic: Demosthenes and His Ancient Commentators.* Berkeley.

Hajdú, I., 2002: *Kommentar zur 4. Philippischen Rede des Demosthenes*. Berlin.

Hamel, D., 1998: *Athenian Generals: Military Authority in the Classical Period*. Leiden.

Hammond, N. G. L., and G. T. Griffith, 1979: *A History of Macedonia*, vol. 2. Oxford.

Hansen, M. H., 1975: *Eisangelia*. Odense.

Hansen, M. H., 1984: "Two Notes on Demosthenes' Symbouleutic Speeches," *Classica et Mediaevalia* 35: 57–70 [reprinted with addenda in M. H. Hansen, *The Athenian Ecclesia II* (Copenhagen, 1989): 283–297].

Hansen, M. H., 1991: *The Athenian Democracy in the Age of Demosthenes*, tr. J. Crook. Oxford.

Harding, P., 1985: *From the End of the Peloponnesian War to the Battle of Ipsus = Translated Documents of Greece and Rome* 2. Cambridge.

Harding, P., 1987: "Rhetoric and Politics in Fourth-century Athens," *Phoenix* 41: 25–39.

Harding, P., 1995: "Athenian Foreign Policy in the Fourth Century," *Klio* 77: 105–125.

Harding, P., 2006: *Didymos: On Demosthenes*. Oxford.

Harding, P., 2008: *The Story of Athens: The Fragments of the Local Chronicles of Attika*. Abingdon.

Harris, E. M., 1996: "Demosthenes and the Theoric Fund," in R. W. Wallace and E. M. Harris (eds.), *Transitions to Empire: Essays in Greco-Roman History, 360–146 BC in Honor of E. Badian*. Norman, OK: 57–76.

Harris, E. M., 2000: "The Authenticity of Andocides *De Pace*: A Subversive Essay," in P. Flensted-Jensen, T. Nielsen, and L. Rubinstein (eds.), *Polis and Politics: Studies in Ancient Greek History*. Copenhagen: 479–506.

Heckel, W., 2005: *Who's Who in the Age of Alexander the Great*. Oxford.

Hornblower, S., 1982: *Mausolus*. Oxford.

Hornblower, S., 2002: *The Greek World 479–323 BC*[3]. London.

Hudson-Williams, H. L., 1951: "Political Speeches in Athens," *Classical Quarterly* 1: 68–73.

Jaeger, W., 1938: *Demosthenes: The Origin and Growth of His Policy*. Berkeley.

Lane Fox, R., 1997: "Demosthenes, Dionysius and the Dating of Six Early Speeches," *Classica et Mediaevalia* 48: 167–203.

Lewis, D. M., 1974: "Entrenchment-clauses in Attic Decrees," in D. W. Bradeen and M. F. McGregor (eds.), *PHOROS: Tribute to Benjamin Dean Meritt*. Locust Valley, NY: 81–89.

Lewis, D. M., 1997: *Selected Papers in Greek and Near Eastern History*. Cambridge.

MacDowell, D. M., 1963: *Athenian Homicide Law in the Age of the Orators*. Manchester.

MacDowell, D. M., 1978: *The Law in Classical Athens*. London.

MacDowell, D. M., 1986: "The Law of Periandros about Symmories" *Classical Quarterly* 36: 438–449.

MacDowell, D. M., 2000: *Demosthenes* On the False Embassy *(Oration 19)*. Oxford.

MacDowell, D. M., 2009: *Demosthenes the Orator*. Oxford.

Mader, G., 2005: "*Pax duello mixta*: Demosthenes and the Rhetoric of War and Peace," *Classical Journal* 101: 11–35.

Mader, G., 2006: "Fighting Philip with Decrees: Demosthenes and the Syndrome of Symbolic Action," *American Journal of Philology* 127: 367–386.

McCabe, D. F., 1981: *The Prose-Rhythm of Demosthenes*. New York.

McQueen, E. I., 1986: *Demosthenes:* Olynthiacs. London.

Meiggs, R., 1972: *The Athenian Empire*. Oxford.

Mitchell, L., 2007: *Panhellenism and the Barbarian in Archaic and Classical Greece*. Swansea.

Montgomery, H., 1983: *The Way to Chaeronea: Foreign Policy, Decision Making and Political Influence in Demosthenes' Speeches*. Bergen.

Moreno, A., 2007: *Feeding the Democracy: The Athenian Grain Supply in the Fifth and Fourth Centuries BC*. Oxford.

Osborne, M., 1983: *Naturalization in Athens*. Brussels.

Parke, H. W., 1933: *Greek Mercenary Soldiers*. Oxford.

Parker R., 2005: *Polytheism and Society in Ancient Athens*. Oxford.

Pickard-Cambridge, A. W., 1914: *Demosthenes and the Last Days of Greek Freedom*. London.

Pritchett, W. K., 1971–1991: *The Greek State at War*, 5 vols. Berkeley.

Radicke, J., 1995: *Die Rede des Demosthenes für die Freiheit der Rhodier (or. 15)*. Stuttgart.

Rhodes, P. J., 1981: *A Commentary on the Aristotelian* Athenaion Politeia. Oxford.

Rhodes, P. J., 1985: "*Nomothesia* in Fourth-century Athens," *Classical Quarterly* 35: 55–60.

Rhodes, P. J., 1986: "Political Activity in Classical Athens," *Journal of Hellenic Studies* 106: 132–144.

Rhodes, P. J., 2006: *A History of the Classical Greek World 478–323 BC*. Oxford.

Rhodes, P. J., and R. Osborne, 2003: *Greek Historical Inscriptions 404–323 BC*. Oxford.

Sallares, R., 1991: *The Ecology of the Ancient Greek World*. London.

Sandys, J. E., 1900: *Demosthenes* On the Peace, Second Philippic, On the Chersonesus *and* Third Philippic. London.

Sandys, J. E., 1910: *The* First Philippic *and the* Olynthiacs *of Demosthenes²*. London.

Sealey, R., 1955: "Dionysius of Halicarnassus and Some Demosthenic Dates," *Revue des Études Grecques* 68: 77–120.

Sealey, R., 1967: "Pseudo-Demosthenes XIII and XXV," *Revue des Études Grecques* 80: 250–255.

Sealey, R., 1993: *Demosthenes and His Time: A Study in Defeat*. Oxford.

Shrimpton, G., 1977: "Theopompus' Treatment of Philip in the *Philippica*" *Phoenix* 31: 123–144.

Shrimpton, G., 1991: *Theopompus the Historian*. Montreal.

Sinclair, R. K., 1988: *Democracy and Participation in Athens*. Cambridge.

Tod, M. N., 1948: *Selection of Greek Historical Inscriptions*, vol. 2. Oxford.

Todd, S. C., 2001: "How to Execute People in Fourth-century Athens," in J. Edmondson and V. Hunter (eds.), *Law and Social Status in Classical Athens*. Oxford: 31–51.

Trevett, J. C., 1992: *Apollodoros the Son of Pasion*. Oxford.

Trevett, J. C., 1994: "Demosthenes' Speech On Organization (Dem. XIII)," *Greek, Roman and Byzantine Studies* 35: 179–193.

Trevett, J. C., 1996: "Did Demosthenes Publish His Deliberative Speeches?" *Hermes* 124: 425–441.

Tuplin, C., 1998: "Demosthenes '*Olynthiacs*' and the Character of the Demegoric Corpus," *Historia* 47: 276–320.

van Wees, H., 2004: *Greek Warfare: Myths and Realities*. London.

Westlake, H. D., 1935: *Thessaly in the Fourth Century*. Manchester.

Whitehead, D., 1983: "Competitive Outlay and Community Profit: *philotimia* in Democratic Athens," *Classica et Mediaevalia* 34: 55–74.

Whitehead, D., 2001: *Hypereides: The Forensic Speeches*. Oxford.

Will, E., 1982: "Zur Datierung der Rede Ps.-Demosthenes XVII," *Rheinisches Museum für Philologie* 125: 202–213.

Wooten, C., 2008: *A Commentary on Demosthenes'* Philippic I. Oxford.

Worthington, I., 2006: *Demosthenes, Speeches 60 and 61, Prologues, Letters* (The Oratory of Classical Greece, vol. 10). Austin.

Worthington, I., 2008: *Philip II of Macedonia*. New Haven.

Worthington, I., C. Cooper, and E. Harris, 2001: *Dinarchus, Hyperides, and Lycurgus* (The Oratory of Classical Greece, vol. 5). Austin.

Yunis, H., 1996: *Taming Democracy: Models of Political Rhetoric in Classical Athens*. Ithaca, NY.

Yunis, H., 2005: *Demosthenes, Speeches 18 and 19* (The Oratory of Classical Greece, vol. 9). Austin.

INDEX

〰〰〰〰〰〰〰〰〰〰〰〰〰〰〰〰〰〰〰〰〰〰〰〰〰〰〰〰〰〰〰〰〰

CPSIA information can be obtained
at www.ICGtesting.com
Printed in the USA
LVHW090526030921
696763LV00015B/165